Hispanics in the United States

A Demographic, Social, and Economic History, 1980–2005

In 1980 the U.S. government began to systematically collect data on Hispanics. By 2005 the Latino population of the United States had become the nation's largest minority; it is projected to comprise about one-third of the total U.S. population in 2050. Using census data and other statistical source materials, this book examines the transformations in the demographic, social, and economic structures of Latino Americans in the United States between 1980 and 2005. Unlike most other studies, this book presents data on transformations over time, rather than a static portrait of specific topics at particular moments. Latino Americans are examined over this twenty-five-year period in terms of their demographic structures, changing patterns of wealth and poverty, educational attainment, citizenship and voter participation, occupational structures, employment, and unemployment, among other themes. The result is a detailed socioeconomic portrait by region and over time that indicates the basic patterns that have led to the formation of a complex national minority group that has become central to U.S. society.

Laird W. Bergad is Distinguished Professor in the Department of Latin American and Puerto Rican Studies at Lehman College and the Ph.D. Program in History at the Graduate Center of the City University of New York. Bergad is the founding and current director of the CUNY Center for Latin American, Caribbean, and Latino Studies at the Graduate Center. His previously published books include *Coffee and the Growth of Agrarian Capitalism in Nineteenth-Century Puerto Rico*; *Cuban Rural Society in the Nineteenth Century: The Social and Economic History of Monoculture in Matanzas*; *The Cuban Slave Market, 1790–1880* (co-author); *The Demographic and Economic History of Slavery in Minas Gerais, Brazil, 1720–1888*; and *The Comparative Histories of Slavery in Brazil, Cuba, and the United States*.

Herbert S. Klein is the author of some 20 books and 155 articles in several languages on Latin America and on comparative themes in social and economic history. Among these books are four comparative studies of slavery, the most recent of which are *African Slavery in Latin America and the Caribbean* (co-author), *The Atlantic Slave Trade*, and *Slavery and the Economy of São Paulo, 1750–1850* (co-author). He has also published books on such diverse themes as *The American Finances of the Spanish Empire, 1680–1809*, and *A Population History of the United States* and is co-author of *Brazil Since 1980* and *Mexico Since 1980*.

Hispanics in the United States

A Demographic, Social, and Economic History, 1980–2005

LAIRD W. BERGAD

*Lehman College and The Graduate Center of the
City University of New York*

HERBERT S. KLEIN

Stanford University

CAMBRIDGE
UNIVERSITY PRESS

CAMBRIDGE UNIVERSITY PRESS
Cambridge, New York, Melbourne, Madrid, Cape Town, Singapore,
São Paulo, Delhi, Dubai, Tokyo, Mexico City

Cambridge University Press
32 Avenue of the Americas, New York, NY 10013-2473, USA

www.cambridge.org
Information on this title: www.cambridge.org/9780521718103

First published 2010

Printed in the United States of America

A catalog record for this publication is available from the British Library.

Library of Congress Cataloging in Publication data
Bergad, Laird W., 1948–
Hispanics in the United States : a demographic, social, and economic history,
1980–2005 / Laird W. Bergad, Herbert S. Klein.
p. cm.
ISBN 978-0-521-88953-7
1. Hispanic Americans – History.   2. Hispanic Americans – Population.
3. Hispanic Americans – Social conditions.   4. Hispanic Americans – Economic
conditions.   I. Klein, Herbert S.   II. Title.
E184.S75B47   2010
973'.0468 – dc22   2009042402

ISBN 978-0-521-88953-7 Hardback
ISBN 978-0-521-71810-3 Paperback

This book is dedicated to our grandchildren
Rafael Joshua Goldstein
and
Benjamin Alexander Klein

Contents

List of Graphs, Tables, and Maps   *page* ix

   Introduction   1

1 Immigration to the United States to 1980   9

2 The Hispanic Population to 1980   36

3 Population Growth and Dispersion, 1980–2005   63

4 The Demography of the Hispanic Population   99

5 Wealth and Poverty   123

6 Educational Attainment   192

7 Citizenship, the Latino Electorate, and Voter Participation   237

8 Occupational Structures, Employment, and
   Unemployment   276

9 English Language Abilities and Domestic Usage   320

10 Hispanic Business Ownership   352

11 Race   364

12 Endogamous and Exogamous Marriage Patterns among
    Latino Household Heads   391

13 Conclusion   406

Bibliography   419

Index   437

List of Graphs, Tables, and Maps

Graphs

1.1 Relative Share of Slaves, Convicts, Indentured Servants and Free Persons Among All People Arriving in British North America, 1607–1819. *page* 10

1.2 Share of European Immigration by American Receiving Country, by Quinquenium, 1821–1915. 14

1.3 Annual Immigration to the United States, 1821–1900. 15

1.4 Origins of Arriving Immigrants to the United States by Decade, 1820–1920. 18

1.5 Age Pyramid of the Foreign-Born Population in 1880. 20

1.6 Age Pyramid of the Foreign-Born Population in 1910. 21

1.7 Fertility Ratio for Non-Hispanic White Population by Nativity, 1875–1929. 23

1.8 Annual Arrival of Immigrants to the United States, 1900–1945. 28

2.1 Distribution of Puerto Ricans by Major States of Residence, 1940–1980. 39

2.2 Distribution of Cubans by Major States of Residence, 1940–1980. 41

2.3 Distribution of Dominicans by State, 1970–1980. 42

2.4 Relative Importance of Major Hispanic Nationalities in 1980. 53

2.5 Age Pyramid of the Foreign-Born Hispanic Population, 1980. 58

2.6 Age Pyramid of the Domestic-Born Hispanic Population, 1980. 59

2.7 Age Pyramid of the Total Hispanic Population, 1980. 59

2.8   Age Pyramid of the Non-Hispanic White Population, 1980.   60

2.9   Infant Mortality by Race/Ethnicity/Hispanic Nationality, 1983.   61

3.1   Hispanics as a Percentage of Total Populations in Selected Western and Southwestern Metropolitan Areas, 1980–2005.   87

3.2   Relative Importance by Nationality of Total Hispanic Population of Miami Metro Area, 2005.   91

3.3   Puerto Rican Population of New York City, 1980–2005.   94

3.4   Non–Puerto Rican Latino Nationalities in New York City, 1980–2005.   96

4.1   Total Fertility Rate by Race/Ethnicity or Latino Nationality, 1990 (births per 100 women ages 15–44).   101

4.2   Changing Relative Share of Total Births in the United States by Race/Ethnicity and Mexicans, 1989–2004.   104

4.3   Total Fertility Rate by Race/Ethnicity and Mexicans, Puerto Ricans, and Cubans, 1989–2004.   106

4.4   Mean Age of Mothers at First Birth by Race/Ethnicity and Selected Latino Nationalities, 1989–2000.   107

4.5   Mean Age at Birth of Third Child by Race/Ethnicity and Latino Nationality, 1989–2000.   108

4.6   Birth Rate of Mexican Women in the United States by Age Cohorts of Mothers, 1980–2003.   110

4.7   Number of Births per Thousand Population by Age of Mother for Hispanics and Non-Hispanics, 2004.   111

4.8   Age Pyramids of the Components of the Hispanic Population, and the Total Population of the United States, 2000.   112

4.9   Distribution of Race/Ethnic Groups and Latino Nationalities by Type of Household, 2000.   116

4.10 Infant Mortality by Race/Ethnicity and Hispanic Nationalities, 1983–2004.   117

4.11 Age-Adjusted Death Rates by Sex, Race, Ethnicity, and Hispanic Nationality, 2003.   122

5.1   Percentage of Households Headed by Females by Race/Ethnicity, 1980–2005.   129

5.2   Median Income of Female-Headed Households as a Percentage of Male-Headed Households by Race/Ethnicity, 1980–2005.   132

5.3   Median Household Income Growth in Percentages for Selected Metropolitan Areas by Race/Ethnicity, 1980–1990 and 1990–2005.   141

5.4   Median Household Income of Households Headed by
      Mexicans in 2005 in Chicago, Houston, Los Angeles,
      and Riverside Metro Areas in Nominal 2005 Dollars and
      Adjusted by Cost-of-Living Index.   149

6.1   Percentage of Population 25 Years of Age and Older
      with an Educational Attainment Level of B.A. or Higher
      by Race/Ethnicity, 1980–2005.   195

6.2   Percentage of Population 25 Years of Age and Older Not
      Graduating High School by Race/Ethnicity,
      1980–2005.   196

6.3   Percentage of Population 25 Years of Age and Older
      with an Educational Attainment Level of B.A. or Higher
      by Latino Nationality, 1980 and 2005.   200

6.4   Percentage of Population 25 Years of Age and Older Not
      Graduating High School by Latino Nationality, 1980
      and 2005.   201

6.5   Percentage of Population 25 Years of Age and Older
      with an Educational Attainment Level of B.A. or Higher
      by Selected Latino Nationality and Domestic- or
      Foreign-Born, 2005.   205

6.6   Percentage of Population 25 Years of Age and Older
      without a High School Diploma by Selected Latino
      Nationality and Domestic- or Foreign-Born, 2005.   210

6.7   Median Total Personal Income by Educational
      Attainment Level by Race/Ethnicity for Population
      25 Years of Age and Older, 2005.   212

6.8   Percentage of Mexican Population 25 Years of Age and
      Older Who Have Achieved a B.A. Degree or Higher in
      Houston, Los Angeles, Chicago, and Riverside,
      1980–2005.   218

6.9   Percentage of Mexican Population 25 Years of Age and
      Older Who Have Not Graduated from High School in
      Houston, Los Angeles, Chicago, and Riverside,
      1980–2005.   219

6.10 Percentage of Mexican Population 25 Years of Age and
      Older Who Were Foreign-Born in Houston, Los Angeles,
      Chicago, and Riverside, 1980–2005.   220

6.11 Median Total Personal Income among Mexicans by
      Educational Attainment Levels in Houston, Los Angeles,
      Chicago, and Riverside, 2005.   224

6.12 Percentage of Miami Cuban Population 25 Years of Age
      and Older Who Were Domestic- or Foreign-Born,
      1980–2005.   227

6.13 Median Total Personal Income among Cubans in Miami by Educational Attainment Levels, 2005. 228

6.14 Percentage of New York Latino Nationalities 25 Years of Age and Older Who Have Achieved a B.A. Degree or Higher by Puerto Ricans, Dominicans, Mexicans, Ecuadorians, and Colombians, 1980–2005. 230

6.15 Percentage of New York Latino Nationalities 25 Years of Age and Older Who Have Not Graduated from High School by Puerto Ricans, Dominicans, Mexicans, Ecuadorians, and Colombians, 1980–2005. 231

6.16 Median Personal Income among New York Latino Nationalities 25 Years of Age and Older by Educational Attainment Level by Puerto Ricans, Dominicans, Mexicans, Ecuadorians, and Colombians, 2005. 235

7.1 Citizenship Data among Latinos in the United States, 1980–2005 (in percentages). 239

7.2 Citizenship Data among Latinos in the United States, 1980–2005 (in absolute numbers). 240

7.3 Percentage of Total Latino Citizens by Selected Latino Nationalities, 1980–2005. 241

7.4 Percentage of All Citizens Who Are Latinos by Metropolitan Area, 1980–2005. 246

7.5 Percentage of Mexicans Who Were Citizens in the Houston, Los Angeles, Chicago, and Riverside Metropolitan Areas, 1980–2005. 248

7.6 Percentage of Mexican Citizens Who Were Naturalized in the Houston, Los Angeles, Chicago, and Riverside Metropolitan Areas, 1980–2005. 249

7.7 Mexicans as Percentage of Total Populations and as Percentage of Total Citizen Populations in the Houston, Chicago, Los Angeles, and Riverside Metropolitan Areas, 1980–2005. 250

7.8 Percentage of Cubans in Miami Who Were Citizens and Percentage of Cuban Citizens Who Were Naturalized, 1980–2005. 252

7.9 Cubans in the Miami Metropolitan Area by Citizenship Status, 1980–2005. 253

7.10 Percentage of Miami Population Who Were Cubans and Percentage of Miami Citizens Who Were Cuban Citizens, 1980–2005. 254

7.11 Percentage of Selected New York Metro Area Latino Nationalities Who Were Citizens, 1980–2005. 255

7.12 Percentage of New York Metro Area Total Citizens Who
Were Naturalized by Selected Latino Nationalities,
1980–2005. 257

7.13 Percentage of Total Latino Electorate Who Were
Naturalized Citizens by Metropolitan Area, 1980–2005. 263

7.14 Percentage of Total National Latino Electorate by State,
2005. 266

7.15 Percentage of Total Electorate Who Were Latinos by
Selected States, 2005. 267

7.16 Percentage of Citizens 18 Years of Age and Older
Registered to Vote in the Presidential Elections of 2000
and 2004 by Race/Ethnicity. 271

7.17 Percentage of Registered Voters Who Voted in the
Presidential Elections of 2000 and 2004 by
Race/Ethnicity. 271

7.18 Percentage of Total Eligible Voting Population Who
Voted in the Presidential Elections of 2000 and 2004 by
Race/Ethnicity. 272

7.19 Percentage of Latino Citizens Aged 18 and Older
Registered to Vote in the Presidential Elections of 2000
and 2004 in California, Texas, Florida, and New York. 273

7.20 Percentage of Registered Latinos Who Voted in the
Presidential Elections of 2000 and 2004 in California,
Texas, Florida, and New York. 274

7.21 Percentage of Latino Citizen Voting-Age Population
Who Voted in the Presidential Elections of 2000 and
2004 in California, Texas, Florida, and New York. 274

8.1 Percentage of the Workforce Employed by Occupational
Category by Race/Ethnicity, 2005. 278

8.2 Percentage of the Latino Workforce Employed by
Occupational Category by Sex, 2005. 279

8.3 Unemployment Rates among Population 16 Years of Age
and Older by Race/Ethnicity, 1980–2005. 299

8.4 Percentage of Population 16 Years of Age and Older Not
in the Labor Force by Race/Ethnicity, 1980–2005. 300

8.5 Unemployment Rates and Percentage of Those Not in
the Labor Force among the Latino Population 16 Years
of Age and Older by Sex, 1980–2005. 301

8.6 Women as Percentages of Total Employed Population,
16 Years of Age and Older by Race/Ethnicity, 1980–2005. 302

8.7 Percentage of All Women 16 Years of Age and Older
Not in the Labor Force by Race/Ethnicity, 1980–2005. 303

8.8 Age-Specific Unemployment Rates among Latinos by
Sex, 2005. 304
8.9 Age-Specific Out-of-the-Workforce Rates among
Latinos by Sex, 2005. 305
8.10 Unemployment Rates and Percentage of Those Not in
the Labor Force among the Latino Population 16 Years
of Age and Older by Nativity and Sex, 2005. 306
8.11 Unemployment Rates by Sex for Population 16 Years
of Age and Older by Latino Nationality, 2005. 309
8.12 Out-of-the-Workforce Rates by Sex for Population
16 Years of Age and Older by Latino Nationality, 2005. 309
8.13 Unemployment Rates among Mexicans Aged 16 and
Older in Houston, Los Angeles, Chicago, and
Riverside, 1980–2005. 314
8.14 Unemployment Rates among Cubans 16 Years of Age
and Older in Miami, 1980–2005. 316
8.15 Unemployment and Out-of-the-Workforce Rates
among Cubans 16 Years of Age and Older in the
Miami Metropolitan Area by Nativity and Sex, 2005. 316
8.16 Unemployment Rates among Puerto Ricans,
Dominicans, Mexicans, Ecuadorians, and Colombians
in New York, 1980–2005. 317
9.1 Median Total Personal Income by Sex and Ability to
Speak English among All Latinos, 2005, Population
25 Years of Age and Older. 344
9.2 Percentage of Latino Household Heads by Nativity,
Who Spoke Spanish at Home, 1980–2005. 346
9.3 Percentage of Latinos Living in Linguistically Isolated
Households, 1990–2005. 349
10.1 Hispanic-Owned Businesses in the United States, 2002. 354
10.2 Revenues Generated per Hispanic-Owned Business in
Six Metro Areas, 1992–2002. 356
10.3 Percentage of Total Hispanic-Owned Businesses by
Latino Nationality Nationwide and Selected States,
2002. 358
10.4 Percentage of Total Hispanic-Owned Businesses by
Latino Nationality in Selected Metro Areas, 2002. 360
10.5 Percentage of Total Hispanic-Owned Businesses by
Sector and State, 2002. 362
10.6 Percentage of Total Revenues Generated by
Hispanic-Owned Businesses by Sector and State,
2002. 363

11.1 Percentage of Latinos Declaring Themselves to Be White
     or Some Other Race by Foreign- or Domestic-Born,
     1980–2005.   372
11.2 Percentage of the Median Household Income of Latinos
     Who Identify as White Earned by Latinos Who Identify
     as Some Other Race and as Black, 1980–2005.   376
11.3 Percentage of Latinos 25 Years of Age or Older Who Did
     Not Graduate from High School or Who Achieved a
     B.A. Degree or Higher by Racial Self-Identification,
     1980–2005.   383
11.4 Percentage of Mexicans 25 Years of Age or Older Who
     Did Not Graduate from High School or Who Achieved a
     B.A. Degree or Higher by Racial Self-Identification,
     1980–2005.   385
11.5 Percentage of Puerto Ricans 25 Years of Age or Older
     Who Did Not Graduate from High School or Who
     Achieved a B.A. Degree or Higher by Racial
     Self-Identification, 1980–2005.   386
11.6 Percentage of Cubans 25 Years of Age or Older Who
     Did Not Graduate from High School or Who Achieved a
     B.A. Degree or Higher by Racial Self-Identification,
     1980–2005.   387
11.7 Percentage of Dominicans 25 Years of Age or Older
     Who Did Not Graduate from High School or Who
     Achieved a B.A. Degree or Higher by Racial
     Self-Identification, 1980–2005.   388
11.8 Percentage of Colombians 25 Years of Age or Older
     Who Did Not Graduate from High School or Who
     Achieved a B.A. Degree or Higher by Racial
     Self-Identification, 1980–2005.   389
12.1 Percentage of Foreign- and Domestic-Born Latino
     Household Heads Married to Other Latinos, by Sex,
     1980–2005.   393
12.2 Percentage of Foreign- and Domestic-Born Latino
     Household Heads Married to Non-Hispanic Whites, by
     Sex, 1980–2005.   394
12.3 Percentage of Heads of Households by Nationality and
     Sex Married to Spouse of Same Nationality in the United
     States, 2005.   400
12.4 Percentage of Heads of Households by Nationality and
     Sex Married to Spouse Who Was a Latino in the United
     States, 2005.   401

12.5 Percentage of Heads of Households by Nationality and
Sex Married to a Spouse of Opposite Sex Who Was
Non-Hispanic White, 2005.　　　　　402
12.6 Percentage of Heads of Households by Nationality and
Sex Married to a Spouse of Opposite Sex Who Was
Non-Hispanic Black, 2005.　　　　　403

Tables

2.1 Distribution of the Hispanic Population by Major State
of Residence in 1980.　　　　　56
3.1 Hispanic Population of the United States 1980–2005 in
Relation to the Total and African American Populations.　　　　　64
3.2 Domestic- and Foreign-Born Hispanics, 1980–2005.　　　　　65
3.3 Domestic and Foreign-Born Components of Hispanic
Population Increase, 1980–2005.　　　　　65
3.4 Percentage Distribution of Hispanic Population by State,
1980–2005.　　　　　66
3.5 Percentage of All Mexicans by State and Mexicans as a
Percentage of Total Hispanic Populations by State,
1980–2005.　　　　　67
3.6 Mexicans and the Increase in Hispanic Populations,
1980–2005, in Arkansas, Georgia, North Carolina,
Oregon, and South Carolina.　　　　　68
3.7 Mexican Domestic- and Foreign-Born by State, 2005.　　　　　70
3.8 Hispanics as a Percentage of State Populations,
1980–2005 (domestic- and foreign-born components in
2005).　　　　　76
3.9 Hispanics as a Percentage of Total Populations of
Chicago, Miami, and New York Metro Areas and
Percentage Importance of Major Hispanic Group in
Miami and New York, 1980–2005.　　　　　88
4.1 Estimated Death Rates from Leading Causes of Death by
Sex, Race, and Hispanic Origin, 2003.　　　　　119
5.1 Median Household Income by Race/Ethnicity,
1980–2005.　　　　　127
5.2 Median Household Income by Latino Nationality,
1980–2005.　　　　　128
5.3 Median Household Income by Sex of Head of
Household by Racial/Ethnic Group, 1980–2005.　　　　　131
5.4 A Median Household Income by Sex of Head of
Household by Latino Nationality, 1980–2005.　　　　　134

5.5 Median Income of Household Head by Foreign- or
Domestic-Born for Selected Latino Nationalities,
1980–2005. 136

5.6 Median Income of Household Head by Foreign- or
Domestic-Born by Sex for Selected Latino Nationalities,
1980–2005. 137

5.7 Median Household Income by Ethnicity/Nationality of
Household Head by Selected Metropolitan Areas,
1980–2005. 139

5.8 Mexican Household Heads as a Percentage of Total
Latino Household Heads in Chicago, Houston, Los
Angeles, and Riverside, 1980–2005. 142

5.9 Selected Latino Nationality Household Heads as a
Percentage of Total Latino Household Heads in the New
York Metro Area, 1980–2005. 142

5.10 Median Household Income among Households by
Mexicans in Chicago, Houston, Los Angeles, and
Riverside Metropolitan Areas, 1980–2005. 143

5.11 Median Income among Mexican Household Heads by
Sex and Foreign- or Domestic-Born, 1908–2005, Los
Angeles, Riverside, Chicago, and Houston. 145

5.12 Median Household Income among Households Headed
by Mexicans in Chicago, Houston, Los Angeles, and
Riverside Metropolitan Areas, 2005. 148

5.13 Median Income among Cuban Household Heads in
Miami by Sex and Foreign- or Domestic-Born,
1980–2005. 151

5.14 Mexican and Cuban Head of Household Median
Incomes in Major Metro Areas by Sex and Domestic-
and Foreign-Born, 2005. 152

5.15 Median Income among Latino Household Heads in New
York Metro Area by Selected Nationalities, Sex, and
Foreign- or Domestic-Born, 1980–2005. 154

5.16 Educational Attainment Levels and Median Household
Incomes among Puerto Rican, Dominican, Mexican,
Ecuadorian, and Colombian Household Heads in the
New York Metro Area, 2005. 157

5.17 Median Incomes of Household Heads in Major Metro
Areas by Sex and Domestic- and Foreign-Born, 2005. 158

5.18 Percentage of Individuals Living at or below the Poverty
Line by Sex and Racial/Ethnic Group, 1980–2005. 160

5.19 Percentage of Each Age Category at or below Poverty
Level by Race/Ethnicity, 1980–2005. 161

5.20 Poverty Rates among Latino Nationalities by Sex,
      1980–2005.   162
5.21 Percentage of Each Age Category at or below Poverty
      Line by Latino Nationality, 1980–2005.   164
5.22 Poverty Rates among Latino Nationalities by Foreign- or
      Domestic-Born, 1980–2005.   165
5.23 Household Income Distribution by Race/Ethnicity,
      1980–2005.   167
5.24 Household Income Distribution by Latino Nationality,
      1980–2005.   170
5.25 Poverty Rates in Percentages by Race/Ethnicity by Major
      Metropolitan Areas, 1980–2005.   172
5.26 Poverty Rates in Percentages by Race/Ethnicity and Sex
      by Major Metropolitan Areas, 1980–2005.   173
5.27 Percentage of Children Aged 1–14 Living at or below the
      Poverty Line by Race/Ethnicity by Metro Area,
      1980–2005.   174
5.28 Poverty Rates among Mexicans in Chicago, Houston,
      Los Angeles, Riverside, and New York, 1980–2005.   175
5.29 Percentage of Mexican Children Aged 1–14 Living at or
      below the Poverty Line in Chicago, Houston, Los
      Angeles, Riverside, and New York Metro Areas,
      1908–2005.   176
5.30 Poverty Rates among Cubans in Miami, 1980–2005.   176
5.31 Poverty Rates among Latino Nationalities in New York,
      1980–2005.   178
5.32 Household Income Distribution Structure by
      Metropolitan Area by Race/Ethnicity, 1980–2005.   179
5.33 Household Income Distribution Structure by
      Metropolitan Area by Race/Ethnicity, 1980–2005.   182
5.34 Mexican Household Income Distribution Structure by
      Metropolitan Area, 1980–2005.   185
5.35 Cuban Household Income Distribution Structure in the
      Miami Metro Area, 1980–2005.   187
5.36 Household Income Distribution Structure in the New
      York Metro Area, 1980–2005, Puerto Ricans,
      Dominicans, Mexicans, Ecuadorians, and Colombians.   189
6.1 Educational Attainment by Race/Ethnicity, 1980–2005.   197
6.2 Educational Attainment by Latino Nationality,
      1980–2005.   202
6.3 Educational Attainment Levels by Latino Nationality,
      Domestic- or Foreign-Born, 1980–2005.   207

6.4 Median Total Personal Income by Educational
Attainment Level by Latino Nationality for Population
25 Years of Age and Older, 2005.   211
6.5 Percentage of Population 25 Years of Age and Older
Who Have Achieved a B.A. Degree or Higher by
Race/Ethnicity in Selected Metropolitan Areas, 2005.   214
6.6 Percentage of Population 25 Years of Age and Older
Who Have Not Graduated from High School by
Race/Ethnicity in Selected Metropolitan Areas, 2005.   214
6.7 Median Personal Incomes of Population 25 Years of Age
and Older Who Have Achieved a B.A. Degree or Higher
and Who Have Not Graduated from High School by
Race/Ethnicity in Selected Metropolitan Areas, 2005.   216
6.8 Education Attainment of Hispanics 25 Years of Age and
Older by Domestic- and Foreign-Born in Selected
Metropolitan Areas, 2005.   216
6.9 Percentage of Mexican Population 25 Years of Age or
Older Who Have Achieved a B.A. Degree or Higher by
Domestic- or Foreign-Born.   221
6.10 Percentage of Mexican Population 25 Years of Age or
Older Who Have Not Graduated from High School by
Domestic- or Foreign-Born.   221
6.11 Percentage of Mexican Population 25 Years of Age or
Older Who Have Achieved a B.A. Degree or Higher by
Sex.   222
6.12 Percentage of Mexican Population 25 Years of Age or
Older Who Have Not Graduated from High School by
Sex.   223
6.13 Percentage of Miami Cuban Population 25 Years of Age
and Older Who Have Achieved a B.A. Degree or Higher
and Who Have Not Graduated from High School by
Sex, 1980–2005.   225
6.14 Percentage of Miami Foreign and Domestic-Born Cuban
Population 25 Years of Age and Older Who Have
Achieved a B.A. Degree or Higher and Who Have Not
Graduated from High School, 1980–2005.   226
6.15 Percentage of Selected New York Latino Nationalities
25 Years of Age and Older Who Have Achieved a B.A.
Degree or Higher by Sex, 1980–2005.   232
6.16 Percentage of Selected New York Latino Nationalities
25 Years of Age and Older Who Have Not Graduated
from High School by Sex, 1980–2005.   232

6.17 Percentage of Selected New York Latino Nationalities 25 Years of Age and Older Who Have Achieved a B.A. Degree by Domestic- or Foreign-Born, 1980–2005. 234

6.18 Percentage of Selected New York Latino Nationalities 25 Years of Age and Older Who Have Not Graduated from High School by Domestic- or Foreign-Born, 1980–2005. 236

7.1 Total Latino Citizenship Status by Selected Latino Nationalities, 1980–2005 (numbers). 243

7.2 Total Latino Citizenship Status by Selected Latino Nationalities, 1980–2005 (percentages). 244

7.3 Percentage of Selected Latino Nationalities Who Are Citizens, 1980–2005. 245

7.4 Total Mexican Citizenship Status by Selected Metropolitan Areas, 1980–2005. 251

7.5 Citizenship Status by Selected Latino Nationalities in the New York Metro Area, 1980–2005. 258

7.6 Citizens 18 Years of Age and Older by Race/Ethnicity, 1980–2005. 259

7.7 Citizens 18 Years of Age and Older by Latino Nationality, 1980–2005. 260

7.8 Percentage of Total Electorate by Metropolitan Area by Race/Ethnicity, 1980–2005. 261

7.9 Percentage of Total Latino Electorate by Selected Latino Nationalities, 1980–2005, in Los Angeles, Riverside, Houston, and Chicago. 264

7.10 Percentage of Total Miami Latino Electorate by Selected Latino Nationalities, 1980–2005. 264

7.11 Percentage of Total New York Latino Electorate by Selected Latino Nationalities, 1980–2005. 265

7.12 National Composition of Latino Electorate in California, Florida, New York, and Texas, 1980–2005. 269

8.1 Occupational Structure by Race/Ethnicity and Sex, 2005. 280

8.2 Median Personal Income by Occupational Category, Sex, and Race/Ethnicity, 2005. 283

8.3 Latino Occupational Structure by Nationality and Sex, 2005. 285

8.4 Latino Occupational Structure by Nationality, Nativity, and Sex, 2005. 288

8.5 Median Personal Income by Occupational Category by Latino Nationality, Nativity, and Sex, 2005. 293

8.6 Latino Occupational Structure by Sex and Metropolitan Area, 2005. 296

8.7 Age-Specific Unemployment Rates by Race/Ethnicity and
     Sex, 2005.   304
8.8 Age-Specific Out-of-the–Labor Force Rates by
     Race/Ethnicity and Sex, 2005.   305
8.9 Unemployment Rates among Population 16 Years of Age
     and Older by Latino Nationality, 1980–2005.   307
8.10 Percentage of Population 16 Years of Age and Older Not
     in the Labor Force by Latino Nationality, 1980–2005.   308
8.11 Unemployment Rates for Population 16 Years of Age
     and Older by Race/Ethnicity and Metropolitan Area,
     2005.   310
8.12 Out-of-the-Workforce Rates for Population 16 Years of
     Age and Older by Race/Ethnicity and Metropolitan
     Area, 2005.   310
8.13 Latino Unemployment and Out-of-the-Workforce Rates
     by Sex and Metropolitan Area, 2005.   312
8.14 Latino Unemployment and Out-of-the-Workforce Rates
     by Nativity, Sex, and Metropolitan Area, 2005.   312
8.15 Mexican Unemployment and Out-of-the-Workforce
     Rates by Nativity, Sex, and Metropolitan Area, 2005.   315
8.16 Unemployment and Out-of-the-Workforce Rates by
     Latino Nativity and Sex in the New York Metropolitan
     Area, 2005.   319
9.1 English Language Ability by Sex and Nativity for
     Population 5 Years of Age and Older, 1980–2005.   322
9.2 English Language Ability by Sex and Nativity for
     Mexican-Origin Population 5 Years of Age and Older,
     1980–2005.   325
9.3 English Language Ability by Sex and Nativity for Puerto
     Rican–Origin Population 5 Years of Age and Older,
     1980–2005.   327
9.4 English Language Ability by Sex and Nativity for
     Cuban-Origin Population 5 Years of Age and Older,
     1980–2005.   330
9.5 English Language Ability by Sex and Nativity for
     Salvadoran-Origin Population 5 Years of Age and Older,
     1980–2005.   332
9.6 English Language Ability by Sex and Nativity for
     Dominican-Origin Population 5 Years of Age and Older,
     1980–2005.   335
9.7 English Language Ability by Sex and Nativity for
     Colombian-Origin Population 5 Years of Age and Older,
     1980–2005.   337

9.8   English Language Ability by Sex and Nativity for
       Peruvian-Origin Population 5 Years of Age and Older,
       1980–2005.   339
9.9   English Language Ability by Sex and Nativity for
       Honduran-Origin Population 5 Years of Age and
       Older, 1980–2005.   341
9.10   Percentage of Population 5 Years of Age and Older
       Who Have Poor English Language Skills and
       Percentage of the Population Who Were Foreign-Born
       by Metro Area, 1980 and 2005.   344
9.11   Percentage of Latino Population That Spoke Spanish at
       Home by Nativity and Sex, 1980–2005.   346
9.12   Percentage of Persons 5 Years of Age and Older Who
       Spoke Spanish at Home by Latino Nationality,
       1980–2005.   347
9.13   Percentage of Latinos Who Spoke Spanish at Home by
       Metro Area, 1980–2005.   348
9.14   Linguistic Isolation by Latino Nationality and Nativity,
       1990–2005.   350
9.15   Median Household Income by Household Head,
       Linguistic Isolation Status, and Latino Nationality,
       2005.   351
10.1   Hispanic Business Ownership in the United States,
       1987–2002.   353
10.2   Number of and Receipts of Hispanic-Owned Firms by
       Selected States, 1987–2002.   355
10.3   Number of and Receipts of Hispanic-Owned Firms by
       Selected Metro Areas, 1992–2002.   357
10.4   Hispanic Businesses by Sector in the United States,
       2002.   361
11.1   Racial Composition of the Latino Population of the
       United States Based on Self-Declarations, 1980–2005.   371
11.2   Percentage of People Declaring Themselves to Be
       White, Some Other Race, or Black by Latino
       Nationality, 2005.   373
11.3   Percentage of Latinos Declaring Themselves to Be
       White, Some Other Race, or Black by Metro Area,
       2005.   375
11.4   Median Household Income among Latinos by Racial
       Self-Declarations, 1980–2005.   376
11.5   Median Household Income among Mexicans by Racial
       Self-Declarations, 1980–2005.   377

11.6   Median Household Income among Puerto Ricans by
       Racial Self-Declarations, 1980–2005.   377
11.7   Median Household Income among Cubans by Racial
       Self-Declarations, 1980–2005.   378
11.8   Median Household Income among Dominicans by
       Racial Self-Declarations, 1980–2005.   378
11.9   Median Household Income among Colombians by
       Racial Self-Declarations, 1980–2005.   379
11.10 Percentage of Latinos Living in Poverty by Racial
       Self-Declarations, 1980–2005.   380
11.11 Percentage of Mexicans Living in Poverty by Racial
       Self-Declarations, 1980–2005.   380
11.12 Percentage of Puerto Ricans Living in Poverty by Racial
       Self-Declarations, 1980–2005.   381
11.13 Percentage of Cubans Living in Poverty by Racial
       Self-Declarations, 1980–2005.   381
11.14 Percentage of Dominicans Living in Poverty by Racial
       Self-Declarations, 1980–2005.   381
11.15 Percentage of Colombians Living in Poverty by Racial
       Self-Declarations, 1980–2005.   381
11.16 Percentage of Foreign- and Domestic-Born Latinos
       Who Did Not Graduate from High School or
       Graduated from College by Race, 2005.   384
12.1   Percentage of Latino Household Heads Married to
       Latinos, Non-Hispanic Whites, Non-Hispanic Blacks,
       and Asians by Sex, 2005.   392
12.2   Percentage of Foreign- and Domestic-Born Household
       Heads and Marriage Partners by Sex and Latino
       Nationality, 1980–2005.   396

Maps

2.1   Distribution of the Mexican Population by State, 1900.   44
2.2   Distribution of the Mexican Population by State, 1980.   46
3.1   Percentage of All Hispanics Who Were Mexicans,
      2005.   69
3.2   Percentage of All Hispanics in Florida Who Were
      Mexicans by Counties, 2005.   73
3.3   Percentage of All Hispanics in New York Who Were
      Mexicans by Counties, 2005.   74
3.4   Percentage of Total Populations Who Were Mexicans,
      2005.   78

3.5 Hispanics as a Percentage of Total Populations by
County and Selected Metro Areas, Texas, 2005.   80
3.6 Hispanics as a Percentage of Total Populations in
California Counties and Selected Metro Areas, 2005.   84
3.7 Hispanics as a Percentage of Total Populations in
California Counties and Selected Metro Areas, 2005.   86
3.8 Hispanics as a Percentage of Total Populations in
Chicago by Community, 2005.   90
3.9 Hispanics as a Percentage of Total Populations in Miami
Metro Area, 2005.   92
3.10 Hispanics as a Percentage of Total Populations in
Selected New York Metro Area Counties, 2005.   97

Introduction

At the beginning of the 21st century the Hispanic, or Latino, population of
the United States replaced African Americans as the single largest minority
in the country and they are projected to increase to about 30% of the
national population by 2050 according to the latest U.S. Census Bureau
estimates. The Hispanic presence in the United States has a long historical
tradition, even though it has been only recently that their demographic,
economic, cultural, and political importance has received a great deal of
public attention. With the end of the Mexican-American War in 1848,
or the War of U.S. Intervention as it is referred to in Mexico, the United
States absorbed a large Mexican population into its national borders
in the Southwest and in California. Additionally, from the early 19th
century on there was a small but steady stream of migrants from the
Hispanic Caribbean who settled mainly in the states of New York and
Florida. This included both political exiles fleeing a repressive Spanish
colonialism, which lasted until 1898 in Cuba and Puerto Rico, and the
migration of Cuban tobacco workers to the cigar industry that developed
in Florida, principally in the Tampa Bay area. There was also a significant
migration of Mexican workers from the late 19th century until the Second
World War who labored in a variety of economic sectors from agriculture
to railroad building, mainly in the Southwestern states along the Mexican
border. Much of this migration was seasonal rather than permanent as
these workers usually returned to their homes in Mexico rather than
settling in the United States.

Thus, the presence of Hispanics within the United States is not a new
phenomenon nor should it be considered unexpected given the common
border with Mexico and the political and economic power wielded by

I

> Seasonal migration of Latinos for labor in practice since 19th C.

the United States in the Americas. What changed during the 20th century was the extraordinary growth of migration from the region in the aftermath of World War II until today, as well as the impressive natural demographic increase of the resident Latino population. Moreover unlike earlier migrations from Europe or Asia to the United States, the settlement patterns of Latin American and Caribbean migrants and their offspring have been more evenly spread across the United States from 1980 on. While the Hispanic population had traditionally been concentrated in the Southwestern states, California, New York, and Florida, by 2010 Latinos had spread in significant numbers to nearly every area of the nation.

It should be made clear at the outset that the Hispanic population of the United States is not one homogenous ethnic or racial group as often perceived by the non-Hispanic public. The term itself may be a convenient label for those who do not understand the complexities of this very diverse population. It is made up of many different national subgroups that arrived in different time periods and for a variety of reasons. It consists of white upper-class Cubans and poor Dominicans and Puerto Ricans with mixed racial backgrounds. Hispanics include northern, predominantly white, Mexicans and Guatemalan Mayan Indians. There were political refugees fleeing the civil wars of Central America or Colombia, which raged in the 1980s and on, and migrants from many nations seeking economic opportunities where few exist in their countries of origin.

The terms "Hispanic" and "Latino" have not historically been used as self-identification references for first-generation migrants. They have conceived of themselves as Mexicans, Cubans, Puerto Ricans, Colombians, Ecuadorians, and other national identities who often have little in common with one another, at least from their perspectives. There may be a shared language and somewhat similar religious beliefs. But these communalities have been overshadowed by the powerful nationalism existing in Latin America and the Caribbean itself, and the sharp rivalries and even animosities that have been reproduced in Latino immigrant communities throughout the United States. Highly romanticized notions of a common identity and political solidarity have been forthcoming from some academics and activists within the various Hispanic subcommunities, to be sure. In our view, however, it would be a mistake to cast overarching and sweeping generalizations about Hispanics in the United States. This is certainly not to deny that second, third, and subsequent generations slowly have embraced the concept of a shared Latino identity, or that Latinos of all nationalities may often define themselves collectively in contrast to the non-Hispanic population in the same way that they are identified by "outsiders." However, even within domestic-born Latino communities, nationality continues to be the first and most important reference point for self-identification, even though sometimes these lines are blurred because of mixed parentage. Among domestic-born Latinos it is now common to find many individuals who have parents of different nationalities.

Some scholars have contended that Latinos are different from previous waves of migrants to the United States. It has been argued that they have held on to their Spanish language usage longer than previous migrant groups who maintained their native languages. Another argument is that Latinos have not been integrated into the mainstream as quickly as prior immigrants because so many are not predominantly "white," have experienced enduring racism and discrimination, and have remained mired in poverty. We emphatically do not hold these views and have found that in fact the evolution of the Hispanic population differs very little in the most fundamental ways from earlier waves of migrants who arrived in the United States from its foundation in the late 18th century. In its patterns of social, cultural, and political integration, language retention, economic and geographic mobility, class structures, multiple impacts upon popular culture, and even return migration, the experiences of Hispanics in the United States are similar to the classic patterns found in all immigrant communities of the 19th and 20th centuries. Only the forced migration of Africans from the 17th to the early 19th century through the slave trade remains an anomaly in the history of migration and the evolution of domestic populations in the United States.

We want to be very clear about our purposes in writing this book. As historians we focus upon what to us is the essence of history – measuring change over time. The ability to "measure" quantitatively how specific population groups have been transformed within U.S. society has been revolutionized by the recent generation and accessibility of extraordinary statistical databases on every population sector in the United States including, of course, Hispanics. We describe these later. Both of us have spent a significant part of our respective careers working with and analyzing similar kinds of voluminous statistical databases. We have also, hopefully, honed our abilities to present the results of data analysis in what we believe are fairly understandable formats.

We have focused much of our individual prior research and writing on demographic, social, and economic history. Thus, it is not surprising that when we discussed this project in its early stages, these themes became the focal points of this book. We do not delve into thematic areas that are currently in vogue and that largely revolve around cultural themes. This is not because we don't feel that these are important. It is rather that so many outstanding scholars from different disciplines have produced so much innovative and pioneering work on the cultural aspects of the Latino experience in the United States. We felt it would be useful to produce a book that would present and analyze time-series quantitative data on demographic, social, and economic themes. One of our purposes in discussing and presenting these quantitative data in many graphs and tables – some admittedly quite dense – is to make available analyzed statistical information that we deem to be important, to other researchers, students, journalists, politicians, and the interested public who may not have the quantitative skills to analyze the voluminous raw databases used for this book.

Our data sets for analyzing the Hispanic population have come from a variety of sources provided by the U.S. Census Bureau and the University of Minnesota, Minnesota Population Center's Integrated Public Use Microdata Series (IPUMS). IPUMS has prepared the raw data files for the Census Bureau's PUMS, or Public Use Microdata Sample, in comparable formats for U.S. decennial censuses from 1850 to the American Community Surveys (ACS) of 2001–2008.[1] We have used the 5% sample files provided by IPUMS for the censuses of 1980, 1990, and 2000, and the American Community Survey 2005 to analyze a wide range of demographic, economic, and social variables. On occasion, and indicated clearly in footnotes, we have utilized data for 1990, 2000, and 2005 from the American FactFinder data sets provided by the Census Bureau at the following Web site: http://factfinder.census.gov/home/saff/main.html?_lang=en. This is primarily because of the difficulty of integrating some of the state-designated PUMS geographical areas into more easily understandable administrative entities such as counties across the United States.[2]

---

[1] See Steven Ruggles, Matthew Sobek, Trent Alexander, Catherine A. Fitch, Ronald Goeken, Patricia Kelly Hall, Miriam King, and Chad Ronnander. *Integrated Public Use Microdata Series: Version 3.0* [machine-readable database]. Minneapolis, MN: Minnesota Population Center [producer and distributor], 2004 found at http://usa.ipums.org/usa/.

[2] PUMS data are collected by the Census Bureau from geographical units designated by each state labeled as Public Use Microdata Areas (PUMAs). For the 1980, 1990, and 2000 censuses these areas had a minimum of 100,000 people. For the 2005 American Community Survey these areas had a minimum of 65,000 people. For a visual representation of each state's PUMAs, see http://www.census.gov/geo/www/maps/sup_puma.htm.

The Census Bureau collected data on households and the population. These data sets represent samples of the population which are weighted to provide profiles for the total population. Although there is unquestionably an undetermined margin of error in each

The data collected for the ACS 2005 have been recognized as both problematic and difficult to compare to earlier census years. Not only were sample data collected exclusively on areas with a minimum of 65,000 people, but they were also collected only on people living in households. Persons living in group quarters were not enumerated. Additionally, different methods were employed in the collection of particular data from one census year to the next such as those on income and other variables.[3] Thus, some of the data presented here for 2005 may be not be as accurate as would be the case had we used the subsequently released ACS data for 2006 and 2007. However, we began this ambitious project in 2006, about a year before the data for that year were released, and had completed the construction of our data sets and their analysis prior to the availability of subsequent data. Despite the problems with the 2005 ACS, we strongly believe that the fundamental statistical trends, tendencies, and structures we present here from 1980 to 2005 may be used with confidence and that they are an accurate depiction of how the variables we focus on changed over time. Since we wrote this book, we have run a series of statistical tests on the 2006 and 2007 ACS data released

of these data sets, the data provided in them are more detailed than those found in the Summary Files released by the Census Bureau and thus permit a more sophisticated analysis of numerous variables than other Census Bureau data files. Scholars working with census data files have generally considered the PUMS data to be reliable.

For a discussion of the 1980 PUMS data sets, see "Chapter 4, Sample Design for the Public-Use Microdata Samples," Census of Population and Housing, 1980: Public-Use Microdata Samples Technical Documentation, U.S. Department of Commerce, Bureau of the Census, Washington, DC, 1983, pp. 35–42, reprinted at http://usa.ipums.org/usa/voliii/1980samp.shtml; for 1990 PUMS data sets see "Chapter 4, Sample Design and Estimation," 1990 Census of Population and Housing: Public-use Microdata Samples Technical Documentation, U.S. Department of Commerce, Bureau of the Census, Washington, DC, 1992, pp. 4–1 to 4–7 reprinted by IPUMS at http://usa.ipums.org/usa/voliii/1990samp.shtml; for 2000 PUMS data sets see "Pums Accuracy of the Data, 2000" found at http://www.census.gov/acs/www/Downloads/C2SS/AccuracyPUMS.pdf; for the ACS 2005 data sets see "Pums Accuracy of the Data, 2005" at http://www.census.gov/acs/www/Downloads/2005/AccuracyPUMS.pdf.

For comparability issues related to the ACS 2005 PUMS data see "Ten Things to Know about the American Community Survey (2005 Edition)" published by the Missouri Census Data Center at http://mcdc2.missouri.edu/pub/data/acs2005/Ten_things_to_know.shtml. Also see "Census 2000 Acs 2005 Comparison Issues" found at the New York State Data Center Web site at http://www.empire.state.ny.us/nysdc/Census_ACS2005_Comparison.pdf.

[3] These problems are considered in "PUMS Accuracy of the Data, 2005" found at http://www.census.gov/acs/www/Downloads/2005/AccuracyPUMS.pdf and in "Census 2000 ACS 2005 Comparison Issues" found on many Web sites including http://dola.colorado.gov/dlg/demog/census/ACS2005comparison.pdf.

by the Census Bureau. These tests confirmed that the basic patterns we describe here, on the variables we focus upon from 1980 through 2005, are accurate.

We want to reiterate that unlike most studies on Hispanics, which are statistically static in that they concentrate upon particular variables in specific years, this study presents and analyzes statistical indicators of change over time. It is clear that the absolute numbers on population, income, educational attainment, and the other topics we consider in detail would obviously have been different and more current had we used later data sets. However, to repeat, the fundamental trends and tendencies between 1980 and 2005 would have remained precisely as presented in this book. As in all quantitative studies, there is an unknown margin of error, and we are aware that the data presented in this book certainly reflect this basic inescapable fact. We are, however, confident that this margin of error is relatively small.

To obtain detailed data on Hispanic national subgroups, we have recalculated the data provided by the census in the Hispanic self-identification section of the Census Questionnaire that has been given since the census of 1980. As several scholars and even the Census Bureau itself have noted, there has been a considerable undercount of national groups because of the use of generic categories such as "Hispanic," "Latino," or "Latin American" by informants. To correct for this, we have categorized a great many of these generic "other Hispanic" category persons into nationality groups by using data provided by the same person as to their place of birth and their first and second ancestry. For example, we have recoded people who define themselves as Hispanic, Latino, or Latin American, but who were born in the Dominican Republic and/or whose parents (ancestry) indicated the Dominican Republic, as Dominican. Thus, through use of the raw data PUMS files, our data for Hispanic national groups are greater than those provided by the Census Bureau in the summary files for each census year.[4]

---

[4] The issues of Hispanic responses to the census questionnaire and recoding issues are discussed in Arthur R. Cresce and Roberto R. Ramírez, "Analysis of General Hispanic Responses in Census 2000" Population Division, U.S. Census Bureau, Washington, DC. 20233, Population Division Working Paper Series No. 72. It is found at the following web site: http://www.census.gov/population/www/documentation/twps0072/twps0072.html. For a detailed analysis of all studies on this issue, see U.S. Department of Commerce, Bureau of the Census. *Simulated Totals For Hispanic National Origin Groups [In Census 2000] By State, Place, County, And Census Tract: [United States]* [computer file]. ICPSR release. Washington, DC: U.S. Dept. of Commerce, Bureau of the Census [producer], 2003. Ann Arbor, MI: Inter-university Consortium for Political and Social

Introduction

[handwritten margin notes: his panic/Latino would also indicate shared colonial past — not actively rational/ ethical to lump colonizers in with colonized]

We have followed several basic rules in our recording of raw PUMS data, and these ought to be carefully noted. All persons of Iberian origin, both from the European mainland or the Atlantic Islands, have been excluded from the Hispanic category. Their inclusion as Hispanics by the Census Bureau is puzzling as the general connotation of the term suggests persons of Latin American and Hispanic-Caribbean origin. Despite the fact that the Census Bureau does not treat Brazilians as Hispanics, we have included them in our data sets for the simple reason that Brazil is in fact a part of Latin America. As a general rule we have excluded anyone listing themselves as with imprecise terms such as *Tejano* or someone from Texas. We have also excluded anyone using terms such as *criollo* or *mestizo* even if written in Spanish. These cases, or records, were not statistically significant. We have grouped all the numerous Mexican type listings into one category – Mexicans. They are the only national group appearing in the census with several alterative designations. For example in the 1990 census the following self-identifications – "Mexican," "Mexican American," "Mexicano/Mexicana," "Chicano/Chicana," "La Raza," "Mexican American Indian," "Mexico" – were grouped together as Mexicans. We use the term "Mexican" throughout this book to refer to persons of Mexican origin whether born in the United States or not. The same principal was used with every Latino national subgroup.

This book builds on the study of Frank Bean and Marta Tienda, which analyzed the Hispanic population in 1980 using the published census data of that year.[5] This was a pioneering work since prior to that year the Census Bureau had not treated Hispanics separately from the non-Hispanic white population; they were only included in enumeration through the use of surname data. Beginning in 1980, however, an imperfect question on "Spanish/Hispanic origin and descent" was added to the Census Bureau's

Research [distributor], 2004 available at http://webapp.icpsr.umich.edu/cocoon/CENSUS-STUDY/03907.xml#methodology. This study addresses issues raised in John Logan, "The New Latinos: Who They Are, Where They Are" available at http://mumford.albany.edu/census/report.html and Robert Suro, "Counting The "Other Hispanics" How Many Colombians, Dominicans, Ecuadorians, Guatemalans And Salvadorans Are There In The United States?" issued by the Pew Hispanic Center and available at http://pewhispanic.org/reports/report.php?ReportID=8. It ought to be underlined that these studies did not use the PUMS data but rather data from the Census 2000 Supplemental Survey and the March 2000 Current Population Survey issued by the Census Bureau. Our recalculations of nationalities using PUMS data differ marginally from the Suro, Logan, and Census Bureau simulation model reports, agreeing with them on the generalized undercount of nationalities.

[5] Frank D. Bean and Marta Tienda, *The Hispanic Population of the United States* (New York: Russell Sage Foundation, 1987).

questionnaire, which began the modern enumeration of Hispanics in the United States.[6] The amount of data on the Hispanic population produced since then by the Census Bureau, the Center for Disease Control, and many other government agencies collecting population data for the nation has been enormous. Yet surprisingly there has been no large-scale and systematic study of the Hispanic population beyond the original work of Bean and Tienda for 1980, except in highly specialized studies. In our presentation of the 1980–2005 data we have concentrated on presenting our basic findings, but without using advanced, and sometimes arcane, statistical procedures that nonspecialists find difficult to understand. Like Bean and Tienda, we have focused on presenting data in a format that we believe is accessible and understandable and that may be used by a wide audience from the general public to specialized researchers.

[6] The Census Bureau has redefined how data on Hispanics are collected in each subsequent decennial census and in the American Community Survey data from 2001 on.

I

Immigration to the United States to 1980

The only native groups residing in the region that would become the United States in 1492 were the 2 million or so Amerindian peoples whose ancestors had migrated from Northeastern Asia some 15 thousand to 25 thousand years before.[1] All subsequent inhabitants and their descendants originated in migration from Europe, Africa, Asia or through migration between different regions of the Americas. The migration process has been an ongoing one, and in fact the foreign-born and their first-generation sons and daughters born in the United States have represented a third or more of the total U.S. population from the foundation of the republic until today. Migration has clearly been one of the most dominant themes in the history of the United States.

The colonial period in the history of the Americas was defined by two distinct and quite different international migrations. The first consisted of the migration of free workers, a large portion having contracted significant debts to pay for transatlantic passage. The second was the forced migration of slaves from Africa. Throughout the Americas the slave trade was numerically greater than the migration of free peoples from the late 17th century until the 1830s.[2] Although this was the case for the Americas as a whole, in British colonial North America the African slave trade was a

[1] Herbert S. Klein and Daniel C. Schiffner, "The Current Debate About The Origins of The Paleoindians of America," *Journal of Social History*, 37:2 (Winter 2003), 483–92.
[2] See David Eltis, *Economic Growth and the Ending of the Transatlantic Slave Trade* (New York: Oxford University Press, 1987); David Eltis, *The Rise of African Slavery in the Americas* (New York: Cambridge University Press, 2000); David Eltis, editor, *Coerced and Free Migration: Global Perspectives* (Stanford, CA: Stanford University Press, 2002).

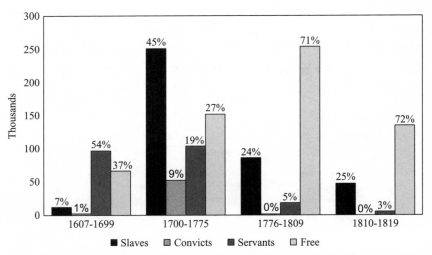

GRAPH 1.1. Relative Share of Slaves, Convicts, Indentured Servants and Free Persons Among All People Arriving in British North America, 1607–1819. *Sources:* Aaron Fogelman, "From Slaves Convicts and Servants to Free Passengers: The Transformation of Immigration in the Era of the American Revolution," *Journal of American History*, 85:1 (June 1998), 43–76 and Herbert S. Klein, *The Atlantic Slave Trade* (New York: Cambridge University Press, 1999).

ꞌ minor part of overall migration, and this pattern continued after independence was achieved in 1783 until 1808 when the slave trade to the United States was permanently closed.[3] The dominant migrants to the future United States during the colonial period were Northern Europeans, primarily from Great Britain and the Germanic states. Many contracted their labor prior to leaving Europe in return for free passage to the Western Hemisphere. Until the end of the 18th century free migrants who paid for their own passage were only a small part of the movement from Europe (see Graph 1.1).[4]

[3] For a survey of this migration see Herbert S. Klein, *The Atlantic Slave Trade* (New York: Cambridge University Press, 1999).

[4] It is estimated that over half of the some 307,000 European immigrants arriving in British North America from 1700 up until the Revolution were indentured laborers, which would have meant that something like 156,000 of them arrived in the period to 1775. Aaron Fogelman, "From Slaves, Convicts and Servants to Free Passengers: The Transformation of Immigration in the Era of the American Revolution," *Journal of American History*, 85:1 (June 1998), 71, Table A3; Aaron Fogelman, "Migrations to the Thirteen British North American Colonies, 1700–1775: New Estimates," *Journal of Interdisciplinary History*, XXII:4 (Spring 1992), 698, Table 1.

Higher wages in the Americas compared with Europe and increasing population density in Northern and Western Europe after 1800 due to the decline of death rates and increasing fertility rates provided an ever-expanding supply of free workers who were willing to pay their own passages or become indentured servants. The introduction of steam vessels in the period after the end of the slave trade in 1808 reduced the length of the Atlantic passage from weeks to days with the resulting decline in mortality on the crossing dropping to under 1%, a figure well below the estimated 15% mortality suffered by slaves during their passage in sailing ships from Africa.

Through the colonial period in British North America migrants from Europe constantly arrived, but the most important factor in the demographic expansion of the future United States was the impressive high rate of natural reproduction among the settled population. This meant that migrants accounted for only a small part of population growth prior to independence. During the 19th century, however, especially after 1830, the flow of international migration to the United States became far greater than in any previous period and had an ever-increasing impact on population growth. Although the natural growth rate of the domestic-born population was a very high 2.5% per annum in this period, it slowly declined. The population as a whole increased at over 3% annually, and this was because of large-scale European immigration after 1830. At the same time, the nation's slaves and its free peoples of color, both population segments increasing at impressive natural rates, declined in relative demographic importance. The total number of African Americans, slave and free, contracted from 19% of the national population in 1790 to 14% by 1860.[5] On the eve of the Civil War in 1860 the foreign-born population represented the same proportion of the population as slaves, about 14%.[6]

This new post-1830 immigration of free workers who paid their own passages was due to major changes within Europe itself. Natural population growth rates were reaching historic proportions and creating population pressures as never before experienced in European history. Most

[5] Campbell Gibson and Kay Jung, *Historical Census Statistics on Population Totals By Race, 1790 to 1990, and By Hispanic Origin, 1970 to 1990, For The United States, Regions, Divisions, and States*, U.S. Census Bureau, Population Division, Working Paper Series No. 56, (Washington, DC: U.S. Census Bureau, September 2002), Tables 1–14.

[6] U.S. Bureau of the Census, *1860 Census of the United States*, vol. 2, p. xxviii. (Washington, DC: Government Printing Office, 1864).

European nations had begun the process of urbanization and industrialization, and populations were increasingly moving out of the countryside and agriculture and into cities and urban occupations. Yet, until the last decades of the 19th century the expansion of European labor markets in both rural and urban areas could not keep up with this historically unparalleled population growth. Increasingly, most nations looked to an international solution to resolve internal population-growth problems, and most of the major European governments favored out-migration as a crucial safety valve for the basic structural changes that were occurring within their own frontiers. Thus, the 19th century would be defined as the first and probably only period of true labor globalization in what became a virtually free international transatlantic labor market.

In turn, the classic American equation of abundant lands and scarce labor, along with increasing exports to Europe to satisfy expanding European markets, guaranteed that wages in the Americas remained higher than those in Europe for most of the 19th century. Thus, the "push" and "pull" factors favoring migration were in place by 1830, and the changing technology and lowered cost of transportation thereafter were the final key elements needed to stimulate the ensuing large-scale migration. The development of railroads in Europe and the introduction of steam shipping by the middle decades of the 19th century drove down the transportation costs of migration to the point where large segments of the European population could pay for their own passage without resorting to indentured servitude. Economic historians have suggested that the indentured labor market would have continued after 1820 if a supply of poorer laborers from Europe could have been found who were unable to pay the transportation costs to come to the United States.[7] But the steep decline in the numbers of poor laborers who were unable to pay their own passages led to the collapse of the indentured system. By 1830 only free and unencumbered workers were crossing the Atlantic to supply labor for the United States market. With the growth of the cotton economy in the South, the ever-expanding production of grains in all other regions, and the development and growth of industrial production and mining, the United States was able to maintain wages that

[7] Farley Grubb, "The End of European Immigrant Servitude in the United States: An Economic Analysis of Market Collapse, 1772–1835," *The Journal of Economic History*, 54:4 (December 1994), 794–824; David W. Galenson, "The Rise and Fall of Indentured Servitude in the Americas: An Economic Analysis," *The Journal of Economic History*, 44:1 (March 1984), 1–26.

could easily compete with the European labor market for most of the 19th century.

The migration of Europeans and others to the United States developed in several stages. From the 1830s to the 1880s migrants came largely from Northwestern Europe, while from the 1880s to the 1920s the "New Immigrants" came mostly from Eastern and Southern Europe, with a small flow of migrants from Asia. In the post–World War II period the "New New Immigrants" came primarily from Asia and Latin America and the Hispanic Caribbean. The overall flow of this migration to 1930 was impressive. From 1821 to 1924 some 44 million Europeans migrated to all of the Americas, of which 31 million or about 70% came to the United States.[8] Until 1855 the majority of immigrants crossing the Atlantic arrived in North America, with the United States as the principal destination. Between 1826 and 1835 Canada absorbed some 40% of all immigrants to North America, but thereafter declined in relative importance. By the post-1836 period two-thirds of all migrants were coming to the United States. Moreover the two other major competitors for transatlantic immigrants, Brazil and Argentina, would not enter the international labor market in a major way until after 1850 (see Graph 1.2).[9]

The volume of transatlantic migration to the United States increased by 8% annually from 1821 to the beginning of the Civil War in 1861, although it varied in volume by decade. The economic crisis of the 1840s led to a decrease in the rate of migration, and during the late 1850s there was an actual decline in total migration. Nevertheless the overall numbers are impressive. By the 1831–35 period migrants to the United States averaged just fewer than 50,000 persons yearly; ten years later the average was almost double that number; and by 1846–50 some 250,000 migrants were coming from Europe to eastern U.S. ports every year. Though this volume fluctuated because of changing European or North American economic and labor-market conditions and especially the emergence of competing demands for European labor by the decade of the 1880s, migration averaged just under a half million persons per annum and would eventually rise to about to 1 million persons annually entering the United States by 1901–05 (see Graph 1.3).

Most of the migration until 1860 was from Northern Europe, which was experiencing what is known as the "demographic transition" or

[8] Imre Ferenczi and Walter F. Willcox, *International Migrations* (New York: National Bureau of Economic Research, 1929–1931), Vol. I, pp. 236–37.

[9] Ferenczi and Willcox, *International Migrations*, Vol. I, pp. 236–37, Table 6.

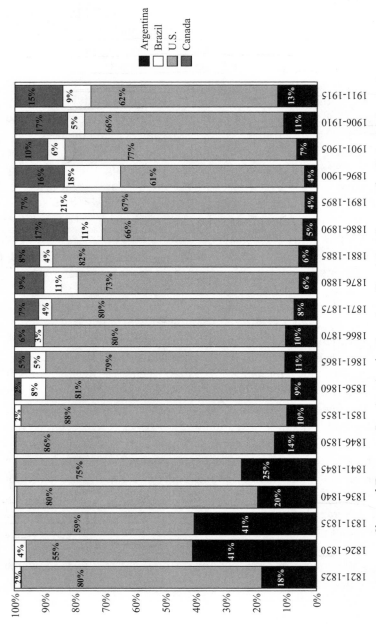

GRAPH 1.2. Share of European Immigration by American Receiving Country, by Quinquenium, 1821–1915. *Source:* Imre Ferenczi and Walter F. Wilcox, *International Migrations, Vol. I. Statistics,* (New York: National Bureau of Economic Research, 1919), pp. 236–37.

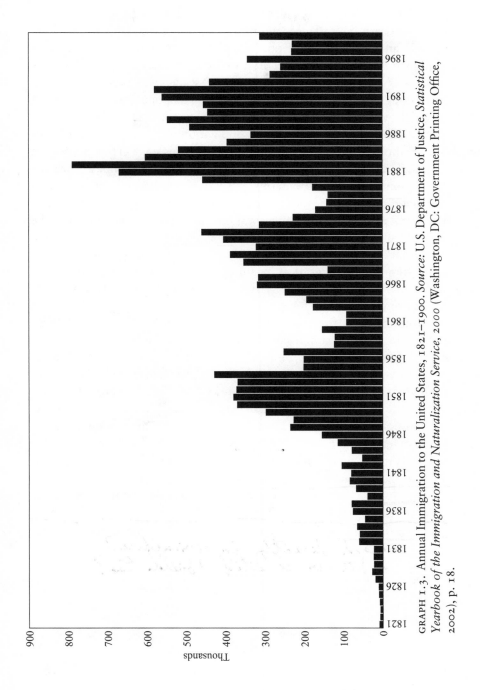

GRAPH 1.3. Annual Immigration to the United States, 1821–1900. *Source:* U.S. Department of Justice, *Statistical Yearbook of the Immigration and Naturalization Service, 2000* (Washington, DC: Government Printing Office, 2002), p. 18.

the shift from high birth rates and high death rates to low birth rates and low death rates. The Scandinavian countries, the United Kingdom, Ireland, and Scotland experienced population growth rates of over 1% per annum.[10] Although rates of increase varied by country and by decade, this trend was nearly identical in all. By 1800 Sweden was experiencing high birth rates and declining mortality rates, and its population was growing at or above 1% yearly. By the 1830s the same was occurring in the United Kingdom, and the German population increased at over 1% per annum through most of the 19th century.[11] At this stage in their respective economic development processes, these countries could not absorb the large number of people entering the workforce because of this rapid population expansion, and a viable solution to the increasing rates of urban poverty and social conflict was out-migration. At the same time the higher wages paid in the Western Hemisphere, the steep decline in the cost of transatlantic passage, and relatively open government policies toward emigration and immigration by European and American governments made migration an option for large numbers of people. This was in fact the age of globalization for labor markets.

Although many foreign immigrants arriving in North America would remain in growing urban centers, the majority found employment in agriculture. The biggest single area to which they migrated was the Middle Atlantic States, with the old Northeastern states in second place.[12] But immigrants were found in all regions of the nation including the South, and before 1860 it was estimated that 15% of the frontier population was foreign-born. In the country as a whole the weight of the foreign-born was impressive. By the census of 1870 foreign-born and second-generation residents (those who had one or more foreign-born parents) represented 34% of the total national population.[13]

In 1860 the United States was still a largely agricultural society. Only 20% of the population resided in towns of 2,500 or more, and 48% of the labor force was still engaged in agriculture. Though manufactures had

[handwritten annotation: engaged directly in agriculture. or in related level than?]

[10] B. R. Mitchell, *International Historical Statistics: Europe, 1750–1993* (3rd ed.; New York: Stockton Press, 1992), pp. 92–101, Table A6.

[11] Jean-Claude Chesnais, *The Demographic Transition: Stages, Patterns, and Economic Implications* (Oxford: Clarendon Press, 1992), Chapter 8.

[12] Peter D. McClelland and Richard J. Zeckhauser, *Demographic Dimensions of the New Republic: American Interregional Migration, Vital Statistics Manumissions, 1800–1860* (Cambridge: Cambridge University Press, 1982), p. 44, Table 3.52.

[13] U.S. Bureau of the Census, *Thirteenth Census of the United States, 1910,* (Washington, DC: n.p., 1918) Vol. 1, Chapter 2, p. 130, Table 8.

been growing, industry still absorbed only 18% of the economically active population. By 1900, however, a complete transformation had occurred. A third of the national population resided in urban areas, and 31% of all persons resided in cities of 100,000 or more inhabitants, an increase from only 10% of the national population in 1860.[14] Additionally, the portion of the economically active population engaged in agriculture had dropped to 37%.[15] This extraordinary shift in residential patterns during the second half of the 19th century meant that the national population was defined as primarily nonrural and nonagricultural, with the trends all moving toward further urbanization and the declining importance of rural occupations in national labor markets. These factors were important in influencing the birth, death, and growth rates of the U.S. population and in making the United States indistinguishable from the other leading industrializing nations of the period from a demographic perspective. It also changed the areas of destination of European migrants arriving after 1880 as immigrants now went primarily to Eastern and Midwestern cities.

Northern Europeans from Great Britain, Scandinavia, and the Germanic regions had predominated until the 1870s; however, after 1880 there was a shift in immigrant origins to Southern and Eastern Europeans. As the demographic transition toward lower birth and death rates began affecting these regions in the second half of the 19th century, population growth in Spain, Portugal, Italy, Greece, the Ottoman regions of the Mediterranean, the western regions of the Russian Empire, and Poland outpaced the capacity of domestic labor markets to absorb expanding working-age populations. At the same time Northern European wages were beginning to reach Western Hemisphere levels, and this resulted in the slowing of emigration from these regions, which had dominated colonial and early 19th-century migration to the United States.[16] By the late 19th century the change in the origins of the migrant population was clearly evident. During the decade of the 1870s immigrants from Southern and Eastern Europe represented just 6% of all immigrants arriving to U.S. ports. In the 1880s these "new immigrants" increased to 18% of all migrants, and then to over half of all arrivals by the 1890s, far surpassing

---

[14] Data taken from U.S. Bureau of the Census, *Historical Statistics of the United States, Colonial Times to 1970* (New York: Basic Books, 1976), Table A pp. 57–72.

[15] Data taken from U.S. Bureau of the Census, *Historical Statistics*, Table F 250–261.

[16] For the latest modeling of this emigration, see Timothy J. Hatton and Jeffrey G. Williamson, "What Drove the Mass Migrations from Europe in the Late Nineteenth Century?" *Population and Development Review*, 20:3 (September 1994), 533–59.

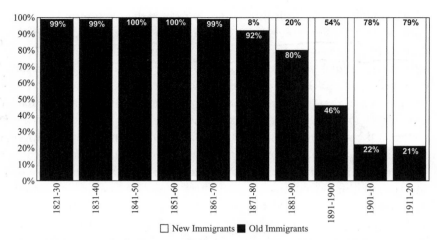

GRAPH 1.4. Origins of Arriving Immigrants to the United States by Decade, 1820–1920. *Source:* U.S. Department of Justice, *Statistical Yearbook of the Immigration and Naturalization Service, 1998* (Washington, DC: Government Printing Office, 2000), p. 19.

the older Northern European–origin countries. By the first decade of the 20th century Southern and Eastern Europeans made up two-thirds of all migrants arriving in the United States (see Graph 1.4).[17]

This flow of new immigrants proved to be even more intense than earlier transatlantic movements. Additionally, most migrants now settled in cities and towns rather than rural areas. The upsurge in the volume of immigration meant that the relative importance of the foreign-born population within the United States also increased. In 1850 the 2.2 million foreign-born residing in the United States represented 10% of the total population, but by 1890 there were 9.2 million foreign-born persons in the United States, and they accounted for 15% of the population, a level that would be maintained until 1910.[18] There was a slight decline by 1930 when the foreign-born were about 13% of the total population. Although this percentage was quite high compared to European countries, it was

[17] U.S. Department of Justice, Immigration and Naturalization Service, *Statistical Yearbook of the Immigration and Naturalization Service, 1998* (Washington, DC: Government Printing Office, 2000), p. 19. For the latest survey of this immigration experience, see Walter Nugent, *Crossings: The Great Transatlantic Migrations, 1870–1914* (Bloomington: Indiana University Press, 1992).

[18] Campbell J. Gibson and Emily Lennon, "Historical Census Statistics on the Foreign-born Population of the United States: 1850–1990," U.S. Census Bureau, Population Division Working Paper No. 29 (Washington, DC: U.S. Census Bureau, February 1999), Table 1.

considerably less than the 22% of the Canadian population that was foreign-born and the 30% foreign-born population of Argentina.[19] *in 1980*

By 1900 the foreign-born and their children (generally labeled "foreign stock") represented 39% of the non-Hispanic white population, and this percentage was maintained in 1910.[20] In the period from 1850 to 1920 they had increased from 10.8 million to 36.4 million persons.[21] In addition to the previously considered change from Northern to Southern Europeans in the migratory flow, the European component itself gradually began to decline. In 1850 92% of the foreign-born came from Europe, and by 1910 Europeans represented 87% of the U.S. foreign-born population. Although European migration began to wane slightly by the early 20th century, and there were signs of a new migration from Latin America and Asia, Eastern and Southern European migrants continued to arrive in the United States until the Great Depression began in 1929. Along with Italians, Poles, and Russians, there was also a steady stream of German and English migrants. Of the 13.7 million foreign-born persons whose language was known in 1920, some 3 million were native English speakers (22% of the total), and there were 2.5 million people who spoke German or about 18% of the foreign-born population. German was the most important language among non-English speakers, followed by 1.6 million people who spoke Italian, a million people who spoke Yiddish, and approximately the same number who spoke Polish. In 1920 some 26.7 million people in the United States spoke a language other than English, and this represented an extraordinary 25% of the total national population.[22]

As was the case with all immigrants in all periods more males than females arrived between 1880 and 1920, and they were primarily working-age adults. Yet after 1880 some characteristics of the migrant population demonstrated a break from the past. There were fewer families, more individuals who traveled alone, and reduced numbers of children. There were also fewer agricultural laborers and far more urban workers.[23] The median age for both foreign-born men and women in

before WWII too? or btw 1880 & WWII?

[19] Niles Carpenter, *Immigrants and Their Children*, 1920, U.S. Bureau of the Census, Census Monographs VII (Washington, DC: GPO, 1927), p. 9.

[20] U.S. Bureau of the Census, *Thirteenth Census of the United States.*

[21] Carpenter, *Immigrants and Their Children*, p. 7.

[22] Carpenter, *Immigrants and Their Children*, pp. 98–99, Table 53.

[23] Charlotte J. Erickson, "Emigration from the British Isles to the USA in 1841: Part 1. Emigration from the British Isles," *Population Studies*, 43 (1989), 380. She argues that there is a general consensus about the differences of the migrants of the 1880s from those of the 1830s.

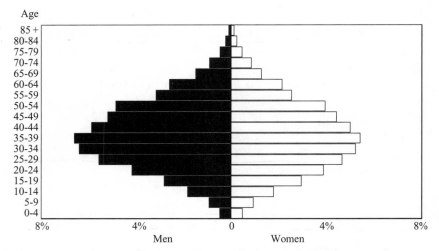

GRAPH 1.5. Age Pyramid of the Foreign-Born Population in 1880. *Source:* Campbell J. Gibson and Emily Lennon, *Historical Census Statistics on the Foreign-born Population of the United States: 1850–1990*, Population Division Working Paper Series No. 29 (February 1999).

1880 was 38 years, and this was 17 years older than the 21-year-old median age of the national population. The immigrant sex ratio was 119 men for every 100 women compared to the 103 male to 100 female sex ratio prevalent among the national population in 1880. This differentiation increased by 1910 as there were 131 male immigrants for every 100 female immigrants, compared to a national average of 106 males per 100 females.[24] The impact of this bias in the age and sex distribution of the immigrant population may be observed in the age pyramids for the foreign-born population in 1880 and in 1910 (see Graphs 1.5 and 1.6).

Although the post-1880 European migrants, like their predecessors settled largely in the northern states – 88% in 1850 and 86% in 1900 – they were beginning to move inland in greater numbers. About 29% of the total foreign-born population lived in Midwestern states according to the 1850 census, and this increased significantly to about 46% by 1900.[25]

This migrant population was also more urban in their settlement patterns than the nonimmigrant population, with only a third living in rural

[24] Gibson and Lennon, "Historical Census Statistics on the Foreign-born," Table 7; U.S. Bureau of the Census, *Historical Statistics*, Tables A143–157, A119–134.
[25] Gibson and Lennon, "Historical Census Statistics on the Foreign-born," Table 14.

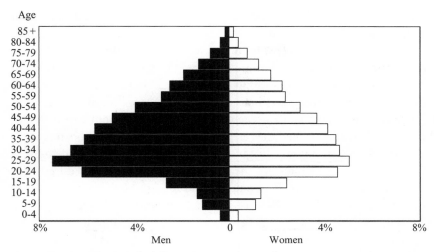

GRAPH 1.6. Age Pyramid of the Foreign-Born Population in 1910. *Source:* Campbell J. Gibson and Emily Lennon, *Historical Census Statistics on the Foreign-born Population of the United States: 1850–1990*, Population Division Working Paper Series No. 29 (February 1999).

areas in 1900 compared to 64% of the domestic-born population. As early as 1870 more than a quarter of the foreign-born resided in cities of 100,000 or more (compared to just 8% of the domestic-born population), and by 1910 some 44% were residing in these large cities compared to 18% of domestic-born residents.[26]

These post-1880 immigrants had both higher mortality and fertility rates compared with the domestic-born population, as was typical of predominantly rural populations.[27] In the Southern and Eastern European countries mortality rates had begun to fall after 1880, but fertility rates were just beginning to decline as a response to rapid population growth.

[26] Gibson and Lennon, "Historical Census Statistics on the Foreign-born," Table 18.
[27] Leading scholars agree that there was consistently higher mortality in the cities, even as late as 1900/02. See Michael R. Haines, "The Urban Mortality Transition in the United States, 1800–1940," (Cambridge, MA: NBER, Historical Research, Paper no. 134, July 2001), p. 2. However, Thompson and Whelpton argue that the difference in the combined male and female life expectancy between urban and rural America was just 8.8 years, in the same period. See Warren S. Thompson and P. K. Whelpton, *Population Trends in the United States* (New York: McGraw-Hill Book Co., 1933), p. 242, Table 67. Also see Michael R. Haines, "The White Population of the United States, 1790–1920," in Michael R. Haines and Richard H. Steckel, *A Population History of North America* (Cambridge: Cambridge University Press, 2000), p. 339.

This pattern would be repeated by later migrants from Asia and Latin America and the Caribbean.

Given their predominantly urban residence in the United States, most first-generation immigrants and their offspring began to emulate domestic-born fertility and family models, and by the second generation their family sizes were sometimes even smaller than domestic-born families in the United States. Consistently over time foreign-born women and their children approached the fertility rates of the domestic-born regardless of national immigrant origins. In a study of domestic- and foreign-born non-Hispanic whites in Chicago from 1920 to 1940, the differential in total fertility between the domestic and foreign-born population constantly decreased. Moreover this decline occurred for all income groups, although it was most rapid for the wealthiest immigrants. By 1920 upper-class immigrants had lower fertility rates than domestic-born non-Hispanic whites of the same socioeconomic standing.[28] A similar process was observed in Detroit between 1920 and 1930, where foreign-born women lowered their fertility rates more rapidly than domestic-born non-Hispanic white women. This decline in fertility among the foreign-born was the most important factor driving down overall birth rates in the city.[29]

In a detailed study of Italian immigrants to the United States in the late 19th and early 20th centuries, Livi Bacci found that immigrant families quickly lowered birth rates to those of domestic-born non-Hispanic whites. In fact, he found that mothers younger than 34 years of age born in Italy, who had fertility rates that were almost double those of domestic-born non-Hispanic whites in 1920, had achieved fertility rates at or below those of domestic-born non-Hispanic whites by the late 1930s.[30] He also estimated that between 1910 and 1940, the fertility of most all immigrant groups at all ages (except for Italians and Mexicans) fell more rapidly than for domestic-born non-Hispanic white women, though none surpassed their low fertility rates.[31]

In the United States as a whole, it is estimated that of the three basic population categories – domestic-born non-Hispanic whites, non-whites, and foreign-born whites – the fertility rates among the foreign-born

[28] Evelyn M. Kitagawa, "Differential Fertility in Chicago, 1920–40," *American Journal of Sociology*, 58:5 (March 1953), 485, Table 1.
[29] Albert Mayer and Carol Klapprodt, "Fertility Differentials in Detroit, 1920–1950," *Population Studies*, 9:2 (November 1955), 154.
[30] Massimo Livi Bacci, *L'immigrazione e l'assimilazione degli italiani negli Stati Uniti secondo le statistiche demografiche americane* (Milano: Giuffrè, 1961), p. 68, Table 23.
[31] Livi Bacci, *L'immigrazione e l'assimilazione*, p. 58. Table 19.

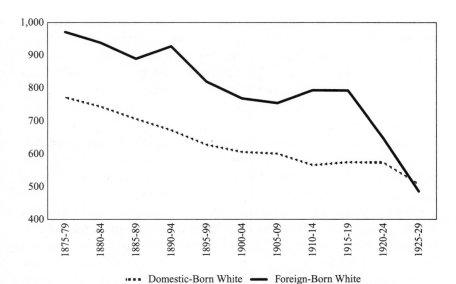

GRAPH 1.7. Fertility Ratio for Non-Hispanic White Population by Nativity, 1875–1929 (Children under 5 Years of Age per Thousand Women Ages 20–44). *Source:* Richard A. Easterlin, "The American Baby Boom in Historical Perspective, *American Economic Review*, LI:5 (December 1961), p. 906, Table A3.

decreased <u>at double the rate of the other two groups</u>. Between 1920 and 1929 fertility rates for women 15 to 44 years of age was estimated to have fallen by 20% among domestic-born non-Hispanic whites, while it fell by almost a third for the foreign-born and just 18% for African Americans.[32] In another study that examined fertility rates by origin, it was suggested that the period 1910–14 showed the largest differential in fertility rates between domestic-born and foreign-born non-Hispanic whites since such data first became available in 1875–79. However, thereafter it fell so rapidly that by 1925–29 the fertility rate of the foreign-born population was actually below that of domestic-born non-Hispanic whites for the first time ever (see Graph 1.7).[33] Moreover, this pattern of initially higher fertility rates of the foreign-born and their progressive decline to levels at

---

[32] Thompson and Whelpton, *Population Trends in the United States*, p. 270, Table 76.
[33] Richard A. Easterlin, "The American Baby Boom in Historical Perspective," *American Economic Review*, LI:5 (December 1961), 906, Table A3. All major immigrant groups in the 1905–09 period had achieved native white rates by the second generation, except for the Italians and non-Jewish Polish immigrants. But even these two groups experienced total fertility rate declines, with the Italians of the second generation having 2 children less than their first-generation parents (or 4.9 children per completed family) and the Catholic Polish immigrants dropping by half a child less – though they remained unusual in the still very high 6.6 children per completed fertility. For a detailed analysis of the

or below those of the domestic-born has been noted in every study and
for every immigrant group arriving in the United States in the 19th and
20th centuries. Regardless of whether they came from Europe in the early
1900s or from Latin America, the Caribbean, or China in the 1980s and
after, this pattern held over time regardless of immigrant group.

In this period the shift from Northern Europeans to Southern and
Eastern Europeans was the major structural change in the origins of the
migrant population. In the 1880s Germany was the leading source of
immigrants followed by the United Kingdom – the two accounting for
2.2 million of the 4.7 million Europeans arriving in this decade. During
the first decade of the 20th century 2.1 million immigrants came from the
Austro-Hungarian Empire; another 2 million came from Italy; followed
by Russia with 1.6 million migrants. More than 70% of all migrants to
the United States came from these three broadly defined regions between
1900 and 1910. From 1910 to 1920 Italy moved into first place as a
source of migrants, followed by Russia, and then the Austro-Hungarian
Empire – the three regions accounting for some 2.9 million of the 4.3
million Europeans arriving, or about 67% of the total, a slight decline
from the previous decade.[34]

The integration of these new immigrants into the United States in the
1880–1920 period established patterns that were to become the norm
for most subsequent migrant groups. Newcomers to the United States
settled in cities, took the lowest-paying unskilled and manual labor jobs,
clustered together in ethnic neighborhoods, spoke their native languages
among one another, and read their own immigrant newspapers. They
entered the labor market in jobs where wages were high relative to their
native countries but low by U.S. standards, and in which opportunities
for social mobility were low. Work was found in occupations generally
avoided by the domestic-born population since these were perceived as
offering little in the way of future improvements.[35] This first generation of

immigrant and native fertility at this time, and the declining fertility rates of second-
generation immigrants by ethnic groups, see S. Philip Morgan, Susan Cotts Watkins,
and Douglas Ewbank, "Generating Americans: Ethnic Differences in Fertility," in Susan
Cotts Watkins, *After Ellis Island: Newcomers and Natives in the 1910 Census* (New
York: Russell Sage Foundation. 1994), pp. 83–124.

[34] U.S. Department of Justice, *Statistical Yearbook 2000*, pp. 19–21, Table 2.

[35] The theory of the dual labor market postulates a basic demand function in advanced
industrial societies for unskilled labor entering into high-risk and low-status occupations
and industries, a market only supplied by non-native immigrants. The emphasis in the
dual labor market theory on immigrant strategies with respect to status and savings in
the mother and host countries is based on the Italian experience before World War I. See

immigrants remained closely connected to their homelands. Repatriation of funds to home countries was high and constant during their early working years in the United States and almost all expected to return to countries of origin. "To make America" was a favorite saying in several languages. This implied both the opportunity to make large sums of money in the United States and to return with their newfound wealth to their countries of origin, thus improving their status and class standing.

The dominant group within the early 20th-century immigration was Italians.[36] They accounted for 22% of the 15 million immigrants who arrived between 1900 and 1920, and Italian was the second-ranking foreign language most frequently spoken in the United States behind German.[37] Like other immigrant groups they settled in cities, but Italian migrants were even more urban and more intensely concentrated in the Northeastern region of the country.[38] Between 1880 and 1920 roughly half of all Italians returned home from all of the Americas: approximately 51% of Italian migrants to Argentina and about 54% of those who migrated to the United States.[39] Brazilian-bound Italian migrants also

but how many actually returned?

Michael J. Piore, *Birds of Passage: Migrant Labor and Industrial Society* (Cambridge, MA: MIT Press, 1979).

[36] They represented 18% of all immigrants from 1881 to 1920, and an extraordinary 23% of all immigrants in the first decade of the 20th century. U.S. Department of Justice, Immigration and Naturalization Service, *Statistical Yearbook of the Immigration and Naturalization Service, 1998* (Washington, DC: Government Printing Office, 2000), p. 19.

[37] In 1910, of the 13 million foreign born, 25% spoke English, 21% spoke German, and 10% spoke Italian. Yiddish was fourth at 8%. If the second generation is included, the total is 32 million, with the ranking the same – English at 31%, German at 28%, and Italian at 7%. U.S. Bureau of the Census, *Thirteenth Census of the United States*, I, Chapter 9, pp. 961, 965, Tables 1, 5. On their ratio of total immigration from 1910 to 1920, see U.S. Bureau of the Census, *Historical Statistics*, I, Table C pp. 89–119.

[38] In 1910 the south and north central states together had 85% of the farm population (as well as 80% of all farm acreage and the total value of all farms) but only 20% of the Italian population. Moreover, since three-quarters or more of the Italians lived in urban areas, probably no more than 60,000 Italian immigrants worked in the agricultural heartland of the United States. In contrast, 69% of the native-born population lived in these two regions. U.S. Bureau of the Census, *Thirteenth Census of the United States*, I, p. 800; U.S. Bureau of the Census, *Historical Statistics*, I, pp. 90–92, 450. For the Italian background experiences of selected U.S.-bound immigrants, see John W. Briggs, *An Italian Passage: Immigrants to Three American Cities* (New Haven, CT: Yale University Press, 1978), Chapter 1; Virginia Yans-McLaughlin, *Family and Community: Italian Immigrants in Buffalo, 1880–1930* (Ithaca, NY: Cornell University Press, 1977), Chapter 1.

[39] We calculated the rate of return from the United States using Livi Bacci's differing decennial estimates for the period 1880–1920 to obtain an overall ratio (*L'immigrazione e l'assimilazion*, p. 35). We calculated the overall estimate of return from Argentina using

repatriated at comparable rates during the period between 1901 and
1920.[40] The return migrants were even more male-dominate than the
arriving immigrants in this period, and this led to a more balanced sex
ratio in the resident Italian-American communities of the United States.

For those who remained because of failure to accumulate savings, or
marriage with other foreigners or to domestic-born partners, rates of
social mobility were quite low. It often took several generations for these
immigrant families to break out of ethnic ghettos and to improve educational attainment levels, which could lead to better jobs and upward social
mobility. Yet, eventually all immigrant groups integrated into U.S. society
to varying degrees. European language retention declined with each generation. There were increasing rates of marriage with domestic-born or
other foreign-born ethnic groups. English became the dominant language
of second and subsequent generations, even though bilingualism may
have persisted for some time. These same dynamics experienced by Italians and other late 19th- and early 20th-century immigrant groups would
be repeated later by immigrants from Latin America and the Caribbean
during the second half of the 20th century and beyond.

The hostility directed toward immigrants, especially the predominantly
southern Italians who made up the majority of the arrivals from Italy, was
widespread. A special investigation by Congress, the famous Dillingham
Commission report (1907–11), was negative in its conclusions about the
potential "Americanization" of these new immigrants. Congress and most

the data in Direccíon General de Inmigración, *Resumen estadístico del movimiento
migratorio en la República Argentina, años 1857–1924* (Buenos Aires: Talleres Gráficos
del Ministerio de Agricultura de la Nación, 1925), p. 8. Recent Italian government statistics, which began to be compiled only in 1905, show even higher trends of repatriation for
the period 1905–1920 than the estimates of Livi Bacci for the United States, though they
correspond more closely to the official Argentine figures. See Italy. Instituto Centrale di
Statistica, *Bolletino mensile di Statistica* (Gennaio, 1975), Anno 5, Appendix 2, pp. 255,
263. Because of his detailed calculations for birth and death rates and his reliance on
the U.S. census for resident populations, we use Livi Bacci's estimates. On the diffi-
culties involved in estimating these rates, see J. D. Gould, "European Inter-Continental
Emigration – The Road Home: Return Migration from the U.S.A.," *Journal of European
Economic History*, 9 (1980), 79–87. For a comparative survey of the relative rates of
Italian immigrants in both countries, see Herbert S. Klein, "The Integration of Italian
Immigrants into Argentina and the United States: A Comparative Perspective," *American
Historical Review*, 88:2 (April 1983), 306–29.

[40] See G. Mortara, "A inmigraçao italiano no Brasil e algumas caracteristicas do grupo
italiano de São Paulo," *Revista Brasileira de Estadística*, 11 (1950), 325. For a comparison of the Italians in Brazil, Argentina, and the United States, see Herbert S. Klein,
"A integração dos imigrantes italianos no Brasil, na Argentina e nos Estados Unidos,"
Novos Estudos CEBRAP (São Paulo), 25 (Outubro, 1989), 95–117.

of the elite-dominated press believed that integration of these semiliterate non-English speaking urban workers and peasants was impossible. This growing nativism in the United States and overwhelming hostility to Italians and Jews among others led to the decision to restrict or close the United States to new immigration. The result was a series of quota laws, which would control the flow of immigration for almost a generation.

The period immediately after World War I was one of major international migration. During the decade of 1911–20, when 5.7 million immigrants entered the United States, some three-quarters came from Europe and the census of 1930 indicated that about 83% of the foreign-born population was of European origin.[41] But the Great Depression of the 1930s slowed the movement of Europeans across the Atlantic considerably, and this occurred just as the United States began to progressively restrict immigration. As early as 1917 the first restrictions were initiated when all illiterates and all Asians were barred from entering the country. Then in 1921 the Immigration Quota Law was enacted; it limited the number of aliens of any nationality entering the United States to 3% of the foreign-born persons of that nationality who lived in the United States in 1910.[42] Approximately 350,000 foreigners were permitted to enter each year, a number well below the yearly average of about one million persons who arrived annually during the 1910–14 period. Then in 1922 the U.S. Congress tightened this quota system even further, reducing the quota of yearly legal immigration to 2% of extant resident nationals, and the year used for calculating eligible immigrant origins was now pushed back to 1890. This was an obvious attempt to reduce the relative importance of Eastern and Southern Europeans in any future immigration, since most had arrived after 1890. With these quota acts the United States finally and effectively closed its doors to mass legal migration for 30 years, and it would not open them again until 1952.[43] By the late 1920s, the flow of immigration dropped to an average of 300,000 migrants annually, and the Great Depression and World War II brought immigration to a halt. After 1930 fewer than 100,000 immigrants per year reached the United States, with only some 38,000 immigrants arriving in 1945 (see Graph 1.8).

[41] Gibson and Lennon, "Historical Census Statistics on the Foreign-born," Table 2; U.S. Department of Justice, *Statistical Yearbook 2000*, p. 19, Table 2.

[42] For a detailed background to the enactment of this act, see John Higham, *Strangers in the Land: Patterns of American Nativism, 1860–1925* (New York: Atheneum Press, 1963), Chapter 11, pp. 300–30.

[43] All immigration data taken from U.S. Department of Justice, *Statistical Yearbook 2000*, p. 18, Table 1.

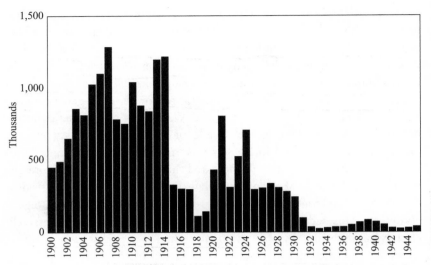

GRAPH 1.8. Annual Arrival of Immigrants to the United States, 1900–1945. *Source:* U.S. Department of Justice, Immigration and Naturalization Service, *Statistical Yearbook of the Immigration and Naturalization Service, 2000* (Washington, DC: Government Printing Office, 2002), p. 18, Table 1.

This major reduction in immigration produced the hoped-for results. In each census conducted after 1920 the percentage of the foreign-born in the total population declined. In 1910 they made up 14.7% of the total population; by 1940 foreign-born persons had declined to 8.8%.[44]

To compensate for the temporary closure of international migration, the expanding northern U.S. economy turned to Southern African Americans for unskilled industrial and manual labor. Confined to the old plantation areas of the South in the aftermath of the Civil War, African Americans did not migrate to other regions of the country until well into the 20th century. This "Great Migration," as it has been labeled, of rural African Americans out of the South, began on a significant scale during and after the Second World War. Limited Southern labor markets and the mechanization of the cotton crop, which progressively destroyed the postemancipation sharecropping system that had given employment to freed slaves, acted as powerful push factors out of the South. Pull factors to the north were related to the decline of foreign immigration from the 1920s onward, which opened up Northern labor markets for semiskilled and unskilled positions to Southern African Americans. In the

---

[44] Gibson and Lennon, "Historical Statistics on the Foreign-born," Table 1.

three decades between 1940 and 1970 over a million African Americans moved northward in each decade, and they settled primarily in cities where jobs were available.[45] As a result, African Americans who had been the most rural sector of the national population until 1950, surpassed non-Hispanic whites as the most urbanized racial/ethnic group of the domestic-born U.S. population. Some 85% of all African Americans lived in urban areas by 1980.[46] They were also no longer confined to the South. In 1920 85% of the African American population resided in the old Southern slave states, but by 1970 some 47% lived in the Northern and Western states.[47]

Not only was the resident population, domestic or foreign-born, moving within the country, but migrants from outside the continental United States had once again begun to arrive. Even in the period of radically reduced international migration in the 1950s and early 1960s, a new type of migrant began arriving in Northeastern cities, principally New York. This was the peak period of Puerto Rican migration. Puerto Ricans had been U.S. citizens since 1917 when the Jones Act was proclaimed by the U.S. Congress as a strategy for making a permanent political connection between the island and the United States. At that time Puerto Rico was a "non-incorporated territory" of the United States, which was an ambiguous legal status since it meant that petitioning for entrance into the United States as a state was legally impossible. Puerto Rico had been occupied by the U.S. military in 1898 and annexed through the Treaty of Paris with Spain in 1900. But until 1917 Puerto Ricans had no citizenship status of any type. The 1917 law bestowing U.S. citizenship upon Puerto Ricans made it completely legal to travel and settle in the United States without any legal documentation, and thus officially Puerto Ricans were not international migrants. During the 1940s some 151,000 Puerto

---

[45] For the most detailed demographic surveys of this migration, see Daniel M. Johnson and Rex R. Campbell, *Black Migration in America: A Socio-Demographic History* (Durham, NC: Duke University Press, 1981); Neil Fligstein, *Going North. Migration of Blacks and Whites from the South, 1900–1950* (New York: Academic Press, 1981). The estimates of the net migration will be found in U.S. Census Bureau, *The Social and Economic Status of the Black Population in the United States, 1790–1978: An Historical View*, Current Population Reports, P-23, No. 80 (Washington, DC: GPO, 1978), p. 15, Table 8.

[46] U.S. Bureau of the Census, *The Social and Economic Status of the Black Population*, p. 14, Table 6; U.S. Bureau of the Census, *1980 Census of the United States*, Summary Volumes, Vol. 1, [PC80-1-B1], pp. 27ff., Table 43. (Washington: U.S. Department of Commerce, Bureau of the Census, 1983).

[47] Frank Hobbs and Nicole Stoops, *Demographic Trends in the 20th Century*, U.S. Census Bureau, Census 2000; Special Reports, Series CENSR-4 (Washington DC: Government Printing Office, 2002), Table 8.

Ricans arrived, most destined for New York City, and this was followed by an impressive 470,000 Puerto Rican arrivals in the 1950s and another 214,000 during the 1960s.[48]

In the same period, a shift toward more tolerant migration laws began to generate new sources of foreign-born immigrants. From the quota laws of the 1920s to the end of World War II foreign immigration to the United States had been progressively declining. The low point was reached during the early 1940s when only some 23,000 legally documented foreign immigrants arrived in the United States. The immediate postwar period saw a rise in immigration, which soon reached the quota limits imposed during the 1920s. The first breach in the wall of legal obstacles to migration was the Immigration Act of 1952, which moved the quota base for each nationality from the 1880s arrivals data to the 1920 resident foreign-born population. By moving the numerical base used to calculate immigration quotas forward chronologically, the bias favoring the older Northern European nations as sources of immigrants was removed.

In October 1965 Congress finally abolished the quota system and allowed anyone to apply for admission to the United States, though it placed the first-ever restrictions on Western Hemisphere immigration by imposing a 120,000 yearly limit.[49] Through this, and subsequent congressional acts, the United States opened itself to new waves of foreign immigration from regions other than the traditional European origin nations. In the 1940s immigrants from Europe still made up 60% of arriving foreigners; by the 1970s they accounted for only 18% of documented

[48] José L. Vázquez Calzada, *La población de Puerto Rico y su trayectoría histórica.* (Río Piedras: Raga Printing, 1988), p. 286.

[49] The entire set of immigration laws from the earliest to the most recent are found at http://www.uscis.gov/portal/site/uscis/menuitem.eb1d4c2a3e5b9ac89243c6a7543f6d 1a/?vgnextoid=dc60e1df53b2fo1oVgnVCM1000000ecd190aRCRD&vgnextchannel= dc60e1df53b2fo1oVgnVCM1000000ecd190aRCRD, which is maintained by the U.S. Citizenship and Immigration Services (USCIS). For the general impact of the 1965 act in its early years, see Richard Polenberg, *One Nation Divisible: Class, Race and Ethnicity in the United States Since 1938* (New York: The Viking Press, 1980), pp. 281–92. But for the first time in immigration history the 1965 act also placed a limit on Western Hemisphere migration, limiting the number of migrants permitted to 120,000 yearly. However Puerto Ricans could migrate without restrictions since they were U.S. citizens, and in 1966 Congress passed the Cuban Adjustment Act, which essentially allowed unrestricted numbers of Cubans to enter the United States. For the negative consequences of this decisions on the pattern of Mexican legal and illegal migration, see Douglas S. Massey, Jorge Durand, and Nolan J. Malone, *Beyond Smoke and Mirrors: Mexican Immigration in an Era of Economic Integration* (New York: Russell Sage Foundation, 1992).

migration to the United States. Two new major migratory movements had developed: that from Latin America and the Caribbean and a second group from Asia. In the 1940s Latin American and Hispanic Caribbean migrants already accounted for over a third of all immigrants when Puerto Ricans are included and Asians were still a relatively small group who made up only 4% of the total. But by the 1970s Asians comprised 35% of documented immigrants while Latin Americans accounted for 44%, and they were the largest single group entering the United States. In the decade of the 1970s Mexicans represented 14% of all documented immigrants and made up a third of all those coming from the Western Hemisphere. The 640,000 Mexicans who legally entered the country were the largest single national contingent arriving in the 1970s, followed by 355,000 people who came from the Philippines.[50]

The new immigration streams that emerged in the 1970s have dominated international migration to the United States until today. In terms of volume, the average annual immigrant flow increased steadily from 180,000 in the late 1940s, to 434,000 in the 1970s, the highest average number of arrivals since the 1920s. As previously observed, there was a shift in the origins of migrants from Europe to Latin America, the Caribbean, and Asia. This major structural change in the source and volume of immigration was reflected in the census of 1980 when, for the first time ever, Europeans were no longer the majority of the foreign-born U.S. population having declined from 62% in 1970 to 39% in 1980. In 1980 Latin Americans "officially" accounted for a third of the foreign-born, an increase from the 19% found in 1970. Asians were 19% of the foreign-born in 1980, having risen from 9% in 1970.

Yet, even these data were an underestimate of the Latin American and Caribbean influence on immigration, since Puerto Ricans were considered American citizens and were not listed as immigrants. If the estimated Puerto Rican migration to the mainland is added to that of officially enumerated Latin Americans in the 1960s and 1970s, predominantly Spanish-speaking migrants made up one-half to two-thirds of all immigrants between 1960 and 1980, accounting for 3.5 million persons coming to the United States in these two decades.[51] Additionally, these data exclude the increasing importance of undocumented immigration from Mexico.

---

[50] U.S. Department of Justice, *Statistical Yearbook 2000*, pp. 18–21, Tables 1, 2.
[51] Gibson and Lennon, "Historical Census Statistics on the Foreign-born," Table 2 (updated 2001).

As had occurred with all of the post-1880 immigration flows, the majority of foreign-born arrivals, and Puerto Ricans, settled in urban areas. In fact, most migrants moved to relatively few cities. It is estimated in 1980 that 40% of the recent immigrant population lived in either the Los Angeles or New York City metropolitan areas.[52] Only Mexican agricultural migrants settled in rural areas, and a large share of these were temporary workers and undocumented persons seeking work in seasonal agricultural activities. The ratio of all Latin Americans and Asians living in cities, or the degree of urbanization, was higher than among the domestic-born non-Hispanic white or black populations. In 1980 about 90% of all Asians and Latin Americans were living in cities.[53]

The surge in Latin American, Caribbean, and Asian immigration reversed the downward trend in the relative number of the foreign-born persons within the national population. From the 1920s to the 1950s the foreign-born became an ever-smaller share of the total U.S. population. By 1940 they had fallen below 10% of the total population and in 1970 comprised only 4.7% of the national population – the lowest percentage in the 20th century.[54] But in the 1970s this decline was not only reversed, but in every subsequent census the percentage of foreign-born within the U.S. population has continually increased.[55]

Of all the Latin American migrants entering the United States, Mexicans had the longest experience of migration. With close family ties along the Texas, New Mexico, Arizona, and California borders, there was a steady movement back and forth across the frontier in this essentially open international border from 1848 until the mid 20th century.[56] But there were distinct periods of large-scale migration and sometimes return migration to Mexico. Prior to the 1920s the flow across the border was fluid and relatively few Mexicans remained in the United States. But from the late 1940s the emigration of Mexicans to the United States

[52] Roger Waldinger, "From Ellis Island to LAX: Immigrant Prospects in the American City," *International Migration Review*, 30:4 (Winter 1996), 1078.
[53] U.S. Bureau of the Census, *1980 Census of the United States*, pp. 27ff., Table 43.
[54] Gibson and Lennon, "Historical Census Statistics on the Foreign-born," Table 1.
[55] U.S. Bureau of the Census, *Vital Statistics of the US 2002*, Part 1, Table 41. By 2000 they were back up to 11.1% of the national total, a level not seen since 1930.
[56] In 1848, through the treaty of Guadalupe Hidalgo, the United States annexed all lands north of the Rio Grande River, or the entire U.S. contemporary Southwest, which had been part of Mexican national territory. This was the settlement exacted from Mexico to conclude the Mexican-American War, or the War of U.S. Intervention, as it is called in Mexico.

grew so dramatically that it actually reduced the indices of natural population growth within Mexico itself.[57] Though migration was ongoing over the course of the 19th and early 20th centuries, Mexicans had been primarily employed as temporary migrant laborers in the United States and relatively few settled permanently. It is estimated that in 1909, for example, they made up 17% of the workforce on the major U.S. railroads. But despite the closing of the United States to competitive Asian unskilled workers in the 1880s and in 1907, permanent Mexican migration remained relatively low until the quota laws of the early 1920s restricted European immigration to the United States. It was only in the 1920s that permanent Mexican migrants began to arrive in significant numbers, and even then this migration would virtually end in the following decade because of the Great Depression.

The principal reason suggested by most scholars for the lack of permanent Mexican migration before the 1920s is that the push factors within Mexico were not sufficient to drive out migrants on a permanent basis. Low natural population growth rates, poor communications, a very high percentage of the economically active population involved in agriculture, and the extensive distribution of lands after the Mexican Revolution, all reduced the potential for migration, despite the open nature of the U.S. frontier and a demand for unskilled labor in the United States. In the decade from 1921 to 1930, some 459,000 Mexicans migrated to the United States, or double the number in the previous decade. But the Great Depression not only reduced this flow to only 22,000 in the 1931–40 period, but between 1929 and 1932 the U.S. government actually repatriated 345,000 Mexicans to Mexico.[58]

Thus, the great migration of Mexicans would become steady only after 1940 when both the push and pull factors were fully in place. Increasing population pressure, urbanization, improved communication in Mexico, and the inability of the Mexican economy to provide employment for an

---

[57] CONAPO, *La situación demográfica de México, 2000*, Chapter 2, p. 12. Thus, the latest estimates for the period 1995–2000 suggest a rate of natural increase of 1.4%, though in fact it was 1.74% once the 0.3% lost to international migration is returned to the national population growth.

[58] On the forced repatriation of Mexicans, see Francisco E. Balderrama and Raymond Rodriguez, *Decade of Betrayal, Mexican Repatriation in the 1930s* (2nd rev. ed.; Albuquerque: University of New Mexico Press, 2006). A recent recalculation of the numbers is provided by Fernando Saúl Alanis Enciso, "¿Cuántos fueron?: La repatriación de mexicanos en los Estados Unidos durante la Gran Depresión: Una interpretación cuantitativa 1930–1934," *Aztlán: A Journal of Chicano Studies*, 32:2 (Fall 2007), 65–91.

expanding labor force, all created the conditions for a steady flow of out migration, which coincided with growing U.S. demands for labor with the end of the Great Depression and the beginning of the Second World War. The United States attempted to resolve this issue by signing a contract with the Mexican government for temporary Mexican migrant workers in 1942. This *bracero* contract, as it was popularly named, lasted until 1964 and resulted in the arrival of about 4.7 million Mexican workers to the United States.[59] But at the same time the flow of undocumented migrants began to approach impressive levels. By 1948 some 293,000 undocumented migrants were captured on the U.S. side of the border, a figure that rose to 885,000 in 1954.[60] By 1980 it was estimated that there were some 2 million undocumented Mexican immigrants residing in the United States.[61]

Between the 200,000 plus Mexicans arriving through the *bracero* contract program each year after 1942, and the migration of undocumented workers, it has been estimated that more migrants found jobs in the United States each year during the 1948–80 period than were being created annually in Mexico itself. Though job creation in Mexico remained high until the early 1980s, it was clearly insufficient to resolve the increased demand for employment resulting from the rapid growth of the working-age Mexican population because of decreasing mortality and increasing fertility rates. In the decade of the 1970s, a period of Mexican economic expansion, some 790,000 jobs per year were being created. But after 1980 this declined to about 150,000 new jobs yearly, an annual growth rate of just 0.7%, which was well below the natural population growth rate. As a rough estimate, it has been suggested that of the deficit in job creation in the 1980s, which was estimated to be on the order of 7.2 million jobs that needed to be generated to incorporate the workforce and were not

---

[59] On the *bracero* program, see Manuel García y Grego, "The Importation of Mexican Contract Laborers to the United States, 1942–1964," in David G. Gutiérrez, ed., *Between Two Worlds: Mexican Immigrants in the United States* (Wilmington, DE: Scholarly Resources, 1996), pp. 45–85.

[60] Gustavo Verduzco, "La migración mexicana a Estados Unidos: Estructuración de una selectividad histórica," in Rodolfo Tuirán, editor, *Migración México-Estados Unidos Opciones de política* (México : Consejo Nacional de Población, 2000). pp. 14–17.

[61] Verduzco, "La migración mexicana a Estados Unidos," p. 19. Mexican government sources estimate that in the decade of the 1960s between 260,000 and 290,000 Mexicans sought temporary work in the United States, and the figure rose to 1.2 million to 1.5 million in the decade of the 1970s. CONAPO, *Índice de Intensidad migratoria México-Estados Unidos, 2000* (México: Consejo Nacional de Población, 2002), p. 30.

created, some 24% of these potential workers found employment in the United States.[62]

Although this new Latin American, Caribbean, and Asian immigration followed many of the classic patterns of all previous migrations, its size ushered in important and lasting demographic transformations in the United States. By 2000, for the first time in the history of the republic, African Americans, having been replaced by the rapidly growing Latin American and Caribbean-origin population, were no longer the single largest minority of the population. Nor is this an ephemeral development, as the comparative growth rates between African Americans and Hispanics, or Latinos imply that by the middle of the 21st century Hispanics will account for about a third of the national population according to 2008 Census Bureau estimates, while African Americans will remain at about 12%. It was this change in both the origins and the volume of the foreign-born – the rise of the Hispanic population – which first led Congress in 1976 to require self-identification questions on Hispanic origin or descent to be included in all government census work. The Census Bureau began enumerating Hispanics as a separate census category for the first time in 1980.[63] This decision finally established a baseline by which to definitely analyze the characteristics of the leading minority population in the United States. In all decennial censuses since 1980, in the American Community Survey sample data collected by the Census Bureau on a yearly basis since 2001, in the annual Current Population Surveys, and in the collections on demographic change of the Center for Disease Control and Prevention (CDC), data on the Latino population have become abundant and comprehensive. These data permit us to develop a more nuanced and systematic examination of demographic, social, and economic changes within the nation's Hispanic population between 1980 and 2005.

[62] Verduzco, "La migración mexicana a Estados Unidos," pp. 23–25.
[63] Bean and Tienda, *The Hispanic Population of the United States*, Chapter 2.

2

The Hispanic Population to 1980

The reform of the quota system in 1965 influenced the flow of immigration to the United States, allowing low-wage and high-fertility countries and regions to begin supplying migrants to the expanding American labor market. The European countries that had been the previous sources of migration to the United States had recovered from the devastation of World War II by the late 1960s, and with their declining fertility, ensuing low population growth rates, and increasingly industrialized urban economies, they were able to absorb most, if not all, of their younger workers entering labor markets. Some European nations even became net importers of foreign labor and in many cases there was labor migration to nearby European countries when higher wages prevailed. But in Latin America and Asia, the beginning of the demographic transition in the postwar period, which was characterized by rapidly declining mortality rates but the maintenance of high pretransition fertility rates, lead to extraordinary rates of natural population growth by historical standards. These expanding populations were surpassing the ability of the local economies to absorb them into their labor markets. The continuing growth of the U.S. economy, now the world's largest, and the end of immigration restrictions in terms of national origins, opened the United States to a new wave of immigration from Asia and Latin America and the Caribbean.

Both regions were sources of migrants to the United States from the mid 19th century on, although the number of migrants was relatively small. There had also been immigrants arriving from the former Spanish colonies of Cuba and Puerto Rico beginning as far back as the early 19th century when economic and political connections were forged

between the Hispanic Caribbean and the United States because of growing
sugar imports from these islands, although this migration was small scale.
Almost all settled in the East. New York and Florida were the principal
states where Cuban and Puerto Rican communities first emerged, and a
Cuban presence was established in Louisiana as well because of the local
sugar industry. The 1898 U.S. intervention in the Cuban War for Independence through a full-scale invasion of Cuba, the subsequent military
occupation of Puerto Rico in the same year, and that island's annexation
to the United States as an "unincorporated territory" in 1900, created new
political conditions for migration.[1] During the early 20th century Puerto
Ricans migrated to Hawaii, recruited as laborers for the sugar industry,
and small Puerto Rican communities evolved in New York City, in Red
Hook, Brooklyn, and later in East Harlem, which came to be known
as *El Barrio*.[2] After 1898, the Cuban presence in Tampa, Florida, also
increased, building upon a foundation that was established much earlier
during the 19th century in the cigar-manufacturing industry.[3]

As demand for skilled and unskilled labor escalated in Northeastern
industrial centers because of the development of a war economy after
the U.S. entrance into the Second World War in 1941, there were new
incentives for migration, especially from Puerto Rico. This marked the
beginning of modern Hispanic-Caribbean migration to the United States.
The first to arrive in significant numbers were Puerto Ricans, who in their
timing matched the Great Migration of African Americans out of the
South toward Northern urban centers. Because they were U.S. citizens,
Puerto Ricans had no legal impediments to migration to the mainland.
Beginning in the early 1940s and lasting until the early 1970s there was
a constant flow of migrants to New York City from Puerto Rico. As we
have already indicated in the previous chapter, during the 1940s some
151,000 Puerto Ricans arrived followed by an impressive 470,000 in the
1950s and another 214,000 in the 1960s.[4] But the decline of fertility

[1] See César J. Ayala and Rafael Bernabe, *Puerto Rico in the American Century: A History since 1898* (Chapel Hill: University of North Carolina Press, 2007).
[2] Virginia Sánchez Korrol, *From Colonia to Community: the History of Puerto Ricans in New York City, 1917–1948* (Westport, CT: Greenwood Press, 1983); Clara E. Rodríguez and Virginia Sánchez Korrol, editors, *Historical Perspectives on Puerto Rican Survival in the U.S.* (Princeton, NJ : Markus Wiener Publishers, 1996).
[3] For a summary, see Chapter 2 "Cubans in Tampa: From Exiles to Immigrants, 1892–1901" in Louis A. Pérez, Jr. *Essays on Cuban History: Historiography and Research* (Gainesville: University of Florida Press, 1995).
[4] José L. Vázquez Calzada, *La población de Puerto Rico y su trayectoria histórica* (Rio Piedras: Raga Printing, 1988) p. 286.

rates on the island and the related slowing of population growth, the expansion of the insular economy, and the reduced job opportunities in the Northeastern U.S. industrial centers where they had previously settled, reduced the Puerto Rican migratory flow after 1970. From that period on, the Puerto Rican population on the U.S. mainland expanded because of natural increase rather than through continued migration.[5]

From a population of about 68,000 in 1930 the number of Puerto Ricans in the United States increased to 246,000 in 1950 of whom 87% resided in New York State, most in New York City. By 1960 they more than tripled to 911,000, and although the growth rate slowed by the end of the decade, in 1970 there were over 1.4 million Puerto Ricans residing on the U.S. mainland.[6] Though their numbers increased dramatically in New York, the state's relative share of all Puerto Ricans gradually declined and would account for slightly less than half of all Puerto Ricans in the United States by 1980 (see Graph 2.1). By then Puerto Ricans had established important communities in Chicago, Philadelphia, and Hartford, Connecticut, as well as in other smaller cities and even suburban centers in the Northeast and the state of Florida. After 1980 the Puerto Rican population sustained its expansion in the United States more through natural increase rather than immigration, and overall population growth rates declined considerably. While Puerto Ricans increased by 9.3% annually between 1950 and 1970, their growth slowed to 3% per annum from 1970 to 1980 and dropped to just over 2% yearly in the 1980s, a rate that would be sustained after 1990. Thus, in many ways Puerto Ricans repeated the experiences of previous immigrant groups, first concentrating in one well-defined geographic area, and later spreading to other regions. As was the case with prior waves of immigrants from Northern, Eastern, and Southern Europe, when migration slowed and then ended, population expansion of particular national groups only

[5] For an analysis of the return migration to Puerto Rico in this period see José Hernández Alvarez, *Return Migration to Puerto Rico*, Population Monographs No. 1 (Berkeley: University of California Press, 1967).

[6] These estimates of the Puerto Rican, Cuban, and Dominican populations resident in the United States include native and foreign-born and are taken from our calculations from the 1900–80 Integrated Public Use Microdata Samples (IPUMS). We have used self-identification, as well as place of birth, parents' place of birth, and ancestry variables to determine the total number of each group. For a survey of the evolution of the Latino community in New York City to 1990, see Gabriel Haslip-Viera, "The Evolution of the Latino Community in New York City: Early Nineteenth Century to the Present," in Gabriel Haslip-Viera and Sherry L. Baver, editors, *Latinos in New York. Communities in Transition* (Notre Dame, IN: University of Notre Dame Press, 1994), pp. 3–29.

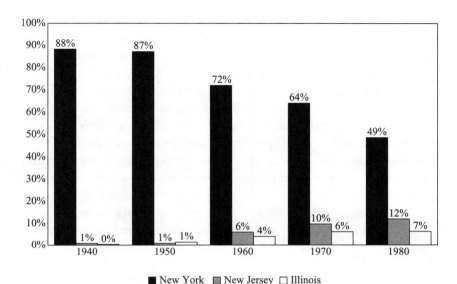

GRAPH 2.1. Distribution of Puerto Ricans by Major States of Residence, 1940–1980.

occurred through natural reproduction. Accordingly, the ratio of foreign-born to domestic-born, or in the case of Puerto Ricans those who were born on the island, shifted in favor of those born in the United States. There are many implications to this universal immigrant experience. Language usage gradually shifted to English, although bilingualism persisted for some time and never completely disappeared. Some degree of integration into a "national" culture evolved even though the immigrants themselves changed that culture. Eventually, political representation of immigrant groups was established, especially at the local level, as domestic-born and naturalized citizens increasingly exercised their rights to vote.

Some of these same patterns may be observed in the second most important postwar Hispanic-Caribbean migration, that of Cubans. Cubans arrived in increasing numbers to the United States during the 1960s as political refugees from the Castro-led 1959 revolution. There was a fundamental difference with earlier Puerto Rican migrants. Puerto Ricans largely came to the United States for socioeconomic reasons, and this would be the case with the post-1980 Dominican migration as well. But Cubans were largely political refugees, at least initially in the 1960s. In 1950 there were only some 41,000 Cubans in the United States and their population had not grown significantly in the small communities that had emerged earlier. But with Castro's victory in 1959 and declaration of socialism in 1961, the United States opened its doors to Cuban migrants seeking to flee the island. Between 1961 and 1970 some 209,000 Cubans arrived in the United States, and in the next decade another 265,000 crossed the Florida Straits.[7] Since Cubans were primarily political refugees and not the traditional economic migrants, they were generally better educated and wealthier compared with prior waves of migration from Europe or even Puerto Rico. Unlike the other contemporary migration flows, the political nature of this post-1959 migration also meant that Cuban immigrants tended to be much older and more balanced by sex.

The socioeconomic composition of Cuban migrants changed significantly after the "Mariel boatlift" of 1980 when some 125,000 Cubans entered the United States between April and October of that year. Unlike the wave of Cuban migrants arriving during the 1960s and 1970s, these "Marielitos," as they were called because they left from the Cuban port of Mariel, were mostly from the working classes. Although they were fleeing the politically repressive Castro regime to be sure, in many ways they were economic refugees who left because of widespread poverty and the absence of any opportunities for social mobility. In this sense, the post-1980 Cuban migration was similar in its class structure to that of Puerto Ricans in the 1950s and 1960s, and to Dominicans during the 1980s and after, although paradoxically most Cubans were better educated because of the fairly extensive Cuban educational system constructed after Castro's 1959 takeover.

As was the case with Puerto Ricans, there were small communities of Cubans in the United States during the first half of the 20th century, primarily located in New York and Florida. By 1960 there were about 122,000 Cubans in the United States. Some had fled the political instability and repression on the island caused by the Batista regime during the 1950s, and the revolutionary upheaval that would bring Castro to power. Others sought economic opportunities in the expanding labor markets of the United States in the same way as Puerto Rican migrants during the 1950s. But after 1959 the U.S. Cuban population soared, increasing at an annual rate of 16.4% during the 1960s. The 1970 census indicated that

7 U.S. Department of Justice, Immigration and Naturalization Service, *Statistical Yearbook of the Immigration and Naturalization Service, 1998* (Washington, DC: Government Printing Office, 2000), pp. 20–23, Table 2.

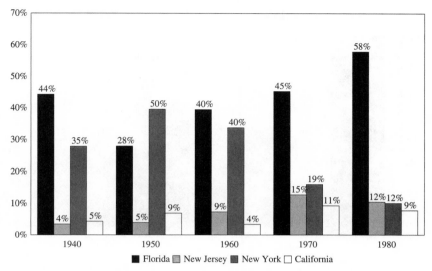

GRAPH 2.2. Distribution of Cubans by Major States of Residence, 1940–1980.

there were a little more than half a million Cubans living in the United States. While their initial settlements were primarily in Florida and New York, the latter state quickly lost population as many Cubans relocated to Florida and also across the Hudson River to New Jersey. In contrast to the pattern of population dispersal away from original regions of settlement which was typical of nearly every preceding immigrant group, the concentration of Cubans in Florida increased after 1980 and in 2005 nearly 70% of the total U.S. Cuban population lived in the state (see Graph 2.2 for the period 1940–1980).[8]

The third major pre-1980 Hispanic-Caribbean migrant group to arrive was from the Dominican Republic, although they only began to come in significant numbers after 1970 when there were about 47,500 Dominicans in the U.S. But by 1980 the Dominican population quadrupled to about 205,000, growing at almost 16% yearly during the decade. Like Puerto Ricans before them Dominicans settled in the East, mainly in the

[8] For the evolution of the Cuban American community see María Cristina García, *Havana USA: Cuban Exiles and Cuban Americans in South Florida, 1959–1994* (Berkeley: University of California Press, 1996); and her more recent survey "Exiles, Immigrants and Transnationals: The Cuban Communities of the United States," in David G. Gutiérrez, *The Columbia History of Latinos in the United States Since 1960* (New York: Columbia University Press, 2004), pp. 146–86.

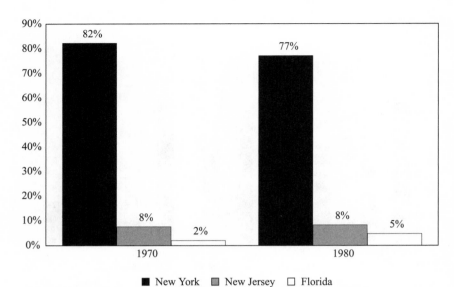

GRAPH 2.3. Distribution of Dominicans by State, 1970–1980.

New York metropolitan area in which about 77% of all Dominicans lived in 1980 (see Graph 2.3).[9]

These pre-1980 Hispanic-Caribbean migrant groups would become progressively more important in subsequent decades and they would be joined by new groups of Latin American immigrants from Central and South America. But no immigrant group compared in either magnitude or in longevity to Mexican migration, which has dominated Latin American migrations to the United States from the mid-19th century until today. Mexicans had a centuries-old presence in the territories of the

[9] For a survey of the evolution of the Dominican community in New York see Ramona Hernández and Silvio Torres-Saillant, "Dominicans in New York: Men, Women and Prospects," in Gabriel Haslip-Viera and Sherry L. Baver, editors, *Latinos in New York. Communities in Transition* (Notre Dame, IN: University of Notre Dame Press, 1994), pp. 30–56; Sherri Grasmuck and Patricia R. Pessar, *Between Two Islands: Dominican International Migration* (Berkeley: University of California Press, 1991), especially Chapter 7, which studies the migration primarily to New York City. Other ethnographies dealing with Dominican migration include Peggy Levitt, *The Transnational Villagers* (Berkeley: University of California Press, 2001), which concentrates on the migration from the town of Miraflores to Boston, and the community study of Los Pinos and its migrants by Eugenia Georges, *The Making of a Transnational Community. Migration, Development and Cultural Change in the Dominican Republic* (New York: Columbia University Press, 1990).

Southwest, which were annexed to the United States in 1848 as part of the Treaty of Guadalupe Hidalgo, which ended the Mexican-American War, or the War of U.S. Intervention as it is called in Mexico. At the conclusion of the war it is estimated that there were about 81,000 Mexicans living in the annexed regions.[10] Nearly a century later, by 1940, the Mexican-origin population was estimated to be approximately 527,000 and accounted for 80% of all Hispanics in the United States. By 1980 the Mexican population had soared to 9 million and despite the growth of the Hispanic-Caribbean population, they still comprised about 61% of the nation's Latino population.[11]

During the 19th century this Mexican immigrant and domestic-born population was concentrated primarily in rural regions of the U.S. Southwest and in the state of California.[12] Even by the census of 1900, when they numbered about a quarter-million people, some 94% of the Mexican-origin population resided in the Southwestern and Western states of Texas, New Mexico, California, and the Arizona territory. (See Map 2.1.) Nearly three-quarters still resided in rural areas in 1900 when only 54% of the national population was considered rural.[13] But this regionally stable and largely farming population began to change slowly by the middle of the 20th century. As we have indicated in the previous chapter, there was a steady seasonal flow of workers across the border for most of the period up to 1920, although few Mexicans became permanent residents. But the quota laws of the 1920s cut off supplies of European unskilled workers, and in the Southwest these were replaced by Mexican migrants who began to settle permanently in the United States in ever-greater numbers. Although the Great Depression and forced repatriation in the 1930s stopped this trend, the renewed growth of the U.S.

---

[10] *Historical Statistics of the United States: Earliest Times to the Present* (5 vols.; Millennial edition: New York: Cambridge University Press, 2006) I: 1–177, Table Aa2189–2215.

[11] All these numbers are based on the data provided in the IPUMS samples for the years considered and from *Historical Statistics of the United States: Earliest Times to the Present*, I: 1–177, Table Aa2189–2215. For a good survery of the history of Mexicans in the United States, see Manuel G. Gonzales, *Mexicans. A History of Mexicans in the United States* (Bloomington: Indiana University Press, 1989).

[12] In the first post–Mexican War census of 1850 they were considered 86% rural. *Historical Statistics of the United States: Earliest Times to the Present* I: 1–177, Table Aa2189–2215.

[13] Total Mexican population and its distribution are calculated from IPUMS 1900 sample, using ancestry, birth, and self-identity to define the total numbers of persons of Mexican origin. For the national population, see *Historical Statistics of the United States: Earliest Times to the Present*, I:1–36, Table Aa22–35.

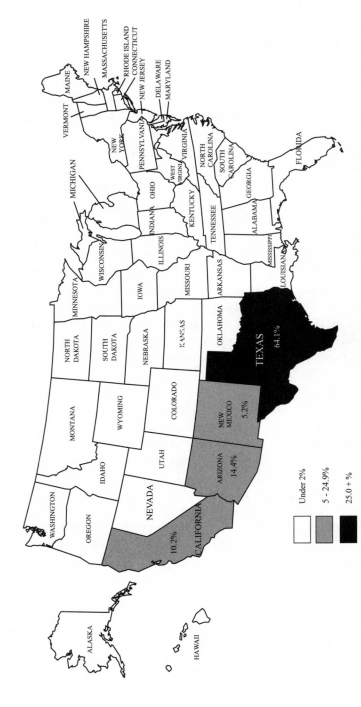

MAP 2.1. Distribution of the Mexican Population by State, 1900.

Under 2%

5 - 24.9%

25.0 + %

TEXAS
64.1%

NEW
MEXICO
5.2%

ARIZONA
14.4%

CALIFORNIA
10.2%

economy in the post–Second World War period created rising labor demands. During the 1950s 300,000 Mexicans arrived in the United States; this number increased to 454,000 in the next decade; to over 660,000 in the 1970s; and finally to more than a million migrants during the 1980s; finally reaching over 2.2 million documented arrivals in the decade of the 1990s.[14]

Yet, Mexican migrants and Mexican Americans born in the United States, much like African Americans before them, began to leave traditional rural areas of settlement in favor of urban areas where economic growth created rising labor demands. In 1960 approximately 80% of the Mexican-origin population was living in urban centers. Although they were still the least urban of any Hispanic-origin national sub-group, their percentage of urban residents steadily rose and stood at about 90% in 1980.[15] They had also begun to move slowly into the Mid-West, especially to the city of Chicago.

In 1950 about 15% of the Mexican and Mexican American population resided outside of the traditional Southwestern and Western states, and this portion increased steadily thereafter. They also began to experience shifts in residential patterns even within the old traditional zones, with California replacing Texas as the largest center of Mexican population concentration by 1970. This shift in settlement patterns would accelerate after 1980 as Mexican and Mexican American migrants moved into every state and region of the nation. See Map 2.2 for Mexican population distribution by major states of settlement in 1980.

This dispersion based on the total Mexican-American population is in fact understated. If we examine the foreign-born Mexican population it becomes apparent that the changes in settlement patterns were even more rapid. By 1970 the foreign-born Mexican origin population in California was double the size of the foreign-born Mexican population in Texas. Additionally, southern states such as Florida and Georgia had emerged as new poles of attraction for recently arrived Mexicans, along with Illinois and Kansas. This slow dispersion became ever more rapid after 1980 and will be considered in detail in Chapter 3.

[14] U.S. Bureau of Citizenship and Immigration Services, Table HS-9. "Immigration by Leading Country or Region of Last Residence: 1901 to 2001," reproduced in U.S. Census Bureau, *Statistical Abstract of the United States: 2003*, Mini-Historical Statistics, p. 16.
[15] Bean and Tienda, *The Hispanic Population*, p. 146, Table 5.5, indicate 80% in 1980 although the PUMS data indicate that about 90% of the Mexican population lived in urban areas.

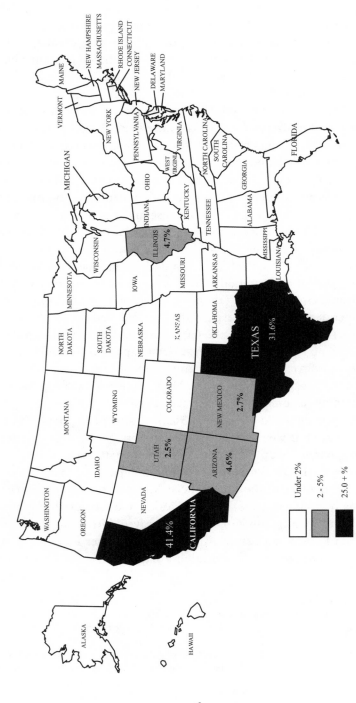

MAP 2.2. Distribution of the Mexican Population by State, 1980.

Under 2%

2 - 5%

25.0 + %

CALIFORNIA
41.4%

TEXAS
31.6%

ILLINOIS
4.7%

NEW MEXICO
2.7%

UTAH
2.5%

ARIZONA
4.6%

WASHINGTON

OREGON

NEVADA

IDAHO

MONTANA

WYOMING

COLORADO

NORTH
DAKOTA

SOUTH
DAKOTA

NEBRASKA

KANSAS

OKLAHOMA

MINNESOTA

IOWA

MISSOURI

ARKANSAS

LOUISIANA

WISCONSIN

MICHIGAN

INDIANA

OHIO

KENTUCKY

TENNESSEE

MISSISSIPPI

ALABAMA

GEORGIA

WEST
VIRGINIA

VIRGINIA

NORTH CAROLINA

SOUTH
CAROLINA

FLORIDA

PENNSYLVANIA

NEW YORK

VERMONT

MAINE

NEW HAMPSHIRE

MASSACHUSETTS

RHODE ISLAND

CONNECTICUT

NEW JERSEY

DELAWARE

MARYLAND

ALASKA

HAWAII

46

Mexicans, who had been the least urban of all the Hispanic national sub-groups, changed in a dramatic way over the course of the 20th century. As expected within the dominant agricultural economy, they had been mainly farmers through most of the 19th century, as owners of rural enterprises or agricultural laborers. But the Mexican population began to move away from rural areas during the 20th century, responding to changes in the structure of the U.S. economy. In 1900 only about 10% of all Mexicans lived in a major metropolitan area. Yet, they were significantly less urbanized than the non-Hispanic white population in the same year, of whom about one-third lived in metro areas. By 1940, however, some 28% of all Mexicans resided in central cities and 43% lived in metropolitan areas compared with about 47% of the white population living in urban areas. Thus, by 1940 similar percentages of Mexicans and non-Hispanic whites lived in cities and towns. This trend continued and by 1980 a greater share of the Mexican population lived in cities (87%) than non-Hispanic whites (79%). Moreover, they were now far more likely to live inside a central city than non-Hispanic whites. By 1980 over a third of urban Mexicans lived in the central cities of large metro areas, compared with 17% of the non-Hispanic white population who had increasingly moved to suburban communities in the post-World War II period.

Given the dominance of Mexicans in the total Hispanic population, it is worthwhile exploring the various factors that motivated the ever-expanding migration of Mexicans to the United States. The push factors were similar for all Latin American and Hispanic-Caribbean migrant groups, except for Cubans. Although mortality had been declining in Mexico since the late 19th century, by the beginning of the 20th century there were few demographic differences from the nation's colonial and early republican past. Until the late 19th century Mexico had a traditional pre-modern demographic structure with high fertility and mortality – both rates averaging in the upper 40s per thousand inhabitants. Life expectancy for both men and women in 1900 was less than 30 years of age.[16] Accordingly, population growth tended to be quite low – on the order of less than 0.5% yearly until the 1880s. The death rate began to decline gradually between 1880 and 1910 with the crude death rate

---

[16] Robert McCaa, "El poblamiento de México: de sus orígenes a la Revolución," in José Gómez de León Cruces and Celia Rabell Romero, editors, *La población de México, tendencias y perspectivas sociodemográficas hacia el siglo XXI* (México: CONAPO & Fondo de Cultura Económica, 2001), p. 63.

dropping into the mid 30s per thousand inhabitants, while fertility remained unchanged. Various estimates put the crude birth rate at between 47 and 51 births per thousand people in 1900 – in all probability about the same rate that prevailed in 1800. It ought to be noted that this same crude birth rate was still at 44 births per thousand inhabitants as late as 1968.

The slow post-1880 decline in mortality was linked to sanitation and transportation improvements begun under the regime of Porfirio Díaz (1876–1911), and this lead to a tripling of the population growth rate to over 1.5% yearly during the last two decades of the 19th century.[17] Although the decline in the crude death rate was significant, life expectancy in the 1920s was only in the upper 20s at birth and infant mortality was still well over 200 deaths per thousand live births. Yet, in the 1920s the decline in mortality began to accelerate. By the 1930s infant mortality dropped to below 200 deaths per thousand live births, and life expectancy at birth finally reached the mid to upper 30s.[18]

Without any serious changes in fertility rates, it was the ever-accelerating pace of declining mortality that drove the changes in population Mexico experienced through most of the 20th century. From 1940 to 1960 life expectancy increased by 20 years and during the 1970s by another 10 years. By 1980 life expectancy reached 71 years of age for women and 64.5 years for men.[19] One of the key causes of increasing life expectancy and declining mortality rates was the drop in infant mortality. By the late 1960s infant mortality rates had fallen to below 100 deaths per thousand live births, and by the mid 1970s it was below 50 deaths per thousand births.[20] The decade of the 1950s was especially crucial for declining mortality rates as Mexico was finally able to inoculate its entire population against such infectious diseases as tuberculosis, polio, diphtheria, and smallpox, and there were major public health campaigns

---

[17] CEED, *Dinamica de la población de México* (2nd ed.; México: El Colegio de México, 1981), Chapter 1.
[18] Sergio Camposortega Cruz, *Análisis demográfico de la mortalidad en México, 1940–1980* (México: El Colegio de México, 1992), pp. 14–16. For a more recent survey of these trends see José Gómez de León Cruces and Virgilio Partida Bush, "Niveles, tendencias y diferenciales de la mortalidad," in Gómez de León Cruces and Cecilia Rabell Romero, editors, *La población de México: Tendencias y perspectivs sociodemográficas hacia el siglo XXI* (México: CONAPO and Fondo de Cultura Económica, 2001), pp. 81–108.
[19] Camposortega Cruz, *Análisis demográfico de la mortalidad*, p. 21.
[20] Camposortega Cruz, *Análisis demográfico de la mortalidad*, p. 36, Cuadro 1.8.

undertaken against malaria as well.[21] While 47% of all deaths in 1930 were due to infectious diseases and parasites, by the end of the century these diseases accounted for only 4% of all deaths.[22] All this was reflected in the crude death rate, which dropped from the upper 20s per thousand people in 1921 to 10 deaths per thousand in 1960.[23] It is estimated that the crude death rate in 1997 was 17% of the rate in 1930.[24]

At the same time, the best estimates available suggest that through most of the 20th century, fertility rates remained at the same high level of some 45+ births per thousand inhabitants. This rose to even higher levels in the late 1950s because of the decline in mortality rates noted previously and the increasing survival rate of female children into child-bearing ages.[25] It is estimated that women who had completed their fertility, or who had given birth to their last child by 1970, were still producing an extraordinary 6.5 children each over the course of their lives.[26] All of this guaranteed a high rate of population growth for most of the 20th century. Except for the decade of the Mexican Revolution, when over a million persons died in the civil wars that raged from 1910 to 1920, the yearly natural growth rate increased from decade to decade.[27] By the 1930s it was approaching 2% per annum; by the 1940s it reached close to 3%

---

[21] Javier Pérez Astorga, "Mortalidad por causas en México, 1950–1980," in Mario Branfman and José Gómez de León, *La mortalidad en México: niveles, tendencias y determinantes* (México: Colmex, 1988), p. 311.

[22] INEGI, *Indicadores Sociodemográficos de México (1930–2000)* (Aguascalientes, Ag., 2001), pp. 150–51. How late this process was with some diseases, is indicated by the fact that diarrhea and other intestinal diseases was still first in importance among all deaths until 1960, and only dropped to second place in 1980. Rosario Cárdenas, "Las causas de muerte en México," in José Gómez de León and Cecilia Rebell Romero, editors, *La población de México: Tendencias y perspectivs sociodemográficas hacia el siglo XXI* (México: CONAPO and Fondo de Cultura Económica, 2001), pp. 122–23, Cuadro 1.

[23] Camposortega Cruz, *Análisis demográfico de la mortalidad*, pp. 358–59, Cuadro 7.1.

[24] Gómez de León and Partida Bush, "Niveles, tendencias y diferenciales de la mortalidad," p. 83.

[25] Marta Mier y Terán, "La fecundidad en México: 1940–1980. Estimaciones derivadas de la información del registro civil y de los census," in Beatriz Figueroa Campos, editor, *Le fecundidad en México: Cambios y perspectivas* (México: El Colegio de México, 1989), pp. 21–23.

[26] Mier y Terán, "La fecundidad en México: 1940–1980," p. 29, Cuadro 5.

[27] In the decade between 1911 and 1921 it is estimated that some 2.7 million persons were lost, or 16% of the potential population that should have existed in 1921 had pre-1911 natural birth and death rates continued through this period. Of this number just under half died in the war, 38% were lost births, 8% were due to migration to the United States, and 5% were migration to Cuba and Guatemala. Gustavo Verduzco, "La migración mexicana a Estados Unidos," p. 14.

annually; and by the late 1970s the Mexican population was increasing at 3.5% yearly, which was its peak. By the 1970s Mexico had one of the highest population growth rates in the world.[28] While this slowly declined in the following decades, it still was near 2% in the mid-1990s. This meant that from 1920, when the postrevolutionary population had finally stabilized at about 14 million, until the end of the 20th century when it reached 97 million, the national population had increased sevenfold in just 80 years. Even despite the rapid drop in birth rates after 1970, the number of women of child-bearing age doubled between 1970 and 1995, thus guaranteeing that population growth continued dynamically. Even as late as 2001, women in their fertile years had increased by 14% from 1995.

This very rapid demographic growth created an ever younger Mexican population, with an increasing dependency ratio as more children survived infancy and early childhood.[29] In 1895, a year of high mortality, some 42% of the population was younger than 15 years of age. Even as late as 1970 the population younger than 15 represented almost half (46%) of the national population despite the impressive decline in morality rates experienced during the 20th century – all because of the continuation of high fertility rates. Subsequently, the decline in fertility, which began in the late 1970s, finally lowered population growth rates. However, the persistence of high numbers of women of child-bearing age in the general population has assured the entry into the labor market of large numbers of people reaching working ages. In fact, even though life expectancy increased markedly, the economically active population increased in relative terms after 1980, and by 2000 some 60% of the total population was in the working ages.[30] While this has meant that more workers were available to take care of the dependent population, the steady expansion of the economically active population has furthered an ever-increasing demand for job creation despite the post-1970 decline in fertility.

Although job creation in Mexico remained high until the 1980s it was clearly insufficient to resolve the growing demand for employment created by the growth of the national population, particularly the working-age population. In the 1970s, a decade of economic expansion in

---

[28] CEED, *Dinamica de la población de Mexico*, p. 6, Cuadro 1–1.
[29] The dependency ratio is an age-population ratio of those not in the labor force, such as younger or older people, and those in the labor force, or the working-age population.
[30] INEGI, *Estadísticas históricas de México,* (3rd ed.; México, 2000), Cuadro 1.5.

Mexico, some 790,000 jobs per year were created. But after the oil-induced crises, which began in the early part of the decade, this declined to about 150,000 new jobs yearly during the 1980s, which meant a growth in new employment possibilities of just 0.7% annually – well below the natural population growth rate. It has been estimated that during the 1980s there was a deficit in employment creation of about 7.2 million jobs and that the resulting structural unemployment stood at about 24% of the workforce. This was a powerful factor leading to migration to the United States where unskilled jobs were readily available.[31] Those who remained behind became a potential pool of future migrants since there was no improvement in the Mexican economic environment, which could have provided employment or adequate salaries to a significant sector of the working-age population. Additionally wage rates were comparatively much higher in the United States even though Mexican migrants were usually employed in the lowest-paying unskilled jobs.

Another factor promoting migration was the major shift in residential patterns within Mexico. As was the case throughout most of Latin America and the Caribbean, Mexico experienced intense urbanization during the 20th century. In 1900 only some 10% of the national population lived in cities with more than 15,000 persons. Urbanization was initially very gradual, and by 1940 this percentage had doubled to 20%. In the post–World War II period, however, the process of rural to urban migration accelerated, and by 1970 45% of the Mexican population resided in urban areas.[32] Though Mexico is still a heavily rural society by Latin American standards, it was clearly one that had experienced significant internal migration, a process that would be extended from the cities of Mexico, where there was rising unemployment, to the farms and urban centers of the United States.

Given the history of an open border and of seasonal migration of agricultural workers to the United States, it was not long before the dynamics of Mexican internal demographic change were providing fundamental incentives for Mexicans to migrate permanently to the United States. The frontier was porous, U.S. employers in the Southwest eagerly sought

[31] Gustavo Verduzco, "La migración mexicana a Estados Unidos," pp. 23–25.
[32] CEED, *Dinamica de la población de México*, p. 118, Cuadro V-1. By the census of 2000, some 61% of the national population lived in cities with a population greater than 15,000 people. INEGI. *Estados Unidos Mexicanos. XII Censo General de Población y Vivienda, 2000. Tabulados Básicos y por Entidad Federativa. Bases de Datos y Tabulados de la Muestra Censal.* (Aguascalientes, Ags., México, 2001), available at http://www.inegi.gob.mx/estadistica/espanol/sociodem/asentamientos/ase_02.html.

Mexican laborers, and the railroad and road transport system provided cheap and efficient means of travel.

Thus, migration to the United States would prove to be a fundamental element in the dynamics of Mexican demography from the 1950s until the present. From the late 1940s the large-scale emigration of Mexicans to the United States reduced the rates of natural population growth within Mexico. The latest estimates for the period 1995–2000 suggests a 1.4% annual rate of demographic increase.[33]

The intensity of Mexican migration rose from decade to decade. It was estimated that only some 61,000 Mexicans legally migrated to the United States on a permanent basis (excluding the temporary worker or *bracero* migrations) in the 1940s; some 300,000 in the 1950s; and 454,000 during the 1960s. The growth of documented migration increased even more intensely in the 1970s when an estimated 640,000 Mexicans migrated; and this nearly tripled to 1.7 million persons during the 1980s. By 1980 Mexican demographers estimated the Mexican and Mexican American population of the United States was a little over 9 million, and the U.S. Census Bureau confirmed this estimate in the 1980 decennial census. Approximately 2.2 million (24%) were foreign-born; another 1.5 million (17%) were estimated to have been domestic-born descendants of the Mexican population that had resided in the U.S. Southwest and West before the annexation in 1848; and some 5.4 million (59%) were estimated to be domestic-born second and third generations of migrants who had arrived in the 20th century.[34]

The Mexican American population was growing at impressively high annual rates, and the volume of immigration of foreign-born Mexicans was rising. However, the arrival of large numbers of Hispanic Caribbean migrants during the 1950s and after temporarily reduced the share of Mexicans both in the total Hispanic population and in their importance among all arriving Latin American and Caribbean immigrants. Accordingly, the relative weight of Mexicans among all Hispanics dropped from

---

[33] When the 0.3% of the population that migrated to the United States is added, the actual population growth rate was 1.7% yearly. CONAPO, *La situación demográfica de México, 2000*, p. 12, Chapter 2.

[34] For estimates of the founding populations and their descendents, as well as second- and third-generation descendents of post-1850 immigrants, see Rodolfo Corona, "Estimación del número de emigrantes permanentes de México a Estados Unidos 1850–1990," in Rodolfo Tuirán, editor, *Migración México-EU,Continuidad y cambio* (México: CONAPO, 1998), Cuadro 3, available at www.conapo.gob.mx/publicaciones/ migra3/03.pdf.

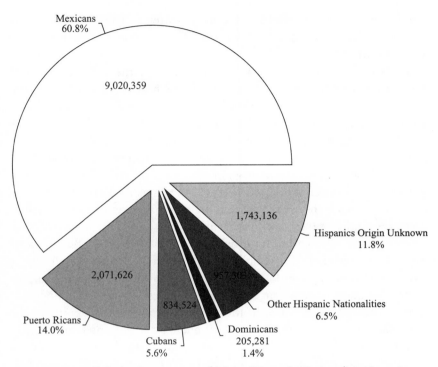

Mexicans
60.8%

9,020,359

1,743,136

Hispanics Origin Unknown
11.8%

2,071,626

957,308

834,524

Other Hispanic Nationalities
6.5%

Puerto Ricans
14.0%

Cubans
5.6%

Dominicans
205,281
1.4%

GRAPH 2.4. Relative Importance of Major Hispanic Nationalities in 1980.

about three-quarters of the total before 1960, to 61% of the total Latino population of the United States in 1980 (see Graph 2.4). Their portion of all arriving migrants from Latin America and the Hispanic Caribbean fell to a low of about a third during the 1950s and 1960s.[35]

The rapid growth of the Hispanic population in the United States meant that Latinos steadily increased their share of the total national population. In 1980 Hispanics numbered about 14.8 million, an increase of 60% from the 9.1 million Latinos found in 1970. They had grown by 6.1% yearly during the 1970s, which dwarfed the growth rate of the other racial/ethnic sectors of the U.S. population.[36] Accordingly Latinos, who were 4.5% of the total national population in 1970, rose to 6.4% in 1980,

[35] Frank D. Bean, Rodolfo Corona, Rodolfo Tuirán, and Karen A. Woodrow-Lafield, "The Quantification of Migration between Mexico and the United States," in *Migration Between Mexico and the United States, Binational Study*, Vol. 1 (Mexico City and Washington, DC: Mexico Ministry of Foreign Affairs; U.S. Commission on Immigration Reform, 1998), Table 6; Bean and Tienda, *The Hispanic Population*, p. 105, Table 4.1.

[36] Bean and Tienda, *The Hispanic Population*, pp. 57–58, and p. 53, Table 2.2.

and this upward trend would continue thereafter. In 1980 Hispanics also comprised an estimated 30% of the total foreign-born population of the United States.[37]

In recognition of this extraordinary increase, the U.S. government began to refine its classification system and methods of data collection for Hispanics. In 1950 the U.S. Census Bureau had classified Puerto Ricans as a separate group for enumeration. Then in the 1969 the Current Population Survey, an annual sampling of the U.S. population conducted by the Census Bureau, self-identification of Hispanic origin was first used. Prior to these first specific efforts at enumeration, estimates of the Hispanic population had been made on the basis of Spanish surnames, language spoken at home, the place of birth of informants or of their parents, and other indirect forms of identification. In 1970 Cubans were added to the specific self-identification question when the Census Bureau conducted its decennial 5% sampling of the overall population. In 1976 Congress passed legislation mandating the reporting of Hispanic origin in all subsequent government-sponsored censuses and surveys, and finally in the 1980 census self-identification of specific national Hispanic origin was made part of the standard questionnaire.[38] The Center for Disease Control and other governmental agencies began to divide the national population not only by race, which had long been enumerated, but also by ethnicity and Hispanic origin. The first systematic vital statistics for Hispanics were collected in 1980 at the national level.[39]

In this context, new race and origin categories were developed for all government-produced statistical materials, and the population was divided into broad racial/ethnic categories: Hispanics, non-Hispanic whites, non-Hispanic blacks, and Asians. Additionally, Hispanics were enumerated by more refined national-origin categories than had existed before, when only Mexicans, Puerto Ricans, and Cubans were counted. Moreover, ever-greater details were provided for Hispanics by nationality and more questions were added to census questionnaires on a variety

[37] Gibson and Lennon, *Historical Census Statistics on the Foreign-born*, Table 2.
[38] Bean and Tienda, *The Hispanic Population*, pp. 37–48.
[39] The Center for Disease Control and Prevention, which produces the vital statistics of the United States, has an often repeated table on fertility rates since 1950 for blacks and whites, but only provides the Hispanic/Non-Hispanic breakdowns for the period since 1980. See for example, CDC, NCHS, *Health, United States, 2005 With Chartbook on Trends in the Health of Americans* (Hyattsville, MD: U.S. Department of Health and Human Services, Centers for Disease Control and Prevention and National Center for Health Statistics, 2005), Table 3. Detailed information about Hispanic origins seems to be available only from the late 1980s, see, for example, "Births: Final Data for 2003," in *National Vital Statistics Reports*, 54:2 (September 8, 2005), 37, Table 6.

of important topics such as specific origin, language spoken at home, linguistic ability in English, date of immigration, citizenship status, and many other variables. This fine-tuning of data collection has provided the basic information needed to define and distinguish the various national subgroups that make up the Hispanic population. This was critical for an understanding of this diverse population as it became evident from all these newly generated materials that Hispanics could not be considered as a homogeneous group.

As we noted previously, the census of 1980 indicated a Hispanic population of 14.6 million of whom 29% were foreign-born, and this compared to only 4% of the non-Hispanic white population that was born outside of the United States. Since over half the 3.7 million Asians resident in the United States were foreign-born, the combined impact of this new migration from Latin America and Asia meant that by 1980 the foreign-born component of the U.S. population (now at 6.2%) had increased for the first time since 1910. The overall foreign-born population would continue to expand in each post-1980 decade, largely driven by the arrival of ever-larger numbers of migrants, documented and undocumented, from Latin America and the Caribbean.[40]

Hispanic settlement patterns had been changing continuously over the course of the 20th century. In 1920 some 48% of all Hispanics lived in urban areas and this increased to 82% by 1960. There was geographical dispersion as well, with New York and Florida becoming important centers of Hispanic settlement because of the Puerto Rican and Cuban migrations we noted previously. In 1960 20% of the Hispanic population lived in the Northeastern part of the country, and the Hispanic presence in the Midwest had increased as well to 7% of all Latinos nationally, largely because of Mexican and Puerto Rican migration to the Chicago metropolitan area.[41]

In 1970 some 9 million Hispanics were enumerated by the census, and about half of them lived in Texas and California. New York was the third largest state with a population of 1.2 million Latinos, most of whom were Puerto Ricans, and Florida was fourth ranked with 437,000 Hispanics, most of whom were Cubans.[42] By 1980 some 71% of the estimated 14.8 million Latinos lived in six states: California, Texas, Florida, Illinois, New York, and New Jersey. These six states accounted for 79% of all

[40] Gibson and Lennon, *Historical Census Statistics on the Foreign-born*, Table 8.
[41] *Historical Statistics of the United States: Earliest Times to the Present*, I, Table Aa2189–2215.
[42] Gibson and Jung, "Historical Census Statistics," table E-5.

TABLE 2.1. *Distribution of the Hispanic Population by Major State of Residence in 1980 (in absolute numbers and percentages)*

States	Mexicans	Puerto Ricans	Cubans	Dominicans	Colombians	Other Hispanics	Total Hispanics
California	3,734,411	93,874	66,020	2,400	21,015	669,591	4,587,311
Texas	2,846,335	23,730	15,130	1,100	5,887	126,675	3,018,857
New York	43,426	1,008,862	85,145	158,450	59,613	341,613	1,697,109
Florida	80,354	102,862	483,303	9,754	31,152	167,321	874,746
Illinois	421,633	133,810	19,595	1,760	6,507	67,467	650,772
New Jersey	14,604	250,920	88,081	16,987	25,421	111,826	507,839
Other States	1,879,596	457,568	77,250	14,830	28,681	1,037,670	3,495,595
TOTAL	9,020,359	2,071,626	834,524	205,281	178,276	2,522,163	14,832,229
California	41%	5%	8%	1%	12%	27%	31%
Texas	32%	1%	2%	1%	3%	5%	20%
New York	0%	49%	10%	77%	33%	14%	11%
Florida	1%	5%	58%	5%	17%	7%	6%
Illinois	5%	6%	2%	1%	4%	3%	4%
New Jersey	0%	12%	11%	8%	14%	4%	3%
Other States	21%	22%	9%	7%	16%	41%	24%
TOTAL	100%	100%	100%	100%	100%	100%	100%

Note: Unless specifically noted all data in this and all subquent tables have been derived from the PUMS data sets for specific years indicated in the introduction.

Mexicans, 78% of Puerto Ricans, 91% of Cubans, and 93% of the Dominican population (see Table 2.1).

By 1980 the Hispanic population in the United States tended to be more concentrated in its residential patterns than the national population. It was also slightly more male: 99 males per 100 females compared to sex ratios of 95 males per 100 females for non-Hispanic whites and 89 males per 100 non-Hispanic black females. The Hispanic population was also more urban than the national population: 89% lived in cities and towns compared with 71% of non-Hispanic whites and an 85% rate among African Americans.[43] Latinos tended to be younger as well. The median age of the Hispanic population was 22 years (18 years for domestic-born and 31 years for foreign-born Hispanics) compared with 31 years of age for non-Hispanic whites. They also had 29% more children than the non-Hispanic population.[44] Because of higher fertility rates and the concentration of newly arrived immigrants in the working ages, the Hispanic population had a more traditional age and sex pyramid than was to be found in the dominant non-Hispanic white population.

Yet, because of migration and high fertility rates there were fundamental differences in the age structures of the foreign- and domestic-born sectors of the Hispanic population in 1980. Among the foreign-born the ratio of children to the total population was small, since most migrants were working-age adults (see Graph 2.5). In contrast domestic-born Hispanics (who represented 68% of the total Hispanic population in 1980) had a classic age-pyramid structure that was heavily influenced by high fertility rates (see Graphs 2.6, 2.7, and 2.8).

Although complete fertility data are unavailable for 1980, the extant information indicates that Latin American and Caribbean migrants had much higher fertility rates than the rest of the population. In the post–World War II rise in fertility – the so-called baby boom – the total fertility rate for women ages 15–44 reached its peak in 1957 at 3.7 children per hundred women in this age cohort. Yet by the early 1960s fertility rates had dropped dramatically, and by 1976 the lowest point was reached in the 20th century with the total fertility rate falling to 1.7 children

---

[43] U.S. Bureau of the Census, *1980 Census of the Population* Vol. 1, Chapter C, Part 1, "United States Summary", PC80·1·C1, Table 75. The census provided detailed origins for only Mexicans, Puerto Ricans, and Cubans and grouped all other Latin Americans as "Other Hispanics."

[44] They had 22% more children than non-Hispanic whites and 1% more than non-Hispanic blacks. Bean and Tienda, *The Hispanic Population,* p. 207, Table 7.1.

Age

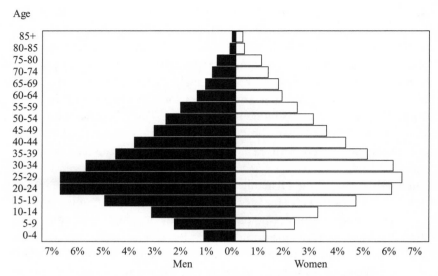

GRAPH 2.5. Age Pyramid of the Foreign-Born Hispanic Population, 1980.

for every hundred women ages 15–44.[45] Although this rate rose slightly
thereafter, the non-Hispanic white population has maintained a fertility
rate below 2.1 children per hundred women in the child-bearing years,
a level recognized by demographers as necessary to maintain a stable
population.

In contrast, when the CDC finally began generating partial data on
Hispanic births for the first time in 1980, the general fertility rate for
Hispanics was the highest for any resident U.S. race or ethnic group,
was close to a third greater than that of non-Hispanic whites, and was
considerably above that of non-Hispanic blacks and American Indians.[46]
Evidence of this differential in fertility rates may be observed in data on
family size and number of children per family. Non-Hispanic whites in
1980 had 1.9 children/household compared with 2.5 children/household

[45] Robert Schoen, "Timing Effects and the Interpretation of Period Fertility," *Demography*,
41:4 (November 2004), 815–16.
[46] The total fertility rate for non-Hispanic whites was 62.4 versus 92.4 for Hispanics (which
given better and more complete data in 1990 shows that this was an underestimate) and
84.9 for blacks and 82.7 for American Indians. See CDC, NCHS, *Health, United States,
2005*, pp. 132–33, Table 3. That these 1980 data are incomplete is seen in the fact
that in 1990 the fertility rate was 107.7 for Hispanics, while the non-Hispanic white,
black, and Amerindian rates in 1990 were much closer to those for 1980 (e.g., 62.8 for
non-Hispanic whites).

Age

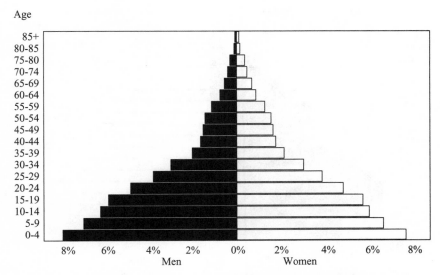

GRAPH 2.6. Age Pyramid of the Domestic-Born Hispanic Population, 1980.

among Mexicans and 2.3 children/household for all Hispanics. The average size of families also was quite distinct for the Hispanic population. Latino families averaged 4.3 persons compared with 3.3 persons among non-Hispanic whites. Almost half (49%) of Mexican families that had

Age

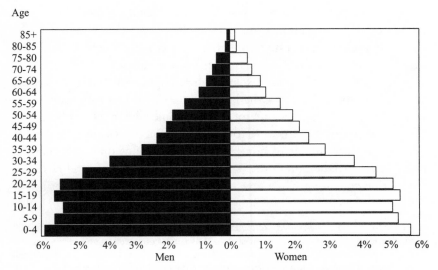

GRAPH 2.7. Age Pyramid of the Total Hispanic Population, 1980.

Age

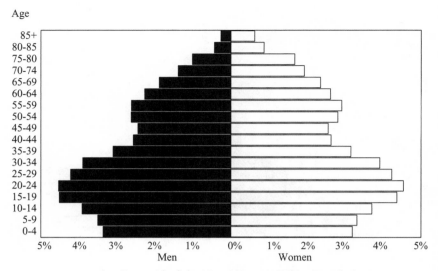

GRAPH 2.8. Age Pyramid of the Non-Hispanic White Population, 1980.

children were made up of 5 or more persons, compared with just 22% of non-Hispanic white families. Some 43% of all Hispanic households were composed of 5 or more people.

Given the bias toward a younger population, Hispanics had a relatively low death rate compared with the other racial/ethnic groups since there were relatively fewer older people within the Latino population. What stands out are the relatively low rates of infant mortality found among the Hispanic population. As may be observed in Graph 2.9, the overall infant mortality rate for all Hispanics in 1983, the first year when such data are available, was less than for the national population and almost identical to the non-Hispanic white population.[47] Moreover, the specific rate for Mexicans – the largest Latino national subgroup – was actually slightly below the rate for non-Hispanic whites. The only serious exceptions to this pattern were found among Puerto Ricans whose mortality rates were similar to non-Hispanic blacks. But time and again in mortality, morbidity, and other such demographic indices, the Hispanic population consistently had lower than expected rates. The lower infant

---

[47] CDC, NCHS, *Health, United States, 2005*, p. 155, Table 19. Even using age-adjusted figures, for example the overall death rate of Hispanics compared to non-Hispanics and the entire population was quite impressive. As late as 2001–03, for example, the overall death rate of Hispanics was a quarter below both the non-Hispanic white and the overall national death rates, see CDC, NCHS, *Health, United States, 2005*, p. 177, Table 28.

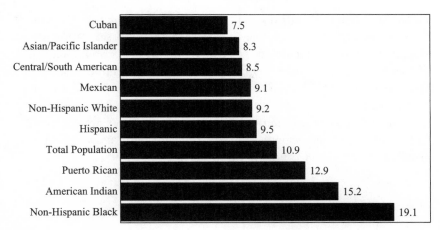

GRAPH 2.9. Infant Mortality by Race/Ethnicity/Hispanic Nationality, 1983 (deaths per thousand live births). *Source: Health United States, 1983* (Washington, DC: National Center for Health Statistics, Public Health Service, 1983), p. 155, Table 19.

mortality finding is particularly noteworthy. Compared with the non-Hispanic white population, Latinos had lower levels of education, poorer paying jobs, and personal and family income below the non-Hispanic white majority. These are factors that historically have been associated with higher rates of infant mortality. Yet, except for Puerto Ricans, infant mortality rates were extremely low. The precise reasons for these patterns are difficult to determine with precision.

Thus, on the eve of its great expansion after 1980, the Hispanic population demonstrated all of the characteristics that would define it in the decades to come. It had relative low mortality and high fertility and was substantially below national averages in terms of education, wealth, and ability to speak English. But of equal importance were the sharp differentiations by national group. Since Mexicans dominated the Hispanic population demographically, they overwhelmingly influenced social, economic, and demographic indicators found among all Hispanics. Puerto Ricans and Central Americans were the poorest of the nationalities in 1980, and Cubans were the wealthiest. Although they were in general a younger population compared with the other racial/ethnic groups because of high birth rates, foreign-born Hispanics exhibited the expected age biases with low numbers of children and elderly people since most immigrants fell into the working-age categories. But like all postwar immigrants, and in sharp contrast to pre-1940 migrations, the foreign-born actually had a balanced sex ratio. In part this was because of U.S. immigration laws that favored the arrival of women, which led to balanced sex ratios for all foreign immigrants arriving in the post–World War II period. Finally, the Hispanic population and their first- and second-generation descendents were concentrated in traditional areas of settlement in the Southwestern and Western states, along with New York and Florida. There was only a marginal presence in the interior of the United States, despite the fact that there had been some growth. These settlement patterns would change significantly after 1980 and will be considered in Chapter 3.

3

Population Growth and Dispersion, 1980–2005

Between 1980 and 2005 the Hispanic-origin population of the United States grew at a faster rate than any of the other nation's racial or ethnic components. Latinos also increased as a percentage of the total population and surpassed African Americans as the country's largest minority group. From a population of slightly more than 14.8 million in 1980, Hispanics nearly tripled to more than 43.1 million in 2005.[1] Latinos accounted

---

[1] We use the terms "Hispanic" and "Latino" interchangeably. Our population estimates on Hispanics differ slightly from other published sources including estimates of the Census Bureau. We have calculated the number of Hispanics using the raw 5% Public Use Microdata Sample data released by the Census Bureau and accessible at the University of Minnesota, Minnesota Population Center's Integrated Public Use Microdata Series, (IPUMS) web site at http://www.ipums.org. We effected our calculations using self-declared origin data as well as birthplace and ancestry data.

However, our approach differs from other studies in that we include Brazilians in our data. Additionally, we have excluded all persons designated as Spaniards or of Spanish descent since the conceptualization of Hispanics in the United States implies Latin American and Caribbean origin. We include Brazilians not only because of their Latin American origins but because the term "Hispanic" is derived from the Roman designation of the Iberian peninsula as *Hispania*, and this included the people of the post-Roman future Kingdom and later independent nation of Portugal from which Brazilians hale.

We have calculated the total population of Hispanics for 2005, using our definitions, at 43,126,900 in the following way: First the 5% PUMS 2005 data derived from the American Community Survey were analyzed producing an estimate of the national population at 288,398,819. This was an undercount in part because of the exclusive enumeration of people living in households. Persons living in group quarters, who may have represented about 3% of the total population, were not included in the 2005 data. The Hispanic total, using our definitions, was 41,961,236 or 14.54972532% of the total population for 2005 according to the PUMS data. We then used the Census Bureau's estimate for the total population of the United States on July 1, 2005, of 296,410,404 and multiplied this number by 14.54972532% to arrive at total Hispanics. These data

TABLE 3.1. *Hispanic Population of the United States 1980–2005 in Relation to the Total and African American Populations*

Year	Total Population	Hispanic Population	Hispanics as % of Total	African-American Population	African-Americans as % of Total
1980	227,021,768	14,832,229	6.5%	26,698,267	11.8%
1990	248,107,628	20,958,680	8.4%	29,821,972	12.0%
2000	281,421,906	35,336,969	12.6%	34,357,836	12.2%
2005	296,410,404	43,126,900	14.5%	39,724,136	13.4%

Sources: For 1980, 1990, 2000, 2005, PUMS data released by the U.S. Census Bureau. For 2005 total population see Table 1. Estimates of the Population by Race Alone or in Combination and Hispanic or Latino Origin for the United States and July 1, 2005, available at http://www.census.gov/Press-Release/www/2006/cb06–123table1.xls. For methodology on calculation of total Hispanics see footnote 1 in this chapter.

for 6.5% of the U.S. population in 1980 and for 14.5% in 2005 (see Table 3.1).

Between 1980 and 2005 the overall population of the United States grew by over 69 million people. About 41% of the total, some 28 million people, was comprised of Hispanics. The role of Hispanics in U.S. population expansion intensified after 2000. From 2000 to 2005 the total population of the United States increased by approximately 15 million persons. About half of this population expansion, or nearly 7.8 million people, was of Hispanic origin. The U.S. Census Bureau has estimated that, if these trends continue, Hispanics will account for about 21% of the overall population of the United States in 2025 and 30% in 2050.[2]

Latino population growth resulted from high rates of natural reproduction as well as immigration after 1980.[3] In 1980 over two-thirds of the

---

are found at http://www.census.gov/Press-Release/www/2006/cb06–123table1.xls. There is an unknown margin of error in these estimates.

We also want to make note of the fact that in subsequent analyses of the Hispanic population found in this chapter for 2005 we use the original 5% PUMS data from the American Community Survey, which produced a total of 41,961,236 Hispanics, again without enumerating people living in group quarters. We do this because the detailed data we present are only available utilizing these data files and are not available from other sources such as the Census Bureau's American FactFinder Web site at http://factfinder.census.gov/home/saff/main.html?_lang=en. Any incongruities in data found in this chapter are due to this factor.

In 2008 the U.S. Census Bureau estimated that the Hispanic population had increased to 45.5 million on July 1, 2007, and over 15% of the total U.S. population.

[2] U.S. Bureau of the Census, Projections of the Population by Sex, Race, and Hispanic Origin for the United States: 2010 to 2050 (NP2008-T4); Release date: August 14, 2008.

[3] We will consider fertility and mortality among Hispanics in comparative perspective later.

TABLE 3.2. *Domestic- and Foreign-Born Hispanics, 1980–2005*

Year	Domestic-Born	% of Total Hispanics	Foreign-Born	% of Total Hispanics	Total
1980	10,499,469	70.8%	4,332,760	29.2%	14,832,229
1990	12,980,543	61.9%	7,978,137	38.1%	20,958,680
2000	20,762,145	58.8%	14,574,824	41.2%	35,336,969
2005	24,524,176	58.4%	17,437,060	41.6%	41,961,236

Note: The differences in the total populations for 2005 indicated here and in Table 3.1 are because of the exclusive use of the PUMS data for 2005, the only data set that may be used to calculate domestic- and foreign-born Hispanics. Also, our estimate of the 1980 domestic-born population is higher than that indicated by the census.

Hispanic population was born in the United States. Because of increased immigration from Latin America and the Caribbean during the decade of the 1980s, the proportion of domestic-born Latinos declined slightly from 62% in 1990 to about 58% in 2005 (see Table 3.2).

If the domestic and foreign-born components of Hispanic population growth are considered over the entire period between 1980 and 2005, about 52% of total Latino demographic increase was from domestic births and 48% was the result of immigration. However, if each inter-census period is examined separately, the increase in immigration from Latin America and the Caribbean after 1980 shows a progressive rise in the foreign-born component of Latino population growth. Between 1980 and 1990 foreign-born Hispanics comprised nearly 41% of the increase in the Hispanic population. This grew to 54% between 1990 and 2000; and almost 57% between 2000 and 2005 (see Table 3.3).

This impressive growth in the Hispanic population between 1980 and 2005 was characterized by major changes in the spatial distribution of Hispanics throughout the country, in their relative proportions within local populations, and in the growth of newer national groups as migration patterns from Latin America and the Caribbean changed over this 25-year period.

TABLE 3.3. *Domestic- and Foreign-Born Components of Hispanic Population Increase, 1980–2005*

Period	Increase in Hispanic Population	% Increase because of Domestic Born	% Increase because of Foreign Born
1980–1990	6,126,451	59.5%	40.5%
1990–2000	14,378,289	45.9%	54.1%
2000–2005	6,624,267	43.2%	56.8%
1980–2005	27,129,007	51.7%	48.3%

TABLE 3.4. *Percentage Distribution of Hispanic Population by State, 1980–2005 (major states of Hispanic population concentration)*

State	1980	1990	2000	2005
California	31%	35%	31%	30%
Texas	20%	20%	19%	19%
New York	11%	10%	8%	8%
Florida	6%	7%	8%	7%
Illinois	4%	4%	4%	4%
Arizona	3%	3%	4%	4%
New Jersey	3%	3%	3%	3%
Colorado	2%	2%	2%	2%
New Mexico	3%	2%	2%	2%
Georgia	0%	0%	1%	2%

However, some fundamental aspects of Hispanic society in the United States remained relatively stable despite the sharp upward population surge. First and foremost was the continued concentration of the vast majority of Latinos in the Western and Southwestern states, and in the two eastern coastal states of New York and Florida. This occurred despite the growth of Hispanic populations in new regions such as the South where they had been only a marginal presence prior to 1980. In 1980 over 51% of the nation's Latinos lived in California and Texas. Another 11.4% resided in New York because of the large-scale Puerto Rican migration of the post–World War II period. Cuban migration to Florida after the Castro revolution's triumph in 1959 resulted in that state accounting for nearly 6% of all Hispanics in 1980. Thus two-thirds of all Latinos lived in these four states.

By 2005 although the relative proportion of Hispanics in Texas and California had decreased slightly to 47.5%, these four states still contained some 64% of all Hispanics. There were declines in New York where a little more than 7% of all Latinos lived in 2005; however, due to the influx of Central Americans, Mexicans, and Latinos who migrated from other states, Florida's Hispanic population increased to more than 8% of all Latinos in the United States by 2005. The political instability of Central America spawned by the triumph of the Sandinista revolution in Nicaragua in 1979, and the civil war in El Salvador of the 1980s, created a tide of immigration, and this was supplemented by large-scale migration of Mexicans into Florida and the relocation of various other Latino nationalities from within the United States (see Table 3.4).

TABLE 3.5. *Percentage of All Mexicans by State and Mexicans as a Percentage of Total Hispanic Populations by State, 1980–2005*

State	Percentage of All Mexicans by State			
	1980	1990	2000	2005
California	41.4%	45.2%	40.4%	38.3%
Texas	31.6%	29.2%	25.6%	25.0%
Arizona	4.6%	4.7%	5.2%	5.6%
Illinois	4.7%	4.5%	5.4%	5.3%
Colorado	2.5%	2.1%	2.3%	2.5%
Florida	0.9%	1.2%	1.7%	2.0%
New Mexico	2.7%	2.5%	1.8%	1.7%
Others	11.7%	10.7%	17.7%	19.6%
TOTAL	100.0%	100.0%	100.0%	100.0%

State	Mexicans as a Percentage of Total Hispanic Populations in the United States and in Selected States			
	1980	1990	2000	2005
United States	60.8%	63.9%	62.8%	64.9%
California	81.4%	82.7%	82.2%	83.6%
Texas	94.3%	92.8%	85.5%	86.9%
Arizona	92.2%	94.1%	88.6%	90.9%
Illinois	64.8%	70.7%	77.7%	79.9%

The second stable factor was the continued overwhelming dominance of Mexicans as the nation's largest Latino nationality. In 1980 Mexicans comprised 61% of all Hispanics in the United States, and this increased to 65% in 2005. Despite their migration to new areas throughout the country that were not previously associated with Mexicans as part of state or local populations, they remained heavily concentrated in the states of California and Texas where 73% of all Mexicans lived in 1980 and 63% in 2005. In the two key states of California and Texas, Mexicans accounted for more than 80% of total Hispanic populations from 1980 through 2005, while in Arizona they accounted for approximately 90%. A large Mexican community resided in Illinois, mostly in Chicago, and Mexicans increased as a portion of all Hispanics in the state from 65 to 80% from 1980 to 2005.[4] (See Table 3.5.)

[4] New Mexico had an extraordinarily high Mexican population as a percentage of all Hispanics. However, the data also indicate a very large number of Hispanics, over 40% in each census year, for whom nationality could not be determined.

TABLE 3.6. *Mexicans and the Increase in Hispanic Populations, 1980–2005,*
in Arkansas, Georgia, North Carolina, Oregon, and South Carolina

States	1980	% of Total State Population	2005	% of Total State Population	% Increase in Hispanic Population 1980–2005	Mexicans as % of all Hispanics 2005
Arkansas	17,178	0.8%	129,512	4.8%	654%	73.5%
Georgia	63,319	1.2%	637,921	7.2%	907%	65.8%
North Carolina	58,562	1.0%	545,786	6.5%	832%	66.4%
Oregon	66,546	2.5%	358,382	10.1%	439%	86.1%
South Carolina	34,163	1.1%	136,968	3.3%	301%	61.2%

Despite the overall stability of the distributions, there were some significant changes as well. Since 1980 Mexicans have begun to settle in
states with high labor demand where Hispanics had only been marginally
important prior to their arrival. The states of Arkansas, Georgia, North
Carolina, South Carolina, and Oregon provide examples of this process.
These states had relatively small Hispanic populations in 1980, less than
3% of total inhabitants in each case. Latinos moved into both rural and
urban areas of these states over the next 25 years and by 2005 both their
absolute numbers had increased sharply as well as their shares of overall
state populations (see Table 3.6).[5]

The increasing spread of Mexicans across the United States by 2005
is indicated in Map 3.1. With the exception of the Northeastern region
of the country, where Puerto Ricans established a major presence during
the 1950s and 1960s and Dominicans in the 1980s and 1990s, Mexicans
accounted for well over 70% of Hispanic populations in most regions.
Another exception is the state of Florida where Cubans after 1959
were the largest Latino subgroup. While lacking detailed survey data to
examine the relative importance of foreign- and native-born Mexicans in

[5] For recent surveys of the changing origin of Mexican migration see Jorge Durand, Douglas
S. Massey, and Fernando Charvet, "The Changing Geography of Mexican Immigration
to the United States: 1910–1996" *Social Science Quarterly*, 81:1 (March 2000), 1–15;
Jorge Durand, Douglas Massey, and René Zentino, "Mexican Immigration to the United
States: Continuities and Changes," *Latin American Research Review* 36:1 (2001), 107–
27; Elizabeth Fussell, "Sources of Mexico's Migration Stream: Rural, Urban, and Border
Migrants to the United States," *Social Forces,* 82:3 (March 2004), 937–67 and the essay
by Jorge Durand, "Origen y destino de una migración centenaria," in Marina Ariza and
Alejandro Portes, editors, *El país transnacional: Migración Mexicana y Cambio Social
a traves de la frontiera* (México: UNAM, 2007), pp. 55–82; and Bryan Roberts and
Erin Hamilton, "La nueva geografía de la emigración: zonas emergentes de atracción y
expansión, continuidad y cambio," in ibid., pp. 83–118.

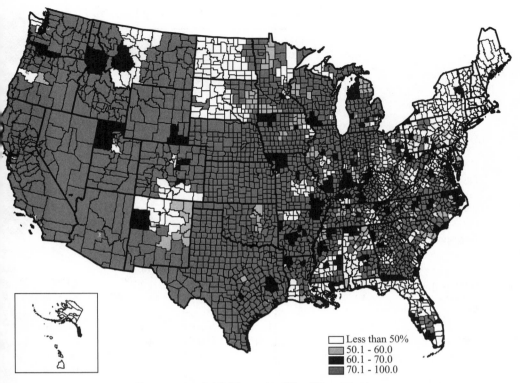

MAP 3.1. Percentage of All Hispanics Who Were Mexicans, 2005.

this expansion, an examination of birthplace information in the census data point to migration from Mexico as the principal factor behind this population expansion in these new regions of Mexican settlement after 1980.[6] Assuming that Mexicans born outside of the United States were more likely to have recently migrated from Mexico, the 2005 data suggest that the Mexican population of these newer areas of settlement were in their majority migrants from Mexico. In South Carolina, Georgia, and North Carolina over 60% of the Mexican population was born outside

---

[6] The PUMS data files for ACS 2005 have two other variables that potentially may be used to measure migration within the United States or from a foreign country by state. These are the "state or country of residence one year ago" and the "migration status, one year" variables. Unfortunately, for each of these variables the vast majority of records were listed as unknown. A little over 80% of the records for Latinos for the "state or country of residence one year ago" were unknown. Slightly over 78% of records for Latinos for the "migration status, one year" were listed as unknown. The high number of unknowns makes these two variables fairly unreliable as measures of migration from abroad or within the United States.

TABLE 3.7. *Mexican Domestic- and Foreign-Born by State, 2005*

State	Domestic-Born	Foreign-Born	Total	% Domestic-Born	% Foreign-Born
Alabama	26,559	35,878	62,437	42.5%	57.5%
Alaska	11,233	1,857	13,090	85.8%	14.2%
Arizona	923,129	592,192	1,515,321	60.9%	39.1%
Arkansas	46,073	49,158	95,231	48.4%	51.6%
California	6,150,103	4,292,470	10,442,573	58.9%	41.1%
Colorado	424,769	244,331	669,100	63.5%	36.5%
Connecticut	14,977	18,047	33,024	45.4%	54.6%
Delaware	11,589	15,609	27,198	42.6%	57.4%
District of Columbia	1,745	3,379	5,124	34.1%	65.9%
Florida	253,315	288,391	541,706	46.8%	53.2%
Georgia	145,745	274,066	419,811	34.7%	65.3%
Hawaii	25,501	7,575	33,076	77.1%	22.9%
Idaho	63,562	53,863	117,425	54.1%	45.9%
Illinois	731,300	712,434	1,443,734	50.7%	49.3%
Indiana	121,341	93,555	214,896	56.5%	43.5%
Iowa	52,525	29,374	81,899	64.1%	35.9%
Kansas	124,414	67,192	191,606	64.9%	35.1%
Kentucky	20,553	23,934	44,487	46.2%	53.8%
Louisiana	27,106	13,556	40,662	66.7%	33.3%
Maine	2,580	304	2,884	89.5%	10.5%
Maryland	22,502	34,270	56,772	39.6%	60.4%
Massachusetts	16,816	15,235	32,051	52.5%	47.5%
Michigan	204,801	83,111	287,912	71.1%	28.9%
Minnesota	67,831	60,454	128,285	52.9%	47.1%
Mississippi	15,772	14,123	29,895	52.8%	47.2%
Missouri	71,379	43,200	114,579	62.3%	37.7%
Montana	13,511	1,399	14,910	90.6%	9.4%
Nebraska	59,926	40,651	100,577	59.6%	40.4%
Nevada	247,258	199,506	446,764	55.3%	44.7%
New Hampshire	3,067	635	3,702	82.8%	17.2%
New Jersey	55,984	92,712	148,696	37.6%	62.4%
New Mexico	346,376	120,397	466,773	74.2%	25.8%
New York	129,649	195,829	325,478	39.8%	60.2%
North Carolina	135,278	226,932	362,210	37.3%	62.7%
North Dakota	5,515	1,275	6,790	81.2%	18.8%
Ohio	89,901	41,225	131,126	68.6%	31.4%
Oklahoma	107,818	76,141	183,959	58.6%	41.4%
Oregon	162,048	146,559	308,607	52.5%	47.5%
Pennsylvania	42,766	47,908	90,674	47.2%	52.8%
South Carolina	26,924	56,953	83,877	32.1%	67.9%
South Dakota	5,935	2,207	8,142	72.9%	27.1%

State	Domestic-Born	Foreign-Born	Total	% Domestic-Born	% Foreign-Born
Tennessee	52,247	62,416	114,663	45.6%	54.4%
Texas	4,515,099	2,302,649	6,817,748	66.2%	33.8%
Utah	109,883	82,973	192,856	57.0%	43.0%
Vermont	794	–	794	100.0%	
Virginia	56,425	57,837	114,262	49.4%	50.6%
Washington	251,606	196,901	448,507	56.1%	43.9%
West Virginia	4,636	1,958	6,594	70.3%	29.7%
Wisconsin	101,284	73,483	174,767	58.0%	42.0%
Wyoming	21,343	5,775	27,118	78.7%	21.3%
TOTAL	16,126,402	11,107,398	27,233,800	59.2%	40.8%

Note: Discrepancies in the total number of Mexicans with other data are due to a small number of missing values.

of the United States in 2005. In Arkansas 52% of all Mexicans were born abroad, and in Oregon 48% of the resident Mexican population in 2005 was foreign-born. At the national level about 41% of all Mexicans were born outside of the United States in 2005 (see Table 3.7).

This finding does not mean that all recently arrived immigrants went directly to the newly established Mexican communities in the South, the Midwest, and the Northwest. In 2005, despite their increasing dispersion throughout the country, 59% of all foreign-born Mexicans still lived in California and Texas and some two-thirds of U.S.-born Mexicans lived in these two states. Thus, Mexicans coming from Mexico in the most recent period, though seemingly more willing to settle in new regions, still had a greater propensity to settle in these two states of historic Mexican population concentration. Whether foreign- or domestic-born, the majority of Mexicans continued to make Texas and California their states of residence by 2005.

Two other states merit special attention when considering changing Mexican settlement patterns after 1980. The first is Florida, which has seen an extraordinary growth of the Mexican population and its dispersion throughout central and northern Florida. In 1980 Mexicans had accounted for just over 9% of the 80,000 or so Hispanics residing in the state. By 2005 there were over 540,000 Mexicans in Florida, and they now represented about 16% of all Florida Latinos. As elsewhere in the South their expansion was linked in part to immigration, since about 53% of Mexicans in Florida in 2005 were foreign-born. Unlike the other

Hispanic national subgroups, Mexicans were more heavily concentrated in central Florida counties, in rural areas of the state, and in the North, where they made up 30% of the total of resident Hispanics (see Map 3.2).

The second state where Mexicans increased significantly after 1980 is New York. New York has always had the most diversified of the Hispanic populations in the United States in terms of national subgroups, but Mexicans were relatively insignificant numerically. In 1980 Mexicans numbered slightly more than 43,000 in the state, and they accounted for less than 3% of all Hispanics. During the next 25 years there was rapid growth, and in 2005 there were over 325,000 Mexicans throughout New York State, about 60% of them foreign-born, and they now represented about 11% of the state's total Latino population. (See Map 3.3 for the spatial distribution of Mexicans in New York State in 2005.)

The growth of the Mexican population throughout the nation between 1980 and 2005 had a major impact on the relative proportion of Latinos making up state and local populations.[7] In the five states in which Hispanics had the largest percentages of total populations in 2005 – New Mexico (42%), California (35%), Texas (35%), Arizona (29%), and Nevada (23%) – Mexicans were overwhelmingly the dominant national Latino subgroup.[8] Florida followed as the sixth ranking state in terms of Hispanics as a percentage of overall populations at 20%, and here the Mexicans were the third most numerous component of Florida's Hispanic population in 2005.[9]

---

[7] A simple linear regression run on the 2005 data for all 5% PUMAs across the United States in which the percentage of Hispanics in total populations was used as the dependent variable and the percentage of Mexicans as the independent variable, produced a correlation coefficient of .85 indicating a very strong association between the two. When the number of total Hispanics was used as the dependent variable and the number of total Mexicans the independent variable, the correlation coefficient was .88.

[8] Mexicans accounted for 91% of all Hispanics in Arizona in 2005, 87% in Texas, 83% in California, 80% in Nevada, and 97% in New Mexico. The New Mexico percentage was calculated by dividing the number of Mexicans by the number of Hispanics with known nationalities. For an undetermined reason there were a larger number of Hispanics in New Mexico (44% of the total) for whom nationality was unknown than in any other state.

[9] The relative decline in the Cuban population of Florida as a percentage of all Hispanics from 1980 ought to be underlined. In 1980 they made up 55% of the total Hispanic population of the state falling to 29% in 2005. In political terms there has been a decisive, if perhaps unrecognized, decline in the potential Cuban voting population of the state as a percentage of all Hispanic potential voters. Cubans older than age 18 who are citizens represented about 53% of total Hispanics in the state who were citizens and thus eligible to vote in 2005. In 1980 they represented 79% of all potential eligible Hispanic voters. It should be noted that there was a large Hispanic population in the state of Florida for

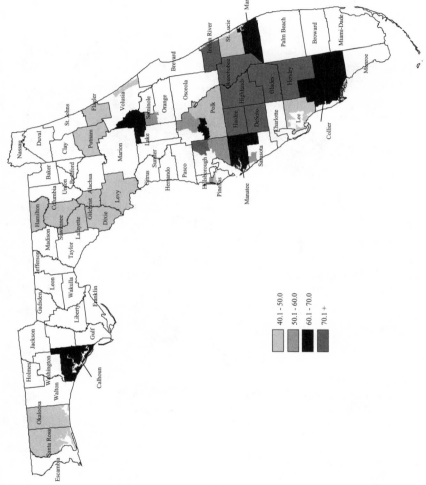

MAP 3.2. Percentage of All Hispanics in Florida Who Were Mexicans by Counties, 2005.

40.1 - 50.0
50.1 - 60.0
60.1 - 70.0
70.1 +

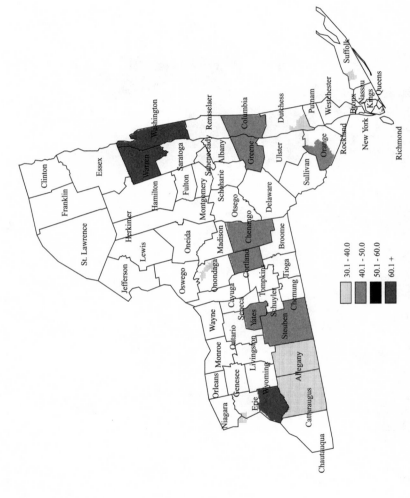

MAP 3.3. Percentage of All Hispanics in New York Who Were Mexicans by Counties, 2005.

In each of these states, the increase in Latinos as a percentage of total populations between 1980 and 2005 was substantial, and except for Florida, this was in large part due to Mexican population growth. These same dynamics were found in the newly emerging regions of Hispanic demographic expansion in the states of Arkansas, Tennessee, Georgia, North Carolina, Alabama, and South Carolina. In 1980 the Latino presence in these states represented just 1% of total populations in each (see Table 3.8). By 2005 Georgia's Latinos increased over tenfold from 63,000 in 1980 to nearly 638,000 and 7.2% of the state population in 2005. In North Carolina, the Southern state with the second largest Hispanic population after Georgia, over the same time frame Hispanics increased from 59,000 to 546,000 and 6.5% of all inhabitants. In both of these states, Hispanic population expansion was closely connected to the arrival of foreign-born migrants among whom Mexicans were the dominant nationality. In Georgia 62% of the state's Hispanics were foreign-born in 2005, and 66% of the total Latino population was of Mexican origin. In North Carolina 58% of the Hispanic population was foreign-born in 2005, and, as in Georgia, 66% of all Latinos were Mexicans. In each of the other Southern states – Arkansas, Tennessee, Alabama, and South Carolina – over 50% of all Hispanics were foreign-born, and over 60% of total Latino populations were Mexicans in 2005.[10]

When we examine the Hispanic community at the county level, patterns of population concentration become even clearer. As we have already noted, the Mexican-origin population accounted for the greatest percentage of Hispanic populations throughout most of the United States in 2005. Aside from their continued importance in counties

whom citizenship data are not available for both 1980 and 2005. Citizenship rates and eligible voters will be taken up in chapter 7.

The standard history of the Miami Cuban has been written by María Cristina García, *Havana USA*; also see her updated essay "Exiles, Immigrants and Transnationals." On second-generation Cubans see Lisandro Pérez, "Growing Up in Cuban Miami: Immigration, the Enclave and New Generations," in Rubén G. Rumnaut and Alejandro Portes, editors, *Ethnicities. Children of Immigrants in America* (New York: Russell Sage Foundation, 2001), pp. 91–126. On specific groups see for example Alejandro Portes and Alex Stepick, "Unwelcome Immigrants: The Labor Market Experiences of 1980 (Mariel) Cuban and Haitian Refugees in South Florida," *American Sociological Review*, 50:4 (August 1985), 493–514. A useful comparative analysis of the Cuban and Mexican immigrant experience is found in Alejandro Portes and Robert Bach. 1985. *Latin Journey: Cuban and Mexican Immigrants in the United States*, (Berkeley: University of California Press, 1985).

[10] In Georgia 65% and in North Carolina 63% of all Mexicans in 2005 were foreign born. See Table 3.5.

TABLE 3.8. *Hispanics as Percentage of State Populations, 1980–2005 (domestic- and foreign-born components in 2005)*

State	Hispanics as % of Total Population 1980	Hispanics as % of Total Population 2005	Domestic-Born 2005	% Domestic born	Foreign-Born 2005	% Foreign Born	Total Hispanics 2005
Alabama	0.9%	2.3%	45,619	45.5%	54,629	54.5%	100,248
Alaska	2.2%	4.3%	23,024	80.8%	5,464	19.2%	28,488
Arizona	16.5%	28.7%	1,028,848	61.7%	638,041	38.3%	1,666,889
Arkansas	0.8%	4.8%	61,446	47.4%	68,066	52.6%	129,512
California	19.3%	35.4%	7,178,360	57.5%	5,316,474	42.5%	12,494,834
Colorado	11.9%	19.1%	593,238	68.3%	275,935	31.7%	869,173
Connecticut	4.2%	11.4%	261,361	68.3%	121,074	31.7%	382,435
Delaware	1.6%	6.1%	28,487	56.7%	21,758	43.3%	50,245
District of Columbia	2.8%	8.6%	18,081	41.4%	25,559	58.6%	43,640
Florida	8.9%	20.0%	1,581,646	45.6%	1,889,030	54.4%	3,470,676
Georgia	1.2%	7.2%	243,525	38.2%	394,396	61.8%	637,921
Hawaii	7.7%	7.7%	83,426	86.3%	13,194	13.7%	96,620
Idaho	4.0%	9.5%	74,605	55.9%	58,763	44.1%	133,368
Illinois	5.7%	14.5%	989,569	54.7%	818,112	45.3%	1,807,681
Indiana	1.5%	4.5%	161,766	59.4%	110,437	40.6%	272,203
Iowa	0.9%	3.6%	62,879	61.2%	39,916	38.8%	102,795
Kansas	2.7%	8.1%	139,780	64.4%	77,327	35.6%	217,107
Kentucky	0.8%	1.6%	33,458	51.4%	31,672	48.6%	65,130
Louisiana	2.4%	2.8%	74,952	61.1%	47,620	38.9%	122,572
Maine	0.4%	1.1%	9,660	68.8%	4,386	31.2%	14,046
Maryland	1.6%	5.8%	131,329	41.4%	186,063	58.6%	317,392
Massachusetts	2.6%	9.4%	316,411	54.1%	268,028	45.9%	584,439
Michigan	1.7%	3.8%	264,550	70.3%	111,894	29.7%	376,444
Minnesota	0.8%	3.7%	95,289	52.1%	87,518	47.9%	182,807

State	%		%		%	
Mississippi	0.9%	26,437	54.4%	22,180	45.6%	48,617
Missouri	1.0%	94,883	61.3%	59,871	38.7%	154,754
Montana	1.4%	17,181	85.6%	2,887	14.4%	20,068
Nebraska	1.8%	71,504	57.9%	52,077	42.1%	123,581
Nevada	6.8%	308,057	55.6%	246,198	44.4%	554,255
New Hampshire	0.5%	16,888	60.4%	11,058	39.6%	27,946
New Jersey	6.9%	728,217	54.3%	612,685	45.7%	1,340,902
New Mexico	36.7%	668,043	83.7%	129,661	16.3%	797,704
New York	9.7%	1,779,356	58.6%	1,257,243	41.4%	3,036,599
North Carolina	1.0%	227,960	41.8%	317,826	58.2%	545,786
North Dakota	0.6%	7,833	71.1%	3,186	28.9%	11,019
Ohio	1.1%	188,193	74.2%	65,351	25.8%	253,544
Oklahoma	1.9%	127,294	57.8%	92,885	42.2%	220,179
Oregon	2.5%	192,773	53.8%	165,609	46.2%	358,382
Pennsylvania	1.3%	365,466	74.1%	127,720	25.9%	493,186
Rhode island	2.1%	58,982	51.4%	55,673	48.6%	114,655
South Carolina	1.1%	54,997	40.2%	81,971	59.8%	136,968
South Dakota	0.7%	8,626	72.7%	3,235	27.3%	11,861
Tennessee	0.8%	78,926	46.4%	91,059	53.6%	169,985
Texas	21.1%	5,157,068	65.7%	2,686,560	34.3%	7,843,628
Utah	4.3%	143,371	54.8%	118,283	45.2%	261,654
Vermont	0.7%	3,552	79.7%	902	20.3%	4,454
Virginia	1.6%	204,140	45.8%	241,346	54.2%	445,486
Washington	8.8%	315,363	58.0%	228,140	42.0%	543,503
West Virginia	0.7%	6,817	73.1%	2,504	26.9%	9,321
Wisconsin	1.4%	141,794	61.6%	88,535	38.4%	230,329
Wyoming	5.2%	29,146	83.0%	5,970	17.0%	35,116
Total United States	6.5%	24,524,176	58.4%	17,435,971	41.6%	41,960,147

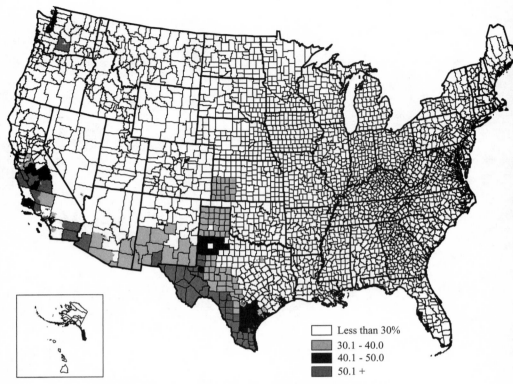

MAP 3.4. Percentage of Total Populations Who Were Mexicans, 2005.

contiguous to the Mexican border (see Map 3.4), they additionally comprised between 30 and 40% of total local populations in a quadrangular region of southwestern Kansas sprawling across some 18 counties. Central California rural counties characterized by large-scale agro industries also had Mexican majority or near-majority populations and a similar situation was found in Yakima County, Washington.[11]

---

[11] Mexicans were the majority of inhabitants in Monterey, San Benito, Fresno, Tulare, Ventura, and the western region of Kern County, California, in 2005.

    For the evolution of the Chicano community of Los Angeles, see the studies by Richard Griswald del Castillo, *The Los Angeles Barrio, 1850–1890: A Social History*, (Berkeley: University of California Press, 1979); Pedro G. Castillo and Antonio Ríos Bustamanete, *México en los Ángeles. Una historia social y cultural, 1781–1985* (México: Alianza Editoria Mexicana, 1989); George Joseph Sánchez, "Becoming Mexican American: Ethnicity and acculturation in Chicano Los Angeles, 1900–1943" (Ph.D. dissertation, Stanford University, 1989; Douglas Monroy, *Rebirth: Mexican Los Angeles from the Great Migration to the Great Depression* (Berkeley: University of California Press, 1999), Ricardo Romo, *East Los Angeles: History of a Barrio* (Austin: University of

County-level data indicate that a significant swath of counties in the nation's Southwestern and Western states had majority or near-majority Hispanic populations in 2005, in large measure because of the historic Mexican presence. Every single county along the Texas-Mexico border had majority Hispanic populations, and these majorities extended to inland counties where Latinos comprised population majorities in all of southwest and south Texas (see Map 3.5). Bexar County, Texas, which encompasses the city of San Antonio, was the second-ranking county in the United States in terms of Hispanics as a percentage of total populations at 57% in 2005, behind Miami-Dade County, Florida.[12]

In the San Antonio metropolitan area the Hispanic-origin population more than doubled between 1980 and 2005 from about 480,000 to 976,000. Mexicans represented 93% of all San Antonio's Latinos in 1980 and 80% in 2005. By 2005 Latinos comprised the majority of the San Antonio metro area's population at 53% of all residents compared with 31% in 1980.

Harris County, Texas, had the third highest absolute number of Latinos in the nation at nearly 1.3 million followed by Los Angeles County,

Texas Press, 1983); and George J. Sánchez, *Becoming Mexican American.* Matt Garcia, *A World of Its Own. Race, Labor and Citrus in the Making of Greater Los Angeles, 1900–1970* (Chapel Hill: University of North Carolina Press, 2001) covers the local industry that attracted so many Chicano workers. For the history of Mexicans in other California areas, see Robert R. Alvarez, *Familia: Migration and Adaptation in Baja and Alta California, 1800–1975* (Berkeley: University of California Press, 1987) and Albert Camarillo, *Chicanos in a Changing Society From Mexican Pueblos to American Barrios in Santa Barbara and Southern California, 1848–1930* (Cambridge, MA: Harvard University Press, 1979). A recent study on Mexican immigrants in Silicon Valley is Stephen J. Pitti, *The Devil in Silicon Valley: Northern California, Race, and Mexican Americans* (Princeton, NJ: Princeton University Press 2002), and a combination ethnography and history of Ventura County Mexicans is found in Martha Menchaca, *The Mexican Outsiders: A Community History of Marginalization and Discrimination in California* (Austin: University of Texas Press, 1995). On the Central American migration to Los Angeles see Nora Hamilton and Norma Stoltz Chinchilla, *Seeking Community in a Global City: Guatemalans and Salvadorans in Los Angeles* (Philadelphia: Temple University Press, 2001).

[12] Included here are only counties with populations of one million or more. In Miami-Dade County, Florida, 61% of all people were of Hispanic origin in 2005. See U.S. Bureau of the Census Internet release of August 4, 2006, *Table 2. Estimates of the Population by Race Alone or in Combination and Hispanic or Latino Origin for Counties with 1,000,000 or more population as of July 1, 2005 sorted by total population size: July 1, 2005,* available at http://www.census.gov/Press-Release/www/2006/cb06–123table2.xls. The San Antonio metro area indicated in Figure 3.5 had a population of over 1.8 million in 2005 of whom 53% were Hispanic. Data for the Census Bureau designated "metro areas" are available on the Census Bureau Web site at http://www.census.gov through the 2005 American Community Survey data available through the FactFinder program.

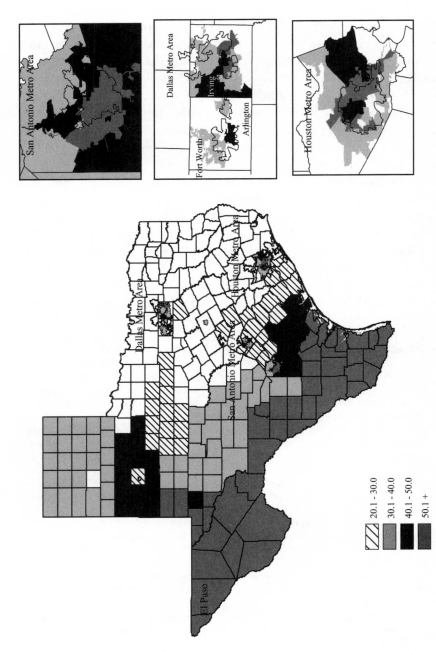

MAP 3.5. Hispanics as a Percentage of Total Populations by County and Selected Metro Areas, Texas, 2005.

San Antonio Metro Area

Dallas Metro Area

Irving

Fort Worth

Arlington

Houston Metro Area

Dallas Metro Area

Houston Metro Area

San Antonio Metro Area

El Paso

20.1 - 30.0
30.1 - 40.0
40.1 - 50.0
50.1 +

California, and Miami-Dade County, Florida. Although Hispanics comprised about 37% of the total population of Harris County, in western and eastern Houston neighborhoods and its suburbs Hispanics made up well over 50% of total populations. From downtown Houston south to the Golfcrest/Reveille super-neighborhood, north to Greater Greenspoint, and east to Northshore, Hispanics were the majority of local populations. This was also the case in western Houston super-neighborhoods in an arc of districts from Sharpstown in the south to Fairbanks Northwest Crossing in the north. It was only in southern Houston neighborhoods that Latinos made up less than 20% of total populations. These included the areas from the Midtown super-neighborhood south of Downtown through University Place, the Medical Center area, and to South Main.

Changes from 1980 to 2005 in the Houston metropolitan area were dramatic. In 1980 the Hispanic population of the Houston standard metropolitan statistical area (hereafter SMSA) represented 13% of the total population and a total of 423,000 inhabitants. Although the geographical definitions and designations had shifted somewhat, the Houston metro area's (MSA) Hispanic population quadrupled to 1,686,000 and 32% of all residents in 2005.[13] In 1980 Mexicans were 88% of the

---

[13] For 1980 see U.S. Bureau of the Census, *1980 Census of the Population*, Vol. 1, Chapter C, Characteristics of the Population, General Social and Economic Characteristics, Table 249. Persons by Spanish Origin and Race for Areas and Places: 1980. In 1980 the Census Bureau used the classification of SMSA which was described as "Each SMSA has one or more central counties containing the area's main population concentration: an urbanized area with at least 50,000 inhabitants. An SMSA may also include outlying counties which have close economic and social relationships with the central counties." For 1980 data we use SMSA designations.

For 1990 the Census Bureau did not enumerate MSAs separately from CMSAs. These both were defined in 1990 as follows: "If an area that qualifies as an MA has more than one million persons, primary metropolitan statistical areas (PMSA's) may be defined within it. PMSA's consist of a large urbanized county or cluster of counties that demonstrates very strong internal economic and social links, in addition to close ties to other portions of the larger area. When PMSA's are established, the larger area of which they are component parts is designated a consolidated metropolitan statistical area (CMSA). Metropolitan Statistical Area (MSA) Metropolitan statistical areas (MSA's) are relatively freestanding MA's and are not closely associated with other MA's. These areas typically are surrounded by nonmetropolitan counties." See Area Classifications, appendix A-6 and A-8 in Technical Documentation for the 1990 census. The data presented here for Albuquerque, Las Vegas, Phoenix, San Antonio, and San Diego are for MSAs; for Chicago, Dallas, Denver, Houston, Los Angeles, Miami, New York, and San Francisco, are for SMSAs.

For 2000 the same situation prevailed in terms of data presentation as was the case in 1990, and the data presented here on MSAs and SMSAs were the same geographical entities as for 1990.

metropolitan area's Hispanics, while in 2005 they had declined to 78% with Salvadorans, at 9%, the second largest Latino nationality.

In Dallas County, Texas, about 36% of the total population was Hispanic in 2005, although in the city itself the neighborhoods in the south and southeast of the city were majority Latino. In a large region to the west of Dallas from Irving in the north extending south past eastern Arlington, Hispanics were over 40% of all inhabitants. This was also the case in the southern districts of Fort Worth.[14] The proportional growth of the Hispanic population of the Dallas-Fort Worth metro area between 1980 and 2005 was substantial. In 1980 Latinos represented only 8% of total inhabitants, while in 2005 they accounted for 26% of the population. The absolute growth of the Hispanic population was one of

In 2005 the American Community Survey collected data on both MSAs and CMSAs and defined the metropolitan statistical area (or metro area as used here) as follows: "Metropolitan statistical area (MSA) – A geographic entity, defined by the Federal OMB for use by Federal statistical agencies, based on the concept of a core area with a large population nucleus, plus adjacent communities having a high degree of economic and social integration with that core. Qualification of an MSA requires the presence of a city with 50,000 or more inhabitants, or the presence of a UA and a total population of at least 100,000 (75,000 in New England). The county or counties containing the largest city and surrounding densely settled territory are central counties of the MSA. Additional outlying counties qualify to be included in the MSA by meeting certain other criteria of metropolitan character, such as a specified minimum population density or percentage of the population that is urban. MSAs in New England are defined in terms of cities and towns, following rules concerning commuting and population density."

There were also consolidated metropolitan statistical areas that were defined as follows: "A geographic entity defined by the Federal Office of Management and Budget (OMB) for use by Federal statistical agencies. An area becomes a CMSA if it meets the requirements to qualify as a metropolitan statistical area (MSA), has a population of 1,000,000 or more, if component parts are recognized as primary statistical metropolitan areas (PMSAs), and local opinion favors the designation. Whole counties are components of CMSAs outside of New England, where they are composed of cities and towns instead."

See http://www.census.gov/acs/www/UseData/index.htm.

Although the CMSA's were larger in geographical scope and in total populations, the data for the percentages of total populations that were Hispanics and for Mexicans as percentages of all Hispanics were similar for both MSAs and CMSAs. As the MSAs were more compact and urban, we chose to present these data.

14 Mexicans were the overwhelming component of these Texas Latino populations. In 2005 they accounted for 80% of Bexar County's Latinos, 77% in Harris County, and 84% in Dallas County. For consideration of Mexican populations in Texas see Mario T. Garcia, *Desert Immigrants: The Mexicans of El Paso, 1880–1920* (New Haven, CT: Yale University Press, 1981); Arnaldo De Leon, *The Tejano Community, 1836–1900* (Dallas: Southern Methodist University Press, 1997); Richard Griswold del Castillo, *La Familia: Chicano Families in the Urban Southwest, 1848 to the Present* (Notre Dame: University of Notre Dame Press, 1984); David Montejano, *Anglos and Mexicans in the Making of Texas, 1836–1986* (Austin: University of Texas Press, 1987).

the largest among Southwestern metropolitan regions increasing fivefold from nearly 249,000 in 1980 to 1,479,000 in 2005.[15] Mexicans remained the most important of the Latinos, comprising 89% of all Hispanics in the Dallas-Fort Worth metro area in 1980 and about 85% in 2005 with Salvadorans the second largest nationality at 6%.

In every New Mexico border-county contiguous to Mexico and Texas the Hispanic population was well over 40% of total populations, and as expected Mexicans were over 80% of all Hispanics. These same demographic structures were found in eastern Arizona counties sharing the Mexican border, and in Pima County the Hispanic population was nearly 35% of all inhabitants. In Yuma County, Arizona, bordering on Southern California, Latinos were over 50% of all inhabitants, and 94% were of Mexican origin.

But for all their significance in these three states, the Southern California counties had the highest concentration of Latinos in the United States. There were over 8 million people of Hispanic origin residing in Los Angeles, San Bernardino, Orange, Riverside, San Diego, and Imperial Counties in 2005, and they accounted for about 85% of California's total Hispanic population. About 80% of these were Mexicans. Los Angeles County itself was home to over 4.6 million Hispanics in 2005, nearly 50% of the total population, and 77% were Mexicans.

Looking at just the urban counties that made up the metropolitan districts, similar patterns of concentration were found. In the city of Los Angeles nearly all of the central and eastern districts of the city were predominantly Hispanic by 2005 (see Map 3.6). The increase in Latinos as a percentage of the total population of the Los Angeles metropolitan area was dramatic in the 25 years between 1980 and 2005. In 1980 the Los Angeles SMSA's Latinos made up 22% of all residents, and 80% of these were Mexicans. By 2005 that percentage had doubled, and Hispanics comprised 44% of the Los Angeles metro area's population. Nearly 80% was of Mexican origin.[16] The Southern California Association of Governments has estimated that by the year 2020 over half of Los Angeles County's population will be of Hispanic origin and that this will increase to 64% by 2040.[17]

[15] In 1980 the nomenclature for the region was the Dallas-Fort Worth SMSA, whereas in 2005 it was the Dallas-Fort Worth-Arlington MSA. See Map 3.5 for the 2005 geographical designation.

[16] The Census Bureau classifies the Los Angeles Metro Area as Los Angeles-Long Beach-Santa Ana, as indicated in the boundaries on Map 3.6.

[17] See the Southern California Association of Governments publication "Population Estimates and Projections by County, Ethnicity, Region, and State, 1990–1996, and 1997–2040" located at http://www.scag.ca.gov/economy/econdata.html.

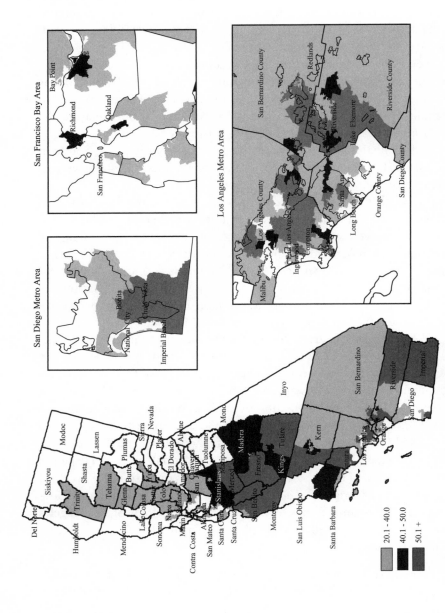

San Francisco Bay Area

San Diego Metro Area

Los Angeles Metro Area

MAP 3.6. Hispanics as a Percentage of Total Populations in California Counties and Selected Metro Areas, 2005.

20.1 – 40.0

40.1 – 50.0

50.1 +

The same kind of Hispanic relative population expansion was found in San Diego and in the San Francisco Bay Area between 1980 and 2005. In the San Diego SMSA 13% of the overall population was Hispanic in 1980, almost 275,000 people of whom 83% were Mexican. The Latino population had increased to 844,000 by 2005 and represented 30% of San Diego's total inhabitants. Some 86% of all Hispanics in San Diego were Mexican in 2005. Additionally, the southern districts of the San Diego metro area from National City to the Mexican border were majority Hispanic.

In the San Francisco-Oakland SMSA only 10% of the population was Latino in 1980, about 352,000 people of whom 53% were Mexican. The Hispanic proportion of the Bay Area's population more than doubled to 795,000 and 20% of the metropolitan area's total population by 2005 and 60% were of Mexican origin. Salvadorans accounted for 11% of the Bay Area's Latinos in 2005.

Four other large Southwestern metropolitan areas merit attention. In Albuquerque, New Mexico, Hispanics made up 27% of the total population in 1980 (164,000 people) and 43% (340,000 people) in 2005. In 2005 the southwestern districts of the city from Armijo to Los Padillas, Hispanics were more than half of local populations. In Denver, Colorado, the percentage of the metro area's population that was Latino increased from 10% and 174,000 to 22% and 505,000 between 1980 and 2005 (nearly 80% Mexicans), while in Las Vegas, Nevada, the corresponding increase was from 7% and only 35,000 in 1980 to 26% and 443,000 in 2005. Close to 80% of the Las Vegas Latino population was Mexican. In Phoenix, Arizona, 12% of the metro area's population was Hispanic in 1980 (200,000 people); 29% of the 1,109,000 persons in 2005 were Hispanic, of whom 90% were of Mexican origin.[18] (See Map 3.7 and Graph 3.1.)

The Chicago, Miami, and New York metropolitan areas are the three other major U.S. urban centers that have been focal points of Latino settlement and culture, although the historical patterns of migration and nationality distribution were different from those found in Western and Southwestern urban areas (see Table 3.9). Because Chicago was much closer to the traditional areas of Mexican settlement compared with New York and Miami, the Hispanic presence in the Chicago metropolitan area was shaped by Mexican migration patterns. Mexican communities

---

[18] In each of these metro areas the Mexican-origin population was over 75% of total Hispanics in both 1980 and 2005.

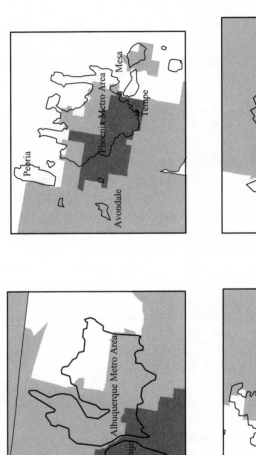

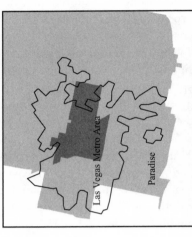

30.1 - 50.0

50.1 +

MAP 3.7. Hispanics as a Percentage of Total Populations in California Counties and Selected Metro Areas, 2005.

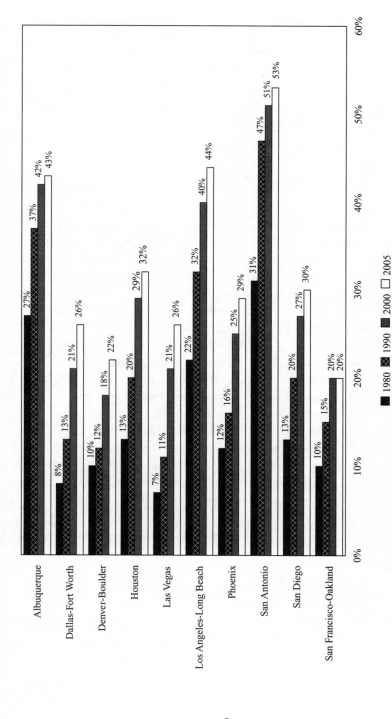

GRAPH 3.1. Hispanics as a Percentage of Total Populations in Selected Western and Southwestern Metropolitan Areas, 1980–2005. *Sources:* AmericanFactfinder data for Metropolitan Statistical Areas, Censuses of 1980, 1990, and 2000; American Community Survey, 2005.

TABLE 3.9. *Hispanics as a Percentage of Total Populations of Chicago,
Miami, and New York Metro Areas and Percentage Importance of Major
Hispanic Group in Miami and New York, 1980–2005*

	Chicago	Miami	New York City	Cubans as % of Miami Hispanics	Puerto Ricans as % of New York Hispanics
1980	8%	26%	14%	70%	61%
1990	11%	33%	15%	56%	50%
2000	16%	40%	18%	45%	37%
2005	19%	38%	21%	42%	36%

were established in Chicago during and after the First World War long
before any other Hispanic nationalities arrived. In this sense Hispanic
Chicago was similar to the Southwestern metro areas, although Mexican
population levels were much smaller than in the cities closer to Mexico,
and Hispanics in general were a fractional part of the Chicago population.
Yet by 1960 Chicago was the third-ranking U.S. city in total numbers of
Mexicans surpassed only by Los Angeles and San Antonio.

In 1980 Latinos made up only 8% of Chicago's total population, and
63% of all Hispanics were of Mexican origin. Puerto Rican migrants to
the United States during the 1950s settled principally in New York, but a
small Puerto Rican community was established in Chicago, and in 1980
Puerto Ricans accounted for 22% of the overall Hispanic population
of the Chicago metropolitan area. The Lincoln Park, West Town, and
Humboldt Park neighborhoods had the greatest concentrations of Puerto
Ricans.[19] After 1980, however, the Puerto Rican community did not
grow significantly in Chicago, while the Mexican population increased

[19] See the Center for Puerto Rican Studies, Hunter College, City University of New York,
special edition of the *Centro Journal*, XIII:2 (Fall 2001), which is devoted to the Puerto
Rican community of Chicago. Also see Felix M. Padilla, *Puerto Rican Chicago* (Notre
Dame, IN: University of Notre Dame Press, 1987); Ana Yolanda Ramos-Zayas, *Nationalist Performances: Race, Class, and Space in Puerto Rican Chicago*, (Chicago: The
University of Chicago Press, 2003); and Elena Padilla, "Puerto Rican Immigrants in
New York and Chicago" (Ph.D. dissertation, University of Chicago. 1947), published
as *Up From Puerto Rico* (New York: Columbia University Press, 1958). On the origins
of the Chicano community in Chicago see the studies of Louise Año Nuevo Kerr, "The
Chicano Experience in Chicago, 1920–1970" (Ph.D. dissertation, University of Illinois,
1976), and her article, "Chicano Settlements in Chicago: A Brief History," *Journal of
Ethnic Studies*, 2:4 (Winter 1975), 22–32. Also see Juan R. Garcia "History of Chicanos in Chicago Heights," *Aztlán: A Journal of Chicano Studies* 7:2 (Summer 1976),
291–306.

markedly. From a population of about 365,000 in 1980, Mexicans in Chicago increased to nearly 1.4 million in 2005, while Puerto Ricans rose only slightly over the same time frame from nearly 130,000 to 176,000 in 2005. By 2005 Hispanics had grown to 19% of the Chicago metro area's population, and Mexicans represented 78% of all Chicago Latinos, while Puerto Ricans had declined to 10%.

Although Latinos accounted for about one-fifth of Chicago's population, there were districts in which they were the majority and these are indicated in Map 3.8. In the neighborhoods to the southwest of the Loop district, from Lower West Side to West Lawn, and in the northern districts of the city from West Town north to Avondale and Portage Park, Latinos were over 50% of neighborhood populations. The largest component in most communities was Mexican.

The national composition of the Miami metropolitan area's Hispanic population in 1980 was in large part determined by Cuban political refugees who settled in South Florida in the aftermath Fidel Castro's revolutionary triumph in 1959. About 26% of the Miami population was Hispanic in 1980, and 70% of all Miami Latinos was of Cuban origin. Another 8% of the total Latino population was Puerto Rican. From about 580,000 in 1980 Miami's Hispanics increased to over 2 million by 2005 and 38% of the total population. Over this time frame, however, migration from other nations in Latin America resulted in a steady decrease in the Cuban population's relative portion of Latino Miami. In 1990 they had declined to 56% and to 42% in 2005. Puerto Ricans were the second largest national Hispanic subgroup in 2005 at 10%, but Miami's Latino population had become increasingly diverse as indicated in Graph 3.2.

In the city of Miami itself, northwest toward Hialeah, west to Tamiami, south through Coral Gables, South Miami, and beyond, Latinos made up majority populations in most neighborhoods as indicated in Map 3.9. This was the case in Key Biscayne as well. In Miami Beach Hispanics were over 40% of all inhabitants, and it was only in the northern areas of the metro area and in a pocket to the south of Cutler, that the Hispanic population was smaller as a percentage of local populations.

The extraordinary diversity of the New York metropolitan area's Hispanic population has made the region the most cosmopolitan of all the Latino cultural areas in the United States. Although during the 19th century there were small communities of Latin American and Caribbean-origin peoples, mostly from Cuba and Puerto Rico, it was the U.S. intervention into the Cuban War for Independence (1895–98), and subsequent

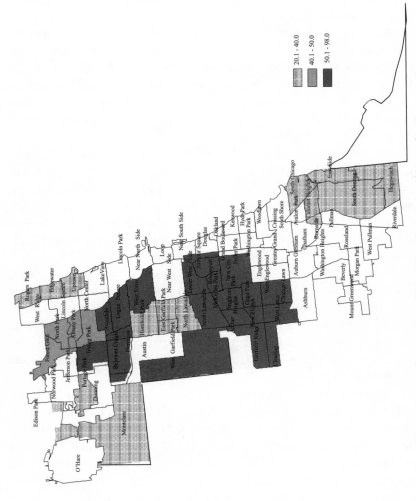

MAP 3.8. Hispanics as a Percentage of Total Populations in Chicago by Community, 2005.

20.1 - 40.0

40.1 - 50.0

50.1 - 98.0

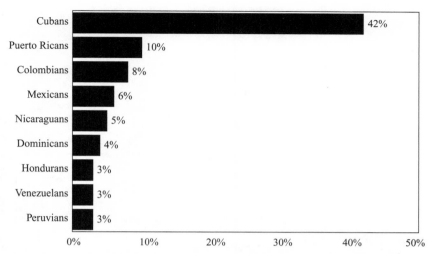

GRAPH 3.2. Relative Importance by Nationality of Total Hispanic Population of Miami Metro Area, 2005. *Sources:* AmericanFactfinder data for Metropolitan Statistical Areas, American Community Survey, 2005.

invasions and military occupations of both islands, that created the conditions for future migration to New York. In 1900 there were only about 1,300 Puerto Ricans in the entire United States, and most of them were in New York.[20] By 1910 Puerto Ricans in the United States had increased to about 2,700 but 90% of the total were concentrated in Hawaii where they had been recruited as workers for the sugar industry of the territory. Through the Jones Act passed by Congress in 1917 the United States decreed that Puerto Ricans were U.S. citizens, and this paved the way for unrestricted migration from the island. By 1920 there were over 19,000 Puerto Ricans in the United States, and nearly 45% of them lived in New York. In 1930 Puerto Ricans dwarfed all other Latino nationalities in New York at over 51,000 compared with 10,000 Cubans, and 76% of all Puerto Ricans in the United States lived in New York State. From this point and until the 1970s Latino culture in New York City was defined by the Puerto Rican presence.

Yet, despite this shift in the locus of Puerto Rican migration and settlement toward New York, in 1930 Latinos comprised only 1.1% of the total population of New York City and less than 1% of the New York

---

[20] Data on the Puerto Rican population of the United States prior to 1970 were derived from the PUMS ancestry data published by the IPUMS, University of Minnesota site used throughout this study.

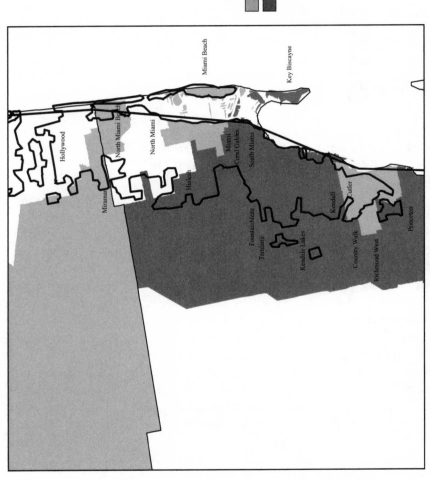

30.1 - 50.0

50.1 +

MAP 3.9. Hispanics as a Percentage of Total Populations in Miami Metro Area, 2005.

92

metropolitan area's total population. These percentages remained nearly unchanged in 1940 despite the gradual increase in the Puerto Rican population because of continued migration. In 1940 there were over 81,000 Puerto Ricans in New York City, and they comprised about 70% of the overall Latino population. The development of a Latino culture that would help define New York in the late 20th century intensified during the 1940s. Employment opportunities during the Second World War and in its aftermath drew increased numbers of Puerto Ricans to the city. By 1950 the number of Puerto Ricans had tripled from 1940 to over 247,000; the overall Latino population had increased from 1% to 3% of all New Yorkers; and Puerto Ricans made up 84% of all Latinos. But it was the large-scale migration from Puerto Rico during the 1950s and 1960s that led to the creation of distinct and sometimes exclusive Puerto Rican enclaves in East Harlem (El Barrio), the Lower East Side of Manhattan, parts of Brooklyn, and the Bronx. In these neighborhoods Spanish became the dominant language, an array of Hispanic-Caribbean cultural forms from music to food were manifest, and these slowly began to impact other areas of the city. By 1970 there were over 1.2 million total Latinos (about 8% of the overall population) of whom 850,000 were Puerto Ricans residing in the New York metropolitan area.[21] (See Graph 3.3.) Cubans were the second most numerous Latino national subgroup in 1970 with a population of over 85,000.

The decade of the 1970s was accompanied by extraordinary changes in New York City's Latino population. First, and foremost by 1980 they had increased to 20% of the city's residents.[22] Second, Puerto Rican migration slowed considerably, and while Puerto Ricans remained the

---

[21] There are no data for Hispanics or Puerto Ricans at the city or metropolitan area levels found in the Public Use Microdata Series data sets for 1960. For 1970 there are data for metropolitan areas but no data at the city level. The New York metropolitan area data cited here includes the counties of northern New Jersey, western Long Island, counties in New York state just north of the City, and western Connecticut counties.

For second-generation immigrants and their adaptation to the city, see Philip Kasinitz, John H. Mollenkopf, and Mary C. Waters, editors, *Becoming New Yorkers. Ethnographies of the New Second Generation* (New York: Russell Sage Foundation, 2004). For the latest survey of these first and second generation immigrants in New York City see Philip Kasinitz, John H. Mollenkopf, Mary C. Waters and Jennifer Holdaway, *Inheriting the City. The Children of Immigrants Come of Age* (New York: Russell Sage Foundation, 2008).

[22] Although there are no accurate Latino city data to compare with 1970, by way of comparison the New York metro area's Latino population increased from 8% in 1970 to 16% of all inhabitants in 1980. It is likely that the New York City's Latino population was somewhere near 10% of the total in 1970, and this soared to 20% in 1980.

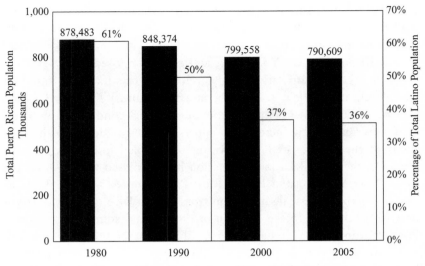

GRAPH 3.3. Puerto Rican Population of New York City, 1980–2005.

dominant Latino national group, their share of the city's total Hispanic population had declined to 61%.[23] In absolute numbers there was only a marginal increase in the Puerto Rican population during the 1970s to nearly 880,000 people. Third, newer migrant groups from Latin America and the Caribbean began to arrive in the 1970s and this lead to an extraordinary diversification of Latino culture in the city.

Foremost among the new were migrants from the Dominican Republic. There were slightly more than 40,000 Dominicans living in the New York metropolitan region in 1970. By 1980 that number had soared to over 153,000, and 150,000 of this Dominican population lived in New York City. They were concentrated in the northern Manhattan communities of Washington Heights/Inwood and made up 10% of the city's Latino population in 1980. Cubans were the next largest group, but their numbers had declined in absolute and relative terms, and they accounted for 5% of all New York City Latinos. The other two national groups that established a significant presence in the city were Ecuadorians (47,000) and Colombians (49,000). The Mexican community in 1980 was still relatively small, at only some 25,000 persons.

The changes set in motion during the 1970s – the relative decrease of Puerto Ricans as a percentage of overall New York City Latinos and the increase in Dominicans and other newer immigrant groups – continued from 1980 through 2005. By 1990, for the first time in the 20th century, the number of Puerto Ricans living in New York City declined from the previous decennial census, and this decline continued through the 1990s and to 2005. In 1990 there were about 850,000 Puerto Ricans in the city and they represented just half of all Latinos in the city. The pace of decline continued in the 21st century. In absolute numbers they were some 790,000 persons in 2005 and now represented 37% of the city's Hispanic population. (See Graph 3.4.)[24]

The explosive growth of the Dominican population characterized the period after 1980, and by 2005 there were over 570,000 Dominicans in New York City representing 26% of all Latino nationalities. If yearly rates of population expansion continue into the future, Dominicans will surpass Puerto Ricans some time after 2020. The growth of the Dominican population was also characterized by spatial expansion outside of upper Manhattan into contiguous neighborhoods in the South Bronx across the East River and also into Brooklyn and Queens. By 2005 more Dominicans lived in the Bronx than in the original area of settlement in upper Manhattan.

Although the numbers of Ecuadorians and Colombians also increased steadily between 1980 and 2005, during the 1990s they were eclipsed in absolute terms by the Mexican population of New York City, which expanded dramatically largely because of immigration from Mexico. By 2005 Mexicans had become the third largest Latino nationality behind Puerto Ricans and Dominicans. Their yearly rate of expansion was so dramatic between 1990 and 2005 that if projected into the future some time after 2030 Mexicans may become the most numerous Latino subgroup in the city.[25]

---

[24] It ought to be noted that the Puerto Rican population of the overall New York metropolitan region also declined over the same period from 909,048 in 1980 to 843,496 in 2005. In 1980 97% of the New York metro's Puerto Rican population lived in New York City, and this relative percentage declined only slightly to 94% in 2005.

[25] Not only are large numbers of Mexicans migrating to New York City and the metropolitan area, but the New York City birth rates among Mexican women dwarfed those of other Latino national groups. In 2005 there were 147 live births per thousand women ages 15–44 among Mexican New Yorkers compared with 85 among Ecuadorians and 66 among Dominicans. See Bureau of Vital Statistics, New York City Department of Health and Mental Hygiene, "Summary of Vital Statistics, 2005," The City of New York, Table 30, p. 44.

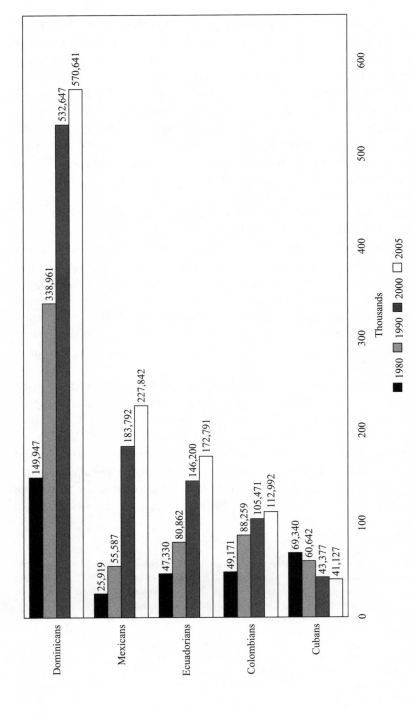

GRAPH 3.4. Non-Puerto Rican Latino Nationalities in New York City, 1980–2005.

■ 1980   ▨ 1990   ■ 2000   □ 2005

Thousands

Dominicans
149,947
338,961
532,647
570,641

Mexicans
25,919
55,587
183,792
227,842

Ecuadorians
47,330
80,862
146,200
172,791

Colombians
49,171
88,259
105,471
112,992

Cubans
69,340
60,642
43,377
41,127

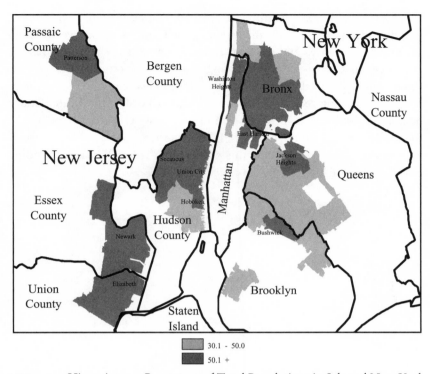

MAP 3.10. Hispanics as a Percentage of Total Populations in Selected New York Metro Area Counties, 2005.

In 2005 the Latino population of New York City had risen to 28% of all inhabitants. In the Bronx over 50% of all residents were Hispanics, and in some South Bronx neighborhoods they were more than 70% as indicated in Map 3.10. In Manhattan and Queens, Latinos were about 26% of all residents. More than 70% of total populations were Latinos in the northern Manhattan communities of Washington Heights and East Harlem; in Jackson Heights, Queens; and in Bushwick, Brooklyn. Across the Hudson River in New Jersey, in the Hudson County cities of Secaucus, Union City, and Hoboken, Latinos were also more than 70% of total populations. This was also the case in the New Jersey cities of Newark, Elizabeth, and Patterson.

The trends and tendencies in Hispanic population expansion found in the various states, metropolitan areas, and cities between 1980 and 2005 will in all likelihood continue into the future. Despite political debates on immigration policy, legalization of extant undocumented persons, and tightened border "security," there is little possibility that migration from

Latin America and the Caribbean, especially along the Mexican border, will diminish in any significant way into the future. Low wages and high unemployment rates within Latin American nations, especially Mexico, are forces that are not likely to change, and these factors will drive continued migration to the United States. Additionally, comparatively higher birth rates among resident Hispanics, whether born in the United States or abroad, will also lead to the continued increase in the percentage of the nation's population who are of Latin American and Caribbean origin, although it is likely that within this population there will be an expanding portion who are born in the United States.

4

The Demography of the Hispanic Population

Hispanics have had a demographic impact on the United States far beyond their relative importance within the total population because of their high fertility rates. In fact, it is quite clear that the United States would have had below population replacement rates of reproduction in the past few decades had it not been for the contribution of the Hispanic population, and above all Mexicans and Central Americans. When the Center for Disease Control first began enumerating Hispanic births in a systematic way in 1990, their fertility rate was already well above national averages. In that year the total fertility rate (defined as births per hundred women ages 15–44) among Hispanic women was 3.2 children, while the comparable rate for non-Hispanic white women was 1.9 children, a rate that had prevailed since the late 1970s.[1] The rapid growth of the Latino population since 1990, and their consistently higher fertility rates compared with the rest of the population, has resulted in the national population growing naturally at or above a total fertility rate of 2.1 children, which is the threshold for the population replacement level. Without this Hispanic population growth U.S. fertility rates would have resembled those of most European countries, which have fallen below population replacement levels.

Because of their relative weight within the Hispanic population, Mexicans, with a fertility rate of 3.0 children, heavily impacted the

---

[1] This and all subsequent numbers come from Brady E. Hamilton, "Reproduction Rates for 1990–2002 and Intrinsic Rates for 2000–2001: United States," *National Vital Statistics Reports*, 52:17 (March 18, 2004), Table 2. The data for Hispanic births in this table was updated in February 2005.

overall Latino fertility rate. Most other Latino national subgroups had total fertility rates that approximated the Mexican rates, with the average in 1990 at 2.9 children. Yet there were nationalities that varied considerably from the Mexican norm. The most extreme was the Cubans whose total fertility rate of 1.5 children in 1990 was the lowest for any major Hispanic national subgroup, even below that of non-Hispanic whites. Puerto Ricans had fertility rates that fell between Cubans and Mexicans and were comparable with those of non-Hispanic blacks. In 1990 the Puerto Rican total fertility rate was 2.3 children, and this compared with a rate of 2.5 children among non-Hispanic blacks (see Graph 4.1).

Despite their high fertility, Mexicans residing in the United States had a fertility rate that was lower than the total 3.4 fertility rate found in Mexico in 1990. Moreover, the five northern and western states in Mexico had fertility rates that were much higher than those found among Mexican migrants and their descendents in the United States, with three of them – Durango, Michoacán, and Zacatecas – having total fertility rates of 3.9 children or more in 1990. Of the seven states that were the next most important centers of out-migration, all but two had fertility rates that were higher than those found among Mexican women ages 15–44 in the United States.[2] Thus, Mexicans who had migrated to the United States were having fewer children than their peers who remained in Mexico. The same was true for Cubans. Although fertility had dropped dramatically in Cuba from 1970 when the total fertility rate was at 3.1 children to 1.8 children in 1990, this was still higher than the rate for Cuban women of child-bearing age in the United States.[3]

Puerto Ricans were the only exception to this pattern of lower fertility rates among Latino national subgroups living in the United States compared with their countries of origin. Those residing on the mainland had higher birth rates than those who lived on the island in 1990. While the gap between mainland and island rates have narrowed among Puerto Ricans, island birth rates in 2001 were still lower than those of Puerto

---

[2] Only Colema and Morelos had rates less than the U.S. resident Mexican average. CONAPO, "Indicadores demográficos, 1990–2050," available at http://www.conapo .gob.mx/index.php?option=com_content&view=article&id=149&Itemid=14. For the ranking of Mexican states by the intensity of their migration to the United Status, see CONAPO, Cuadro A. "Indicadores sobre migración a Estados Unidos, índice y grado de intensidad migratoria por entidad federativa, 2000," available at http://www.conapo .gob.mx/publicaciones/migra4.htm.

[3] Libia López Nistal, Miriam A. Gran Álvarez, and Ana Maria Felipe Ramos, "Evolución de la fecundidad en Cuba en las últimas cinco décadas," *Revista Temas Estadísticos de Salud* (Habana), No 2 (Diciembre 2006), 4, Cuadro 2.

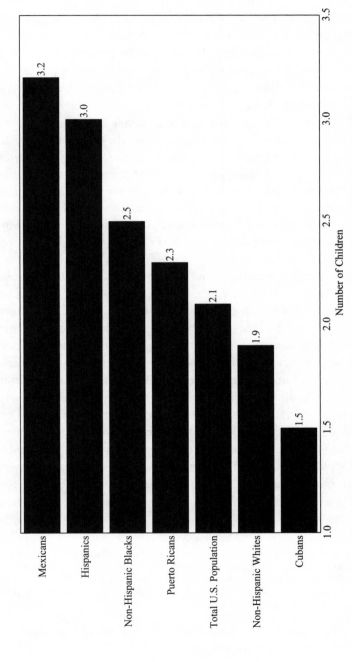

GRAPH 4.1. Total Fertility Rate by Race/Ethnicity or Latino Nationality, 1990 (births per hundred women ages 15–44).

Ricans residing in the United States.[4] Recent studies have suggested that post–World War II migrating Puerto Rican women were poorer and less educated than those who remained at home, and that this accounted for the differentiation in birth rates.[5] Although most Latin American and Caribbean immigrants to the United States came from the working classes, except the earliest post-Castro Cubans, their economic and educational levels were probably higher than their nonmigrating compatriots. This does not seem to have been the case with Puerto Rican migrants. Puerto Ricans who came to the mainland tended to mimic the poorest group in the United States – non-Hispanic blacks – and they seem to share less in common in terms of fertility and mortality with other Latin American and Caribbean migrants. The lack of any legal restrictions to migration for Puerto Ricans, and the availability of inexpensive airline service to the U.S. mainland, permitted an even poorer socioeconomic class of workers to arrive in the United States than was possible from the other Latin American countries where the costs of entry into the United States were much higher.

The higher fertility patterns found among all foreign-born Latinos in the United States in 1990 have remained relatively constant to 2005 and continue to be well above those of the non-Hispanic white population. Although individual Latino subgroups experienced declines in fertility toward non-Hispanic white levels, a pattern typical for all previous immigrant groups in American history, among the demographically dominant Mexicans there was no decline whatsoever. Despite some variation in the late 1990s, the fertility rate among Mexicans in the United States has remained high and returned to a level at or above 3.0 children. There was a modest, if temporary, decline of fertility among Mexicans toward the end of the 1990s, when rates dropped below 3 births per hundred women of child-bearing age. This seemed to suggest a movement toward the fertility rates among non-Hispanic whites. But since then the total fertility rate has risen to 3.0 children. Thus, Mexicans are producing on

---

[4] The crude birth rate on the island in 1990 was 18.9 births per thousand persons, and for Puerto Ricans on the mainland it was 21.6 births per thousand persons. For the island rates, see CDC, NCHS, *Vital Statistics of the United States, 2001*, I, "Natality," Table 3–1, "Live Births and Birth Rates: Puerto Rico, 1943–2001" and *National Vital Statistics Reports*, 54:2 (September 8, 2005), 37, Table 6.

[5] CDC, NCHS, "Topics in Minority Health: Childbearing Patterns Among Puerto Rican Hispanics in New York City and Puerto Rico," CDC, *Morbidity and Mortality Weekly Report*, 36:3 (January 30, 1987), 34, 39–41.

average about 1.2 children above the non-Hispanic white reproductive rate. But it also means, surprisingly, that they have now reversed their statistical relationship to the birth rates in Mexico itself. The total fertility rate of Mexicans in the United States is now higher than the national rate in Mexico, and this is the case for every Mexican state, all of which are now well below the 3.0-child total fertility rate of Mexicans in the United States.[6]

This high and relatively stable fertility rate among Mexicans in the United States, along with the increasing volume of Mexican immigration has meant that the Mexicans had an impact not only on fertility rates among all Hispanics, but also on national birth rates. In 2004, when the latest available data for births are available, Hispanics accounted for 23% of all births in the United States, with Mexicans alone accounting for 17% of total births, both figures well above their 14% (Hispanics) and 9% (Mexicans) representation, respectively, within the total population in 2005.[7] Moreover the Hispanic portion of total births has constantly been increasing since they were first systematically recorded, rising steadily each year from 1989 when Hispanics accounted for 13% of all births, with Mexicans at 8%. Over the same period Mexicans births rose from 60% to 70% of all Hispanic births. By way of comparison, in 1989 non-Hispanic white mothers accounted for 65% of all births in the United States, but this had fallen to 56% in 2004. For non-Hispanic blacks the decline was less dramatic, from 16% of all births in 1989 to 14% in 2004 (see Graph 4.2).[8]

---

[6] The Mexican government estimated that the overall total fertility rate of Mexico in 2000 at 2.4 children per thousand women in the 15–44 age group, which was already below the U.S. Mexican rates. Also most states in Mexico were at or below this rate. Rodolfo Tuirán, Virgilio Partida, Octavio Mojarro, and Elena Zúñiga, "Tendencias y perspectivas de la fecundidad," in *La situación demográfica de México, 2002* (México: CONAPO, 2002), p.30. It also projected the 2005 Mexican total fertility rate to be 2.1 children and estimated that even the state with the highest such rate, Guerrero, would only have a total fertility rate of 2.6 children, again, all this well below the Mexican residents in the United States. See Bush et al., "Situación actual y perspectivas demográficas" in *La situación demográfica de México, 2000* (2nd rev. ed., México: CONAPO, 2001), p. 51, Cuadro 5. Also see the latest projections for 2006 and 2007 – again both well below U.S. rates – at CONAPO, *Indicadores demográficos, 1990–2050*.

[7] Joyce A. Martin et al., "Births: Final Data for 2004," *National Vital Statistics Reports*, 55:1 (September 29, 2006), 54, Table 13. For the representation of Hispanics and Mexicans in the total population in 2005, see American Community Survey of 2005 summary tables available at http://www2.census.gov/acs2005/SPP/Race_Ancestry_Hispanic_Origin/Mexican/.

[8] Martin et al., "Births: Final Data for 2004," p. 55, Table 14.

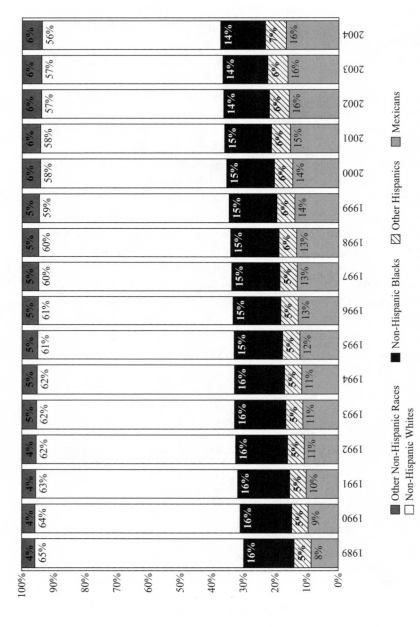

GRAPH 4.2. Changing Relative Share of Total Births in the United States by Race/Ethnicity and Mexicans, 1989–2004. *Source:* CDC, NCHS, *National Vital Statistics Reports,* 55:1 (September 29, 2006), p. 41, Table 5.

When data are examined in states where Mexicans were large percentages of overall populations, these birth rates were even more significant. In New Mexico, Hispanics (mostly Mexicans) accounted for 53.4% of all births in 2004 compared to 42% in 2000. In California as well, Hispanics accounted for the majority of total births at 51.2% in 2004 (Mexican mothers alone giving birth to 44.8% of all California-born infants). This was proportionally much greater than their one-third share of the total state population. In Texas, where Hispanics also represented a third of the state population, Latinos accounted for 49.4% of all births in 2004; and in Arizona, where they were a quarter of the state population in 2004, 44.2% of all births were to Hispanic mothers.[9]

Even though overall Hispanic birth rates remained high, not all Latino national subgroups experienced the same trends. In contrast to Mexicans, most of the other nationalities were slowly moving toward the rates prevailing among non-Hispanic whites, which was the traditional pattern for most immigrant groups in the United States. Puerto Rican fertility rates have approximated the non-Hispanic white birth rate in the same way that non-Hispanic black birth rates have declined. Even Cubans, despite extraordinarily low birth rates, have seen a slow rise in the 21st century toward the non-Hispanic white rate. (See Graph 4.3.) The slight rise in birth rates among Cubans is due to the fact that the foreign-born among them declined in importance and the native-born, who were generally younger, increased. This reduced both the average age of Cubans in the United States and resulted in a modest increase in fertility. Thus, the traditional pattern of convergence of immigrant fertility toward non-Hispanic white rates was experienced by most Latino national subgroups. Mexicans stand out as the major exception with the persistence of high fertility rates compared not only to U.S. non-Hispanic whites but also, as previously noted, to the resident population in Mexico.

Not only were Hispanics in general having more children than non-Hispanic whites and blacks, but they were also having them at younger ages. For Mexicans, and indeed for all Latinos, the average age of mothers at the birth of their first child was 3.1 years younger than non-Hispanic whites in 1989. The differential increased to 3.7 years in 2000

---

[9] Martin et al. "Births: Final Data for 2004," p. 54, Table 13. The percentage of Hispanics in the total population in the Census of 2000 was 32.4% for California, 32.0% for Texas, and 25.3% for Arizona. See American FactFinder, Census 2000, "GCT-P6: Race and Hispanic or Latino: 2000 . . . Summary File 1 . . . United States – States; and Puerto Rico."

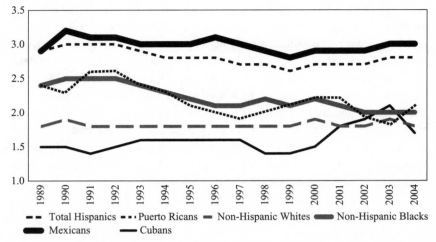

GRAPH 4.3. Total Fertility Rate by Race/Ethnicity and Mexicans, Puerto Ricans, and Cubans, 1989–2004.

and to 4.1 years by 2004.[10] (See Graph 4.4.) While Mexicans and Hispanic mothers in general were having their first children earlier, they were also having their third child at younger ages, thus often completing their families before non-Hispanic whites. However, Cubans and Central and South Americans did not fit the general Hispanic pattern. (See Graph 4.5.) Additionally, Hispanic women at the end of their reproductive years had lower rates of childlessness compared with the rest of the population. In 2004 Hispanic women ages 40–44 had the lowest reported rate of any major group with only 14% never having given birth to a child, compared to 18% for Asian women and 20% for both non-Hispanic-black and non-Hispanic white women – with the national average at 19%.[11] All these patterns in the timing and incidence of fertility seem to suggest that in their fertility behavior Hispanics were very different from the patterns found among the predominant non-Hispanic white population.

However, some changes in fertility patterns have begun to occur among Hispanic women. As has been the case within nearly all racial/ethnic groups, Latinas in the United States are progressively bearing children

[10] Martin et al., "Births: Final Data for 2004," p. 51, Table 10.
[11] U.S. Department of the Census, "Fertility of American Women, Current Population Survey – June 2004," Table 7, available at http://www.census.gov/population/www/socdemo/fertility/cps2004.html.

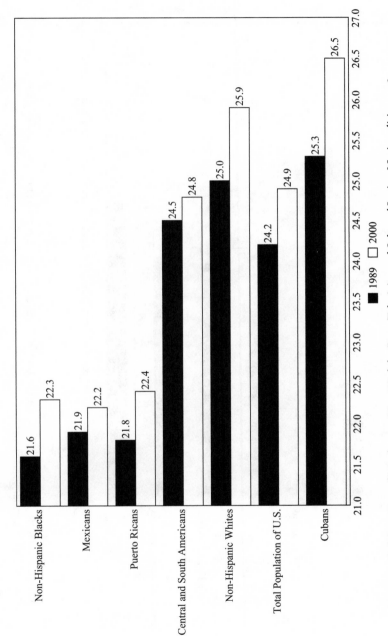

GRAPH 4.4. Mean Age of Mothers at First Birth by Race/Ethnicity and Selected Latino Nationalities, 1989–2000. *Source:* CDC, NCHS, *National Vital Statistics Reports*, 51:1 (December 11, 2002), pp. 6–8, Tables 1 & 2.

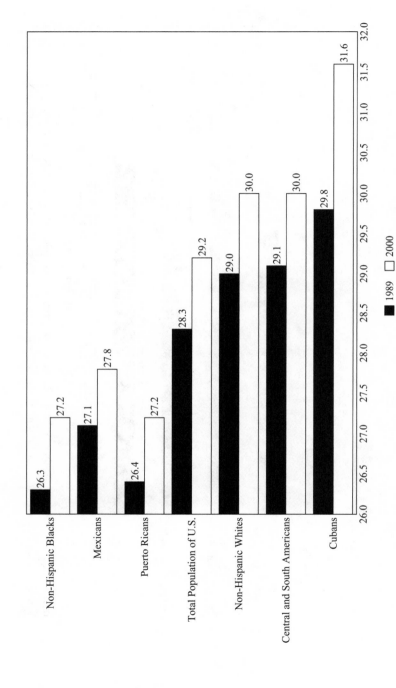

GRAPH 4.5. Mean Age at Birth of Third Child by Race/Ethnicity and Latino Nationality, 1989–2000. *Source:* CDC, NCHS, *National Vital Statistics Reports,* 51:11 (December 11, 2002), pp. 6–8, Tables 1 & 2.

at older ages. Accordingly, the relative importance of younger women – between 15 and 19 years of age – in the births of Hispanic children has steadily declined from their peaks in the early 1990s and the number of births to women in the older age cohort of 30–34 year olds, has replaced the 15–19 year old mothers in importance (see Graph 4.6). Even with these declines in births among younger Hispanic women, they are still producing greater numbers of children in the 15–19 year old age category than all other race and ethnic groups. Moreover in 2004, the latest year for complete national birth data, Hispanics achieved their maximum fertility in the 20–24 year old age category, while non-Hispanic whites, still the majority of the national population, peaked in the older 25–29 year old age group. Only Asians did not reach their maximum fertility levels until 30–34 years of age, and this was similar to Cubans, the only Hispanic national subgroup for which this was the case. The age-specific fertility patterns among non-Hispanic blacks were similar to Hispanics, but they had fewer children (see Graph 4.7). Some 46% of all Hispanic births were to mothers under 25 years of age, while the rate was only 30% for non-Hispanic whites. There were also significant differences when the age of the mother at the time of the first birth is considered. In 2004 some 71% of Hispanic mothers had their first child before they reached 25 years of age, where fewer than half of non-Hispanic white mothers who gave birth to their first child were this young.[12]

In one area Hispanic mothers were not very different from other racial/ethnic groups and that is in birth rates outside of formal marriage. Among mothers who were not legally married, Hispanics had nearly double the rate of births (46%) compared to non-Hispanic whites (25%). By way of comparison, some two-thirds of non-Hispanic black births were to single women. Nevertheless, despite fairly high rates of births to single mothers among the Latino population, in 2000 households headed by single mothers with children under 18 years of age represented only 12% of all Hispanic households. This compared to a 19% rate among non-Hispanic blacks and 5% among non-Hispanic whites. This suggests that a higher portion of single mothers were living in households headed by a male, most probably the father of their children. There were of course sharp differences among different Latino national subgroups. Among Mexicans about 10% of all households were headed by single mothers, while for Puerto Ricans the rate was 18%. Dominicans had the highest

[12] Joyce A. Martin et al. "Births: Final Data for 2004," pp. 42–43, Table 6.

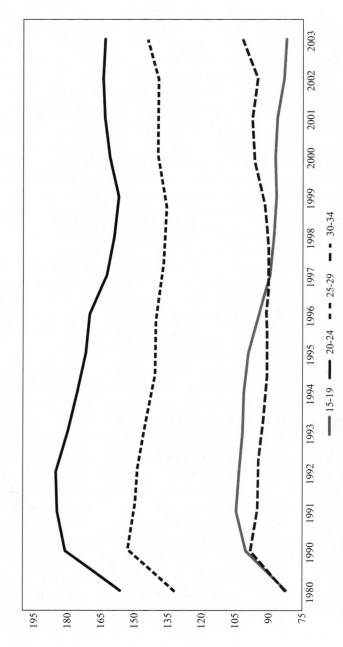

GRAPH 4.6. Birth Rate of Mexican Women in the United States by Age Cohorts of Mothers, 1980–2003 (births per thousand women in each age group). *Source:* CDC, NCHS, *National Vital Statistics Reports*, 51:12 (August 4, 2000), Table 2.

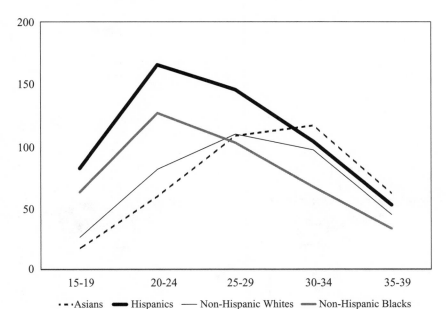

GRAPH 4.7. Number of Births per Thousand Population by Age of Mother for Hispanics and Non-Hispanics, 2004.

percentage of all households with children headed by single mothers at 23%.[13]

The generally high rate of fertility shown by the Hispanic population in all recent censuses has had a direct impact on its age structure. By 2000 Hispanics had a greater population in younger age categories than almost all other components of the U.S. population, and this resulted in an age pyramid that was quite unusual compared with other population sectors and modern industrial societies in general. For the non-Hispanic population, as for all contemporary industrial country populations that had experienced the transition to low birth and mortality rates, the distribution of ages by sex resulted in a jar-shaped pyramid structure with fewer children and a greater aged population compared to the working-age cohorts (see Graph 4.8). This distinctive age pyramid among Hispanics

[13] Census 2000, Summary File 2, "PCT9. Household Size, Household Type, And Presence Of Own Children – Universe: Households." Also see Graph 4.9. A recent study argues, however, that Mexican-born immigrants have shown low levels of female household heads, while domestic-born Mexicans tended to have higher rates of female-headed households and are following the trend line of non-Hispanic blacks. See Elizabeth Wildsmith, "Race/Ethnic Differences in Female Headship: Exploring the Assumptions of Assimilation Theory," *Social Science Quarterly*, 85:1 (March 2004), 89–106.

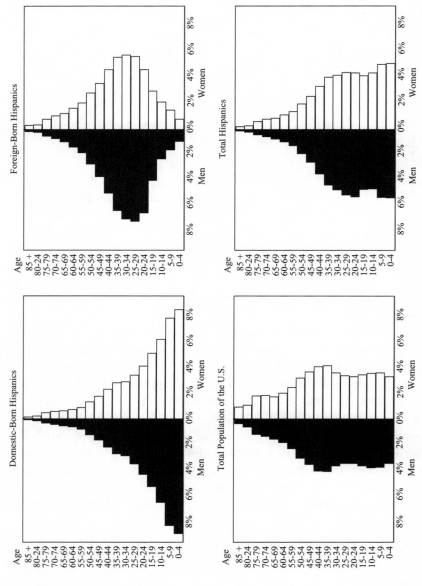

GRAPH 4.8. Age Pyramids of the Components of the Hispanic Population, and the Total Population of the United States, 2000.

was not due to higher mortality rates, for as we will see Hispanics had lower mortality rates than the national population. Rather it was because of the high rates of immigration of younger people, as well as comparatively high fertility rates among Hispanic women. These factors meant that the Hispanic age pyramid looked more like the demographic structures found in preindustrial societies. These had large numbers of children, larger numbers of working-age men and women, and relatively smaller numbers of older people in relation to these younger sectors of the population. Even if only the domestic-born Hispanic population is examined, and the foreign-born are excluded, the Latino age structure exhibits traits that were more common to preindustrial societies because of the large percentage of children (see Graph 4.8).

An examination of median age data is revealing. The median for all Hispanics in 2000 was 25 years of age, some 14 years younger than the 39-year-old median age for non-Hispanic whites. However, this masked a sharp difference between the median ages of foreign-born Hispanics at 33 years of age and 17 years of age for domestic-born Latinos. This comparatively younger age structure also had an impact on the dependency ratio, which is the number of persons in the working ages compared to retired persons (65 years and older) and young people (younger than 18 years). Hispanics had fewer workers in relation to nonworking older or younger dependents than non-Hispanic whites in 2000. The national dependency ratio was 60%, but among Hispanics it was 65%. The key difference was that children accounted for a much higher ratio of Hispanic dependents, compared to the national population where most of the dependents were retired persons. In the general U.S. rate, children accounted for 67% of all dependents, while they made up a very high 88% of the total dependent population among Hispanics. Thus, while Latinos had more people dependent on fewer workers than the national average, this had less of a potential impact than it would seem, since most of these dependents were children who would eventually enter the workforce. In contrast, the non-Hispanic population has been supporting a constantly increasing ratio of nonproductive retirees, thus putting ever-increasing pressures on social services while the tax base was shrinking because of fewer people in the labor force. Again there were the expected differences among Hispanic national subgroups, with Mexicans having some 37% of their population younger than 18 years of age, and Cubans at the other extreme with 21% in this age category. The majority of Hispanics were closer to the Mexican pattern than the Cuban one, but all were larger than the 25% of the national population that was younger than 18 years of age.

With their high fertility, it would be expected that family size was also different for Hispanics compared with the other race and ethnic groups in U.S. society. By 2000 the average family size (mean) among Hispanics was 4.3 persons, and there was no difference between families headed by domestic-born or foreign-born individuals. In the nation as a whole, the average family size was 3.3 persons while median family size was 3 persons. In fact, the non-Hispanic white rate was even lower than this with the average at 3.0 persons per family. The Hispanic means and medians were higher than almost all other major race and ethnic groups – the non-Hispanic black rate was a mean of 3.4 and a median of 3 persons in each family. An important minority of Hispanics also had large families. In fact, Latinos had the highest percentage of families with 5 or more persons compared with the other racial/ethnic groups. In 2005 some 19% of all domestic-born Latino families had 5 or more persons, while among the foreign-born it was an extraordinary 33% of all families. Some 41% of both domestic and foreign-born Mexicans had family sizes of 5 or more persons, the highest rate for any ethnic, racial, or Hispanic national subgroup in the United States.

Despite large family sizes, the adult Hispanic population (those 15 years of age and older) tended to have more persons who never married than non-Hispanic whites. Surprisingly, the ratios were much higher among native-born than among foreign-born Hispanic adults. Some 43% of domestic-born Hispanics ages 15 years or older were unmarried, compared to only 28% of foreign-born Hispanic adults in 2000. In this regard foreign-born Hispanics were more similar to the national population, whereas the domestic-born were closer to the non-Hispanic black ratio. Given the more balanced sex ratio of adult domestic-born Hispanics (97 males per 100 females) in contrast to the highly male-biased foreign-born Hispanic adult population (111 males per 100 females) this pattern is difficult to explain. One would expect the opposite result, with a more balanced sex ratio among native-born Hispanics leading to higher rates of marriage, especially if endogamy was practiced. But clearly foreign-born males were often marrying non-Hispanics, and they were marrying at much higher rates than second- and third-generation domestic-born Hispanics. This sharp variation in marriage rates between the domestic- and foreign-born groups is also found in 2005. Given their high fertility and the low numbers of women who were childless, it was inevitable that birth rates out of formal marriage for domestic-born Hispanics would be quite high given relatively low marriage rates. In contrast, the foreign-born had low levels of births outside of marriage despite the fact that they had lower ratios of persons never having been married. It may be that the domestic-born adopted a more lenient attitude toward nonmarital births than more tradition-bound immigrants.

Like non-Hispanic blacks, Latinos had a significantly higher percentage of female-headed households than the non-Hispanic white population. They also had a higher percentage of female-headed households with children than the non-Hispanic white majority in 2000. But in one area there were nearly verbatim similarities with non-Hispanic whites, and that was in the ratio of married couples to total household types. Hispanics and non-Hispanic whites had the same 54% of all households defined as headed by two-parent families. For non-Hispanic blacks it was significantly lower at 31%. There was, of course, some variation by Latino national subgroup. Mexicans, at 58%, had among the highest percentage of households headed by married couples, whereas Dominicans and Puerto Ricans had less half of all households designated as headed by a traditional married couple. Even with high levels of births outside of marriage, the stability of the family was impressive among Hispanics compared with other racial/ethnic groups in American society.[14] (See Graph 4.9.)

If fertility among Hispanics has been unusually high in the recent past, an even more surprising factor is the mortality experienced by Hispanics compared with all other racial/ethnic groups. Because of their concentration in the working classes and their predominance in the poorest strata of American society in terms of income and education, Hispanics should demonstrate health outcomes that would be comparable to non-Hispanic blacks who have similar socioeconomic structures. This, in fact, is the case with Puerto Ricans. But it is not the case with the majority of Hispanics. In fact, with respect to health, Latinos seem to be better off than even non-Hispanic whites. This has led to a major discussion in the academic literature as to the causes, consequences, and even validity of what has become known as the "Hispanic Paradox" in health – that is their indices of disease and death are close to and sometimes even better than those of non-Hispanic whites.

First and foremost, Hispanics have consistently had lower infant mortality rates than non-Hispanic whites and much lower rates than non-Hispanic blacks. Using the standard measure of infant mortality – deaths

---

[14] Census 2000, Summary File 2, "PCT9. Household Size, Household Type, And Presence Of Own Children – Universe: Households." It should also be noted that Mexicans resident in the United States had much lower marriage rates than Mexicans living in their country of origin.

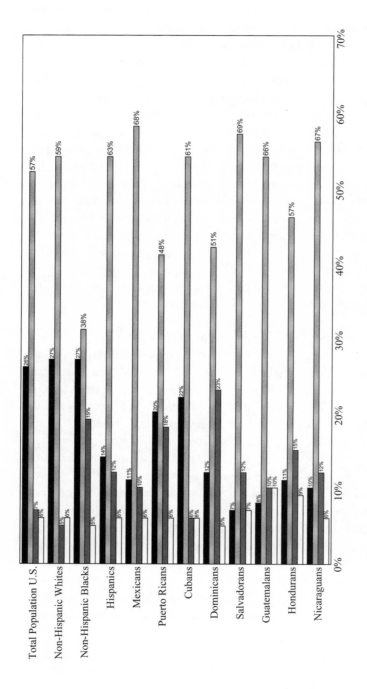

GRAPH 4.9. Distribution of Race/Ethnic Groups and Latino Nationalities by Type of Household, 2000. *Source:* U.S. Bureau of the Census, *2000 Census of Population and Housing,* Summary File 2, "PCT9, Household Size, Household Type, and Presence of Own children – Universe: Households."

■ 1-person households ▨ Married-couple family ▤ Female householder with own children □ Nonfamily households under 18 years

116

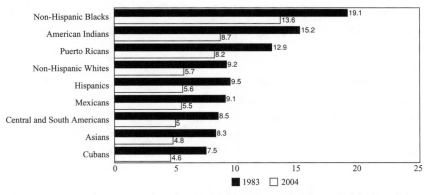

GRAPH 4.10. Infant Mortality by Race/Ethnicity and Hispanic Nationalities, 1983–2004 (infant deaths per thousand live births). *Source:* CDC, NCHS, *National Vital Statistics Reports*, 54:13 (April 19, 2006), Table 5.

of infants under 1 year of age per thousand live births – data from 2004 show that all Hispanics, and Mexicans specifically, have had an infant mortality rate slightly below non-Hispanic whites (see Graph 4.10). Non-Hispanic blacks have consistently had higher infant mortality rates than Latinos, and among all of the Hispanic national subgroups, only Puerto Ricans have had higher infant mortality rates than the non-Hispanic white population. Based on these data the Latino population appears to be healthier and has a lower mortality rate than most of the other racial/ethnic groups in the United States.

It should also be stressed that the infant mortality rate of Mexicans in the United States in 1983 was a fifth of the same rate in Mexico itself and remained well below the Mexican national rate even as late as 2004 (5.9 infant deaths per thousand births for Mexicans in the United States compared to a rate of 19.7 infant deaths per thousand births in Mexico).[15] Along with these low mortality rates, a recent study of all births in the

---

[15] For the comparable 1980s figures for Mexico see José Gómez de León Cruces and Virgilio Partida Bush, "Niveles, tendencias y diferenciales de la mortalidad," in Gómez de León Cruces and Romero, *La población de México*, p. 100, Cuadro 3. Moreover even the best of the state rates in the 1980–85 period, was still 23.3 deaths per thousand births – and this was the Distrito Federal. For the Mexican national rate for 2004, see CONAPO, "República Mexicana: Indicadores demográficos, 1990–2050," table downloaded on December 26, 2006, from http://www.conapo.gob.mx/oocifras/ooindicadores .htm. Moreover even in the best of Mexican states in 2004, again the Distrito Federal, the infant mortality rate was double that experienced by Mexicans in the United States in 2004. See INEGI, "Tasa de mortalidad infantil por entidad federativa, 2000 a 2006," table downloaded on December 26, 2006, from http://www.inegi.gob.mx/est/contenidos/ espanol/rutinas/ept.asp?t=mpob55&c=3232.

United States in 2004 found that the percentage of Hispanic children born with low birth weights, a key indicator of potential health problems, was below that of non-Hispanic whites, and was half the rate of non-Hispanic blacks.[16]

There were also extraordinary differences by race/ethnicity when the leading causes of death for adults in the United States are considered. As may be observed in Table 4.1, all Hispanics, except for Puerto Ricans, have experienced lower adult death rates in all the major diseases that lead to death in the United States. They only exceed the national and non-Hispanic white rates in the less quantitatively important national causes of death, which are diabetes, chronic liver disease and cirrhosis, HIV, and homicides. But in all of the major diseases that lead to death, such as cancer, stroke, and heart disease, their mortality rates are extraordinarily low compared with non-Hispanic whites.

These phenomena have puzzled scholars. In almost all nations, socio-economic status has had a direct impact on mortality levels. However, among Latinos in the United States this standard correlation does not hold. It clearly prevails for non-Hispanic blacks and for Cubans and Puerto Ricans residing on the mainland. But this is not the case for the demographically dominant Mexican population and other Hispanic national subgroups. Many explanations have been offered for these indicators of better health among Latinos. These have included the possibility of errors in data coding because of possible erroneous identification of ethnicity (now generally rejected after numerous careful studies); the open frontier for Mexicans, which permits a "salmon" effect (i.e., that Mexican migrants return to Mexico to die and thus reduce the influence of morbidity and mortality at higher ages), a factor that would primarily affect foreign-born Hispanics; and the relationship among specific ethnic, cultural, and social network arrangements that mitigate the impact of social class and socioeconomic status for Hispanics on adult mortality. It has also been argued that there is a self-selection process through which Latin American and Caribbean migrants are healthier in general terms than nonmigrating populations from which they originate. Finally almost all scholars agree that foreign-born Hispanics, as well as all migrants arriving in the United States, are initially healthier than they are after 5 years of residence. But most of these origin effects disappear after a few years, as immigrants consume the same diet as the majority of the U.S. population, with its heavy emphasis on high-calorie fast foods

[16] Martin et al. "Births: Final Data for 2004," p. 81, Table 34.

TABLE 4.1. *Estimated Death Rates from Leading Causes of Death by Sex, Race, and Hispanic Origin, 2003 (per 100,000 people)*

	United States	Non-Hispanic Blacks	American Indians	Asians	Hispanics	Non-Hispanic Whites	Hispanic Rates as % of Non-Hispanic Whites
All causes	832.7	1,065.9	685.0	465.7	621.2	826.1	75%
Diseases of heart	232.3	300.2	160.2	127.6	173.2	230.9	75%
Ischemic heart disease	162.9	195.0	114.1	92.8	130.0	163.3	80%
Cerebrovascular diseases	53.5	74.3	34.6	45.2	40.5	51.7	78%
Malignant neoplasms	190.1	233.3	119.3	113.5	126.6	192.4	66%
Trachea, bronchus, and lung	54.1	60.8	31.3	26.9	23.2	56.7	41%
Colon, rectum, and anus	19.1	26.4	11.8	12.1	13.4	18.8	71%
Prostate	26.5	57.4	17.8	10.9	20.2	24.6	82%
Breast	25.3	34.0	14.0	12.6	16.1	25.2	64%
Chronic lower respiratory diseases	43.3	30.1	31.7	16.2	20.2	47.0	43%
Influenza and pneumonia	22.0	23.3	24.1	17.3	18.4	22.0	84%
Chronic liver disease and cirrhosis	9.3	8.4	22.6	3.0	14.7	9.0	163%
Diabetes mellitus	25.3	49.2	43.7	17.3	35.0	22.1	158%
Human immunodeficiency virus (HIV) disease	4.7	21.3	2.5	0.7	5.9	2.0	295%
Unintentional injuries	37.3	36.1	56.4	18.0	30.6	38.8	79%
Motor vehicle–related injuries	15.3	14.9	28.1	8.4	15.1	15.5	97%
Suicide	10.8	5.2	10.0	5.6	5.6	12.7	44%
Homicide	6.0	21.0	7.3	2.9	7.7	2.7	285%

Source: CDC, NCHS, *Health, United States, 2006 With Chartbook on Trends in the Health of Americans* (Hyattsville, MD, U.S. Department of Health and Human Services, Centers for Disease Control and Prevention and National Center for Health Statistics, 2006), pp. 177–78, Table 28.

that have been shown to cause obesity and other serious health problems. There is now agreement among scholars studying all of this that there is a real difference exhibited in the mortality data, and the cultural/network argument is now widely accepted as an explanation, although there have been no definitive conclusions.[17]

Still, the trends and tendencies for general and infant mortality continue to appear in estimates on other related demographic variables. A recent finding for 2006 suggested that the average 65-year-old foreign-born Hispanic woman would live 1.1 years longer than the average non-Hispanic female.[18] Although there is still some debate about the Hispanic health paradox in adult mortality and the possibility of data biases, these would still not account for the low infant mortality and relatively low incidence of low birth weight children. These conclusions are based on far more complete data on both domestic- and foreign-born Hispanics and do not involve any question of selection or the issue of return migration.

---

[17] An interesting early testing of this hypotheses was carried out analyzing the subset of Puerto Ricans and Cubans (groups either not affected by return migration or whose return migrants were included in the U.S. mortality data). These groups were still found to have mortality rates lower than non-Hispanic whites. See Ana F. Abraido-Lanza, Bruce P. Dohrenwend, Daisy S. Ng.-Mak, and J. Blake Turner, "The Latino Mortality Paradox: A Test of the 'Salmon Bias' and Healthy Migrant Hypotheses," *American Journal of Public Health* 89:10 (October 1999), 1543–48. For the latest challenge questioning the quality of the data proving the validity of the lower Mexican-American mortality rates, see Kushang V. Patel, Karl Eschbach, Laura A. Ray, and Kyriakos S. Markides, "Evaluation of Mortality Data for Older Mexican Americans: Implications for the Hispanic Paradox," *American Journal of Epidemiology*, 159:7 (2004), 707–15. A very good summary of this long and complex debate is found in Alberto Palloni and Elizabeth Arias, "Paradox Lost: Explaining the Hispanic Adult Mortality Advantage," *Demography*, 41:3 (August 2004), 385–415. They note that "In summary, the findings of [almost all] previous studies offer general support for the existence of a Hispanic adult mortality advantage. When grouped, Hispanic adults exhibit lower mortality rates than non-Hispanic whites even after pertinent demographic and socioeconomic characteristics are taken into account. An important revelation of this review is that findings regarding the Hispanic mortality advantage have been fairly uniform across two distinct data sets, the NLMS and NHIS-MCD. This revelation is significant because findings that are based on linked data sets are not affected by the problem of ethnic misidentification, a shortcoming that is inherent in vital statistics," ibid., p. 387.

[18] *New York Times*, January 3, 2007, p. A16. As Turra concluded in his dissertation, "foreign-born Hispanics have lower mortality than U.S.-born Hispanics and non-Hispanic whites, and this advantage remains unaffected up to age 100," see Cassio Maldonado Turra, "Living and Dying at Older Ages: Essays on the Hispanic Mortality Paradox and the Annuity Puzzle in the United States," (Ph.D. dissertation, Department of Sociology, University of Pennsylvania, 2004).

The recognized mortality advantage of Hispanics has had a direct impact on life expectancy. One recent study found that for Hispanic males and females, with the exception of Cubans and Puerto Ricans, "the male and female advantages are far from trivial, since adult mortality rates among foreign-born Mexicans and other Hispanics are 35%–47% lower than those among non-Hispanic whites. The corresponding relative risks translate into additional years of life expectancy at age 45 of approximately five to eight years." At age 80 the differences would be 7.5 to 9.3 years of additional longevity for Latinos.[19]

With mortality, as with all other demographic factors, there were differences among the Latino national subgroups, and these may be related to socioeconomic variables. Puerto Ricans have had the worst mortality rates because of generally recognized poorer origin backgrounds and lower living standards than the other Hispanic nationalities. In contrast, Cubans had lower age-adjusted death rates, and this may have been connected to higher educational attainment levels and income, and generally better living conditions.[20] Yet, for the demographically dominant Mexicans and many other Latino national subgroups, mortality was low when compared with the non-Hispanic white population. Moreover these low mortality rates were even more pronounced for females than for males, though again there were differences among Mexicans, Puerto Ricans, and Cubans. Puerto Rican women had the highest age-adjusted mortality rates and Cuban women the lowest. Hispanic women of all origins and backgrounds (even Puerto Rican women) had lower age-adjusted death rates than all non-Hispanic groups in the population (see Graph 4.11).

Thus, when examining fertility and family size, or disease and mortality, the Latino population exhibited characteristics that were different

[19] Palloni and Arias, "Paradox Lost," pp. 397–98. Another recent study has reduced these estimates, but still found a significant difference as "Hispanic men aged 65 can expect to live 1.3 years longer, on average, than can non-Hispanic white men, and Hispanic men aged 80 can expect to live 0.4 year longer, on average, than can non-Hispanic white men. Among women, the difference in life expectancy at age 65 is less pronounced but still substantial. Hispanic women can expect to live 0.9 year longer at age 65 and 0.5 year." Irma T. Elo, Cassio M. Turra, Bert Kestenbaum, and B. Reneé Ferguson, "Mortality among Elderly Hispanics in the United States: Past Evidence and New Results," *Demography*, 41:1 (February 2004), 118.
[20] All rates have been adjusted to a normalized American age population so as to eliminate the biases that would occur because of differing age structures of the comparative populations. Using age-adjusted numbers makes the death rates numbers comparable across groups.

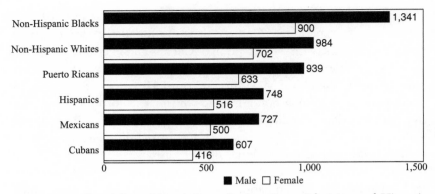

GRAPH 4.11. Age-Adjusted Death Rates by Sex, Race, Ethnicity, and Hispanic Nationality, 2003 (age-adjusted rates per 100,000 persons). *Source:* CDC, NCHS, *National Vital Statistics Reports*, 54:13 (April 19, 2006), Table 5.

from the other racial/ethnic groups in the United States. They generally had higher fertility rates, lower mortality rates, and disease profiles that were different from the non-Hispanic population. At the same time Latinos were not homogenous. In all the demographic indicators we have considered, there were major distinctions among the different Latino national subgroups.

5

Wealth and Poverty

There has been a long debate in the academic literature about the relative skill levels of Latino immigrants, their wages compared to domestic-born workers, and whether or not they have depressed salaries for unskilled and semiskilled laborers, particularly African Americans. There has also been considerable discussion about whether there has been economic and social mobility within Latino communities, especially for second- and third-generation children of Mexican and other immigrants.[1] Some

---

[1] This debate has involved two conflicting schools, with little consensus so far. Borjas and Katz have argued that Mexican immigrants, because of their low education level, have low income and low job status and their employment in the U.S. labor market negatively affects the wages of poorer domestic-born workers. See for example George J. Borjas and Lawrence F. Katz, "The Evolution of the Mexican-Born Workforce in the United States," in Geogre J. Borjas, ed., *Mexican Immigration to the United States* (Chicago: University of Chicago Press, 2007): George J. Borjas, "The Labor Demand Curve Is Downward Sloping: Reexamining the Impact of Immigration on the Labor Market," *Quarterly Journal of Economics*, 118 (November 2003), 1335–74; George J. Borjas, Jeffrey Grogger, and Gordon H. Hanson, "Immigration and African-American Employment Opportunities: The Response of Wages, Employment, and Incarceration to Labor Supply Shocks," NBER Working Paper 12518 (September 2006). It is even suggested that immigrants have increased the levels of inequality of male workers, see Deborah Reed, "Immigration and Males' Earnings Inequality in the Regions of the United States," *Demography*, 38:3 (August 2001), 363–73. For a counterposition, see David Card, "Is the New Immigration Really So Bad?" NBER Working Paper 11547 (August 2005); Gianmarco I. P. Ottaviano and Giovanni Peri, "Rethinking the Gains from Immigration: Theory and Evidence from the U.S.," NBER Working Paper 11672 (September 2005). The latter argue that in fact low-skilled immigrants have had a positive effect on native low-skilled wages. It has also been shown that grouping all immigrants into single categories, rather than breaking them into skill and education levels has a direct impact on estimating mobility. See Maude Toussaint-Comeau, "The Occupational Assimilation of Hispanic Immigrants in the U.S.: Evidence from Panel Data," *International Migration Review*, 40:3 (Fall 2006), 508–536;

have assumed that part of the story of Latin American and Caribbean immigration is economic stagnation and low levels of social mobility over time. Others have argued that the experiences of Latino populations are unique and that they are unlike previous waves of migrants and their descendants in the United States in terms of integration or acculturation levels into the dominant society.

An unfortunate and inaccurate image of enduring poverty has emerged and this has obfuscated the fact that from a historical perspective the Latino population of the United States is very much like every racial and ethnic group with respect to social and economic stratification, as well as mobility. Additionally, there are extraordinary similarities when Hispanics are compared with prior waves of migration to the United States in the 19th and 20th centuries. The large-scale arrival of immigrants from Latin America and the Caribbean after 1980, many of them coming from impoverished rural environments, has surely exacerbated the problem of poverty within Latino communities. Yet, a solid and growing Latino middle class has emerged and high-income-earning individuals, families, and households exist within each national group and in every major region of Hispanic population concentration. An examination of income data since 1980 reveals the difficulty of making sweeping and often impressionistic generalizations about Latino economic performance.

There are three general ways in which income may be measured using data from the U.S. Census Bureau. These are household income, family income, and personal income.[2] Although family income may be as valid

Anh Nguyenn, Getinet Hailenn, and Jim Taylor, "Ethnic and Gender Differences in Intergenerational Mobility: A Study of 26-Year-Olds in the USA," *Scottish Journal of Political Economy*, 52:4 (September 2005), 554–64. For a contrary negative view of Mexican assimilation by sex and across generations see Gretchen Livingston & Joan R Kahn, "An American Dream Unfulfilled: The Limited Mobility of Mexican Americans," *Social Science Quarterly*, 83:4 (September 2002), 1003–12, who adopt the Borjas position of nonlinear mobility across generations. Others have challenged the Borjas assumption that Mexican immigrants are less skilled and educated than those who did not migrate: see Cynthia Feliciano, "Educational Selectivity in U.S. Immigration: How Do Immigrants Compare to Those Left Behind? *Demography*, 42:1 (February 2005), 131–52.

[2] The Census Bureau defines the various ways in which income is measured as follows:

"Income of Households – This includes the income of the householder and all other individuals 15 years old and over in the household, whether they are related to the householder or not. Because many households consist of only one person, average household income is usually less than average family income. Although the household income statistics cover the past 12 months, the characteristics of individuals and the composition of households refer to the time of enumeration. Thus, the income of the household does not include amounts received by individuals who were members of the household during all or part

an indicator of wealth and poverty as the other two measures, there are no data provided by the Census Bureau on heads of families. On the other hand, we can examine our nativity, national origin, and sex variables using both personal income and household income. Total personal income data permit a detailed examination of individuals and especially the impact on income of factors such as educational attainment, citizenship, sex, and nativity. We can do this with household income as well, but only for heads of households. Like the personal income data, this permits us to analyze the influence of these same variables on the income of Hispanic households. We will also be using the median income of household heads when we provide broad comparisons between Latinos as a group and other sectors of society, as well as when we compare Latino nationalities.

The most useful point of departure is to examine changing household income patterns among Latino household heads in comparative

of the past 12 months if these individuals no longer resided in the household at the time of enumeration. Similarly, income amounts reported by individuals who did not reside in the household during the past 12 months but who were members of the household at the time of enumeration are included. However, the composition of most households was the same during the past 12 months as at the time of enumeration.

Income of Families – In compiling statistics on family income, the incomes of all members 15 years old and over related to the householder are summed and treated as a single amount. Although the family income statistics cover the past 12 months, the characteristics of individuals and the composition of families refer to the time of enumeration. Thus, the income of the family does not include amounts received by individuals who were members of the family during all or part of the past 12 months if these individuals no longer resided with the family at the time of enumeration. Similarly, income amounts reported by individuals who did not reside with the family during the past 12 months but who were members of the family at the time of enumeration are included. However, the composition of most families was the same during the past 12 months as at the time of enumeration.

Income of Individuals – Income for individuals is obtained by summing the eight types of income for each person 15 years old and over. The characteristics of individuals are based on the time of enumeration, even though the amounts are for the past 12 months.

Median Income – "The median divides the income distribution into two equal parts: one-half of the cases falling below the median income and one-half above the median. For households and families, the median income is based on the distribution of the total number of households and families including those with no income. The median income for individuals is based on individuals 15 years old and over with income. Median income for households, families, and individuals is computed on the basis of a standard distribution."

See U.S. Bureau of the Census, "American Community Survey, Puerto Rico Community Survey, 2005 Subject Definitions," p. 46 available at http://www.census.gov/acs/www/Downloads/2005/usedata/Subject_Definitions.pdf.

perspective between 1980 and 2005. The concentration on the head of household rather than on the entire family – which is the more standard way the U.S. Census Bureau reports these findings – is because of our need to examine household income data along with demographic and origin data and these are available only for the heads of households. Our principal concern is to analyze such factors as race/ethnicity, Latino nationality, sex, educational attainment levels, and nativity, and the influence they exerted on household income patterns over time. Since we will be concentrating only on the incomes of household heads, the data we will present in this chapter vary somewhat from other published statistics on household income, and from the data that may be generated using Census Bureau Internet sources such as American FactFinder because they do not include every income-earner in each household. Yet, isolating household heads is the only strategy that may be utilized to accurately parse the different factors affecting the comparative household income patterns that we analyze throughout this chapter.

Latino-headed households across the United States had median incomes that were significantly lower than those of Asians and non-Hispanic whites between 1980 and 2005, but they were higher than among the non-Hispanic black or African American population.[3] (See Table 5.1.) However, Latino household income increased in real terms at 0.6% annually over this 25-year period, the same rate of growth experienced by non-Hispanic black households, and this was below the 0.8% yearly growth rate among non-Hispanic whites in the same period. Asian household income rose at 1% yearly between 1980 and 2005. This meant the gap in median household income found between Latino households and those of non-Hispanic whites and Asians gradually increased over this 25-year period.

When we examine these data by national origins, it turns out that in 2005 Ecuadorian, Colombian, Cuban, and Peruvian household heads earned the highest median household incomes, all between $53,000 and

---

[3] By 2005 Hispanic households were composed of an average number of families (1.22 per household), which was greater than among non-Hispanic whites (1.11 families per household), non-Hispanic blacks (1.14 families per household), and Asians (1.13 families per household). This was in all likelihood the result of the surge in migration from Latin America and the Caribbean after 1980 and the propensity for families established in the United States for some time, to offer housing to recently arrived family members. All income values in this chapter for all years have been converted into 2005 dollars using the consumer price indexes generated by the U.S. Department of Labor Bureau of Labor Statistics available at http://www.bls.gov/cpi/home.htm.

TABLE 5.1. *Median Household Income by Race/Ethnicity, 1980–2005 (in 2005 dollars adjusted for inflation)*

Racial/Ethnic Group	1980	1990	2000	2005
Non-Hispanic Whites	50,347	55,138	59,883	61,120
Non-Hispanic Blacks	32,430	35,846	40,489	37,996
Hispanics	37,671	41,827	44,232	43,905
Asians	56,169	66,793	70,208	72,529

Racial/Ethnic Group	Yearly Rate of Growth 1980–2005	Yearly Rate of Growth 1980–1990	Yearly Rate of Growth 1990–2000	Yearly Rate of Growth 2000–2005
Non-Hispanic Whites	0.8%	0.9%	0.8%	0.4%
Non-Hispanic Blacks	0.6%	1.0%	1.2%	−1.3%
Hispanics	0.6%	1.1%	0.6%	−0.1%
Asians	1.0%	1.7%	0.5%	0.7%

Note: Current dollar values for 1980, 1990, and 2000 were converted to 2005 dollars using the U.S. Department of Labor, Bureau of Labor Statistics, CPI Inflation Calculator, at http://www.bls.gov/data/home.htm.

$55,000. These incomes were considerably greater than the $43,905 median household incomes found among all Latino household heads in 2005 (see Table 5.1), and in fact were closer to the incomes of non-Hispanic white households than to the poorest Latino households, Dominicans and Mexicans. Puerto Rican–headed households in the United States enjoyed the highest rate of median household income growth among Latinos between 1980 and 2005 (1.9% annually) followed by Ecuadorians (1.2%), Salvadorans (1.1%), and Dominicans (1.1%), who despite remaining as the Hispanic national group with the lowest median household income in 2005, enjoyed a fairly significant rate of income increase after 1980. Given these stark contrasts in levels and growth of income among Hispanic heads of households of different origins, it is evident that there are difficulties in generalizing about wealth and poverty among Latinos in the United States. (See Table 5.2.)

One of the basic determinants of household-head income among all racial/ethnic groups was the sex of the head of household, since in general adult females earned significantly less than males. Between 1980 and 2005 there was a steady increase in the number of households headed by females among all sectors of the U.S. population, although the increase was most dramatic among non-Hispanic blacks. In 1980 women headed about 44% of all African American households, and this percentage rose

TABLE 5.2. *Median Household Income by Latino Nationality, 1980–2005*
(in 2005 dollars adjusted for inflation)

Nationality	1980	1990	2000	2005
Colombian	43,908	52,299	52,171	54,673
Cuban	46,055	51,498	51,944	53,989
Dominican	28,470	37,040	39,695	37,691
Ecuadorian	40,541	52,299	55,188	55,008
Guatemalan	37,849	42,661	46,500	45,738
Honduran	36,545	38,851	44,232	43,701
Mexican	37,932	40,049	43,098	41,969
Peruvian	47,442	53,495	57,842	53,276
Puerto Rican	27,948	38,851	42,644	45,229
Salvadoran	35,584	43,278	47,407	46,655

Nationality	Yearly Rate of Growth 1980–1990	Yearly Rate of Growth 1990–2000	Yearly Rate of Growth 2000–2005	Yearly Rate of Growth 1980–2005
Colombian	1.8%	0.0%	0.9%	0.9%
Cuban	1.1%	0.1%	0.8%	0.6%
Dominican	2.7%	0.7%	−1.0%	1.1%
Ecuadorian	2.6%	0.5%	−0.1%	1.2%
Guatemalan	1.2%	0.9%	−0.3%	0.8%
Honduran	0.6%	1.3%	−0.2%	0.7%
Mexican	0.5%	0.7%	−0.5%	0.4%
Peruvian	1.2%	0.8%	−1.6%	0.5%
Puerto Rican	3.3%	0.9%	1.2%	1.9%
Salvadoran	2.0%	0.9%	−0.3%	1.1%

to nearly 60% in 2005. Patterns among Hispanic households were very different and paralleled those found among non-Hispanic whites. In 1980 26% of non-Hispanic white households were headed by females compared with 27% of Hispanic households. By 2005 42% of non-Hispanic white households and 43% of Latino households were headed by women. Asians had the lowest percentage of female-headed households: 21% in 1980 and 35% in 2005. (See Graph 5.1.)

For all racial/ethnic groups, women heading households had lower median incomes than male household heads, with Hispanic female-headed households experiencing the lowest level for any group. But these households headed by Latina women experienced an extraordinary transformation in income-earning capacity between 1980 and 2005. Whereas in 1980, they earned only 44% of the median income earned by male household heads, by 2005 female Hispanic household heads earned 74%

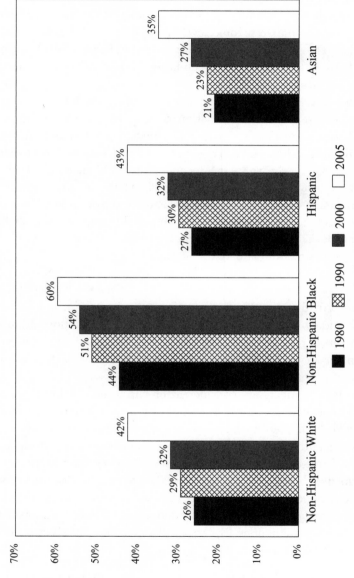

GRAPH 5.1. Percentage of Households Headed by Females by Race/Ethnicity, 1980–2005.

of the median incomes earned by their male counterparts, and this was the highest level among women who headed households in the major racial/ethnic groups. Non-Hispanic white women heading households earned just two-thirds of the median incomes earned by their male counterparts, which was a significant increase from 1980, but still considerably lower than relative income levels among Hispanic female-headed households. The same pattern occurred for non-Hispanic black women heading households and Asian female-headed households (see Table 5.3 and Graph 5.2).[4]

Although there were significant improvements in the median incomes of female-headed households in relation to those headed by males between 1980 and 2005 among Latino households, median incomes for both male- and female-headed households lagged considerably behind non-Hispanic whites and Asians. In 1980 the median household incomes of male-headed Latino households were about 77% of the incomes generated by non-Hispanic white male household heads, and this declined by 2005 to 72%. Nevertheless, Hispanic male household heads earned slightly more than households headed by non-Hispanic black males: 107% of median incomes in 1980 and 101% in 2005.

Among Latino female household heads there was a slight improvement in relation to non-Hispanic white women who headed households: in 1980 they earned 75% and in 2005 79% of the median income levels of non-Hispanic white female household heads. There was more dramatic improvement in relative median female household incomes in relation to non-Hispanic black female household heads: 101% of median income levels in 1980 and 124% in 2005. (See Table 5.3.)

When these numbers are considered for Latino national groups, it is Colombian-, Ecuadorian-, and Peruvian-origin female household heads who earned the highest median incomes in both 1980 and 2005, while Puerto Rican and Dominican female household heads earned the lowest. Among all Latino nationalities there was a steady decrease in the differential in median household incomes earned by female-headed households in relation to male-headed households between 1980 and 2005, although there were sharp disparities among Dominicans and Puerto Ricans compared to other nationalities. By 2005 all other households headed by

---

[4] This extraordinary transformation in the median incomes of female-headed households in relation to males was linked to rising educational attainment levels, which will be considered later in this chapter.

TABLE 5.3. *Median Household Income by Sex of Head of Household by Racial/Ethnic Group, 1980–2005 (in inflation adjusted 2005 dollars)*

Race/Ethnicity	Male-Headed Households Median Income	Female-Headed Households Median Income	Total Households Median Income	% of Household Heads Males	% of Household Heads Females	Median Income of Female-Headed Households as % of Male-Headed Households
1980						
Non-Hispanic White	49,280	22,102	42,248	74.2%	25.8%	44.9%
Non-Hispanic Black	35,584	16,399	25,837	55.6%	44.4%	46.1%
Hispanic	37,956	16,612	31,814	73.5%	26.5%	43.8%
Asian	53,027	26,596	47,406	79.1%	20.9%	50.2%
1990						
Non-Hispanic White	54,382	26,942	46,322	70.8%	29.2%	49.5%
Non-Hispanic Black	40,414	18,977	28,391	48.8%	51.2%	47.0%
Hispanic	41,839	22,414	35,862	70.3%	29.7%	53.6%
Asian	64,247	37,357	57,649	77.3%	22.7%	58.1%
2000						
Non-Hispanic White	58,182	32,323	49,903	68.3%	31.7%	55.6%
Non-Hispanic Black	44,232	24,384	32,210	45.8%	54.2%	55.1%
Hispanic	42,984	27,220	37,427	67.6%	32.4%	63.3%
Asian	67,482	40,829	59,429	73.3%	26.7%	60.5%
2005						
Non-Hispanic White	59,592	39,728	50,933	57.7%	42.3%	66.7%
Non-Hispanic Black	42,377	25,569	31,579	40.3%	59.7%	60.3%
Hispanic	42,988	31,579	38,506	57.5%	42.5%	73.5%
Asian	70,288	50,944	63,157	65.2%	34.8%	72.5%

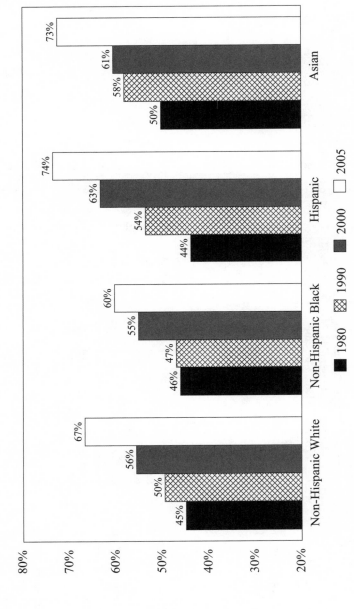

GRAPH 5.2. Median Income of Female-Headed Households as a Percentage of Male-Headed Households by Race/Ethnicity, 1980–2005.

Latino females earned greater than 70% of the median incomes of male-headed households, whereas Dominican women earned 55% the median incomes of men, while Puerto Rican women earned 60% of the median incomes of Puerto Rican male-headed households in 2005. (See Table 5.4.)

To fully understand the major household income disparities existing within the nation's Hispanic population, a further variable that must be considered is the differentiation in income found among foreign-born and domestic-born Latinos. By 2005 at the national level, foreign-born Latinos earned about 87% of the median household incomes of their domestic-born counterparts although there were significant variations by Latino nationality. Foreign-born Mexicans earned about 83% of the median household income levels found among domestic-born Mexicans. Cubans households headed by the foreign-born earned 59% the median income levels of domestic-born Cuban-headed households. Within the Dominican population the foreign-born earned only 65% the household incomes of the domestic-born. Foreign-born Colombian-headed households earned 79% of the income levels of the domestic born, while for Peruvians it was 78% and for Ecuadorians it was 72%. In general, domestic-born male–headed households earned higher median incomes than all other household heads (see Tables 5.5 and 5.6).

There were sharp regional variations in median household income levels among Latinos. These may be brought into focus by examining differentials found in the six major metropolitan areas in which Latino populations were the largest in the United States and in which Latinos make up significant percentages of metro area populations: Los Angeles; New York; Chicago; Riverside, CA; Houston; and Miami.[5] Of the six metropolitan areas, Latinos earned the highest median household incomes

[5] In 2005 the Los Angeles-Long Beach (here labeled Los Angeles) metropolitan area had the largest Latino population in the United States at 4,602,111 persons who accounted for 47% of the total population. The New York-Northeastern New Jersey metropolitan area (here labeled New York) was the second-ranking metro area for Latinos who numbered 2,444,570 and 26% of the total population. The Chicago-Gary-Lake, IL, metropolitan area (here labeled Chicago) was the third-ranking center for Latinos with a population of 1,669,058 and 20% of all residents. Riverside-San Bernardino, CA (here Riverside), was slightly behind Chicago at 1,662,299 people who were 43% of the total population. Houston-Brazoria, TX (here Houston), had the fifth largest concentration of Latinos at 1,552,164 and 34% of the total population. Finally, Miami-Hialeah, FL (Miami), had the sixth largest Latino population concentration at 1,419,910 and 62% of the total population.

TABLE 5.4. *Median Household Income by Sex of Head of Household by Latino Nationality, 1980–2005 (in 2005 dollars adjusted for inflation)*

Nationality	Male-Headed Households Median Income	Female-Headed Households Median Income	Total Households Median Income	% Household Heads Males	% Household Heads Females	Median Income of Female-Headed Households as % of Male-Headed Households
1980						
Mexican	37,090	17,703	32,750	77.9%	22.1%	47.7%
Puerto Rican	32,928	12,415	23,727	59.3%	40.7%	37.7%
Cuban	44,134	18,510	37,956	76.8%	23.2%	41.9%
Dominican	30,853	14,715	23,727	54.5%	45.5%	47.7%
Salvadoran	32,573	19,719	28,470	67.9%	32.1%	60.5%
Guatemalan	36,551	20,116	32,039	71.1%	28.9%	55.0%
Honduran	35,596	19,849	29,667	65.8%	34.2%	55.8%
Colombian	42,699	23,158	36,331	74.2%	25.8%	54.2%
Ecuadorian	41,821	20,069	36,539	76.1%	23.9%	48.0%
Peruvian	44,798	23,727	40,209	78.2%	21.8%	53.0%
Total Latinos	37,956	16,612	31,849	73.5%	26.5%	43.8%
1990						
Mexican	39,312	22,294	34,812	74.3%	25.7%	56.7%
Puerto Rican	44,828	17,931	32,500	55.9%	44.1%	40.0%
Cuban	48,144	23,310	41,262	72.2%	27.8%	48.4%
Dominican	41,839	19,425	30,530	49.2%	50.8%	46.4%
Salvadoran	39,417	27,727	36,117	71.8%	28.2%	70.3%
Guatemalan	41,120	27,719	36,798	73.1%	26.9%	67.4%
Honduran	37,357	25,178	31,771	60.4%	39.6%	67.4%
Colombian	49,759	31,566	44,529	69.4%	30.6%	63.4%
Ecuadorian	51,268	29,213	44,828	70.1%	29.9%	57.0%
Peruvian	50,799	33,684	45,193	72.7%	27.3%	66.3%
Total Latinos	41,750	22,414	35,862	70.4%	29.6%	53.7%

2000

Mexican	40,829	27,254	37,314	72.2%	27.8%	66.8%
Puerto Rican	45,366	23,590	34,064	53.0%	47.0%	52.0%
Cuban	47,271	27,446	40,376	67.3%	32.7%	58.1%
Dominican	42,531	24,498	32,862	46.7%	53.3%	57.6%
Salvadoran	43,098	30,395	39,695	69.7%	30.3%	70.5%
Guatemalan	41,964	29,488	38,561	73.0%	27.0%	70.3%
Honduran	39,922	28,354	35,385	61.6%	38.4%	71.0%
Colombian	50,243	32,664	43,954	63.9%	36.1%	65.0%
Ecuadorian	51,037	34,818	45,933	68.7%	31.3%	68.2%
Peruvian	53,305	38,561	48,814	69.4%	30.6%	72.3%
Total Latinos	42,984	27,220	37,427	67.6%	32.4%	63.3%

2005

Mexican	40,747	31,273	37,181	60.5%	39.5%	76.7%
Puerto Rican	47,877	28,523	36,672	46.9%	53.1%	59.6%
Cuban	49,915	35,613	43,803	57.1%	42.9%	71.3%
Dominican	42,657	23,633	30,917	40.2%	59.8%	55.4%
Salvadoran	43,497	33,616	39,728	61.1%	38.9%	77.3%
Guatemalan	41,765	32,597	38,709	63.6%	36.4%	78.0%
Honduran	38,709	30,866	35,246	53.7%	46.3%	79.7%
Colombian	52,309	37,691	46,553	56.6%	43.4%	72.1%
Ecuadorian	50,933	40,747	46,553	58.3%	41.7%	80.0%
Peruvian	49,477	40,747	45,840	59.5%	40.5%	82.4%
Total Latinos	42,957	31,579	38,506	57.5%	42.5%	73.5%

TABLE 5.5. *Median Income of Household Head by Foreign- or Domestic-Born for Selected Latino Nationalities, 1980–2005 (adjusted for inflation in 2005 dollars)*

	1980		1990		2000		2005	
	Domestic-Born	Foreign-Born	Domestic-Born	Foreign-Born	Domestic-Born	Foreign-Born	Domestic-Born	Foreign-Born
Mexican	34,648	29,656	37,252	32,687	40,035	35,159	41,358	34,329
Cuban	35,596	37,968	49,311	40,405	54,439	37,994	64,176	37,691
Dominican	28,577	23,727	38,009	29,885	37,994	31,983	45,565	29,541
Salvadoran	42,770	28,470	47,816	36,161	43,098	39,695	44,821	39,524
Guatemalan	39,574	32,027	41,839	36,609	47,634	37,994	47,216	37,691
Honduran	35,584	29,193	39,920	31,379	41,510	35,159	35,093	35,246
Colombian	37,968	36,201	47,408	44,387	49,449	43,098	57,045	44,821
Ecuadorian	31,090	36,770	41,839	44,828	54,099	45,366	63,565	45,738
Peruvian	51,248	40,078	48,280	45,170	56,821	48,315	58,064	45,025
Total Latinos	35,276	31,885	37,058	35,713	39,695	36,746	41,867	36,468

TABLE 5.6. Median Income of Household Head by Foreign- or Domestic-Born by Sex for Selected Latino Nationalities, 1980–2005 (adjusted for inflation in 2005 dollars)

	1980				1990			
	Domestic-Born Males	Foreign-Born Males	Domestic-Born Females	Foreign-Born Females	Domestic-Born Males	Foreign-Born Males	Domestic-Born Females	Foreign-Born Females
Mexican	40,327	32,881	18,438	16,375	43,632	35,563	22,414	21,348
Cuban	42,497	44,466	23,679	18,095	58,276	47,816	31,645	22,414
Dominican	32,181	30,853	22,589	14,715	47,835	41,561	24,723	19,425
Salvadoran	48,331	31,802	25,962	19,126	55,288	39,222	29,885	27,793
Guatemalan	43,185	36,551	23,727	19,743	51,470	40,922	27,662	27,686
Honduran	40,327	35,596	17,330	19,873	46,173	37,357	28,690	24,655
Colombian	47,442	42,236	24,130	23,134	53,196	49,777	36,236	31,379
Ecuadorian	50,240	41,762	13,292	20,549	46,322	52,178	37,132	29,386
Peruvian	51,248	44,703	50,839	23,727	57,529	50,805	41,391	32,948
Total Latinos	40,837	35,810	18,984	17,964	43,650	39,150	22,414	23,372

	2000				2005			
	Domestic-Born Males	Foreign-Born Males	Domestic-Born Females	Foreign-Born Females	Domestic-Born Males	Foreign-Born Males	Domestic-Born Females	Foreign-Born Females
Mexican	47,067	37,540	28,354	26,085	47,877	37,100	34,635	27,576
Cuban	62,151	45,003	41,294	24,951	69,545	44,465	56,842	28,523
Dominican	49,052	41,964	29,545	23,817	50,933	40,747	35,653	22,411
Salvadoran	48,315	43,098	37,081	30,055	45,840	42,886	43,803	33,107
Guatemalan	51,037	41,283	39,015	28,779	47,725	40,849	44,821	30,560
Honduran	46,954	39,814	37,427	27,787	36,163	38,709	34,227	30,560
Colombian	55,573	49,903	42,871	31,416	57,045	51,952	57,045	35,653
Ecuadorian	61,358	50,129	46,103	33,457	61,630	50,628	63,565	36,672
Peruvian	65,214	52,171	46,500	37,427	68,760	47,877	48,387	40,645
Total Latinos	47,067	40,149	28,354	27,220	48,896	40,441	35,144	29,643

137

in Chicago from 1990 through 2005 and the lowest in New York in all years from 1980 on.[6]

Although Latinos lagged considerably behind non-Hispanic whites and Asians in median household income in all six metropolitan areas, they earned more than non-Hispanic blacks in Houston, Los Angeles, Miami, Riverside, and Chicago between 1980 and 2005. In New York, however, Latino households had median incomes that were lower than those of non-Hispanic blacks, and indeed Latinos earned the lowest incomes of the major racial/ethnic groups in the city. The precise reasons for this fundamental difference in comparative income levels found in New York are difficult to ascertain. Educational attainment levels among Latinos in New York did not lag behind those found in the five other metro areas.[7] Additionally, while New York has been a destination of constant immigration from Latin America and the Caribbean between 1980 and 2005, only 51% of households among Latinos were headed by foreign-born individuals. This compares with 62% Houston, 67% in Los Angeles, 54% in Riverside, 63% in Chicago, and 83% in Miami. As indicated earlier, New York's Latino households earned the lowest median incomes of the six metropolitan areas. (See Table 5.7.)

There were some improvements in real median income levels among Latino-headed households between 1980 and 1990, although economic performance varied by metropolitan area. However, in Houston there was a decline of −14% in the 1980s. Between 1990 and 2005 there was only a significant improvement in median household income levels in Chicago (+8%), Riverside (+8%), and Miami (+12%). There was absolutely no increase in real income levels among Latino-headed households in New York; a 3% rise in Houston; and a −3% decline in Latino median household incomes in Los Angeles from 1990 to 2005. By comparing

---

[6] The data presented in this section are in 2005 dollars adjusted for inflation. Later in this chapter we will present data on metro areas adjusted by cost-of-living indexes. In 1980 Houston Latinos earned higher median household incomes than in the other five metro areas. It is likely that Chicago metro area Latino household heads worked in higher-skilled and thus better-paying jobs than in the other major metro areas. We examined the percentage of foreign-born versus domestic-born household heads in each metro area to determine if there were any major differentials that could explain differences in median household incomes and found no major differences comparing Chicago with the other metro areas. We also examined educational attainment levels for Latino household heads as a possible factor that could explain Chicago's higher median household incomes among Latinos and also found no major differences with the other four metro areas.

[7] Slightly over 16% of New York's Latino household heads over 25 years of age earned B.A. degrees or higher compared with 12% in Houston, 11% in Los Angeles, 10% in Riverside, 15% in Chicago, and 28% in Miami.

TABLE 5.7. *Median Household Income by Ethnicity/Nationality of Household Head by Selected Metropolitan Areas, 1980–2005 (in 2005 dollars adjusted for inflation)*

1980

Metro Area	Non-Hispanic White	Non-Hispanic Black	Latino	Asian
Chicago	54,129	29,656	38,074	56,489
Houston	56,596	33,213	40,327	52,197
Los Angeles	47,027	28,909	34,410	47,726
Miami	40,814	26,098	33,272	39,082
New York	44,134	25,861	23,727	40,837
Riverside	42,734	33,213	37,956	43,316

1990

Metro Area	Non-Hispanic White	Non-Hispanic Black	Latino	Asian
Chicago	60,069	34,219	42,501	61,859
Houston	58,276	29,885	34,613	52,299
Los Angeles	62,759	38,156	41,839	60,219
Miami	51,854	29,896	35,568	47,879
New York	59,173	37,357	31,799	52,299
Riverside	52,299	41,902	43,334	57,380

2000

Metro Area	Non-Hispanic White	Non-Hispanic Black	Latino	Asian
Chicago	68,049	38,901	47,181	68,049
Houston	63,739	34,138	36,860	57,842
Los Angeles	61,902	35,833	37,540	55,573
Miami	56,140	31,756	36,701	47,657
New York	61,579	36,293	32,437	49,222
Riverside	52,058	40,829	41,283	58,522

2005

Metro Area	Non-Hispanic White	Non-Hispanic Black	Latino	Asian
Chicago	68,251	35,552	45,840	72,224
Houston	67,640	33,616	35,653	61,528
Los Angeles	64,711	36,672	40,543	56,027
Miami	58,828	29,541	39,728	53,989
New York	65,195	37,691	31,945	53,989
Riverside	56,256	45,840	46,881	61,207

the contiguous metro areas of Los Angeles and Riverside, the sharp differences in economic performance between inner city and more sub-urbanized Latino populations may be brought into focus. Real median household incomes among Latinos in Los Angeles declined between 1990 and 2005, while they rose substantially in more heavily suburbanized Riverside.

Compared with the other major racial/ethnic groups, Latino median household income growth was favorable between 1980 and 1990 in all major urban areas with the exception of Houston as indicated previously. In Chicago and New York the overall percentage increase in median household income during the 1980s was about the same among Latinos as for non-Hispanic whites, although in absolute terms Latino-headed households lagged behind. Although the increase in Los Angeles was lower than among non-Hispanic whites, it was still a substantial 22% in the 1980s. In Riverside there was a similar pattern as median incomes of Latino-headed households increased by 14% between 1980 and 1990, but this increase was significantly lower than the 22% rise found among non-Hispanic whites. In Miami, Latino median household incomes increased by only 7%, which was much lower than all other racial/ethnic groups. (See Graph 5.3.)[8]

However, the pace of these increases among Latinos slowed substan-tially in the 15 years after 1990 both in absolute terms and in relation to the higher-income households headed by non-Hispanic whites and Asians. The exceptions to these patterns were in Miami where Latino households experienced a 12% rise in median incomes between 1990 and 2005 compared with 13% among non-Hispanic whites and 13% among Asians; and in Riverside where Latino households increased their median incomes by 8%, which was greater than the increase experienced by non-Hispanic white and Asian households, yet slightly lower than the 9% rise found among non-Hispanic black–headed households. In the four other major metropolitan centers, there was a notable decrease in economic performance among Latino-headed households between 1990 and 2005 compared with the 1980–90 period as indicated previously.

Comparative aspects of median household incomes by Latino nation-ality among these six metropolitan areas must be addressed with cau-tion because of the great differences in the national origins of Latino

---

[8] It is likely that this comparative slower growth in median household income among Miami Latinos was related to the sharp influx of Central American immigrants fleeing the civil wars in El Salvador and Nicaragua during the decade.

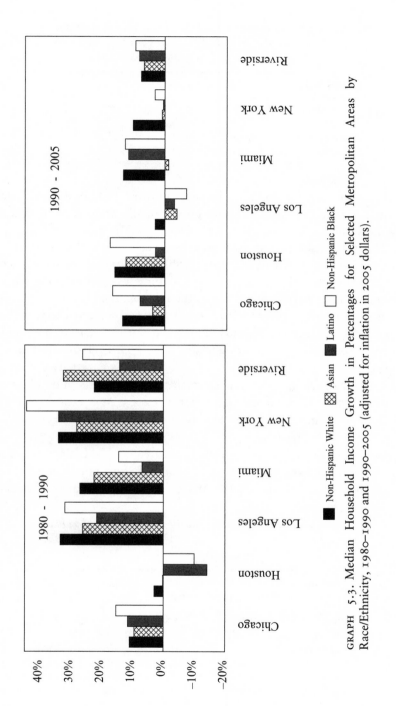

GRAPH 5.3. Median Household Income Growth in Percentages for Selected Metropolitan Areas by Race/Ethnicity, 1980–1990 and 1990–2005 (adjusted for inflation in 2005 dollars).

TABLE 5.8. *Mexican Household Heads as a Percentage of
Total Latino Household Heads in Chicago, Houston,
Los Angeles, and Riverside, 1980–2005*

Metro Area	1980	1990	2000	2005
Chicago	60%	65%	74%	74%
Houston	89%	82%	79%	76%
Los Angeles	78%	76%	74%	74%
Riverside	87%	89%	86%	86%

populations found in each. In Chicago, Houston, and Los Angeles, Mexicans accounted for nearly 75% or greater of all Latino household heads by 2005, and in Riverside they were 86%. (See Table 5.8.)

This was in sharp contrast with the east coast New York and Miami metropolitan areas where Hispanic Caribbean migrants and their descendants dominated the demographic structures of Latino communities, although there were major shifts in the national composition of Latino household heads in these metro areas between 1980 and 2005. In New York, Puerto Ricans headed just under two-thirds of Latino households in 1980, but they declined to 41% by 2005. This relative decline was linked to large-scale Dominican migration to New York City during the 1980s and 1990s. Accordingly, Dominicans headed a tenth of all Latino households in 1980 and almost a quarter in 2005. Mexicans were 7% of all New York metro area households in 2005 followed by Ecuadorians and Colombians. (See Table 5.9.)

In Miami, Cubans declined from 73% to 56% of all Latino household heads between 1980 and 2005 as Miami's Latino population became more diversified because of the arrival of migrants from other Latin

TABLE 5.9. *Selected Latino Nationality Household Heads
as a Percentage of Total Latino Household Heads in the
New York Metro Area, 1980–2005*

Nationality	1980	1990	2000	2005
Puerto Rican	60%	52%	42%	41%
Dominican	10%	17%	22%	23%
Mexican	2%	3%	6%	7%
Ecuadorian	3%	4%	6%	6%
Colombian	4%	6%	5%	5%
Cuban	6%	5%	3%	3%
Others	14%	13%	15%	14%

TABLE 5.10. *Median Household Income among Households Headed by Mexicans in Chicago, Houston, Los Angeles, and Riverside Metropolitan Areas, 1980–2005 (in 2005 dollars adjusted for inflation)*

Metro Area	1980	1990	2000	2005
Chicago	40,357	43,772	47,634	45,738
Houston	39,485	34,847	36,973	35,552
Los Angeles	34,422	42,437	38,561	40,747
Riverside	37,956	42,655	41,056	46,288

American and Caribbean regions. Still, even in 2005 Cubans, Dominicans (4%), and Puerto Ricans (6%) headed about two-thirds of all Miami's Latino households. Colombians (7%) and Nicaraguans (6%) were the other two largest Latino household heads.

Among Mexican household heads in the four metropolitan regions in which they were demographically dominant among Latinos, there were clear differences in median household incomes. In the Riverside and Chicago metro areas, Mexican household heads earned median incomes that were higher in absolute terms than those found in Los Angeles and Houston. In, fact from 1990 on the lowest median household incomes among Mexicans was found in Houston, at least in incomes adjusted for inflation using 2005 dollars.[9] It is also worth noting that in more suburbanized Riverside median household income among Mexicans was significantly higher than in the more urbanized Los Angeles metro area. (See Table 5.10.)

It is difficult to determine the underlying reasons for these metropolitan area income differentials among Mexican households. Clearly, better salaries in higher-paying occupations in Riverside and Chicago compared with Los Angeles and Houston are the factors that accounted for these household income differences.[10] Yet, a key indicator of job-market preparation – educational attainment – reveals no meaningful discrepancies between the four metropolitan areas. About 11% of Chicago metro area Mexican household heads 25 years of age and over earned a B.A. degree or higher in 2005 compared with 9% in both Houston and Los Angeles and 8% in Riverside. A broader consideration of educational attainment data that includes all Mexican household heads 25 years of age or older

[9] The issue of cost-of-living indexes will be considered later in this chapter.
[10] An analysis of occupational data provided by the Census Bureau for the 2005 American Community Survey is problematic because of the extraordinary high percentage of household heads for which information was not available.

who have attended or graduated from college also suggest no significant disparities. In Riverside 33% of all Mexican household heads had at least some college compared with 29% in Chicago and Los Angeles, and 27% in Houston in 2005. The slightly higher educational participation rate at the college level found among Mexican household heads in Riverside in 2005 may be suggestive of slightly higher skill levels, but this small differential is not convincing as an overall explanation.

There were some differences in the sex distribution of Mexican household heads in the four metro areas, and although this factor should not be discounted in determining the underlying causes for metro area household income disparities, these differences were not large.[11] About 67% of Mexican households were headed by males in Chicago in 2005, and this may help explain the relatively higher overall median household incomes found among Chicago's Mexican households compared with the other metro areas. In Houston, males headed 61% of all Mexican households, 60% in Los Angeles, and 63% in Riverside in 2005.

One other factor that may be considered in examining disparities in median household incomes is whether household heads were domestic- or foreign-born. In general, foreign-born household heads earned about 83% of the median income levels compared with domestic-born household heads at the national level in 2005 among all Mexican-headed households. If urban Los Angeles and suburban Riverside are compared, it is striking that 47% of Mexican household heads in Riverside were domestic-born compared with 37% in Los Angeles. Additionally, in Los Angeles foreign-born Mexican household heads earned 76% the incomes of domestic-born household heads; in Riverside it was 80%. Thus, among Mexican-headed households in more urbanized Los Angeles, male or female, there were a significantly greater percentage of foreign-born Mexicans compared with suburbanized Riverside, and they earned less than their domestic-born counterparts. (See Table 5.11.)

Until now, comparative aspects of median household income have been examined using 2005 dollar amounts adjusted for inflation for the earlier years. Another factor that must be considered is the differentiation

---

[11] This is an important factor since Mexican female-headed households generally earned about 80% of the household incomes earned by male-headed households at the national level and in each of the four metro areas. In Chicago female-headed Mexican households earned 83% the median household incomes of male-headed Mexican households in 2005. In Houston and Los Angeles the corresponding figure was 81%, and in Riverside it was 75%.

TABLE 5.11. *Median Income among Mexican Household Heads by Sex and Foreign- or Domestic-Born, 1980–2005, Los Angeles, Riverside, Chicago, and Houston*

	1980		1990		2000		2005	
	% of Household Heads	Median Income in 2005 Dollars	% of Household Heads	Median Income in 2005 Dollars	% of Household Heads	Median Income in 2005 Dollars	% of Household Heads	Median Income in 2005 Dollars
Los Angeles								
Domestic-Born Males	31.4%	47,454	24.1%	60,420	19.2%	55,573	18.9%	56,027
Domestic-Born Females	12.6%	22,980	12.6%	33,993	12.7%	33,696	18.4%	40,747
Foreign-Born Males	45.2%	34,399	49.7%	41,839	50.9%	39,015	40.7%	40,747
Foreign-Born Females	10.8%	18,510	13.7%	26,717	17.1%	26,409	21.9%	31,344
TOTAL	100.0%	34,648	100.0%	42,485	100.0%	38,561	100.0%	40,747
Riverside								
Domestic-Born Males	58.5%	46,885	39.4%	55,376	29.9%	54,093	26.5%	61,120
Domestic-Born Females	16.2%	16,310	15.7%	27,584	15.7%	29,488	20.4%	43,090
Foreign-Born Males	20.6%	36,308	37.1%	40,494	43.8%	40,943	36.9%	45,840
Foreign-Born Females	4.8%	16,778	7.8%	23,908	10.6%	26,085	16.2%	32,597
TOTAL	100.0%	37,956	100.0%	42,881	100.0%	41,056	100.0%	46,288
Chicago								
Domestic-Born Males	26.0%	50,501	18.8%	55,288	15.2%	58,749	15.0%	57,555
Domestic-Born Females	10.3%	18,622	9.6%	32,266	9.1%	39,695	13.5%	42,784
Foreign-Born Males	56.0%	42,699	60.9%	44,716	62.0%	48,995	52.1%	46,248
Foreign-Born Females	7.7%	21,355	10.8%	29,736	13.6%	36,293	19.4%	36,672
TOTAL	100.0%	41,086	100.0%	43,961	100.0%	47,634	100.0%	45,738
Houston								
Domestic-Born Males	53.9%	47,442	38.0%	46,359	27.5%	49,903	22.3%	49,813
Domestic-Born Females	11.9%	23,727	14.8%	26,194	13.1%	31,870	20.4%	34,635
Foreign-Born Males	30.2%	35,608	39.9%	32,243	48.0%	36,293	38.5%	33,616
Foreign-Born Females	4.1%	23,264	7.3%	21,218	11.4%	24,186	18.8%	26,740
TOTAL	100.0%	40,114	100.0%	35,006	100.0%	36,973	100.0%	35,552

in cost-of-living indexes in the metropolitan areas under consideration.[12] Using these indexes it is possible to produce a more accurate approximation of comparative living standards between metropolitan areas by converting current 2005 dollar median household incomes into cost-of-living-adjusted incomes that reflect purchasing power. These data reveal with more clarity the real meaning of differences in Mexican household income levels in urban Los Angeles and suburban Riverside. Median household incomes in 2005 among Mexicans in Riverside ($46,288) were 14% higher than those in Los Angeles ($40,747). However, when income is adjusted using metropolitan area cost-of-living indexes published by the U.S. Census Bureau, Mexican households in Riverside in 2005 earned median household incomes ($36,134), which were 41% higher than in Los Angeles ($25,627).[13] Thus, there were even starker contrasts in comparative standards of living between Mexican households in these two contiguous metropolitan areas than the unadjusted household income data for 2005 suggest.

Among Mexican-born household heads in Chicago there were sharp differences in demographic profiles compared with the other three metro areas. Most striking was the fact that about 72% of all Chicago metro area Mexican household heads were foreign-born in 2005, and this is the highest percentage among the four metropolitan areas. Yet, the association of generally lower median household incomes in Los Angeles and Riverside with foreign-born household heads is not apparent in Chicago. Despite the predominance of foreign-born Mexican-headed households, all Chicago metro area Mexican-headed households earned higher median incomes in 2005 than the Mexican-headed households in Los Angeles and Houston, and only slightly less than in Riverside. One reason is that Chicago area households headed by foreign-born Mexicans earned 86% the median incomes of domestic-born Mexican household heads. This was significantly higher than the 76% found in Los Angeles and Houston and the 80% in Riverside. Additionally, as indicated

---

[12] Cost of living indexes for metropolitan areas for the fourth-quarter 2005 are found on the U.S. Census Bureau's Web site at http://www.census.gov/compendia/statab/2007/prices/consumer_price_indexes_cost_of_living_index.html. These data are from the Census Bureau's *Statistical Abstract: 2007 Edition*, Table 709. These indexes are as follows and are based on the nationwide average which is 100: Chicago, 117.4; Houston, 88.8; Riverside; 128.1; Los Angeles, 159; New York, 146.6 (based on Queens); and Miami, 116.2.

[13] The formula used to calculate these cost-of-living-adjusted incomes is (median household income/cost of living index)*100.

previously, a greater portion of Chicago's Mexican household heads were males (67%) who generally earned higher incomes than females.

It is likely that Chicago foreign-born Mexican household heads had higher skill levels than found in the other metro areas and were drawn to the region by employment opportunities in better paying jobs.[14] Evidence on educational attainment suggests this. As we indicated previously, Chicago area Mexican household heads had higher college graduation rates in 2005 (11%) than were found in Los Angeles (9%), Houston (9%), and Riverside (8%). Additionally, job market data suggest that a slightly greater percentage of Chicago Mexican household heads were employed (73%) compared with the employment rates in Los Angeles (69%), Houston (71%), and Riverside (68%).

For a more accurate portrayal of comparative living standards these Chicago income data also must be converted by using the cost-of-living indexes previously utilized to examine Riverside and Los Angeles. In absolute terms Mexican household heads in Chicago earned slightly lower median incomes ($45,738) than in Riverside ($46,288). However, when converted into incomes using the cost-of-living indexes for 2005, Chicago's Mexican headed households earned slightly more ($38,959) than in Riverside, ($36,134).

The importance of using cost-of-living indexes to determine comparative household income levels is brought into sharp focus by examining Mexican household heads in the Houston metro area. In absolute terms median household income was significantly lower than in the other three metropolitan areas as indicated in Table 5.10. This is despite the fact that when the three major variables that we have considered are examined – sex of the household head, birthplace (foreign- or domestic-born), and educational attainment levels of the household head – there were no significant factors that would adversely influence household income levels compared with Chicago, Los Angeles, and Riverside. Houston had a lower percentage of Mexican households headed by foreign-born individuals in 2005 (57%) compared with Chicago (72%) and Los Angeles (63%), while in Riverside the corresponding figure was 53%. Males headed about 61% of Houston's Mexican households, which was not significantly different from the percentage found in Chicago (67%), Los Angeles (60%), and Riverside (63%). Educational attainment levels among Houston's

---

[14] It is unfortunate that the occupational data in the American Community Survey of 2005 has such a large number of cases for which data are not available, which makes an accurate portrayal of occupational data difficult.

TABLE 5.12. *Median Household Income among Households Headed by Mexicans in Chicago, Houston, Los Angeles, and Riverside Metropolitan Areas, 2005 (nominal and adjusted by cost of living indexes)*

Metro Area	Nominal Household Income in 2005 Dollars	Cost-of-Living Index Fourth Quarter 2005	Adjusted for Cost-of-Living Index in 2005 Dollars
Houston	35,552	88.8	40,036
Chicago	45,738	117.4	38,959
Riverside	46,288	128.1	36,134
Los Angeles	40,747	159.0	25,627

Mexican-headed households were not very different either as about 9% had achieved a B.A. degree or higher by 2005 compared with 9% in Los Angeles, 8% in Riverside, and 11% in Chicago, as we indicated previously. Despite these demographic similarities, Houston's Mexican-headed households had median household income levels that lagged behind the other three metro areas in absolute terms. However, when adjusted by the 2005 cost-of-living index, in fact Mexican-headed households in Houston earned the highest median income levels of the four metro areas under consideration in 2005. (See Table 5.12 and Graph 5.4.) These data highlight the importance of taking into consideration cost-of-living factors when income levels are compared in different regions in the United States.

From the 1960s on, Cubans have dominated the Miami metropolitan area. But since 1980, their demographic preponderance has diminished considerably from 73% of all Latinos to 56% in 2005. The profile of Cuban household heads in Miami has few similarities compared with the Mexican household heads considered previously. First and foremost, females headed an extraordinarily high percentage (44%) of Miami's Cuban households. Second, when compared to all Latino national subgroups in metro areas in the United States, educational attainment levels were the highest among Cuban household heads. An astounding 25% had achieved a B.A. degree or higher by 2005, and nearly 50% of all Cuban household heads in Miami had attended or graduated college. Only 28% had not graduated from high school. There were also no significant differences in educational attainment levels between Cuban male and female household heads. About 22% of Miami female-headed Cuban households had achieved a B.A. degree or higher compared with 24% among male-headed households. Yet, despite these higher educational

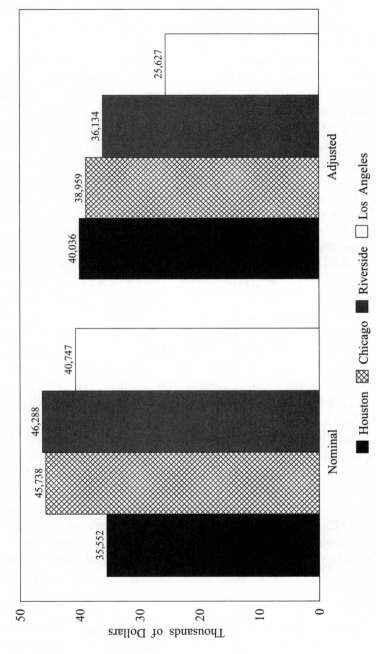

GRAPH 5.4. Median Household Income of Households Headed by Mexicans in 2005 in Chicago, Houston, Los Angeles, and Riverside Metro Areas in Nominal 2005 Dollars and Adjusted by Cost-of Living Index.

attainment levels, Cuban households in Miami did not have significantly greater median incomes than Mexicans in the four metro areas considered previously either in nominal 2005 dollars or in income adjusted by the cost-of-living index.

The key to understanding the lower median household incomes found among Miami's Cuban households in comparative perspective is in the extraordinarily distorted ratio of foreign-born to domestic-born household heads that has been the case since 1980. In 1980 97% of Miami Cuban household heads were foreign-born, and even though this had declined somewhat to 86% in 2005, their generally lower median incomes pulled down the averages among all Cuban households considerably. Domestic-born Cuban households had median incomes in 2005 of $69,167, but they represented only 14% of household heads. By way of contrast Cuban foreign-born household heads earned median incomes of $34,584 or 50% of their domestic-born counterparts.

Additionally and perhaps critical, foreign-born females headed 38% of Miami's Cuban households in 2005, and their median household income was at a level well below that of median incomes found for every other demographic category. By way of comparison, households headed by domestic-born Cuban females earned median incomes of $60,101, but they represented only 6% of all Cuban household heads. Domestic-born male-headed Cuban households earned higher median incomes in 2005, but they were only 7% of all Miami Cuban households. Foreign-born male Cuban household heads, 49% of total Cuban household heads, earned median incomes of about 50% of domestic-born Cuban males. (See Table 5.13.)

Finally, it is important to transform Miami nominal incomes into cost-of-living-adjusted incomes to compare standard-of-living differentiations between Latino nationalities in the major metro areas. In 2005 Miami Cubans heading households had median incomes of $38,709 that when adjusted by the cost-of-living index of 116.2 results in a real median income of $33,312. Given the image, which has been popularly advanced, that Cuban households are fairly well off among Latino nationalities, this is an important finding. In real adjusted income all Cuban households earned more than Mexican households in Los Angeles, but less than Mexican household heads in Houston, Chicago, and Riverside. (See Table 5.12.)

However, these general data must be considered with a great deal of caution because they do not indicate how particular subgroups of Mexicans or Cubans have performed economically. In fact, domestic-born

TABLE 5.13. Median Income among Cuban Household Heads in Miami by Sex and Foreign- or Domestic-Born, 1980–2005

	1980		1990		2000		2005	
	% of Household Heads	Median Income in 2005 Dollars	% of Household Heads	Median Income in 2005 Dollars	% of Household Heads	Median Income in 2005 Dollars	% of Household Heads	Median Income in 2005 Dollars
Domestic-Born Males	1.8%	39,236	2.7%	55,288	4.4%	65,781	7.4%	80,679
Domestic-Born Females	0.7%	16,612	1.1%	40,946	2.6%	45,366	6.5%	60,101
Foreign-Born Males	75.2%	40,825	69.1%	43,112	61.8%	41,635	48.6%	49,543
Foreign-Born Females	22.2%	15,255	27.0%	20,273	31.2%	22,910	37.6%	26,587
TOTAL	100.0%	34,529	100.0%	37,177	100.0%	36,293	100.0%	38,709

TABLE 5.14. *Mexican and Cuban Head of Household Median Incomes in Major Metro Areas by Sex and Domestic- and Foreign-Born, 2005*

	Nominal 2005 Dollars				
	Los Angeles Mexicans	Riverside Mexicans	Chicago Mexicans	Houston Mexicans	Miami Cubans
Domestic-Born Males	56,027	61,120	57,555	49,813	80,679
Domestic-Born Females	40,747	43,090	42,784	34,635	60,101
Foreign-Born Males	40,747	45,840	46,248	33,616	40,543
Foreign-Born Females	31,344	32,597	36,672	26,740	26,587
	Cost-of-Living Adjusted 2005 Dollars				
	Los Angeles Mexicans	Riverside Mexicans	Chicago Mexicans	Houston Mexicans	Miami Cubans
Domestic-Born Males	35,237	47,713	49,025	56,096	69,431
Domestic-Born Females	25,627	33,637	36,443	39,003	51,722
Foreign-Born Males	25,627	35,785	39,394	37,856	34,891
Foreign-Born Females	19,713	25,447	31,237	30,113	22,880

Cuban household heads of both sexes in Miami enjoyed much higher incomes than their Mexican counterparts in the four metro areas considered previously, in both absolute terms and when adjusted by cost-of-living indexes. However, they comprised only 14% of all Cuban household heads as we stressed earlier. This again underscores the complexity of the Latino experience in the United States as well as the difficulty of advancing sweeping generalizations about Latinos in general or particular national groups. (See Table 5.14.)

The New York metropolitan area has the second largest concentration of Latinos in the United States behind Los Angeles and is the most diverse in its composition by Latino nationality. As we have already noted (see Table 5.9), the overwhelming predominance of Puerto Ricans has diminished considerably since 1980, and the Dominican population has increased dynamically. If current demographic trends continue, Dominicans will be the New York metro area's largest Latino nationality some time after 2020. Ecuadorian and Colombian migration during the 1980s and 1990s and Mexican migration during the 1990s and after 2000 have led to an important presence of these national groups, and recently the Mexican population has been the fastest growing of all the Latino nationalities in New York.

When examining the median incomes of household heads by the largest Latino national groups in the New York metro area, the first, and perhaps most important, factor that must be considered is the extraordinarily high number of households headed by women among the two largest national groups, Puerto Ricans and Dominicans. In 2005 64% of all Dominican households and 56% of all Puerto Rican households were headed by women. This compares with 35% among Mexicans, 40% among Ecuadorians, and 49% among Colombians.

Among Dominicans, an extraordinary 57% of all households were headed by foreign-born Dominican women in 2005. This factor is of critical importance in examining median household incomes in the New York metro area because foreign-born female Dominican household heads, and Puerto Rican female household heads who were born in Puerto Rico had the lowest median household incomes of any specific demographic category among any Latino national group. Puerto Rican female household heads who were born in Puerto Rico (14% of all Puerto Rican household heads in 2005) earned a median household income of $14,771, which was about 50% of the level earned by Puerto Rican women household heads born in the United States. Foreign-born Dominican women (57% of all Dominican household heads) earned median incomes of $19,711 in 2005, or 45% the level of Dominican domestic-born women. Although foreign-born Mexican, Ecuadorian, and Colombian women who were household heads also had median incomes much lower than domestic-born women of the same nationalities, they were not a large percentage of total household heads. (See Table 5.15.)

The data on Ecuadorians and Colombians for 2005 stand out because of the extraordinary fact that foreign-born female household heads had median incomes that were greater than or equal to domestic- and foreign-born male household heads. One critical factor was their educational attainment levels. By 2005 17% of foreign-born female Colombian household heads had achieved a B.A. degree or higher, while 47% had at least some college education. Perhaps even more significant was the fact that only 28% had not graduated high school. These data may be compared to the lowest median income-earning categories among household heads: females from the Dominican Republic and females born in Puerto Rico. Almost half of Dominican-born female household heads in the New York metro area did not graduate from high school, and an extraordinary 55% of female household heads born in Puerto Rico had not graduated from high school in 2005. Although some Dominican-born and Puerto Rican–born female household heads had achieved B.A. degrees or higher,

TABLE 5.15. *Median Income among Latino Household Heads in New York Metro Area by Selected Nationalities, Sex, and Foreign- or Domestic-Born, 1980–2005*

	1980		1990		2000		2005	
	% of Household Heads	Median Income in 2005 Dollars	% of Household Heads	Median Income in 2005 Dollars	% of Household Heads	Median Income in 2005 Dollars	% of Household Heads	Median Income in 2005 Dollars
Dominicans								
Domestic-Born Males	1.1%	32,181	2.0%	55,288	2.8%	44,232	4.9%	50,832
Domestic-Born Females	0.7%	22,589	2.8%	18,745	4.7%	30,622	7.0%	44,312
Foreign-Born Males	50.2%	28,897	40.5%	40,061	37.2%	38,561	31.0%	35,857
Foreign-Born Females	48.0%	14,241	54.7%	17,916	55.2%	22,683	57.0%	19,711
TOTAL	100.0%	22,719	100.0%	27,857	100.0%	29,488	100.0%	26,485
Puerto Ricans								
U.S. States-Born Males	32.1%	35,596	35.1%	46,471	38.1%	45,366	35.8%	44,363
U.S. States-Born Females	21.3%	16,043	30.4%	23,070	37.4%	27,220	42.5%	28,523
Males Born in Puerto Rico	23.6%	28,470	15.5%	38,851	10.3%	33,117	8.0%	29,185
Females Born in Puerto Rico	23.0%	11,816	19.0%	13,856	14.2%	14,801	13.6%	14,771
TOTAL	100.0%	23,727	100.0%	31,968	100.0%	32,664	100.0%	32,190

Mexicans								
Domestic-Born Males	37,351	30.4%	44,828	14.9%	59,543	8.3%	47,042	5.9%
Domestic-Born Females	18,035	23.9%	43,334	9.5%	41,056	6.0%	37,283	8.1%
Foreign-Born Males	35,590	35.7%	44,753	60.5%	39,979	62.9%	37,589	59.4%
Foreign-Born Females	16,079	10.0%	36,036	15.1%	30,622	22.8%	24,346	26.6%
TOTAL	28,482	100.0%	43,481	100.0%	39,468	100.0%	32,628	100.0%
Ecuadorians								
Domestic-Born Males	100,279	0.7%	29,885	1.4%	49,336	2.6%	48,285	5.7%
Domestic-Born Females	31,458	0.4%	18,895	0.8%	45,933	2.7%	65,042	4.5%
Foreign-Born Males	36,545	71.2%	46,980	63.2%	45,366	64.2%	42,122	54.5%
Foreign-Born Females	18,984	27.7%	28,391	34.6%	31,756	30.5%	35,348	35.2%
TOTAL	32,561	100.0%	40,345	100.0%	41,964	100.0%	40,747	100.0%
Colombians								
Domestic-Born Males	45,070	1.6%	57,454	2.4%	57,501	3.1%	49,915	6.7%
Domestic-Born Females	30,865	0.7%	47,816	1.0%	55,573	2.8%	50,933	3.9%
Foreign-Born Males	37,570	66.4%	47,942	61.0%	48,428	52.8%	51,443	44.2%
Foreign-Born Females	23,442	31.3%	32,052	35.6%	33,911	41.3%	31,579	45.3%
TOTAL	33,148	100.0%	42,437	100.0%	43,098	100.0%	41,867	100.0%

the median incomes of female-headed households were dragged down-ward by low-income- earning women without high school diplomas. (See Table 5.16.)

The complexity of the Latino experience in the United States is brought into sharp focus by comparing these New York metro area data (adjusted by cost-of-living indexes for 2005) with those for Mexicans in Los Angeles, Riverside, Chicago, and Houston and Cubans in Miami. (See Table 5.17.) These data reveal with clarity why Miami Cubans are pop-ularly associated with being more prosperous than other Latino groups. In fact, domestic-born Cuban male and female household heads had the highest median household incomes of any other demographic cohort in any of the six metropolitan areas, despite making up only a small per-centage of Cuban household heads in the Miami metro area. However, this fact may not be used to generalize about all Cuban household heads in Miami, or elsewhere. In fact, foreign-born Cuban household heads in Miami were no better off than foreign-born Mexican household heads in Riverside, Chicago, and Houston, although they earned higher median incomes than Mexican household heads in Los Angeles and nearly every foreign-born household head in every Latino nationality in New York when adjusted using cost-of-living indexes.

It is also impossible to make any sweeping generalizations about Mex-ican median household income patterns. In 2005 Chicago and Houston domestic-born Mexican household heads earned median incomes, ad-justed by cost-of-living indexes that were well above those earned by nearly every other Latino demographic cohort in the metropolitan areas considered here.

New York Puerto Rican, Dominican, and Mexican household heads, domestic- and foreign-born, earned the lowest median household incomes of any Latino nationality in the six metro areas, and their cost-of-living adjusted incomes were below those of Los Angeles Mexican household heads. In the New York metropolitan area only Colombian and Ecuado-rian household heads had median income levels that were somewhat comparable with those earned by Mexicans in Los Angeles, Riverside, Chicago, and Houston and Cubans in Miami.

The preceding examination of household-head median incomes may be used to compare the relative economic performances of the major racial/ethnic groups and Latino subgroups that have been considered nationally and in the largest metropolitan areas of Latino population concentration. We now turn to the issue of poverty among Latinos in

TABLE 5.16. *Educational Attainment Levels and Median Household Incomes among Puerto Rican, Dominican, Mexican, Ecuadorian, and Colombian Household Heads in the New York Metro Area, 2005*

Educational Attainment	Puerto Ricans	Median Household Income	Dominicans	Median Household Income	Mexicans	Median Household Income	Ecuadorians	Median Household Income	Colombians	Median Household Income
Did Not Graduate High School	38.9%	11,715	43.7%	19,253	51.9%	29,338	33.4%	35,450	23.3%	28,115
High School Graduate	26.3%	30,560	21.6%	27,504	24.6%	31,986	25.4%	35,653	25.2%	35,195
Some College, No Degree	15.3%	44,821	14.7%	33,922	8.0%	46,349	19.1%	45,331	15.9%	40,747
Associates Degree	7.1%	46,859	6.1%	39,117	2.7%	62,139	7.5%	56,027	10.4%	42,020
B.A. or Higher	12.4%	66,234	13.8%	52,971	12.8%	76,400	14.6%	58,573	25.2%	65,093
TOTAL	100.0%	28,523	100.0%	26,485	100.0%	34,125	100.0%	40,747	100.0%	42,122

TABLE 5.17. *Median Incomes of Household Heads in Major Metro Areas by Sex and Domestic- and Foreign-Born, 2005*

Nominal 2005 Dollars

	Los Angeles Mexicans	Riverside Mexicans	Chicago Mexicans	Houston Mexicans	Miami Cubans	New York Puerto Ricans	New York Dominicans	New York Mexicans	New York Ecuadorians	New York Colombians
Domestic-Born Males	56,027	61,120	57,555	49,813	80,679	44,363	50,832	47,042	48,285	49,915
Domestic-Born Females	40,747	43,090	42,784	34,635	60,101	28,523	44,312	37,283	65,042	50,933
Foreign-Born Males	40,747	45,840	46,248	33,616	40,543	29,185	35,857	37,589	42,122	51,443
Foreign-Born Females	31,344	32,597	36,672	26,740	26,587	14,771	19,711	24,346	35,348	31,579

Cost-of-Living-Adjusted 2005 Dollars

	Los Angeles Mexicans	Riverside Mexicans	Chicago Mexicans	Houston Mexicans	Miami Cubans	New York Puerto Ricans	New York Dominicans	New York Mexicans	New York Ecuadorians	New York Colombians
Domestic-Born Males	35,237	47,713	49,025	56,096	69,431	30,261	34,674	32,089	32,937	34,048
Domestic-Born Females	25,627	33,637	36,443	39,003	51,722	19,456	30,226	25,432	44,367	34,743
Foreign-Born Males	25,627	35,785	39,394	37,856	34,891	19,908	24,459	25,641	28,732	35,090
Foreign-Born Females	19,713	25,447	31,237	30,113	22,880	10,076	13,445	16,607	24,112	21,541

Note: For Puerto Ricans the foreign born are those born in Puerto Rico. For New York there are two cost-of-living indexes, one for Manhattan borough, 204.3, and one for Queens borough, which is 146.6. Since most Latinos in New York lived outside of Manhattan, the Queens cost-of-living index is used here.

comparative perspective with the other major demographic groups and the differentiations found between the principal Latino nationalities.

There are two ways in which this complex issue will be addressed. The first is through the use of poverty indexes developed by the U.S. Census Bureau.[15] These indexes permit the general categorization of individuals within families and households who are considered to be below a poverty level calculated by the Census Bureau based on family size and income during each census year. The second method will utilize household income structures and how they changed from 1980 through 2005. This permits a more nuanced examination of how household income was distributed within the major racial/ethnic groups and Latino nationalities. This second method permits poverty to be considered from the broader perspective of how the poor compare to those who were not living below poverty income levels.[16]

First and foremost, between 1980 and 2005 non-Hispanic blacks and Latinos had poverty rates that were more than twice the rates of non-Hispanic whites and Asians. Non-Hispanic blacks had the greatest percentage of populations living below the poverty "line." Second, there was only a very slight decline in the overall poverty rates of the major racial/ethnic groups over this 25-year period, although there was a meaningful decline among African-American females from 32% in 1980 to 27% in 2005. In general, females had higher rates of poverty among each racial/ethnic group. By 2005 nearly 25% of African Americans were living in poverty at the national level compared 29% in 1980. Among Latinos approximately 21% lived in poverty in 2005, which was a marginal decline from 24% in 1980. About 11% of Asians and 8% of non-Hispanic whites were living below the poverty level in 2005. (See Table 5.18.)

The correlation between age and poverty in the United States reveals much about the great socioeconomic chasm that separates non-Hispanic blacks and Latinos from non-Hispanic whites and Asians. Among non-Hispanic blacks an astounding 40% of children lived in poverty in 1980 and this had declined only marginally in 2005, more than four decades after the Civil Rights Act was passed. Among Hispanics, 31% of children 14 years of age or younger lived in poverty in 1980, and this had also

[15] For a detailed list of poverty thresholds and how they have been determined by the Census Bureau for each census year see http://www.census.gov/hhes/www/poverty/threshld .html.

[16] By focusing on poverty alone, wealth is explicitly ignored within each racial/ethnic category and Latino nationality.

TABLE 5.18. *Percentage of Individuals Living at or below the Poverty Line by Sex and Racial/Ethnic Group, 1980–2005*

Racial/Ethnic Group	1980			1990		
	Males	Females	Total	Males	Females	Total
Non-Hispanic Black	26.0%	32.4%	29.4%	26.0%	32.6%	29.5%
Hispanic	21.4%	25.5%	23.5%	23.3%	27.4%	25.4%
Asian	12.8%	12.5%	12.7%	13.0%	12.9%	13.0%
Non-Hispanic White	7.6%	10.0%	8.9%	7.9%	10.5%	9.2%

Racial/Ethnic Group	2000			2005		
	Males	Females	Total	Males	Females	Total
Non-Hispanic Black	22.2%	27.1%	24.8%	22.2%	26.7%	24.7%
Hispanic	21.4%	24.5%	22.9%	19.6%	23.2%	21.4%
Asian	12.2%	12.4%	12.3%	10.3%	10.6%	10.5%
Non-Hispanic White	7.4%	9.4%	8.5%	7.3%	9.3%	8.3%

fallen only slightly to 29% by 2005. By way of comparison, 11% of non-Hispanic whites and 16% of Asian children 14 years of age or younger lived in poverty in 1980, and these percentages declined significantly by 2005. (See Table 5.19.)

In 2005 Dominicans had the greatest percentage of people living in poverty, some 27% of the total Dominican population in the United States, although this was somewhat lower than the 33% rate for Dominicans in 1980. Mexicans had the second largest percentage of Latino nationalities living in poverty in 2005 at 23%, and this was nearly exactly the same as in 1980. The third most impoverished Latino nationality in 2005 was Puerto Ricans at 23%, and this was substantially lower than the 36% of all Puerto Ricans living in poverty in 1980. The decline in the poverty rate among Puerto Ricans between 1980 and 2005 was the largest among any Latino national group. Cubans, Colombians, Ecuadorians, and Peruvians had the lowest poverty rates among the Latino national groups. In 2005 these rates (see Table 5.20) were closer to those prevailing among Asians and non-Hispanic whites than to the high-poverty-rate Latino nationalities. The poverty rate among Salvadorans was between the lower-end nationalities and higher-end national groups at about 17% in 2005, although this was an improvement from the 22% of 1980.

Among every Latino nationality, females had higher poverty rates than males. The most extreme differential was among Dominicans of whom

TABLE 5.19. *Percentage of Each Age Category at or below Poverty Level by Race/Ethnicity, 1980–2005*

1980

Age Category	Non-Hispanic White	Non-Hispanic Black	Asian	Hispanic
0–14	11.4%	39.6%	15.6%	30.7%
15–44	8.0%	24.6%	12.7%	20.4%
45–59	5.6%	21.1%	7.2%	15.6%
60+	11.0%	32.0%	12.1%	23.7%

1990

Age Category	Non-Hispanic White	Non-Hispanic Black	Asian	Hispanic
0–14	12.7%	42.5%	16.5%	33.7%
15–44	8.6%	24.5%	13.2%	22.7%
45–59	5.8%	19.2%	7.9%	16.5%
60+	9.8%	30.2%	10.1%	22.1%

2000

Age Category	Non-Hispanic White	Non-Hispanic Black	Asian	Hispanic
0–14	11.3%	35.7%	14.7%	29.4%
15–44	8.8%	21.7%	13.2%	21.3%
45–59	5.9%	17.2%	7.9%	15.5%
60+	7.7%	22.6%	11.0%	18.9%

2005

Age Category	Non-Hispanic White	Non-Hispanic Black	Asian	Hispanic
0–14	10.8%	36.6%	11.5%	28.6%
15–44	9.4%	23.5%	11.4%	19.8%
45–59	5.9%	16.5%	7.3%	13.4%
60+	7.3%	20.3%	10.6%	17.9%

TABLE 5.20. *Poverty Rates among Latino Nationalities by Sex, 1980–2005*

Total Population				
Nationality	1980	1990	2000	2005
Dominican	32.7%	32.0%	27.5%	27.3%
Mexican	23.2%	26.8%	24.0%	23.0%
Puerto Rican	36.2%	30.2%	25.4%	22.9%
Honduran	20.7%	28.7%	25.5%	22.2%
Salvadoran	22.3%	25.3%	20.7%	16.9%
Cuban	13.0%	14.1%	14.6%	13.9%
Ecuadorian	17.9%	15.7%	16.5%	13.8%
Colombian	14.5%	14.6%	16.6%	11.9%
Peruvian	13.9%	13.6%	12.3%	11.0%

Males				
Nationality	1980	1990	2000	2005
Dominican	29.2%	28.0%	24.6%	23.6%
Mexican	21.5%	25.0%	22.7%	21.2%
Puerto Rican	32.1%	26.3%	22.4%	20.4%
Honduran	18.9%	26.8%	23.1%	19.1%
Salvadoran	20.3%	23.0%	18.6%	14.9%
Cuban	11.5%	12.8%	13.6%	12.3%
Ecuadorian	16.8%	13.6%	15.0%	12.2%
Colombian	13.3%	12.3%	15.0%	10.8%
Peruvian	12.8%	11.6%	11.0%	9.7%

Females				
Nationality	1980	1990	2000	2005
Dominican	35.6%	35.6%	29.9%	30.3%
Honduran	22.0%	30.3%	27.9%	25.2%
Puerto Rican	40.0%	33.8%	28.1%	25.1%
Mexican	25.0%	28.8%	25.5%	24.9%
Salvadoran	24.0%	27.7%	23.0%	18.9%
Cuban	14.3%	15.4%	15.6%	15.4%
Ecuadorian	19.0%	17.7%	18.0%	15.3%
Colombian	15.5%	16.6%	18.0%	12.8%
Peruvian	15.0%	15.4%	13.5%	12.3%

30% of all females lived in poverty in 2005 compared to 24% of all Dominican males. Puerto Ricans had the next highest disparity as 25% of all females lived in poverty compared with 20% of Puerto Rican males.

Childhood poverty has remained an extraordinary problem within each Latino national subgroup. About 36% of all Dominican children

14 years of age and younger lived in poverty in 2005, and although this was intolerably high it was an improvement from the dreadful 48% of Dominican children living in poverty in 1980. Among Puerto Ricans, who had the second highest incident rate of childhood poverty at 30% in 2005, there was also a substantial decline from the lamentable 48% of Puerto Rican children living in poverty in 1980. Childhood poverty rates among Mexicans showed absolutely no improvement between 1980 (29%) and 2005 (30%). There were also only slight improvements in childhood poverty rates among other Latino national groups as indicated in Table 5.21. There was not necessarily a correlation between birthplace and poverty rates among Latino nationalities. Among Mexicans, Puerto Ricans, and Cubans poverty rates among the foreign-born, or those born in Puerto Rico, were slightly higher in 2005 than among those born in the United States. However, among the other Latino national groups, poverty rates among the domestic-born were slightly higher than among the foreign-born. (See Table 5.22.)

But poverty, however dire, was not the normal lot for most Hispanics in the United States. An examination of the way in which income was distributed shows some startling patterns, but only because of the unfortunate stereotypical image of Latino poverty. Unquestionably there were solid middle and even higher income sectors among Latino households and an economic and social structure that was in many ways similar to the stratification found within the other major racial/ethnic groups in the United States.[17] There are two related ways we will address the question of income distribution. The first is to examine the percentage of households found in four income categories we have defined: (1) those earning less than $20,000 yearly; (2) those earning between $20,000 and $39,999; (3) those earning between $40,000 and $74,999; and (4) those households whose incomes were above $75,000. The second is to consider the percentage of total income earned by each of these household categories, which will indicate the relative levels of wealth concentration.

The first general observations that may be made is that non-Hispanic blacks and Latinos had proportionally more households earning less than $20,000 and fewer households earning greater than $75,000 than non-Hispanic whites or Asians from 1980 through 2005. Latinos generally were better off than non-Hispanic blacks in terms of income distribution with a smaller percentage of households in the lower income bracket and

---

[17] This section will examine household income by the race/ethnicity and Latino nationality of household heads.

TABLE 5.21. Percentage of Each Age Category at or below Poverty Line by Latino Nationality, 1980–2005

Age Category	Mexican	Puerto Rican	Cuban	Honduran	Salvadoran	Colombian	Ecuadorian	Peruvian	Dominican
1980									
0–14	29.3%	48.3%	15.5%	26.6%	24.3%	17.7%	22.7%	15.1%	47.7%
15–44	20.0%	31.0%	10.7%	19.4%	23.2%	13.9%	17.1%	13.4%	29.0%
45–59	16.5%	23.3%	9.0%	13.9%	15.2%	11.2%	12.8%	12.8%	23.3%
60+	25.2%	28.9%	22.0%	18.1%	14.6%	15.3%	18.0%	16.3%	29.9%
1990									
0–14	34.3%	42.4%	17.7%	34.0%	29.6%	17.9%	23.0%	15.0%	43.7%
15–44	23.9%	25.3%	11.3%	28.3%	24.3%	14.2%	14.2%	13.4%	28.4%
45–59	18.2%	19.8%	10.2%	19.4%	19.1%	10.3%	9.5%	10.0%	22.5%
60+	23.7%	26.6%	20.3%	22.5%	22.2%	16.4%	16.4%	16.8%	25.5%
2000									
0–14	30.1%	33.5%	16.6%	33.3%	26.0%	19.6%	19.8%	15.1%	36.3%
15–44	22.4%	22.4%	12.3%	24.1%	19.7%	17.1%	16.1%	12.0%	24.9%
45–59	15.8%	19.2%	12.4%	20.0%	16.5%	12.6%	13.0%	9.6%	21.2%
60+	18.8%	23.7%	18.6%	20.6%	19.7%	15.4%	16.8%	12.8%	26.7%
2005									
0–14	30.3%	30.2%	15.6%	28.3%	23.7%	14.8%	18.0%	15.7%	36.2%
15–44	21.3%	20.4%	11.6%	20.8%	15.2%	11.4%	13.6%	10.1%	24.1%
45–59	14.0%	17.2%	9.7%	15.8%	11.8%	8.4%	7.1%	6.2%	19.6%
60+	17.5%	22.1%	19.4%	21.3%	17.0%	14.7%	15.6%	15.2%	30.8%

TABLE 5.22. *Poverty Rates among Latino Nationalities by Foreign- or Domestic-Born, 1980–2005*

	Mexican	Puerto Rican	Cuban	Honduran	Salvadoran	Colombian	Ecuadorian	Peruvian	Dominican
1980									
Domestic-Born	22.2%	22.6%	12.6%	22.5%	18.4%	16.6%	21.2%	11.9%	42.4%
Foreign-Born	26.4%	35.4%	12.9%	20.1%	23.0%	14.1%	17.1%	14.6%	30.4%
1990									
Domestic-Born	25.3%	25.1%	13.1%	25.9%	25.3%	15.3%	18.9%	10.4%	37.9%
Foreign-Born	29.8%	30.2%	14.3%	29.5%	25.0%	14.3%	14.4%	14.3%	29.3%
2000									
Domestic-Born	22.2%	22.8%	12.1%	28.2%	23.3%	14.1%	14.9%	12.0%	30.7%
Foreign-Born	26.6%	26.3%	15.7%	24.8%	19.9%	17.4%	17.0%	12.4%	26.0%
2005									
Domestic-Born	21.9%	21.2%	11.6%	25.2%	20.8%	12.7%	13.9%	12.6%	29.8%
Foreign-Born	24.9%	23.8%	15.4%	20.9%	15.0%	11.6%	13.7%	10.5%	25.5%

Note: For Puerto Rico, foreign-born means born in Puerto Rico; domestic-born means born in the United States.

a larger percentage at the highest income level over $75,000 between 1980 and 2005.

The second general conclusion is that the overall percentage of households earning less than $20,000 annually declined to varying degrees among all racial/ethnic groups. In 1980 21% of non-Hispanic white households were in the lower income category, while by 2005 the corresponding figure was 17%. For Asians in 1980 19% of all households earned less than $20,000, and this fell to 14% in 2005. Among non-Hispanic blacks an extraordinarily high 39% of all households fell into the lowest income-earning category in 1980, and in 2005 this had fallen to 32%, the highest percentage among the major racial/ethnic groups. For Latino households there were about 30% earning less than $20,000 in 1980 and 23% in 2005. Although there were proportionally more Latino households earning less than $20,000 than non-Hispanic blacks, Latino households at this lower income level were more similar to non-Hispanic whites (17%) than to non-Hispanic blacks (32%).

At the top of the household income-earning hierarchy there were considerable improvements among all racial and ethnic groups. Among Latinos some 10% of all households earned more than $75,000 in 1980, and this rose to 19% in 2005. Thus, about a fifth of all Latino households were fairly well off in terms of income in 2005, and if we add together all of those households earning greater than $40,000 yearly, about 49% of Latino households were above this income level. These data underline the importance of not making sweeping conclusions about poverty among Latino households. Previously it was indicated that about 21% of Latinos lived in poverty in 2005. By way of contrast, 19% of Latino households earned more than $75,000 in the same year. There were proportionally more households headed by non-Hispanic whites (32%) and Asians (43%) earning more than $75,000 annually in 2005. Among non-Hispanic blacks 16% of all households were in this income category. (See Table 5.23 for complete data.)

The progressive concentration of wealth in the hands of upper-income-earning households was a characteristic of each racial/ethnic group between 1980 and 2005, although it was most extreme among non-Hispanic whites and Asians. By 2005 some 64% of all household income among non-Hispanic whites was concentrated in households earning more than $75,000 (32% of all households), and for Asians it was an extraordinary 74% (43% of all households). Although much lower levels of wealth concentration were found among Latinos and non-Hispanic blacks, it was still indicative of the great disparities between rich and poor

TABLE 5.23. Household Income Distribution by Race/Ethnicity, 1980–2005 (in 2005 dollars adjusted for inflation)

Income Level	Non-Hispanic Whites		Non-Hispanic Blacks		Asians		Latinos	
	% of Income	% of Households	% of Income	% of Households	% of Income	% of Households	% of Income	% of Households
1980								
Less Than 20,000	5.1%	21.2%	12.0%	39.4%	3.8%	18.6%	8.5%	29.8%
20,000–39,999	15.4%	25.6%	23.9%	27.8%	11.9%	22.2%	22.9%	30.2%
40,000–74,999	38.8%	34.5%	38.9%	24.3%	33.9%	33.7%	41.6%	29.8%
75,000+	40.7%	18.7%	25.2%	8.5%	50.5%	25.6%	27.0%	10.2%
TOTAL	100.0%	100.0%	100.0%	100.0%	100.0%	100.0%	100.0%	100.0%
1990								
Less Than 20,000	3.8%	19.0%	9.4%	36.8%	2.2%	14.3%	6.5%	26.4%
20,000–39,999	12.0%	23.4%	19.3%	25.5%	7.6%	18.4%	17.9%	27.8%
40,000–74,999	30.8%	32.2%	35.0%	24.8%	23.4%	30.0%	35.9%	29.8%
75,000+	53.4%	25.3%	36.3%	12.9%	66.8%	37.3%	39.7%	16.1%
TOTAL	100.0%	100.0%	100.0%	100.0%	100.0%	100.0%	100.0%	100.0%
2000								
Less Than 20,000	2.9%	16.4%	7.1%	31.1%	2.0%	14.3%	5.3%	23.4%
20,000–39,999	10.2%	22.9%	17.3%	26.7%	6.6%	17.7%	16.9%	28.7%
40,000–74,999	25.8%	31.1%	31.4%	25.9%	19.6%	28.0%	32.2%	29.4%
75,000+	61.2%	29.6%	44.1%	16.3%	71.8%	40.1%	45.6%	18.4%
TOTAL	100.0%	100.0%	100.0%	100.0%	100.0%	100.0%	100.0%	100.0%
2005								
Less Than 20,000	2.9%	16.9%	7.7%	32.4%	1.8%	13.6%	5.3%	23.3%
20,000–39,999	9.4%	21.8%	17.4%	26.2%	5.9%	16.5%	16.2%	27.9%
40,000–74,999	24.1%	29.6%	31.3%	25.1%	18.2%	27.0%	31.8%	29.3%
75,000+	63.6%	31.8%	43.5%	16.3%	74.1%	42.9%	46.8%	19.4%
TOTAL	100.0%	100.0%	100.0%	100.0%	100.0%	100.0%	100.0%	100.0%

within these respective populations. Among non-Hispanic blacks 44% of income was concentrated in the hands of household heads earning greater than $75,000 yearly (16% of all households), while among Latinos it was 47% (19% of all households). (See Table 5.23.)

One of the important conclusions that may be advanced is the absolute impossibility of generalizing about the distribution of wealth or poverty among the Latino population in the United States from 1980 on because of a very clear and demarcated social hierarchy. While it is unfortunate that some 20% of individuals lived in poverty in 2005, there was about the same percentage of households with considerable wealth, and these controlled nearly half of the income earned by all Latino households. The vast majority of Latino households were somewhere between these extremes of wealthier and poor, as was the case with each of the other racial/ethnic groups.

Among Latino nationalities, Dominicans (32%) and Puerto Ricans (29%) had the greatest percentage of households earning less than $20,000 yearly in 2005, although this represented a significant improvement from 1980 when 40% of the households in both subgroups were found in this income category. Salvadorans (18%), Colombians (17%), Ecuadorians (17%), and Peruvians (15%) had the lowest portion of households found earning below $20,000 annually. Among Mexicans 23% of households earned $19,999 or less in 2005, and this was a decline from the 28% found in 1980.

Cubans illustrate with clarity the economic cleavages found within all Latino nationalities. Although, every Latino nationality experienced declines in the percentage of households at the bottom of the income-earning hierarchy between 1980 and 2005, this was not the case among Cubans. Some 25% of all Cuban households earned less than $20,000 in 1980, and about the same percentage was found 25 years later in 2005. There were more Cuban households in the lowest income bracket than Mexicans, and the percentage of Cubans in relative poverty was closer to Dominicans and Puerto Ricans than to the Andean nationalities or even Salvadorans. There is no question that this persistence of lower-income-earning households was connected to the arrival of relatively poorer Cuban immigrants in the Mariel boatlift. However, Cubans also had the greatest percentage of households earning over $75,000 (28%) than any other Latino nationality in 2005. This percentage was much closer to non-Hispanic whites in the same income category in 2005 (32%) than to most other Latino national groups.

Every Latino nationality had more households earning more than
$75,000 in 2005 inflation-adjusted income than in 1980, and this was
the case even among the poorest nationalities, Dominicans (16% in 2005)
and Puerto Ricans (21% in 2005). These data once again illustrate the
difficulties of generalizing about poverty or wealth within any Latino subgroup. Among Colombian, Ecuadorian, and Peruvian over one-quarter
of all household heads earned more than $75,000 in 2005. The com-
parative percentage of these high-income-earning households was lower
among Salvadorans (19%), Mexicans (17%), and Hondurans (14%).

The concentration of wealth in households earning more than $75,000
increased considerably among all Latino nationalities between 1980 and
2005, and this tendency was similar to the processes found among non-
Hispanic whites. The most extreme example was found among Cuban
households. By 2005 63% of all income accruing to Cuban-headed
households was concentrated in the more than $75,000 income category.
This compares with 38% in 1980. Among Colombians, Ecuadorians,
Peruvians, and Puerto Ricans over half of all income earned by households headed by individuals of these nationalities was found in the higher
income category in 2005. Within Mexican, Salvadoran, and Dominican
households slightly more than 40% of total household income was concentrated in the wealthiest households. The 1990s economic expansion
and equities-market boom impacted the income distribution structure
and concentration of wealth among Hispanics in the same way as it
affected the other racial/ethnic group in the United States. These data are
summarized in Table 5.24.

We now turn to the comparative dimensions of poverty in the major
metropolitan areas of Latino population concentration. Extraordinary
differentials in the poverty rates found among non-Hispanic blacks and
Latinos compared with non-Hispanic whites in each of the six metropolitan areas examined – Chicago, Houston, Los Angeles, Miami, New York,
and Riverside – reflected national-level data. With respect to Asians there
were divergences from national trends in Miami and Riverside where
Asians had poverty rates that approached those of Latinos, although in
the four other metro areas Asian poverty rates were much lower, and this
also reflected national patterns.

In 1980 Latinos in the New York metropolitan area had the highest
poverty rate (35%) found among all of the racial/ethnic groups in the
six metro areas, and indeed this was far higher than the 21% of all
Latinos living in poverty in Chicago and Los Angeles. Latinos in Houston

Percentage of Income

TABLE 5.24. *Household Income Distribution by Latino Nationality, 1980–2005 (in 2005 dollars adjusted for inflation)*

Income Level	Mexican	Puerto Rican	Cuban	Honduran	Salvadoran	Colombian	Ecuadorian	Peruvian	Dominican
1980									
Less Than 20,000	8.3%	14.4%	6.0%	9.1%	9.9%	5.9%	6.4%	4.6%	15.3%
20,000–39,999	23.8%	27.5%	17.5%	27.0%	30.1%	21.5%	22.6%	18.3%	31.3%
40,000–74,999	43.3%	39.3%	38.9%	37.9%	40.1%	40.3%	44.5%	39.8%	37.2%
75,000 +	24.6%	18.9%	37.7%	26.0%	19.9%	32.3%	26.6%	37.3%	16.2%
TOTAL	100.0%	100.0%	100.0%	100.0%	100.0%	100.0%	100.0%	100.0%	100.0%
1990									
Less Than 20,000	7.0%	7.7%	5.0%	7.6%	6.0%	3.7%	4.1%	3.4%	8.5%
20,000–39,999	19.8%	17.3%	12.5%	23.8%	22.1%	14.5%	13.7%	13.0%	19.5%
40,000–74,999	37.6%	36.5%	29.8%	33.3%	39.6%	33.3%	35.7%	32.2%	37.1%
75,000 +	35.7%	38.5%	52.7%	35.4%	32.3%	48.6%	46.5%	51.4%	34.9%
TOTAL	100.0%	100.0%	100.0%	100.0%	100.0%	100.0%	100.0%	100.0%	100.0%
2000									
Less Than 20,000	5.5%	6.5%	4.7%	6.0%	4.8%	3.7%	3.3%	2.7%	6.9%
20,000–39,999	18.4%	16.0%	11.5%	18.3%	17.5%	12.8%	12.8%	11.7%	18.7%
40,000–74,999	33.8%	31.4%	24.4%	34.1%	34.9%	28.7%	30.2%	30.1%	32.5%
75,000 +	42.3%	46.0%	59.4%	41.7%	42.9%	54.8%	53.7%	55.5%	41.9%
TOTAL	100.0%	100.0%	100.0%	100.0%	100.0%	100.0%	100.0%	100.0%	100.0%
2005									
Less Than 20,000	5.7%	6.0%	4.3%	6.0%	4.6%	3.1%	3.4%	3.0%	7.9%
20,000–39,999	18.2%	13.7%	9.9%	22.8%	18.6%	11.9%	11.8%	12.3%	17.8%
40,000–74,999	34.4%	28.9%	22.4%	37.1%	34.2%	29.1%	30.0%	26.9%	31.4%
75,000 +	41.7%	51.4%	63.4%	34.1%	42.6%	55.9%	54.7%	57.8%	42.8%
TOTAL	100.0%	100.0%	100.0%	100.0%	100.0%	100.0%	100.0%	100.0%	100.0%

(17%), Riverside (18%), and Miami (18%) had about half the poverty rate compared with Latinos in New York where the Hispanic population was dominated by Puerto Ricans. The poverty rate among New York metro area Latinos declined to 27% by 2005; however, this was still the highest rate among Latinos in the six metro areas, although in Houston some 25% of Latinos lived in poverty. These Houston data represent a worsening of the economic situation among the poorest Latinos. In 1980 17% of Houston Latinos lived below the poverty line.

Indeed, there were no great strides made in combating poverty between 1980 and 2005 among Latino communities in Los Angeles where 21% of all Latinos lived in poverty in 1980 and in 2005. In Chicago there was a decline in the poverty rate from 21% in 1980 to 16% in 2005; in Miami there was a marginal reduction from 17% in 1980 to 15% in 2005; and in Riverside the decrease was small as well from 18% in 1980 to 16% in 2005. In every metropolitan area we have examined, Latino females had higher poverty rates then males. (See Tables 5.25 and 5.26.)

The poverty rate for Latino children 14 years of age and younger was an extraordinary 49% in the New York metro area in 1980, and although this had declined to 37% by 2005, it was the highest rate among the metropolitan areas considered here followed by Houston where 33% of all Latino children lived in poverty in 2005. The Houston data represent a serious worsening of impoverishment among children from 1980 when 21% of the Latino population 14 years of age and younger was below the poverty threshold. In Los Angeles and Riverside there were absolutely no advances in eliminating childhood poverty among Latinos between 1980 and 2005. Some 27% of Los Angeles Latino children lived in poverty in 1980 and 29% in 2005, while in Riverside the corresponding figures for children were 23% in 1980 and 21% in 2005. Childhood poverty in Houston and Los Angeles was about the same in 2005 for Latinos and non-Hispanic blacks. The rate among Latinos in Chicago and Miami was considerably lower than for non-Hispanic blacks and marginally lower in Riverside. Only in the New York metro area were childhood poverty rates among Latinos significantly higher at 37% in 2005 than among non-Hispanic blacks (29%). (See Table 5.27.) Thus, despite the much heralded "War on Poverty" declared by President Lyndon Johnson in early 1964, impoverished Latinos in major urban settings, and especially poor Latino children, continue to live in conditions that have not changed significantly in the 25 years from 1980 to 2005.

As we have indicated previously Mexicans were the principal Latino nationality in Chicago, Houston, Los Angeles, and Riverside, and they

TABLE 5.25. *Poverty Rates in Percentages by Race/Ethnicity by Major Metropolitan Areas, 1980–2005*

1980

Metro Area	Non-Hispanic White	Non-Hispanic Black	Asian	Hispanic
Houston	5.2%	22.4%	15.6%	17.3%
Los Angeles	7.4%	23.5%	12.7%	20.8%
Chicago	4.9%	29.3%	8.8%	21.2%
Miami	8.3%	30.9%	14.2%	17.3%
New York	8.1%	28.5%	12.7%	35.0%
Riverside	8.9%	18.2%	15.0%	18.0%

1990

Metro Area	Non-Hispanic White	Non-Hispanic Black	Asian	Hispanic
Houston	6.5%	28.5%	12.9%	26.2%
Los Angeles	6.4%	20.8%	12.5%	23.2%
Chicago	4.6%	29.3%	9.4%	20.1%
Miami	7.8%	30.6%	9.3%	20.0%
New York	7.7%	22.4%	14.5%	31.4%
Riverside	7.9%	20.3%	15.3%	19.6%

2000

Metro Area	Non-Hispanic White	Non-Hispanic Black	Asian	Hispanic
Houston	6.2%	21.9%	11.2%	22.4%
Los Angeles	8.5%	25.1%	13.1%	24.7%
Chicago	4.3%	24.2%	8.7%	16.7%
Miami	9.6%	28.7%	15.1%	17.7%
New York	10.2%	23.9%	17.8%	30.0%
Riverside	9.5%	22.1%	14.5%	21.4%

2005

Metro Area	Non-Hispanic White	Non-Hispanic Black	Asian	Hispanic
Houston	6.4%	23.8%	10.4%	24.6%
Los Angeles	6.7%	19.4%	10.9%	21.0%
Chicago	4.5%	26.2%	6.7%	15.6%
Miami	8.8%	27.0%	14.5%	15.0%
New York	9.3%	20.1%	15.8%	27.1%
Riverside	7.4%	18.8%	10.3%	15.9%

TABLE 5.26. *Poverty Rates in Percentages by Race/Ethnicity and Sex by Major Metropolitan Areas, 1980–2005*

1980

Metro Area	Non-Hispanic Whites		Non-Hispanic Blacks		Asians		Hispanics	
	Males	Females	Males	Females	Males	Females	Males	Females
Houston	4.4%	6.1%	19.4%	25.2%	15.9%	15.3%	16.4%	18.3%
Los Angeles	6.4%	8.2%	21.2%	25.6%	12.8%	12.6%	19.5%	22.0%
Chicago	4.2%	5.7%	26.1%	32.1%	8.6%	9.0%	19.2%	23.4%
Miami	7.0%	9.6%	27.7%	33.7%	14.3%	14.2%	15.8%	18.6%
New York	6.9%	9.1%	25.7%	30.8%	12.3%	13.1%	31.3%	38.2%
Riverside	7.7%	10.0%	15.0%	21.5%	14.8%	15.1%	16.1%	20.0%

1990

Metro Area	Non-Hispanic Whites		Non-Hispanic Blacks		Asians		Hispanics	
	Males	Females	Males	Females	Males	Females	Males	Females
Houston	5.6%	7.3%	25.6%	31.1%	13.0%	12.8%	24.5%	27.9%
Los Angeles	5.7%	7.0%	19.0%	22.4%	12.2%	12.9%	21.7%	24.7%
Chicago	3.9%	5.4%	26.7%	31.5%	9.4%	9.3%	18.1%	22.2%
Miami	7.0%	8.5%	27.2%	33.4%	9.9%	8.7%	18.2%	21.6%
New York	6.7%	8.6%	20.2%	24.1%	14.2%	14.8%	27.4%	34.9%
Riverside	6.6%	9.1%	17.2%	23.3%	15.1%	15.4%	18.5%	20.8%

2000

Metro Area	Non-Hispanic Whites		Non-Hispanic Blacks		Asians		Hispanics	
	Males	Females	Males	Females	Males	Females	Males	Females
Houston	5.4%	6.9%	20.7%	22.9%	10.8%	11.6%	21.1%	23.7%
Los Angeles	7.9%	9.0%	23.7%	26.3%	12.8%	13.3%	23.2%	26.2%
Chicago	3.8%	4.8%	22.5%	25.6%	8.5%	8.9%	15.9%	17.5%
Miami	9.0%	10.2%	26.4%	30.7%	14.2%	15.9%	16.1%	19.2%
New York	9.5%	10.8%	22.3%	25.2%	17.3%	18.2%	27.1%	32.6%
Riverside	8.3%	10.5%	19.9%	24.2%	13.6%	15.3%	20.2%	22.7%

2005

Metro Area	Non-Hispanic Whites		Non-Hispanic Blacks		Asians		Hispanics	
	Males	Females	Males	Females	Males	Females	Males	Females
Houston	5.5%	7.2%	22.1%	25.1%	9.8%	10.9%	22.3%	26.7%
Los Angeles	6.1%	7.2%	17.7%	20.7%	10.5%	11.2%	19.4%	22.4%
Chicago	3.9%	5.0%	24.3%	27.6%	6.0%	7.3%	14.0%	17.3%
Miami	7.4%	10.1%	24.3%	29.2%	16.7%	12.9%	12.4%	17.2%
New York	8.6%	10.0%	18.3%	21.5%	15.1%	16.5%	23.6%	30.1%
Riverside	6.8%	7.9%	17.6%	19.8%	9.5%	11.0%	14.3%	17.4%

TABLE 5.27. *Percentage of Children Aged 1–14 Living at or below the Poverty Line by Race/Ethnicity by Metro Area, 1980–2005*

1980

Metro Area	Non-Hispanic Whites	Non-Hispanic Blacks	Asians	Hispanics
Houston	5.6%	28.7%	17.9%	21.2%
Los Angeles	10.4%	33.6%	15.8%	27.1%
Chicago	6.2%	41.0%	9.2%	27.1%
Miami	9.2%	39.2%	19.8%	22.2%
New York	11.8%	40.8%	14.0%	48.9%
Riverside	13.5%	27.1%	18.5%	22.9%

1990

Metro Area	Non-Hispanic Whites	Non-Hispanic Blacks	Asians	Hispanics
Houston	7.7%	39.0%	14.5%	32.7%
Los Angeles	8.2%	32.8%	15.9%	30.1%
Chicago	5.7%	44.5%	8.6%	26.7%
Miami	10.6%	42.1%	5.8%	26.6%
New York	11.7%	33.4%	16.0%	44.7%
Riverside	11.1%	30.3%	20.1%	24.4%

2000

Metro Area	Non-Hispanic Whites	Non-Hispanic Blacks	Asians	Hispanics
Houston	6.8%	29.5%	12.7%	28.0%
Los Angeles	10.4%	37.0%	15.4%	32.2%
Chicago	4.5%	34.6%	9.9%	21.0%
Miami	12.5%	38.8%	17.2%	21.8%
New York	15.0%	33.2%	21.4%	39.5%
Riverside	13.0%	32.1%	17.3%	27.8%

2005

Metro Area	Non-Hispanic Whites	Non-Hispanic Blacks	Asians	Hispanics
Houston	8.7%	35.5%	12.3%	33.1%
Los Angeles	6.6%	30.0%	12.3%	29.2%
Chicago	4.1%	38.1%	4.9%	20.1%
Miami	8.7%	37.7%	14.3%	16.7%
New York	13.4%	28.9%	18.8%	36.6%
Riverside	9.0%	26.9%	8.7%	21.3%

TABLE 5.28. *Poverty Rates among Mexicans in Chicago, Houston,*
Los Angeles, Riverside, and New York, 1980–2005

Metro Area	1980			1990		
	Males	Females	Total	Males	Females	Total
Chicago	17.4%	20.6%	18.9%	16.7%	20.0%	18.2%
Houston	16.9%	18.7%	17.7%	24.8%	28.2%	26.4%
Los Angeles	20.3%	22.7%	21.5%	21.7%	24.4%	23.0%
Riverside	16.3%	20.1%	18.2%	18.7%	21.3%	20.0%
New York	26.0%	29.0%	27.5%	20.1%	25.8%	22.5%

Metro Area	2000			2005		
	Males	Females	Total	Males	Females	Total
Chicago	16.0%	17.3%	16.6%	14.1%	17.5%	15.8%
Houston	21.5%	24.0%	22.7%	23.3%	28.0%	25.7%
Los Angeles	23.6%	26.6%	25.1%	19.7%	23.0%	21.3%
Riverside	20.6%	23.1%	21.8%	14.6%	17.9%	16.2%
New York	29.1%	34.1%	31.2%	25.9%	34.8%	30.0%

had risen to become New York's third largest Latino national group by 2005. With the exception of Riverside, where there was a marginal decline from 18% to 16% between 1980 and 2005, poverty rates among Mexicans in these metropolitan areas showed no significant improvements, and in fact there were greater percentages of Mexicans living below the poverty line in Houston and New York in 2005 than in 1980. Mexican females had significantly higher rates of poverty than males. (See Table 5.28.)

The poverty rate among Mexican children ages 14 years of age and younger did not improve significantly in any of the metro areas, remained about the same, or in the case of Houston worsened considerably from 22% in 1980 to 34% in 2005. New York had the highest percentage of Mexican children living in poverty: 40% in both 1980 and 2005. In Los Angeles 30% of Mexican children lived in poverty in 2005 compared with 21% in neighboring Riverside. Finally, in Chicago 20% of Mexican children lived below the poverty line. (See Table 5.29.)

Miami Cubans had significantly lower poverty rates than Mexicans in the five metro areas considered previously, and there were no great changes in these rates between 1980 and 2005 despite the demographic impact of the 125,000 or so Cubans who left the island to settle in South Florida between April and October 1980 in the Mariel boatlift. There was

TABLE 5.29. *Percentage of Mexican Children Aged 1–14 Living at or below the Poverty Line in Chicago, Houston, Los Angeles, Riverside, and New York Metro Areas, 1980–2005*

Metro Area	1980	1990	2000	2005
Chicago	23.5%	24.2%	20.8%	20.4%
Houston	21.6%	33.2%	28.3%	34.4%
Los Angeles	28.1%	29.9%	32.4%	29.7%
Riverside	23.1%	24.6%	28.0%	21.3%
New York	40.4%	32.6%	39.3%	40.2%

a very small increase in those living in poverty between 1980 and 1990; however, the percentage of Miami Cubans living below the poverty line in 1980 did not change in 2005. Childhood poverty declined somewhat from 16% in 1980 to 13% in 2005. (See Table 5.30.)

Among the New York metropolitan area's Latino nationalities, only Puerto Ricans and Ecuadorians experienced significant decreases in poverty rates between 1980 and 2005, although despite this Puerto Ricans continued to have one of the highest poverty rates in the region. An extraordinary 42% of all Puerto Ricans lived in poverty in 1980 and among Puerto Rican children 14 years of age and younger the rate was an astounding 56%. By 2005 the Puerto Rican overall poverty rate had declined to 30%, and the percentage of Puerto Rican children living in poverty had dropped to 39%, still extraordinarily high. The Ecuadorian poverty rate fell from 21% in 1980 to 17% in 2005, and Ecuadorian children living in poverty decreased from 30% to 25% over the same period.

Dominicans experienced no significant decline in the poverty rate in the New York metro area from 1980 (36%) to 2005 (33%) and by 2005 had the greatest percentage of the total population living in poverty among the New York Latino nationalities. Dominicans also had the highest rate of children living in poverty in 2005 at 44% compared with a 53% rate

TABLE 5.30. *Poverty Rates among Cubans in Miami, 1980–2005*

	1980	1990	2000	2005
Males	13.1%	14.2%	14.5%	12.3%
Females	16.1%	17.5%	17.4%	16.8%
TOTAL	14.7%	15.9%	16.0%	14.7%
Children Ages 14 and Younger	16.4%	18.6%	17.2%	13.4%

in 1980. Although this was an improvement to some extent, Dominican children in the New York metropolitan area were among the nation's poorest.

With the large-scale Mexican migration to the New York region, especially after 1990, there was an increase in the overall poverty rate from 28% in 1980 to 30% in 2005, while among Mexican children 14 years of age and younger the poverty rate remained exactly the same at 40% in both 1980 and 2005.

Colombians, who were at the lower end of the Latino nationalities living in poverty, experienced a slight increase in the overall poverty rate from 14% to 17% between 1980 and 2005. There was a small decline in the percentage of Colombian children living in poverty from 19% in 1980 to 17% in 2005. (See Table 5.31.)

We now turn to how income was distributed in the major metropolitan areas of Latino population concentration. By a significant margin the New York metropolitan area had the highest percentage of Latino-headed households earning less than $20,000 annually. There was a marked decline from 1980 when 42% of all Latino-headed households in New York were in this lower income bracket, to 2005 when the corresponding figure was 34%. However, this latter figure was well above the 25% of Latino households in Miami, 23% in Houston, 21% in Los Angeles, 16% in Chicago, and 15% found in Riverside at the lower end of the income-earning hierarchy. The disparities in the percentage of households found earning less than $20,000 between urbanized Los Angeles (21%) and sub-urbanized Riverside (15%) ought to the noted. Additionally, New York Latino-headed households had a higher percentage in the lowest income category in 2005 (34%) compared with non-Hispanic blacks (29%), non-Hispanic whites (15%), and Asians (16%). In every other metropolitan area, Latino-headed households had lower percentages in the less than $20,000 income category than non-Hispanic blacks, although they were consistently above non-Hispanic whites and Asians. (See Table 5.32.)

With the exception of Houston, there were significant increases in the percentages of Latino households earning more than $75,000 yearly between 1980 and 2005 in the other five metropolitan areas. This suggests that while there was enduring poverty in all of the metro areas considered here by examining income distribution, and previously through using the poverty index developed by the Census Bureau, there were clearly opportunities for upward social mobility among Latino households. In Los Angeles 11% of Latino-headed households earned $75,000 or more in 1980, and there were 21% in 2005. In Chicago the corresponding

TABLE 5.31. *Poverty Rates among Latino Nationalities in New York, 1980–2005*

Nationality	1980				1990			
	Males	Females	Total	Children Ages 14 and Younger	Males	Females	Total	Children Ages 14 and Younger
Puerto Ricans	37.8%	45.5%	42.0%	55.9%	32.7%	40.9%	37.1%	51.0%
Dominicans	32.0%	38.9%	35.8%	52.5%	32.7%	41.2%	37.3%	50.5%
Mexicans	26.0%	29.0%	27.5%	40.4%	20.1%	25.8%	23.1%	32.6%
Ecuadorians	20.2%	22.5%	21.4%	30.2%	17.6%	23.2%	20.5%	32.4%
Colombians	11.9%	16.0%	14.1%	18.7%	12.8%	18.4%	15.7%	19.4%

Nationality	2000				2005			
	Males	Females	Total	Children Ages 14 and Younger	Males	Females	Total	Children Ages 14 and Younger
Puerto Ricans	30.4%	37.0%	34.0%	44.0%	26.7%	33.4%	30.4%	38.6%
Dominicans	29.7%	35.0%	32.6%	42.4%	28.7%	36.4%	33.1%	44.1%
Mexicans	29.1%	34.1%	31.2%	39.3%	25.9%	34.8%	30.0%	40.2%
Ecuadorians	19.2%	24.4%	21.7%	27.2%	14.7%	19.1%	16.9%	24.9%
Colombians	17.5%	21.9%	19.9%	24.3%	14.6%	18.9%	17.1%	22.2%

TABLE 5.32. *Household Income Distribution Structure by Metropolitan Area by Race/Ethnicity, 1980–2005 (in percentages of total households in 2005 dollars adjusted for inflation)*

Non-Hispanic Whites

1980

Income Category	Houston	Los Angeles	Chicago	Miami	New York	Riverside
Less than 20,000	11.9%	19.2%	14.2%	23.4%	21.8%	21.2%
20,000–39,999	19.8%	23.0%	19.8%	24.6%	22.9%	24.6%
40,000–74,999	36.9%	31.8%	36.5%	29.8%	31.6%	35.1%
75,000+	31.4%	26.1%	29.5%	22.3%	23.7%	19.1%
TOTAL	100.0%	100.0%	100.0%	100.0%	100.0%	100.0%

1990

Income Category	Houston	Los Angeles	Chicago	Miami	New York	Riverside
Less than 20,000	12.4%	13.0%	11.9%	17.6%	16.6%	16.0%
20,000–39,999	19.2%	16.9%	17.9%	20.3%	16.9%	21.0%
40,000–74,999	32.0%	29.1%	32.8%	28.3%	27.7%	32.8%
75,000+	36.4%	41.0%	37.3%	33.8%	38.8%	30.2%
TOTAL	100.0%	100.0%	100.0%	100.0%	100.0%	100.0%

2000

Income Category	Houston	Los Angeles	Chicago	Miami	New York	Riverside
Less than 20,000	10.9%	14.2%	9.7%	15.6%	16.1%	16.5%
20,000–39,999	17.9%	17.7%	16.0%	19.7%	16.7%	21.9%
40,000–74,999	28.9%	26.2%	29.0%	27.2%	25.2%	29.3%
75,000+	42.4%	41.9%	45.2%	37.5%	42.1%	32.4%
TOTAL	100.0%	100.0%	100.0%	100.0%	100.0%	100.0%

2005

Income Category	Houston	Los Angeles	Chicago	Miami	New York	Riverside
Less than 20,000	11.7%	13.6%	10.8%	16.4%	15.4%	15.6%
20,000–39,999	15.9%	16.4%	16.1%	18.6%	16.0%	19.6%
40,000–74,999	26.6%	26.0%	27.5%	24.5%	24.1%	27.7%
75,000+	45.8%	44.0%	45.7%	40.6%	44.5%	37.1%
TOTAL	100.0%	100.0%	100.0%	100.0%	100.0%	100.0%

Non-Hispanic Blacks

1980

Income Category	Houston	Los Angeles	Chicago	Miami	New York	Riverside
Less than 20,000	29.8%	33.6%	35.1%	37.4%	38.5%	27.5%
20,000–39,999	27.8%	28.3%	24.5%	29.3%	29.1%	29.2%
40,000–74,999	30.9%	26.3%	27.6%	25.1%	24.2%	30.1%
75,000+	11.5%	11.8%	12.7%	8.2%	8.2%	13.3%
TOTAL	100.0%	100.0%	100.0%	100.0%	100.0%	100.0%

1990

Income Category	Houston	Los Angeles	Chicago	Miami	New York	Riverside
Less than 20,000	33.8%	26.7%	32.2%	33.2%	27.3%	23.1%
20,000–39,999	27.0%	23.6%	22.9%	26.0%	23.4%	24.2%
40,000–74,999	26.8%	28.0%	28.0%	27.0%	27.7%	29.6%
75,000+	12.4%	21.7%	16.9%	13.7%	21.7%	23.2%
TOTAL	100.0%	100.0%	100.0%	100.0%	100.0%	100.0%

2000

Income Category	Houston	Los Angeles	Chicago	Miami	New York	Riverside
Less than 20,000	27.8%	29.0%	26.4%	30.5%	27.8%	24.8%
20,000–39,999	27.4%	23.9%	23.4%	28.0%	24.2%	23.8%
40,000–74,999	27.1%	26.0%	27.8%	26.8%	26.7%	27.5%
75,000+	17.8%	21.1%	22.4%	14.7%	21.3%	23.9%
TOTAL	100.0%	100.0%	100.0%	100.0%	100.0%	100.0%

2005

Income Category	Houston	Los Angeles	Chicago	Miami	New York	Riverside
Less than 20,000	30.5%	27.5%	30.0%	34.3%	28.5%	21.1%
20,000–39,999	25.8%	24.6%	23.9%	28.1%	22.8%	22.0%
40,000–74,999	27.0%	25.6%	26.3%	24.5%	26.5%	27.3%
75,000+	16.7%	22.3%	19.8%	13.0%	22.3%	29.6%
TOTAL	100.0%	100.0%	100.0%	100.0%	100.0%	100.0%

(continued)

179

TABLE 5.32 *(continued)*

Asians

	1980						1990					
Less than 20,000	15.9%	17.7%	11.6%	25.5%	20.3%	21.1%	14.9%	12.9%	12.5%	15.8%	15.6%	12.9%
20,000–39,999	18.6%	21.4%	18.4%	23.6%	27.3%	20.3%	19.4%	18.0%	16.1%	20.1%	20.9%	19.2%
40,000–74,999	35.7%	34.4%	38.9%	32.7%	31.0%	39.4%	32.1%	30.0%	32.2%	34.5%	29.8%	31.1%
75,000+	29.8%	26.5%	31.2%	18.2%	21.4%	19.1%	33.7%	39.1%	39.2%	29.6%	33.7%	36.8%
TOTAL	100.0%	100.0%	100.0%	100.0%	100.0%	100.0%	100.0%	100.0%	100.0%	100.0%	100.0%	100.0%

	2000						2005					
Less than 20,000	13.3%	16.0%	10.8%	18.1%	18.7%	14.6%	13.0%	16.2%	9.7%	12.5%	17.9%	11.7%
20,000–39,999	19.0%	19.0%	15.3%	22.7%	20.9%	16.6%	17.3%	17.8%	15.6%	23.1%	19.2%	18.5%
40,000–74,999	28.9%	28.1%	28.5%	27.8%	27.3%	30.1%	29.0%	27.1%	26.2%	34.6%	26.7%	28.7%
75,000+	38.7%	37.0%	45.4%	31.4%	33.2%	38.7%	40.7%	38.9%	48.5%	29.8%	36.3%	41.1%
TOTAL	100.0%	100.0%	100.0%	100.0%	100.0%	100.0%	100.0%	100.0%	100.0%	100.0%	100.0%	100.0%

Hispanics

	1980						1990					
Less than 20,000	19.4%	24.9%	22.9%	28.6%	42.1%	24.2%	24.2%	19.2%	18.5%	27.3%	33.2%	18.1%
20,000–39,999	29.1%	31.8%	27.8%	28.7%	30.0%	27.5%	32.1%	27.9%	27.0%	26.8%	24.2%	27.4%
40,000–74,999	36.8%	32.1%	35.1%	29.4%	21.7%	36.2%	30.2%	33.0%	36.1%	28.5%	27.3%	35.0%
75,000+	14.7%	11.2%	14.3%	13.4%	6.2%	12.1%	13.5%	20.0%	18.3%	17.4%	15.3%	19.5%
TOTAL	100.0%	100.0%	100.0%	100.0%	100.0%	100.0%	100.0%	100.0%	100.0%	100.0%	100.0%	100.0%

	2000						2005					
Less than 20,000	20.9%	22.4%	15.0%	25.7%	32.4%	19.3%	21.1%	23.3%	16.1%	24.5%	33.6%	15.2%
20,000–39,999	32.1%	29.6%	25.4%	26.8%	25.0%	28.2%	27.9%	31.8%	26.3%	25.0%	23.6%	26.3%
40,000–74,999	30.9%	29.1%	34.8%	27.3%	25.6%	32.3%	30.9%	29.0%	34.8%	28.3%	24.2%	33.6%
75,000+	16.1%	19.0%	24.8%	20.3%	17.0%	20.2%	20.0%	15.9%	22.8%	22.2%	18.6%	25.0%
TOTAL	100.0%	100.0%	100.0%	100.0%	100.0%	100.0%	100.0%	100.0%	100.0%	100.0%	100.0%	100.0%

figures were 14% in 1980 and 23% in 2005; in Miami 13% in 1980 and 22% in 2005; in Riverside 12% in 1980 to 25% in 2005; and even in New York, with its high poverty rates among Latinos, the percentage of higher-income-earning Latino households increased from 6% in 1980 to 18% in 2005. In Houston there was little change in the percentage of Latino households earning more than $75,000 annually from 1980 (15%) to 2005 (16%). (See Table 5.32.)

As the percentage of higher-income-earning Latinos increased from 1980 to 2005, there was a parallel process of greater wealth concentration in the households that earned more than $75,000 within every metropolitan area we have considered, although it was not as extreme as the concentration of wealth among non-Hispanic whites and Asians. In 2005 Miami metropolitan area Latino-headed households earning $75,000 or more accounted for 54% of all Latino household income, and this was a significant increase from the 35% found in 1980. Riverside's upper-earning Latino household heads earned only 28% of all income in 1980 and this soared to 51% in 2005. The New York metropolitan area's Latino-headed households in the more than $75,000 income category earned only 20% of total Latino household income in 1980 and this increased to 49% in 2005. In Chicago the corresponding percentages were 33% in 1980, 47% in 2005; in Los Angeles, 28% in 1980 and 47% in 2005. Houston's Latino upper-income bracket accounted for 41% of total Latino-headed household income in 2005, an increase from the 32% in 1980.

These data serve as important counterweights to the poverty data we have examined previously. While poverty rates did not erode significantly among Latino households in the metro areas we have examined between 1980 and 2005, there was a clear increase in both the numbers and relative percentages of Latino households earning more than $75,000 annually and in the portion of overall Latino income that they controlled. Thus, as was the case in each of the other major racial/ethnic groups in the United States, the process of social and economic stratification among Latinos between 1980 and 2005 was accompanied by enduring poverty at the bottom of the social hierarchy and the concentration of wealth at the top. (See Table 5.33.)[18]

---

[18] The concentration of wealth among Latino household was not nearly as extreme as among non-Hispanic whites where near 70% or greater of total household income was in the hands of $75,000+ income earners in 2005 in each of the metro areas considered here. A similar pattern of wealth concentration was found among Asian households. Latino household income concentration resembled that of non-Hispanic blacks rather than Asians or non-Hispanic whites.

TABLE 5.33. *Household Income Distribution Structure by Metropolitan Area by Race/Ethnicity, 1980–2005 (in percentages of total income in 2005 dollars adjusted for inflation)*

Non-Hispanic Whites

1980

Income Category	Houston	Los Angeles	Chicago	Miami	New York	Riverside
Less than 20,000	2.2%	4.1%	2.8%	5.2%	4.7%	5.3%
20,000–39,999	9.5%	12.0%	9.8%	13.9%	12.7%	14.7%
40,000–74,999	33.3%	31.4%	34.1%	31.6%	32.7%	39.6%
75,000+	55.1%	52.5%	53.4%	49.2%	49.9%	40.3%
TOTAL	100.0%	100.0%	100.0%	100.0%	100.0%	100.0%

1990

Income Category	Houston	Los Angeles	Chicago	Miami	New York	Riverside
Less than 20,000	2.0%	1.9%	2.0%	2.9%	2.4%	3.1%
20,000–39,999	8.1%	6.3%	7.4%	8.6%	6.4%	9.9%
40,000–74,999	24.9%	20.3%	25.4%	22.4%	19.9%	29.5%
75,000+	65.0%	71.5%	65.3%	66.1%	71.2%	57.5%
TOTAL	100.0%	100.0%	100.0%	100.0%	100.0%	100.0%

2000

Income Category	Houston	Los Angeles	Chicago	Miami	New York	Riverside
Less than 20,000	1.5%	1.8%	1.3%	2.1%	1.9%	3.0%
20,000–39,999	6.3%	5.8%	5.4%	6.6%	5.2%	9.6%
40,000–74,999	18.7%	16.2%	18.3%	17.3%	14.9%	24.3%
75,000+	73.5%	76.1%	75.0%	74.0%	77.9%	63.1%
TOTAL	100.0%	100.0%	100.0%	100.0%	100.0%	100.0%

2005

Income Category	Houston	Los Angeles	Chicago	Miami	New York	Riverside
Less than 20,000	1.5%	1.7%	1.4%	2.3%	1.8%	2.6%
20,000–39,999	5.3%	5.2%	5.3%	6.2%	4.7%	7.8%
40,000–74,999	16.6%	15.7%	17.1%	15.5%	13.8%	21.2%
75,000+	76.6%	77.4%	76.1%	76.1%	79.8%	68.4%
TOTAL	100.0%	100.0%	100.0%	100.0%	100.0%	100.0%

Non-Hispanic Blacks

1980

Income Category	Houston	Los Angeles	Chicago	Miami	New York	Riverside
Less than 20,000	7.8%	9.7%	9.1%	11.3%	11.9%	7.8%
20,000–39,999	20.8%	21.4%	18.4%	24.5%	24.9%	20.1%
40,000–74,999	42.9%	37.3%	39.2%	39.1%	38.8%	40.2%
75,000+	28.5%	31.6%	33.3%	25.1%	24.4%	31.9%
TOTAL	100.0%	100.0%	100.0%	100.0%	100.0%	100.0%

1990

Income Category	Houston	Los Angeles	Chicago	Miami	New York	Riverside
Less than 20,000	8.5%	5.7%	6.9%	8.3%	11.9%	7.8%
20,000–39,999	20.4%	13.7%	15.5%	18.9%	24.9%	20.1%
40,000–74,999	37.5%	30.7%	35.6%	36.8%	38.8%	40.2%
75,000+	33.7%	49.9%	41.9%	36.0%	24.4%	31.9%
TOTAL	100.0%	100.0%	100.0%	100.0%	100.0%	100.0%

2000

Income Category	Houston	Los Angeles	Chicago	Miami	New York	Riverside
Less than 20,000	6.2%	5.8%	5.0%	7.4%	5.1%	5.1%
20,000–39,999	17.1%	13.7%	13.4%	18.9%	14.1%	13.1%
40,000–74,999	31.9%	27.7%	29.6%	33.8%	28.8%	29.0%
75,000+	44.7%	52.8%	52.0%	39.9%	52.1%	52.8%
TOTAL	100.0%	100.0%	100.0%	100.0%	100.0%	100.0%

2005

Income Category	Houston	Los Angeles	Chicago	Miami	New York	Riverside
Less than 20,000	7.1%	5.6%	6.4%	9.6%	5.5%	4.0%
20,000–39,999	16.5%	13.6%	14.8%	20.7%	13.2%	11.0%
40,000–74,999	32.4%	27.0%	30.3%	33.9%	28.7%	26.2%
75,000+	44.0%	53.8%	48.5%	35.8%	52.6%	58.9%
TOTAL	100.0%	100.0%	100.0%	100.0%	100.0%	100.0%

Asians

	1980						1990					
Less than 20,000	3.0%	3.7%	1.9%	6.0%	4.6%	4.8%	2.4%	2.0%	1.7%	2.9%	2.6%	2.2%
20,000–39,999	9.5%	11.3%	8.8%	15.1%	15.8%	12.3%	8.6%	7.2%	6.5%	10.0%	9.1%	8.4%
40,000–74,999	34.2%	34.1%	34.9%	37.4%	33.2%	43.3%	26.3%	23.1%	24.1%	30.9%	24.3%	25.7%
75,000+	53.3%	50.9%	54.4%	41.5%	46.4%	39.5%	62.6%	67.7%	67.7%	56.1%	63.9%	63.8%
TOTAL	100.0%	100.0%	100.0%	100.0%	100.0%	100.0%	100.0%	100.0%	100.0%	100.0%	100.0%	100.0%

	2000						2005					
Less than 20,000	1.9%	2.4%	1.3%	3.1%	2.9%	2.2%	1.8%	2.5%	1.1%	1.7%	2.5%	1.7%
20,000–39,999	7.4%	7.5%	5.2%	10.2%	8.5%	6.4%	6.4%	6.7%	5.3%	9.8%	7.3%	7.4%
40,000–74,999	21.0%	21.0%	18.2%	23.4%	21.0%	22.1%	20.3%	19.3%	16.7%	27.1%	19.6%	21.7%
75,000+	69.8%	69.1%	75.3%	63.2%	67.7%	69.3%	71.5%	71.4%	76.9%	61.4%	70.6%	69.3%
TOTAL	100.0%	100.0%	100.0%	100.0%	100.0%	100.0%	100.0%	100.0%	100.0%	100.0%	100.0%	100.0%

Hispanics

	1980						1990					
Less than 20,000	4.8%	7.2%	5.4%	7.4%	14.2%	6.5%	6.4%	4.6%	4.0%	6.3%	7.7%	4.3%
20,000–39,999	18.9%	22.7%	18.6%	20.2%	28.2%	19.1%	21.5%	16.2%	16.2%	16.4%	16.9%	16.0%
40,000–74,999	43.8%	42.4%	43.3%	38.0%	37.4%	46.1%	37.6%	35.6%	39.7%	32.8%	35.3%	38.2%
75,000+	32.4%	27.7%	32.7%	34.5%	20.1%	28.3%	34.5%	43.7%	40.0%	44.5%	40.2%	41.5%
TOTAL	100.0%	100.0%	100.0%	100.0%	100.0%	100.0%	100.0%	100.0%	100.0%	100.0%	100.0%	100.0%

	2000						2005					
Less than 20,000	5.1%	5.3%	3.0%	5.4%	7.0%	4.5%	6.3%	5.0%	3.4%	5.0%	7.4%	3.2%
20,000–39,999	19.4%	17.2%	13.1%	14.7%	16.1%	16.1%	19.6%	15.7%	14.3%	13.1%	15.0%	13.6%
40,000–74,999	34.3%	31.5%	33.4%	28.1%	30.6%	34.3%	33.0%	32.7%	35.3%	27.7%	28.8%	32.5%
75,000+	41.2%	45.9%	50.5%	51.7%	46.3%	45.2%	41.1%	46.5%	47.0%	54.3%	48.8%	50.6%
TOTAL	100.0%	100.0%	100.0%	100.0%	100.0%	100.0%	100.0%	100.0%	100.0%	100.0%	100.0%	100.0%

Among Mexican households in the five metropolitan areas where they were either dominant demographically, or growing rapidly as was the case with New York, there were great disparities in how those households earning less than $20,000 changed quantitatively between 1980 and 2005. In suburban Riverside some 24% of Mexican-headed households earned less than $20,000 in 1980, and this declined to 16% by 2005. In more urbanized Los Angeles the decline among poorer Mexican households was not as significant. A quarter were in the lower-income category in 1980 and this declined only marginally to 21% in 2005, highlighting the differences we have already pointed out previously between inner city Mexican communities and their more suburbanized counterparts. Mexican-headed households in the Houston metropolitan area experienced an increase in families at the bottom of the income-earning hierarchy between 1980 (20%) and 2005 (23%). Chicago had the lowest portion of Mexican-headed households earning less than $20,000 in 2005 at 14%, which was a decrease from 20% in 1980. The New York metro area's Mexican-headed households had the highest percentage falling into the less than $20,000 income bracket in 2005, although this figure of a quarter of all Mexican headed households represented a decline from the 35% of 1980 when the New York Mexican community was still numerically very small. (See Table 5.34).

However, poverty was only one part of the Mexican household economic dynamic. There were fairly dramatic changes in higher income-earning Mexican-headed households. The most impressive was in Riverside where the percentage of households earning $75,000 or more increased sharply from 11% in 1980 to 24% in 2005. Thus, in the case of Riverside Mexicans, a much higher percentage of household heads were found at the highest income bracket than at the lowest (16%). A similar pattern was found in Chicago where Mexican-headed households in the $75,000 and more income category increased from 15% in 1980 to 21% in 2005. As was the case in Riverside, relatively more Mexican families earned over $75,000 than those earning under $20,000 (14%). There were also significant increases in higher income-earning Mexican households in Los Angeles (from 11% in 1980 to 20% in 2005) and in New York (from 10% in 1980 to 18% in 2005). Only in Houston was there relative stagnation between 1980 when 14% of Mexican households earned more than $75,000 compared with 15% in 2005. (See Table 5.34.) Thus, when examining the economic dynamics of Mexican households at the metropolitan level, it is important to move beyond

TABLE 5.34. *Mexican Household Income Distribution Structure by Metropolitan Area, 1980–2005 (in percentages in 2005 dollars adjusted for inflation)*

Percentage of Total Households

Income Category	1980					1990				
	Houston	Los Angeles	Chicago	New York	Riverside	Houston	Los Angeles	Chicago	New York	Riverside
Less than 20,000	19.7%	24.7%	19.9%	35.0%	24.0%	24.2%	18.4%	15.4%	17.8%	17.9%
20,000–39,999	29.5%	32.1%	27.7%	27.9%	27.7%	32.2%	27.4%	28.4%	24.6%	28.0%
40,000–74,999	37.1%	32.4%	37.6%	27.0%	37.0%	30.6%	33.8%	37.8%	35.6%	35.0%
75,000+	13.7%	10.8%	14.8%	10.1%	11.3%	13.0%	20.3%	18.4%	22.0%	19.1%
TOTAL	100.0%	100.0%	100.0%	100.0%	100.0%	100.0%	100.0%	100.0%	100.0%	100.0%

Income Category	2000					2005				
	Houston	Los Angeles	Chicago	New York	Riverside	Houston	Los Angeles	Chicago	New York	Riverside
Less than 20,000	20.9%	21.7%	13.5%	21.0%	19.4%	23.1%	20.8%	14.4%	24.5%	15.5%
20,000–39,999	32.0%	29.5%	26.1%	28.0%	28.4%	32.8%	27.7%	27.6%	31.0%	26.2%
40,000–74,999	31.5%	29.6%	35.7%	29.4%	32.6%	29.6%	31.7%	37.1%	26.4%	34.5%
75,000+	15.5%	19.2%	24.6%	21.5%	19.6%	14.6%	19.8%	20.9%	18.1%	23.8%
TOTAL	100.0%	100.0%	100.0%	100.0%	100.0%	100.0%	100.0%	100.0%	100.0%	100.0%

Percentage of Total Income

Income Category	1980					1990				
	Houston	Los Angeles	Chicago	New York	Riverside	Houston	Los Angeles	Chicago	New York	Riverside
Less than 20,000	5.0%	7.2%	4.7%	10.6%	6.5%	6.5%	4.4%	3.5%	3.9%	4.3%
20,000–39,999	19.7%	23.2%	18.1%	21.6%	19.4%	22.1%	15.8%	17.1%	13.6%	16.5%
40,000–74,999	45.2%	43.1%	45.1%	39.3%	47.3%	39.0%	36.2%	41.1%	36.0%	38.6%
75,000+	30.2%	26.5%	32.2%	28.5%	26.8%	32.4%	43.5%	38.2%	46.5%	40.6%
TOTAL	100.0%	100.0%	100.0%	100.0%	100.0%	100.0%	100.0%	100.0%	100.0%	100.0%

Income Category	2000					2005				
	Houston	Los Angeles	Chicago	New York	Riverside	Houston	Los Angeles	Chicago	New York	Riverside
Less than 20,000	5.3%	5.2%	2.8%	4.4%	4.5%	6.5%	5.0%	3.2%	5.7%	3.4%
20,000–39,999	19.8%	17.2%	13.5%	15.3%	16.3%	21.2%	15.7%	15.6%	18.0%	13.9%
40,000–74,999	35.9%	32.1%	34.3%	29.7%	34.9%	35.1%	33.7%	38.8%	29.0%	34.0%
75,000+	39.1%	45.5%	49.4%	50.6%	44.2%	37.2%	45.6%	42.4%	47.2%	48.7%
TOTAL	100.0%	100.0%	100.0%	100.0%	100.0%	100.0%	100.0%	100.0%	100.0%	100.0%

poverty data to consider the distribution of income. When this is examined, a more nuanced vision of Mexican communities emerges, underlining the theme we have continually emphasized: among Mexicans and other Latino national groups socioeconomic stratification was similar to the patterns found among the nation's other principal racial and ethnic groups.

The concentration of wealth among Mexican-headed households in the $75,000+ income bracket was most extreme in Los Angeles, Riverside, New York, and Chicago where more than 42% of household income accrued to these households in 2005. This was a significant increase from the 26% to 32% range found in 1980. Mexican-headed households in Houston had slightly lower income concentration patterns as 37% of total household income was earned by the upper income-earning category in 2005 compared with 30% in 1980. (See Table 5.34.)

Income distribution patterns among Cuban-headed households in Miami were somewhat different from those found among Mexicans in the five metro areas examined previously. There was absolutely no change in the percentage of poorer Cuban households as exactly 28% of household heads earned less than $20,000 in 1980, 1990, 2000, and 2005. These data correspond precisely to the poverty rates found in Miami among all Cubans over the same period when there was no change whatsoever between 1980 and 2005. In both years the poverty rate was 15% of Miami's total Cuban population. However, Cuban-headed households earning more than $75,000 increased steadily from 14% to 24% of all Cuban households from 1980 to 2005. Income concentration also accrued to these wealthier Cuban households who controlled 35% of total Cuban income in 1980 and 59% in 2005. This increase represents a much higher concentration of income than found among Mexican households in the other metro areas we have examined, where the most extreme concentration of income in the highest income bracket was in Riverside at 48%. (See Table 5.35.)

The economic stratification of Puerto Rican– and Dominican-headed households in the New York metropolitan area was the most extreme of any Latino subgroup in any of the metro areas we have examined. The percentage of households earning less than $20,000 was the highest among these national groups in all years, despite a slight decline between 1980 and 2005. Some 49% of Puerto Rican–headed households were in the lowest income bracket in 1980, and this had decreased to 41% by 2005. Among Dominicans, 43% of household heads earned less than $20,000 annually in 1980 and 38% in 2005. By way of comparison, 25%

TABLE 5.35. *Cuban Household Income Distribution Structure in the Miami Metro Area, 1980–2005*
(in percentages in 2005 dollars adjusted for inflation)

Income Category	1980		1990		2000		2005	
	% Income	% Households	% Income	% Households	% Income	% Households	% Income	% Households
Less than 20,000	7.0%	28.1%	6.2%	28.0%	5.7%	28.1%	5.4%	28.0%
20,000–39,999	19.5%	28.0%	14.6%	24.7%	13.4%	24.7%	11.6%	22.6%
40,000–74,999	38.2%	30.0%	31.2%	28.0%	26.2%	25.7%	24.5%	25.2%
75,000+	35.3%	14.0%	48.1%	19.3%	54.7%	21.5%	58.5%	24.2%
TOTAL	100.0%	100.0%	100.0%	100.0%	100.0%	100.0%	100.0%	100.0%

of Mexican households, 21% of Ecuadorian households, and 21% of Colombian households were found in this lower income-earning category in 2005, all considerably lower than the rate among Puerto Ricans and Dominicans. (See Table 5.36.)

Yet, despite the enduring poverty suggested by these household income data and the poverty index data cited previously, there was a clear pattern of upward social mobility among sectors of the Puerto Rican and Dominican communities, which again underlines the process of social stratification experienced within both national groups. In 1980 only 4% of Puerto Rican households earned more than $75,000, and this steadily increased to 18% in 2005. Among Dominican households there were also only 4% found in the highest income bracket in 1980, and 12% in 2005. Although this was an improvement to be sure, New York metro area Dominicans had the lowest percentage of households in the upper income category compared with the other national groups. (See Table 5.36.)

Ecuadorian and Colombian households in the New York metro area did not experience major decreases in the percentages of families earning less than $20,000 between 1980 and 2005. Among Ecuadorians the decline was from 27% in 1980 to 21% in 2005, while among Colombians it was from 22% to 21%. Thus, poorer Ecuadorian and Colombian households continued at about one-fifth of the total. However, the increase in upper income-earning households was impressive. Only 8% of Ecuadorian-headed households earned more than $75,000 in 1980, and this soared to 22% in 2005. There was a similar rise in wealthier Colombian households. In 1980 9% of Colombian-headed households were found in the highest income bracket; 25% in 2005.[19]

Finally, as the percentage of higher income-earning sectors of each Latino subgroup in the New York metropolitan area increased, so did the concentration of income. The most exaggerated example was among Colombians. In 1980 22% of all income was concentrated in Colombian-headed households earning more than $75,000. This rose to 55% in 2005. In 1980 Ecuadorian-headed households in the highest income category earned 20% of the total income among Ecuadorian households; 50% in 2007. Among Mexican-headed households the corresponding percentages were 29% in 1980 and 47% in 2005. Within Dominican households 13% of income accrued to the $75,000+ category in 1980, 35% in 2005. The most extreme example of change in income concentration was among

[19] Mexican households in New York were considered previously.

TABLE 5.36. *Household Income Distribution Structure in the New York Metro Area, 1980–2005, Puerto Ricans, Dominicans, Mexicans, Ecuadorians, and Colombians (in percentages in 2005 dollars adjusted for inflation)*

Income Category	1980		1990		2000		2005	
	% Income	% Households	% Income	% Households	% Income	% Households	% Income	% Households
Puerto Ricans								
Less than 20,000	18.6%	49.2%	9.8%	40.1%	9.3%	39.9%	8.9%	40.6%
20,000–39,999	31.0%	28.7%	17.8%	22.6%	16.5%	22.8%	13.9%	20.2%
40,000–74,999	36.1%	18.3%	35.9%	24.6%	30.7%	22.5%	27.8%	21.5%
75,000+	14.3%	3.9%	36.5%	12.8%	43.6%	14.8%	49.4%	17.7%
TOTAL	100.0%	100.0%	100.0%	100.0%	100.0%	100.0%	100.0%	100.0%
Dominicans								
Less than 20,000	17.0%	43.2%	10.1%	37.0%	8.3%	34.1%	10.6%	38.1%
20,000–39,999	33.2%	33.0%	20.7%	26.1%	20.3%	28.3%	20.6%	26.7%
40,000–74,999	36.7%	19.9%	37.8%	25.8%	32.1%	24.6%	34.1%	23.1%
75,000+	13.2%	3.9%	31.4%	11.0%	39.3%	13.0%	34.6%	12.1%
TOTAL	100.0%	100.0%	100.0%	100.0%	100.0%	100.0%	100.0%	100.0%
Mexicans								
Less than 20,000	10.6%	35.0%	3.9%	17.8%	4.4%	21.0%	5.7%	24.5%
20,000–39,999	21.6%	27.9%	13.6%	24.6%	15.3%	28.0%	18.0%	31.0%
40,000–74,999	39.3%	27.0%	36.0%	35.6%	29.7%	29.4%	29.0%	26.4%
75,000+	28.5%	10.1%	46.5%	22.0%	50.6%	21.5%	47.2%	18.1%
TOTAL	100.0%	100.0%	100.0%	100.0%	100.0%	100.0%	100.0%	100.0%

(continued)

TABLE 5.36 (continued)

Income Category	1980		1990		2000		2005	
	% Income	% Households	% Income	% Households	% Income	% Households	% Income	% Households
Ecuadorians								
Less than 20,000	8.6%	27.4%	5.3%	22.9%	4.3%	19.8%	4.8%	20.7%
20,000–39,999	30.0%	36.2%	15.3%	25.1%	15.7%	26.9%	15.3%	27.8%
40,000–74,999	41.1%	28.7%	37.5%	33.1%	34.9%	32.5%	30.2%	29.0%
75,000+	20.2%	7.7%	41.9%	18.8%	45.1%	20.8%	49.7%	22.4%
TOTAL	100.0%	100.0%	100.0%	100.0%	100.0%	100.0%	100.0%	100.0%
Colombians								
Less than 20,000	7.1%	22.1%	4.4%	18.2%	4.1%	20.5%	4.2%	20.8%
20,000–39,999	28.8%	38.3%	16.5%	27.8%	13.4%	25.3%	12.5%	24.4%
40,000–74,999	41.8%	30.5%	36.4%	33.6%	30.8%	31.6%	28.1%	30.0%
75,000+	22.3%	9.1%	42.7%	20.3%	51.7%	22.7%	55.2%	24.7%
TOTAL	100.0%	100.0%	100.0%	100.0%	100.0%	100.0%	100.0%	100.0%

Puerto Rican households. The highest income bracket accounted for 14% of total income in 1980 and 49% in 2005. These data serve as an important counterweight to the exclusive image of poverty that has been unfortunately projected for New York Puerto Ricans and Dominicans.

Latinos across the nation exhibited distinctive economic performance patterns by nationality and geographical region; however, it is clear that the process of social and economic stratification was ongoing, although each nationality demonstrated different dynamics in the relative percentages found living in the extremes of wealth or poverty between 1980 and 2005. It is impossible to make sweeping generalizations about these processes among Latinos, and it is particularly difficult to consider impoverishment without analyzing the process of upward social mobility and the accumulation of wealth. Among each Latino national group, particular sectors remained mired in poverty to be sure. Others took advantage of opportunities to move ahead in their lives in the same way the previous generations of immigrants to the United States did. Latinos of all nationalities were dynamic and ambitious, and learned how to make the most of the ever-changing possibilities to improve themselves and their family's lives. Nowhere is this more evident than in the changing educational attainment patterns among Latinos, which are so closely tied to income-earning possibilities. These are examined in the following chapter.

6

Educational Attainment

We suggested in the last chapter how educational attainment levels are closely linked to household income and also to the possibilities of upward social mobility in the United States. While historically some immigrants arrived in the United States with levels of education which may have been greater than those found among long-standing domestic- or foreign-born residents, in general immigrants had lower educational attainment levels than found among the resident population.[1] At the same time most of

---

[1] There is a lively debate in the academic literature about the impact of the levels of education of arriving immigrants and subsequent social mobility of their children and grandchildren over many generations. Borjas has argued that there is a direct correlation between these two factors, which has a negative impact on mobility over the course of several generations: see George. J. Borjas, "Long-Run Convergence of Ethnic Skill Differentials: The Children and Grandchildren of the Great Migration," *Industrial and Labor Relations Review*, 47:4 (July 1994), 553–73. For a contrary position, see Richard Alba, Amy Lutz, and Elena Vesselinov, "How Enduring Were the Inequalities among European Immigrant Groups in the United States?" *Demography*, 38:3 (August 2001), 349–56. Also see the previously cited work of David Card on this issue. Borjas' immediate response to this critique was negative: see George J. Borjas, "Long-run Convergence of Ethnic Skill Differentials, Revisited," *Demography*, 38:3 (August 2001), 357–61. But in more recent work, Borjas has modified his position somewhat and shown that the impact of first-generation immigrant levels of wages and skills decline over the second and even more over the third generation, or as he put it "ethnic skill differentials have a half-life of one generation." Nevertheless he argues that the current post–World War II immigrant generation is different from previous ones and he expects there to be a more positive correlation for skill levels between first and second generation among Hispanics, and especially in Mexicans with its negative impact on mobility. He finds Hispanic immigrants unique because of their relative importance in the foreign-born population. But aside from incorrectly giving immigrant data on the 1920 census (the immigrants from the British Islands were the largest group, with Germans and not Italians second), he offers no systematic proof that the 30% Mexican representation among today's foreign-born

these immigrants, including those from Latin America and the Caribbean, tended to be better educated than the nonmigrating resident populations of their countries of origin.[2]

In this chapter we will examine educational attainment of all major racial/ethnic groups since 1980, with special attention to educational attainment levels among foreign- and domestic-born Latinos. As is standard for the U.S. Census Bureau, we have adopted the procedure of analyzing the educational attainment levels only for adults 25 years of age and older, that is; the majority of those who have completed their educations. We also will compare domestic-born Latinos to their immigrant parents and then examine different generations to see if change has occurred and how quickly.

When we compare the educational performance of Latinos in the United States between 1980 and 2005, it is striking that the Hispanic population has consistently had the lowest percentage of adult men and women who have completed a B.A. degree or higher, as well as the highest percentage who have not completed high school. This is despite the fact that there were clear improvements in educational attainment levels

---

in the United States influences mobility. See George J. Borjas, "Making It in America: Social Mobility in the Immigrant Population," NBER Working Paper No. 12088 (March 2006). Others have argued that labor market conditions in different localities had more of an impact on social mobility patterns than initial educational or skill levels. See for example the interesting study of Maria Ioannis Benis Baganha, "The Social Mobility of Portuguese Immigrants in the United States at the Turn of the Nineteenth Century," *International Migration Review*, 35:2 (1999), 277–99; and also Klein, "Integration of Italian Immigrants into Argentina and the United States," 306–29.

[2] Borjas has argued that this was not the case in countries that had relatively high wages paid to professional and skilled workers and great inequality, which thus meant that less-skilled would migrate and better-skilled people would stay at home, which, he implied, was the case for Mexico. As he noted: "if the income distribution in the sending country is more unequal than that of the United States (and the correlation in earnings is positive and strong [in the United States]), emigrants will be chosen from the lower tail of the income distribution in the country of origin." See George J. Borjas, "Self-Selection and the Earnings of Immigrants," *American Economic Review*, 77 (1987), 531–53. Recent work has challenged this assumption and shown that Mexican emigrants were in fact better educated than nonmigrating Mexicans. See Daniel Chiquiar and Gordon H. Hanson, "International Migration, Self-Selection, and the Distribution of Wages: Evidence from Mexico and the United States," *Journal of Political Economy*, 113:2 (2005), 239–81. Their findings are duplicated in Cynthia Feliciano, "Educational Selectivity in U.S. Immigration?" 131–52. An attempt to reconcile the two contrasting findings is found in the recent essay by David McKenziea and Hillel Rapoport, "Self-selection Patterns in Mexico-U.S. Migration: The Role of Migration Networks," World Bank, Policy, Research Working Paper No. WPS 4118 (August 2006), available at http:// econ.worldbank.org/external/default/main?pagePK=6.

over these 25 years. In 1980 about 8% of all Latino adults had achieved a B.A. degree or higher, and this increased by 2005 to nearly 14%. Over the same period non-Hispanic blacks experienced an increase from 8% to 18% of populations 25 years of age and older with B.A. degrees or greater. Among non-Hispanic whites the rise was from 17% in 1980 to 30% in 2005; and among Asians, who were the most educated of all the racial/ethnic groups in the United States, 33% of adults had a B.A. degree or higher in 1980 and an astounding 49% in 2005 (see Graph 6.1). There were only slight differences in educational attainment by sex among all Latinos by 2005 when 14% of adult females had completed a B.A. degree or higher compared with 13% of Latino males. Among African Americans, proportionally more women 25 years of age and older had completed college (19%) by 2005 compared with males (17%). Yet, non-Hispanic white males had higher college graduation rates (32%) than females (28%), and Asian males had a significantly higher proportion of those who had achieved a B.A. degree or higher (53%) than among Asian females (46%) in 2005.

Clearly Hispanics had advanced educationally during this quarter century. Whereas some 56% of all Latinos had not completed a high school degree in 1980, this figure stood at 39% in 2005. However, the percentage of Hispanics who had not graduated from high school was significantly greater than every other racial/ethnic group. Among non-Hispanic blacks 21% had not graduated from high school in 2005, down from 49% in 1980. For non-Hispanic white adults 31% had not finished high school in 1980, and this fell to 11% in 2005. Among Asians, 25% of adults were not high school graduates in 1980; 14% had not graduated from high school in 2005. (See Graph 6.2.)

This same pattern was evident among Hispanics with some college or who had achieved a B.A. degree or higher. There had been improvements between 1980 and 2005, but they were not as great as those found among the other Latino national sub-groups. The percentage of Hispanic adults having completed at least some college education, including having graduated with a degree, rose from a fifth of adults in 1980 to 36% in 2005. Yet, this rate lagged considerably behind each of the other racial/ethnic groups. Among non-Hispanic blacks 47% had at least some college education, and among non-Hispanic whites the rate was 58% in 2005. For Asians an extraordinary 70% had attended college or graduated. (See Table 6.1.)

But there were significant differences within the Latino population when we examine the different national subgroups. As with all our categories of analysis, some groups did better and others did far worse than

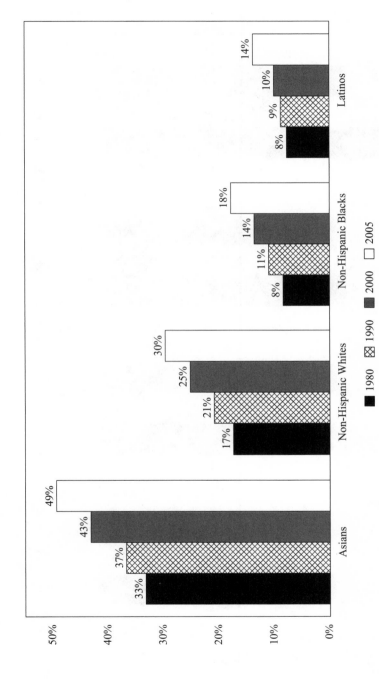

GRAPH 6.1. Percentage of Population 25 Years of Age and Older with an Educational Attainment Level of B.A. or Higher by Race/Ethnicity, 1980–2005.

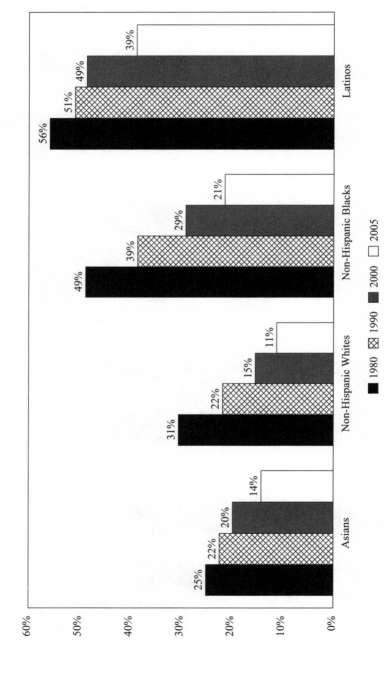

GRAPH 6.2. Percentage of Population 25 Years of Age and Older Not Graduating from High School by Race/Ethnicity, 1980–2005.

TABLE 6.1. *Educational Attainment by Race/Ethnicity, 1980–2005 (in percentages of total population ages 25 and older)*

1980

	Non-Hispanic Whites			Non-Hispanic Blacks			Hispanics			Asians		
	Males	Females	Total	Males	Females	Total	Males	Females	Total	Males	Females	Total
Did Not Graduate from High School	29.7%	31.1%	30.5%	49.3%	48.4%	48.8%	54.4%	57.4%	55.9%	21.1%	28.6%	25.1%
High School Graduate	32.1%	39.5%	36.0%	28.2%	30.1%	29.3%	22.6%	26.1%	24.4%	21.2%	27.6%	24.6%
Some College	16.4%	15.8%	16.1%	14.1%	13.2%	13.6%	13.6%	10.5%	11.9%	17.3%	16.8%	17.0%
Associates Degree	na	na	na	na	na	na	na	na	na	na	na	na
B.A. Degree or Higher	21.7%	13.6%	17.4%	8.4%	8.3%	8.4%	9.5%	6.0%	7.7%	40.4%	27.1%	33.3%
TOTAL	100.0%	100.0%	100.0%	100.0%	100.0%	100.0%	100.0%	100.0%	100.0%	100.0%	100.0%	100.0%

1990

	Non-Hispanic Whites			Non-Hispanic Blacks			Hispanics			Asians		
	Males	Females	Total	Males	Females	Total	Males	Females	Total	Males	Females	Total
Did Not Graduate from High School	21.4%	22.1%	21.8%	39.6%	37.9%	38.6%	51.1%	50.7%	50.9%	18.5%	25.9%	22.4%
High School Graduate	29.6%	34.7%	32.3%	28.1%	27.7%	27.8%	20.5%	22.6%	21.6%	16.6%	20.5%	18.7%
Some College	19.0%	18.6%	18.8%	17.2%	17.8%	17.6%	14.2%	13.7%	13.9%	15.1%	13.6%	14.3%
Associates Degree	5.8%	6.6%	6.2%	4.6%	5.4%	5.0%	4.6%	4.9%	4.8%	7.5%	7.9%	7.7%
B.A. Degree or Higher	24.2%	17.9%	20.9%	10.5%	11.3%	11.0%	9.6%	8.1%	8.8%	42.3%	32.0%	36.8%
TOTAL	100.0%	100.0%	100.0%	100.0%	100.0%	100.0%	100.0%	100.0%	100.0%	100.0%	100.0%	100.0%

(continued)

TABLE 6.1 (*continued*)

2000

	Non-Hispanic Whites			Non-Hispanic Blacks			Hispanics			Asians		
	Males	Females	Total	Males	Females	Total	Males	Females	Total	Males	Females	Total
Did Not Graduate from High School	15.5%	15.3%	15.4%	30.6%	27.9%	29.1%	50.3%	46.8%	48.6%	16.8%	22.3%	19.8%
High School Graduate	30.0%	32.4%	31.3%	31.5%	28.9%	30.1%	21.6%	22.4%	22.0%	14.8%	17.5%	16.3%
Some College	21.2%	21.9%	21.5%	20.5%	22.7%	21.7%	14.7%	15.9%	15.3%	14.8%	13.6%	14.2%
Associates Degree	6.0%	7.0%	6.6%	5.0%	6.0%	5.6%	3.8%	4.6%	4.2%	6.2%	7.1%	6.6%
B.A. Degree or Higher	27.2%	23.4%	25.2%	12.5%	14.5%	13.6%	9.7%	10.3%	10.0%	47.4%	39.5%	43.2%
TOTAL	100.0%	100.0%	100.0%	100.0%	100.0%	100.0%	100.0%	100.0%	100.0%	100.0%	100.0%	100.0%

2005

	Non-Hispanic Whites			Non-Hispanic Blacks			Hispanics			Asians		
	Males	Females	Total	Males	Females	Total	Males	Females	Total	Males	Females	Total
Did Not Graduate from High School	11.5%	10.9%	11.2%	22.1%	20.9%	21.4%	40.2%	37.5%	38.8%	11.4%	16.5%	14.2%
High School Graduate	29.4%	31.5%	30.5%	34.0%	30.3%	31.9%	26.1%	25.5%	25.8%	14.8%	17.3%	16.2%
Some College	20.7%	21.3%	21.0%	20.7%	22.7%	21.9%	15.4%	16.9%	16.2%	13.7%	12.3%	13.0%
Associates Degree	6.9%	8.2%	7.6%	6.4%	7.5%	7.0%	5.0%	5.9%	5.5%	6.7%	7.7%	7.2%
B.A. Degree or Higher	31.5%	28.0%	29.7%	16.8%	18.5%	17.8%	13.4%	14.2%	13.8%	53.2%	46.2%	49.4%
TOTAL	100.0%	100.0%	100.0%	100.0%	100.0%	100.0%	100.0%	100.0%	100.0%	100.0%	100.0%	100.0%

the average data indicate. We have noted that there were extraordinary overall improvements in the percentage of adults acquiring B.A. degrees or higher between 1980 and 2005 among most nationalities. But Salvadorans, Mexicans, and Hondurans lagged well behind the other Latino national subgroups and experienced only marginal advances in college graduation rates. In 1980 7% of Salvadoran adults had achieved a B.A. degree or higher rising only slightly to 9% in 2005. Among Mexicans the corresponding numbers were 5% in 1980, 10% in 2005. For Hondurans there was a small increase from 10% of adults acquiring B.A. degrees or greater in 1980 to 13% in 2005. Moreover, given the weight of Mexicans among Latinos, their lack of improvement in college graduation rates weighed heavily on the total Latino figures.

Among the smaller groups of Latino immigrants, the improvements in educational attainment were impressive. By 2005 the percentage of Colombian (34%) and Peruvian (31%) adults acquiring a B.A. or higher was greater than found among non-Hispanic whites (30%), and Cubans, at 27%, were not far behind. Dominicans, Puerto Ricans, and Ecuadorians experienced impressive increases in college graduation rates between 1980 and 2005 as well. Among Dominicans only 5% of adults had achieved a B.A. degree or higher in 1980 and this increased to 16% in 2005. This paralleled the educational attainment improvements experienced by Puerto Ricans who experienced a rise from 6% to 17% of adults 25 years of age or older who had graduated from college between 1980 and 2005. Among Ecuadorians who had completed college the increase was from 10% in 1980 to 22% in 2005. (See Graph 6.3.)

The percentage of adults who had not graduated from high school was the inverse of the college graduate rate. Among Mexicans, Hondurans, and Salvadorans, between 45% and 53% of all adults had not graduated from high school in 2005, and there had been little improvement since 1980. Only 12% of Peruvian adults and 16% of Colombians had not graduated from high school in 2005, and these rates were similar to Asians (14%) and non-Hispanic whites (11%). Among Cubans, Ecuadorians, and Puerto Ricans between 25% and 27% of all adults did not finish high school in 2005, and these data represent major decreases from 1980, especially among Puerto Ricans of whom 60% had not graduated from high school in that year. Dominicans had a higher rate of non–high school graduates in 2005, 37%, but this was also an extraordinary decline from the 69% of Dominicans older than 25 years of age without a high school diploma in 1980. (See Graph 6.4.) The detailed breakdown of these graduation and educational attainment rates among Latino nationalities between 1980 and 2005 is found in Table 6.2.

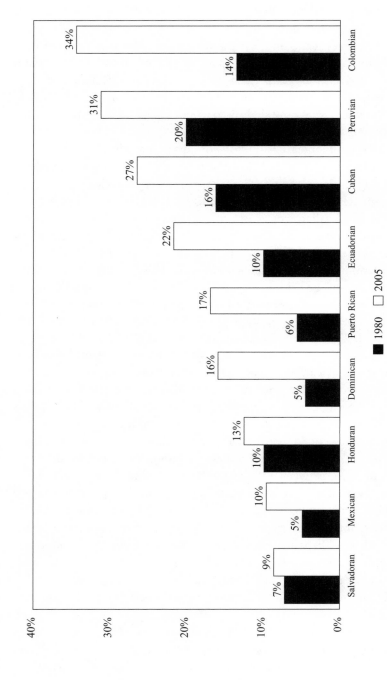

GRAPH 6.3. Percentage of Population 25 Years of Age and Older with an Educational Attainment Level of B.A. or Higher by Latino Nationality, 1980 and 2005.

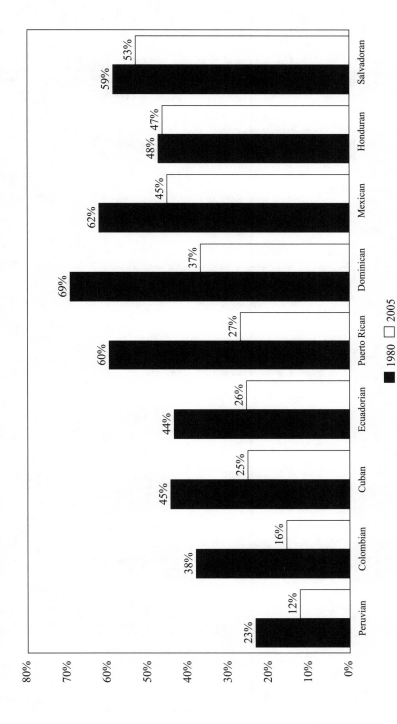

GRAPH 6.4. Percentage of Population 25 Years of Age and Older Not Graduating from High School by Latino Nationality, 1980 and 2005.

TABLE 6.2. *Educational Attainment by Latino Nationality, 1980–2005 (in percentages of total population 25 years of age and older)*

		1980					1990				
Nationality	Sex	Did Not Graduate from High School	High School Graduate	Some College	Associates Degree	B.A. Degree or Higher	Did Not Graduate from High School	High School Graduate	Some College	Associates Degree	B.A. Degree or Higher
Mexican	Males	60.8%	20.8%	12.2%	na	6.2%	57.2%	19.4%	12.9%	4.0%	6.4%
	Females	63.6%	24.0%	8.7%	na	3.6%	56.4%	21.6%	12.5%	4.1%	5.4%
	TOTAL	62.2%	22.4%	10.5%	na	4.9%	56.8%	20.5%	12.7%	4.1%	5.9%
Puerto Rican	Males	58.5%	23.8%	11.2%	na	6.6%	45.7%	24.7%	15.3%	4.5%	9.7%
	Females	60.8%	25.2%	9.2%	na	4.7%	45.5%	24.6%	14.9%	5.2%	9.8%
	TOTAL	59.7%	24.6%	10.1%	na	5.6%	45.6%	24.7%	15.1%	4.9%	9.8%
Cuban	Males	41.9%	23.0%	15.3%	na	19.8%	43.5%	17.8%	15.1%	5.8%	17.8%
	Females	46.8%	27.3%	12.8%	na	13.2%	45.2%	20.4%	13.4%	6.6%	14.4%
	TOTAL	44.5%	25.3%	13.9%	na	16.2%	44.4%	19.2%	14.2%	6.2%	16.0%
Honduran	Males	45.0%	25.6%	17.4%	na	11.9%	51.5%	19.0%	14.9%	5.0%	9.6%
	Females	49.1%	27.9%	14.5%	na	8.5%	50.0%	22.1%	13.5%	6.7%	7.6%
	TOTAL	47.5%	27.0%	15.7%	na	9.9%	50.6%	20.9%	14.0%	6.0%	8.4%
Salvadoran	Males	53.7%	21.1%	15.7%	na	9.5%	64.8%	16.2%	9.7%	4.1%	5.3%
	Females	62.2%	21.2%	11.1%	na	5.5%	67.5%	16.2%	8.2%	3.9%	4.3%
	TOTAL	58.7%	21.2%	13.0%	na	7.2%	66.2%	16.2%	8.9%	4.0%	4.7%
Colombian	Males	32.5%	27.8%	20.9%	na	18.8%	30.2%	25.2%	17.5%	7.2%	19.9%
	Females	42.9%	31.3%	16.6%	na	9.2%	35.7%	27.4%	16.2%	7.4%	13.2%
	TOTAL	38.2%	29.7%	18.6%	na	13.5%	33.2%	26.5%	16.8%	7.3%	16.2%
Ecuadorian	Males	40.4%	26.1%	19.1%	na	14.4%	37.0%	24.1%	18.4%	6.2%	14.4%
	Females	46.5%	33.5%	13.9%	na	6.1%	38.4%	26.7%	16.6%	7.4%	10.9%
	TOTAL	43.6%	30.0%	16.3%	na	10.0%	37.7%	25.5%	17.4%	6.8%	12.5%
Peruvian	Males	19.0%	30.5%	25.6%	na	24.9%	19.6%	24.9%	23.6%	7.3%	24.6%
	Females	27.5%	37.1%	19.9%	na	15.5%	23.6%	30.0%	20.7%	9.1%	16.6%
	TOTAL	23.4%	33.9%	22.7%	na	20.1%	21.7%	27.5%	22.1%	8.3%	20.5%
Dominican	Males	66.1%	19.3%	8.8%	na	5.7%	53.5%	19.5%	13.1%	4.5%	9.3%
	Females	71.7%	18.0%	6.7%	na	3.6%	58.0%	19.3%	10.9%	4.7%	7.2%
	TOTAL	69.4%	18.6%	7.6%	na	4.5%	56.0%	19.4%	11.8%	4.6%	8.1%

Nationality	Sex	Did Not Graduate from High School	High School Graduate	Some College	Associates Degree	B.A. Degree or Higher	Did Not Graduate from High School	High School Graduate	Some College	Associates Degree	B.A. Degree or Higher
Mexican	Males	56.5%	20.5%	13.1%	3.2%	6.7%	46.8%	26.0%	13.9%	4.2%	9.1%
	Females	53.2%	21.3%	14.5%	3.7%	7.3%	43.9%	25.5%	15.8%	4.8%	10.1%
	TOTAL	54.9%	20.9%	13.8%	3.5%	6.9%	45.3%	25.7%	14.8%	4.5%	9.6%
Puerto Rican	Males	38.7%	26.8%	18.0%	4.9%	11.5%	27.5%	30.4%	19.7%	6.6%	15.7%
	Females	36.0%	25.3%	19.2%	6.6%	12.9%	26.8%	26.9%	20.4%	8.2%	17.9%
	TOTAL	37.3%	26.0%	18.6%	5.8%	12.3%	27.1%	28.5%	20.1%	7.4%	16.9%
Cuban	Males	37.6%	20.2%	16.0%	5.1%	21.2%	25.8%	23.2%	16.8%	6.8%	27.4%
	Females	37.6%	20.0%	15.9%	6.1%	20.4%	24.9%	24.0%	17.2%	8.2%	25.7%
	TOTAL	37.6%	20.1%	15.9%	5.6%	20.8%	25.3%	23.7%	17.0%	7.5%	26.5%
Honduran	Males	59.5%	18.5%	10.8%	2.8%	8.4%	50.5%	23.8%	10.0%	4.1%	11.6%
	Females	51.7%	22.1%	12.8%	4.2%	9.2%	43.1%	25.2%	13.2%	5.3%	13.2%
	TOTAL	55.4%	20.4%	11.9%	3.5%	8.8%	46.5%	24.6%	11.7%	4.7%	12.5%
Salvadoran	Males	64.2%	17.3%	10.7%	2.6%	5.2%	52.5%	22.8%	12.5%	3.1%	9.1%
	Females	64.3%	17.7%	10.2%	2.5%	5.2%	53.8%	22.7%	10.8%	4.6%	8.1%
	TOTAL	64.2%	17.5%	10.4%	2.5%	5.2%	53.1%	22.7%	11.7%	3.9%	8.6%
Colombian	Males	25.0%	23.8%	20.5%	6.4%	24.3%	13.8%	23.4%	19.8%	6.8%	36.3%
	Females	28.5%	25.3%	18.1%	6.7%	21.4%	17.1%	23.7%	16.7%	9.5%	32.9%
	TOTAL	27.0%	24.6%	19.2%	6.6%	22.6%	15.7%	23.6%	18.1%	8.4%	34.4%
Ecuadorian	Males	37.4%	23.7%	19.6%	5.1%	14.2%	27.2%	26.0%	19.3%	7.3%	20.2%
	Females	34.6%	25.0%	19.4%	5.9%	15.0%	24.1%	24.5%	19.6%	8.6%	23.2%
	TOTAL	36.0%	24.4%	19.5%	5.5%	14.6%	25.6%	25.2%	19.4%	8.0%	21.7%
Peruvian	Males	18.6%	26.2%	24.2%	5.7%	25.3%	11.7%	25.4%	22.5%	6.9%	33.5%
	Females	19.9%	27.8%	22.5%	7.6%	22.2%	12.9%	26.0%	21.8%	10.0%	29.2%
	TOTAL	19.3%	27.0%	23.3%	6.7%	23.7%	12.4%	25.7%	22.1%	8.6%	31.2%
Dominican	Males	50.8%	20.6%	14.7%	3.6%	10.3%	35.7%	26.0%	15.9%	6.1%	16.3%
	Females	48.9%	20.3%	15.0%	5.5%	10.3%	37.8%	22.7%	17.3%	6.5%	15.6%
	TOTAL	49.7%	20.4%	14.9%	4.7%	10.3%	37.0%	24.0%	16.8%	6.3%	15.9%

Not only were there significant differences among Latino national subgroups, but there were also disparities by generation, which may be measured by considering educational attainment levels by nativity. This is brought into focus because of the extraordinary increases in the percentage of domestic-born Latinos who had achieved a B.A. degree or higher between 1980 and 2005. But first let us examine foreign-born Latinos as a strategy of highlighting how significant the advances in educational attainment were among those Latinos born in the United States.

Educational performance varied significantly by nationality. Among the dominant Mexican community there was only marginal change in the percentage of the foreign-born who had achieved a B.A. degree or higher after 1980. In 1980 some 3% of foreign-born Mexican adults had graduated from college, and by 2005 this stood at 6%. Although many foreign-born Mexicans who had been in the United States for some time went on to improve their educational attainment levels, the constant arrival of Mexican immigrants who did not have the requisite time frame to enroll in high schools or college meant that the overall percentage of college graduates among the foreign-born did not improve significantly. This was also the case with Hondurans and Salvadorans. In 1980 9% of foreign-born Honduran adults had graduated college and this rose to only 11% by 2005. Among Salvadorans there was almost no change as well. About 7% of the foreign-born had achieved a B.A. degree or higher in 1980 and only 8% had done so in 2005. (See Graph 6.5.)

Within the Latino nationalities there was a divergent pattern in educational attainment levels for the foreign-born. National subgroups that experienced ongoing large-scale migration, such as Mexicans, Hondurans, and Salvadorans, did not experience significant improvements in the percentage of college graduates.[3] However, nationalities whose overall

---

[3] There is a debate about whether the education gap between immigrants and the domestic-born has narrowed or grown over time. The deterioration of foreign-born Mexican educational levels compared to U.S.-born Mexicans over time is taken by Zadia M. Feliciano, "The Skill and Economic Performance of Mexican Immigrants," 386–409. This has led to some studies showing declining mobility and wages from the immigrant generation to the second and third generations. See Livingston and Kahn, "An American Dream Unfulfilled," 1003–12. Others have argued that within-group variations are in fact stronger than comparative mobility across groups. See Leslie Mccall, "Explaining Levels of Within-Group Wage Inequality in U.S. Labor Markets," *Demography*, 37:4 (2000), 415–30. Still others have rejected these findings altogether and using different sources have shown that mobility between generations was higher for Mexicans than for other groups in U.S. society. See Nguyenn, Hailenn, and Taylor, "Ethnic and Gender Differences in Intergenerational Mobility," 544–64.

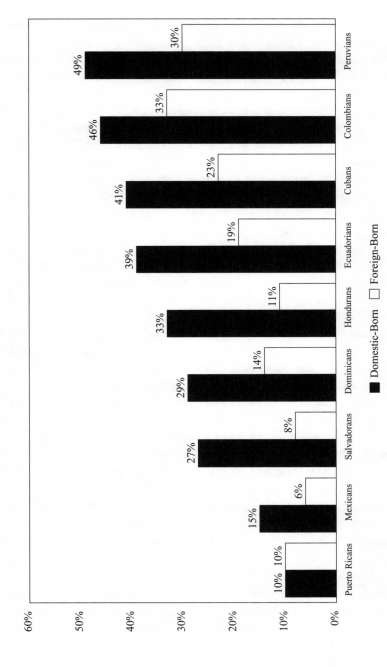

GRAPH 6.5. Percentage of Population 25 Years of Age and Older with an Educational Attainment Level of B.A. or Higher by Selected Latino Nationality and Domestic- or Foreign-Born, 2005.

numbers were not impacted by large numbers of migrants after 1980 experienced marked advances in college graduation rates. This was the case with foreign-born Cubans, Colombians, Ecuadorians, and Peruvians above all. Each of these national subgroups experienced significantly rising educational attainment levels among the foreign-born between 1980 and 2005. Among foreign-born Cuban adults 16% of the foreign-born had achieved a B.A. degree or higher in 1980, while 23% had graduated from college in 2005. For foreign-born Colombians the increase was more dramatic: from 13% to 33% over the same period. Foreign-born Ecuadorians graduating from college rose from 10% to 19% of all adults 25 years of age and older between 1980 and 2005, and for Peruvians the corresponding figures were 20% in 1980 and 30% in 2005. (See Table 6.3 for all nationalities.)

Domestic-born Mexicans more than doubled their rate of college graduation (from 6% to 15%) between the census of 1980 and the American Community Survey data of 2005, and domestic-born Dominican college graduates rose from 12% to 29% among adults over the same period. This latter figure was about the same as for non-Hispanic whites. In turn, domestic-born Peruvian adults had achieved a level of graduation in 2005 (49%) equal to Asians, who were the most educated race/ethnicity/national-origin group in the United States. Domestic-born Colombian adults were not far behind as 46% had graduated from college; among Cubans it was 41%; and 39% of Ecuadorians 25 years of age or older had achieved a B.A. degree or higher in 2005. The corresponding figures were 27% for Salvadorans and 33% for domestic-born Hondurans. Only among Puerto Ricans was there relative parity between those adults born in Puerto Rico and on the U.S. mainland, each with about 15% having achieved a B.A. degree or higher in 2005, and this was the lowest rate among all U.S.-born Latino nationalities. (See Graph 6.6 for data on non–high school graduation rates by nativity.)

These data suggest that second, third, and subsequent generations of Latino immigrant families, irrespective of nationality, take advantage of higher educational opportunities in the same way as more-established racial/ethnic groups in the United States, or as was the case with previous immigrants to the United States in the 19th and 20th centuries. Domestic-born Latinos tend to have much higher educational attainment achievements than non-Hispanic blacks; many surpass the educational attainment levels of non-Hispanic whites; and some nationalities approach the educational attainment levels of Asians, who are the most educated race/ethnicity in the United States.

TABLE 6.3. *Educational Attainment Levels by Latino Nationality, Domestic- or Foreign-Born, 1980–2005*

1980

		Mexican	Cuban	Puerto Rican	Honduran	Salvadoran	Colombian	Ecuadorian	Peruvian	Dominican
Domestic-Born	Did not a High School Graduate	53%	34%	55%	32%	25%	28%	23%	17%	50%
	High School Graduate	28%	28%	25%	26%	31%	23%	19%	38%	23%
	1–3 Years College	13%	19%	12%	20%	23%	23%	31%	22%	15%
	4 Years College	6%	20%	8%	22%	21%	25%	27%	23%	12%
	TOTAL	100%	100%	100%	100%	100%	100%	100%	100%	100%
Foreign-Born	Did not a High School Graduate	78%	45%	66%	49%	60%	39%	44%	23%	70%
	High School Graduate	12%	25%	22%	27%	21%	30%	30%	34%	18%
	1–3 Years College	6%	14%	8%	15%	13%	18%	16%	23%	7%
	4 Years College	3%	16%	4%	9%	7%	13%	10%	20%	4%
	TOTAL	100%	100%	100%	100%	100%	100%	100%	100%	100%

1990

		Mexican	Cuban	Puerto Rican	Honduran	Salvadoran	Colombian	Ecuadorian	Peruvian	Dominican
Domestic-Born	Did Not Graduate from High School	41%	18%	50%	23%	32%	15%	15%	14%	32%
	High School Graduate	28%	22%	22%	18%	19%	22%	17%	16%	20%
	Some College, No Degree	18%	24%	14%	30%	22%	21%	27%	27%	23%
	Associates Degree	5%	9%	5%	6%	10%	9%	9%	8%	8%
	B.A. or Higher	8%	26%	9%	22%	16%	33%	31%	35%	18%
	TOTAL	100%	100%	100%	100%	100%	100%	100%	100%	100%

(continued)

TABLE 6.3 *(continued)*

1990

		Mexican	Cuban	Puerto Rican	Honduran	Salvadoran	Colombian	Ecuadorian	Peruvian	Dominican
Foreign-Born	Did Not Graduate from High School	76%	47%	54%	52%	67%	34%	39%	22%	58%
	High School Graduate	12%	19%	22%	21%	16%	27%	26%	28%	19%
	Some College, No Degree	7%	13%	11%	13%	9%	17%	17%	22%	11%
	Associates Degree	3%	6%	4%	6%	4%	7%	7%	8%	4%
	B.A. or Higher	3%	15%	8%	8%	4%	16%	12%	20%	8%
	TOTAL	100%	100%	100%	100%	100%	100%	100%	100%	100%

2000

		Mexican	Cuban	Puerto Rican	Honduran	Salvadoran	Colombian	Ecuadorian	Peruvian	Dominican
Domestic-Born	Did Not Graduate from High School	32%	14%	48%	24%	28%	11%	10%	9%	19%
	High School Graduate	29%	19%	22%	17%	19%	15%	16%	15%	22%
	Some College, No Degree	22%	23%	15%	24%	24%	25%	29%	28%	28%
	Associates Degree	6%	10%	4%	8%	7%	11%	11%	8%	10%
	B.A. or Higher	11%	34%	10%	28%	22%	39%	33%	39%	22%
	TOTAL	100%	100%	100%	100%	100%	100%	100%	100%	100%
Foreign-Born	Did Not Graduate from High School	71%	42%	47%	57%	65%	28%	38%	20%	52%
	High School Graduate	15%	20%	24%	21%	17%	25%	25%	28%	20%
	Some College, No Degree	8%	15%	14%	11%	10%	19%	19%	23%	14%
	Associates Degree	2%	5%	4%	3%	2%	6%	5%	7%	4%
	B.A. or Higher	4%	18%	10%	8%	5%	21%	13%	22%	9%
	TOTAL	100%	100%	100%	100%	100%	100%	100%	100%	100%

		Mexican	Cuban	Puerto Rican	Honduran	Salvadoran	Colombian	Ecuadorian	Peruvian	Dominican
Domestic-Born	Did Not Graduate from High School	25%	8%	39%	20%	18%	7%	5%	7%	11%
	High School Graduate	30%	18%	26%	23%	18%	15%	16%	13%	23%
	Some College No Degree	23%	23%	16%	16%	27%	22%	25%	23%	27%
	Associates Degree	7%	10%	5%	8%	10%	10%	15%	9%	10%
	B.A. or Higher	15%	41%	14%	33%	27%	46%	39%	49%	29%
	TOTAL	100%	100%	100%	100%	100%	100%	100%	100%	100%
Foreign-Born	Did Not Graduate from High School	61%	30%	37%	49%	55%	17%	28%	13%	41%
	High School Graduate	22%	25%	26%	25%	23%	25%	27%	27%	24%
	Some College, No Degree	8%	15%	16%	11%	11%	18%	19%	22%	15%
	Associates Degree	3%	7%	6%	4%	4%	8%	7%	9%	6%
	B.A. or Higher	6%	23%	15%	11%	8%	33%	19%	30%	14%
	TOTAL	100%	100%	100%	100%	100%	100%	100%	100%	100%

Note: For Puerto Ricans foreign-born means born in Puerto Rico.

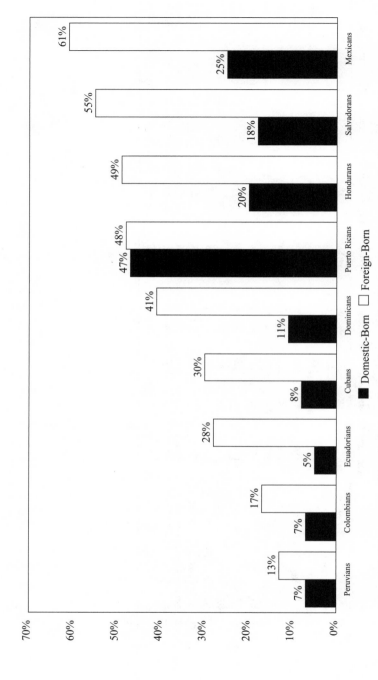

GRAPH 6.6. Percentage of Population 25 Years of Age and Older without a High School Diploma by Selected Latino Nationality and Domestic- or Foreign-Born, 2005.

TABLE 6.4. *Median Total Personal Income by Educational Attainment Level by Latino Nationality for Population 25 Years of Age and Older, 2005*

	Did Not Graduate from High School	High School Graduate	Some College, No Degree	Associates Degree	B.A. or Higher
Cuban	14,246	22,891	34,451	37,618	60,482
Puerto Rican	14,403	24,187	31,459	33,996	51,950
Mexican	15,396	21,998	29,608	32,927	47,711
Peruvian	13,838	21,001	27,228	28,392	45,510
Ecuadorian	17,513	21,098	28,979	32,621	45,018
Colombian	16,018	20,786	28,459	29,999	44,375
Dominican	15,254	19,608	26,230	28,080	42,923
Salvadoran	17,030	22,484	28,360	31,214	40,851
Honduran	15,526	19,697	23,460	23,763	35,281

The relationship between educational attainment levels and income is unquestionable.[4] We examined this theme briefly in the previous chapter by considering the educational attainment levels of heads of households and their relationship to median household income. The connection between education and income is brought into better focus by examining educational attainment among the adult population 25 years of age and older, and total personal income, which is another way that the U.S. Census Bureau measures income. As would be expected, there was a direct correlation between educational attainment levels and the median personal income of individuals among the major racial/ethnic groups and among Latino national subgroups, and this is revealed with clarity in Graph 6.7 and Table 6.4.

Among all racial and ethnic groups in the United States, those who had graduated from college earned more than twice the annual incomes as those without a high school diploma. Although Asians had the greatest share of the adult population having achieved a B.A. degree or higher in 2005, non-Hispanic whites who had graduated from college had the highest median total personal incomes. Latinos and non-Hispanic blacks

---

[4] This holds for all ethnic and racial groups. See for example Barry R. Chiswick, "Differences in Education and Earnings Across Racial and Ethnic Groups: Tastes, Discrimination, and Investments in Child Quality," *The Quarterly Journal of Economics*, 103: 3. (1988), 571–97. Chiswick has also found a high correlation between language proficiency in English, education, skills, and income. See Barry R. Chiswick and Paul Miller, "Immigrant Earnings, Language Skills, Linguistic Concentration and the Business Cyle," *Journal of Population Economics* 15 (2002), 31–57.

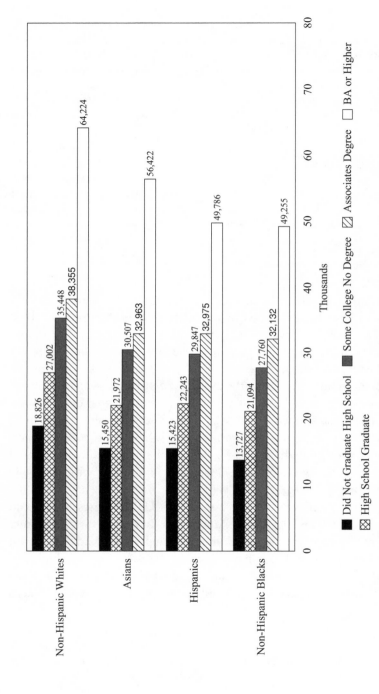

GRAPH 6.7. Median Total Personal Income by Educational Attainment Level by Race/Ethnicity for Population 25 Years of Age and Older, 2005.

with B.A. degrees or higher lagged behind both non-Hispanic whites and Asians in median incomes in 2005.

Among Latino nationalities the same kind of stratification of educational attainment and income levels was found, although the differential between those who had graduated from college and those who had not finished high school was greater than among the major racial/ethnic groups. Those adults 25 years of age and older who had achieved a B.A. degree or higher earned more than three times the personal incomes of those who had not finished high school for Cubans, Puerto Ricans, Mexicans, and Peruvians, and more than two times among the other nationalities.

Cubans graduating from college earned the highest median personal incomes of all the Latino nationalities with the same educational attainment levels in 2005. Ranking second and third were Puerto Ricans and Mexicans. This is of extraordinary significance because both national subgroups not only had among the lowest college graduation rates among Latino nationalities with Mexicans at 10% and Puerto Ricans at 17% but also had among the highest poverty rates as well. Yet, when they graduated from college Mexicans and Puerto Ricans did quite well economically, and this fact underlines the well-known importance of higher education in the quest for upward social mobility.

We now turn to educational achievement patterns found in the six major metropolitan areas of Latino population concentration.[5] There were significant variations among the major metropolitan areas where Latinos were concentrated. But in general the percentage of Latinos 25 years of age and older achieving a B.A. degree or higher by 2005 was lower than among every other major racial or ethnic group in all the major urban centers with the exception of Miami. Additionally, the percentage of those Latino adults who had not graduated from high school was consistently far higher than non–high school graduates found among the other racial/ethnic groups in every metropolitan area. (See Tables 6.5 and 6.6.)

The norm was for Latinos with college degrees to be less than 20% of the adult Latino population. Miami was the exception with some 24% of adult Latinos graduating from college in 2005, and this in turn was a marked improvement from 1980 when the rate was 14%. New York was the second highest metropolitan area in terms of Latino higher educational performance with 16% of Latinos having acquired a B.A. or

[5] About 32% of the total Latino population of the United States was concentrated in these six metropolitan areas in 2005.

TABLE 6.5. *Percentage of Population 25 Years of Age and Older Who Have Achieved a B.A. Degree or Higher by Race/Ethnicity in Selected Metropolitan Areas, 2005*

	Non-Hispanic Whites	Non-Hispanic Blacks	Asians	Hispanics
Miami	47%	14%	53%	24%
New York	48%	21%	44%	16%
Chicago	42%	19%	65%	13%
Houston	41%	23%	56%	11%
Los Angeles	43%	22%	49%	9%
Riverside	26%	20%	43%	8%

higher degree in 2005. This was almost three times the rate that prevailed in 1980 among New York Latinos. In Chicago 13% of the adult Latino population had achieved a B.A. degree by 2005, a rise from the 6% of 1980. In Houston the corresponding rate for 2005 was 11%, an increase from the 7% found in 1980. The poorest performing metro areas were those of California. In Los Angeles only 9% of adult Latinos had achieved a college degree in 2005 compared with 8% in suburbanized Riverside. In both metro areas only 6% had graduated from college in 1980. Thus, the 2005 data do not indicate significant advances in college graduation rates over this 25-year period.

Improvements in higher educational attainment rates among Latinos in these metropolitan areas was overshadowed by the extraordinarily high percentage of adult Latinos who had not graduated from high school compared with the other racial/ethnic groups. Miami was the only metro area in which Latino adults not graduating from high school (26%) were

TABLE 6.6. *Percentage of Population 25 Years of Age and Older Who Have Not Graduated High School by Race/Ethnicity in Selected Metropolitan Areas, 2005*

	Non-Hispanic Whites	Non-Hispanic Blacks	Asians	Hispanics
Houston	8%	17%	12%	48%
Los Angeles	7%	15%	13%	47%
Riverside	9%	10%	13%	43%
Chicago	7%	19%	8%	42%
New York	10%	21%	22%	37%
Miami	7%	28%	16%	26%

similar to non-Hispanic blacks (28%) in 2005. In every other metropolitan area, the percentage of Latinos 25 years of age and older who had not graduated from high school dwarfed that of every other racial/ethnic group. These data underline the educational and social stratification found among Latinos throughout the United States and in the major metropolitan areas of Hispanic population concentration. Although there were clear, and laudable, improvements in the college graduation rates among Latinos, the percentage of those adults who had not graduated from high school remained extraordinarily high.

With such low rates of educational advancements both at the national and metropolitan levels among such a large segment of the Latino population, it was inevitable that income levels would also show such relative stagnation. The high percentage of adult Latinos who had not graduated from high school led to Latinos having comparatively low overall median personal income levels. This was despite the fact that Latinos with college degrees did extremely well compared to all other racial/ethnic groups. The extraordinary differentiation in median personal income levels between those who had not graduated from high school compared to those who had achieved a B.A. degree or higher by metropolitan area are indicated in Table 6.7.

Lower relative educational achievement among all Latinos has a great deal to do with the ongoing large-scale arrival of Latin American and Caribbean immigrants to local metropolitan areas. This may be observed when we compare domestic- and foreign-born Latinos, as indicated previously in this chapter. The former, in fact, have been consistently increasing their educational attainment levels, but the overall ratios continue to be quite low because of the heavy migration of less-educated migrants. In 2005, in every metropolitan region with the exception of New York, the percentage of foreign-born Latinos older than 25 years of age who had not graduated from high school was more than double the rate of domestic-born Latinos. Even in the case of New York where the rates of non–high school graduation among domestic-born Latinos were the highest among the six metropolitan areas (33% of all adults), they still did better than the 41% non–high school graduates among the foreign-born. This exceptionally high rate was due to the large number of U.S.-born Puerto Ricans, the dominant Latino subgroup in New York City, who had not graduated from high school (see Table 6.8).

It is clear that second-generation Latinos did better than foreign-born Latinos in terms of university education when we consider data at the metropolitan level. In Los Angeles, Riverside, and Chicago the

TABLE 6.7. *Median Personal Incomes of Population 25 Years of Age and Older Who Have Achieved a B.A. Degree or Higher and Who Have Not Graduated from High School by Race/Ethnicity in Selected Metropolitan Areas, 2005*

	B.A. Degree or Higher			
	Non-Hispanic Whites	Non-Hispanic Blacks	Asians	Hispanics
Houston	77,563	49,349	53,529	52,294
Miami	76,607	42,573	54,512	50,175
Riverside	64,288	54,791	48,236	49,734
Los Angeles	79,287	56,914	50,524	49,176
New York	86,108	51,566	57,370	48,816
Chicago	74,737	49,920	54,678	45,459

	Have Not Graduated from High School			
	Non-Hispanic Whites	Non-Hispanic Blacks	Asians	Hispanics
Houston	19,739	13,342	14,987	15,314
Miami	24,217	13,006	11,516	12,872
Riverside	21,871	18,833	13,445	18,013
Los Angeles	23,832	14,844	12,186	15,416
New York	21,541	16,329	13,570	13,887
Chicago	23,816	13,664	13,856	17,810

percentage of domestic-born Latinos who had achieved a B.A. degree or higher in 2005 was two times or more the percentage of such foreign-born Latino adults. In Houston and Miami there were significant differentials in graduation rates between domestic- and foreign-born Latinos; only in New York was there more parity.

TABLE 6.8. *Education Attainment of Hispanics 25 Years of Age and Older by Domestic- and Foreign-Born in Selected Metropolitan Areas, 2005*

	Have Not Graduated from High School		B.A Degree or Higher	
	Domestic-Born	Foreign-Born	Domestic-Born	Foreign-Born
Houston	29%	58%	14%	9%
Los Angeles	22%	59%	16%	6%
Chicago	23%	51%	20%	10%
Miami	14%	29%	32%	23%
New York	33%	41%	17%	15%
Riverside	24%	58%	12%	6%

As we have noted repeatedly, the differences among the various Latino national subgroups were substantial. Examining the largest Latino nationalities in the six metropolitan areas, first as total national groups and then considered by whether they were foreign- or domestic-born, many of the trends we have observed previously are accentuated. Among all Mexicans in Houston, Los Angeles, Riverside, and Chicago the overall data suggest a slight improvement in college graduation rates between 1980 and 2005, although they were much lower among Mexicans in all four metro areas compared with the other racial/ethnic groups. Mexicans in Chicago had the highest college graduation rate at 10% in 2005, while in Houston and Los Angeles it was 8%, and in Riverside 7% (see Graph 6.8). Additionally, while the percentages of Mexican adults not completing high school fell somewhat between 1980 and 2005, these rates were still extraordinarily high in comparison with the other demographic sectors of the population. (See Graph 6.9.)

However, when disaggregated into domestic- and foreign-born Mexican adults, the image of educational attainment changes considerably. College graduation rates among domestic-born Mexicans 25 years of age and older increased steadily between 1980 and 2005. They were twice those of foreign-born Mexicans in Houston in 2005 and approximately three times as high in Los Angeles, Chicago, and Riverside. In contrast, foreign-born Mexican adults exhibited only slight improvements in college graduation rates in each metro area (see Graph 6.8). Thus, continued immigration from Mexico during the 1980s and later radically affected the overall educational attainment rate, which masks the real improvements found among second, third, and subsequent generations of Mexican Americans. In every metropolitan area considered here, Mexican adults 25 years of age and older who were born in Mexico increased in absolute and relative terms between 1980 and 2005. In Houston they rose from 34% of all Mexicans in 1980 to 61% in 2005; in Los Angeles, from 57% to 65%; in Chicago from 65% to 73%; and in Riverside from 26% in 1980 to 57% in 2005 (see Graph 6.10 and Table 6.9).

As we previously noted, these Mexican-born migrants experienced gradually improved high school graduation rates. Nevertheless, they had consistently lower rates of high school completion than U.S.-born Mexicans and all other racial/ethnic groups. Among foreign-born adult Mexicans the rates of non–high school graduates declined slightly between 1980 and 2005, but they were extraordinarily higher than among the domestic-born. Between 58% and 64% of adult foreign-born Mexicans had not graduated high school in 2005 in Houston, Chicago, Los Angeles,

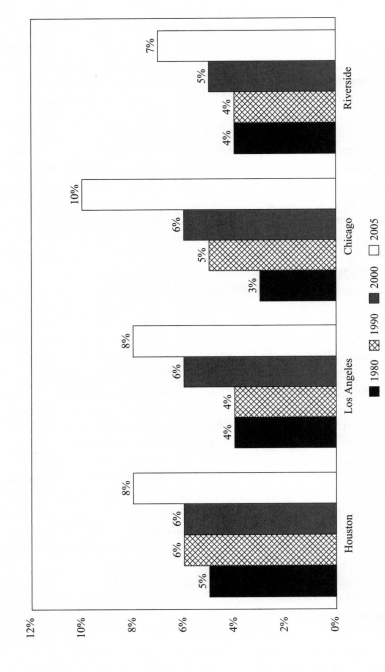

GRAPH 6.8. Percentage of Mexican Population 25 Years of Age and Older Who Have Achieved a B.A. Degree or Higher in Houston, Los Angeles, Chicago, and Riverside, 1980–2005.

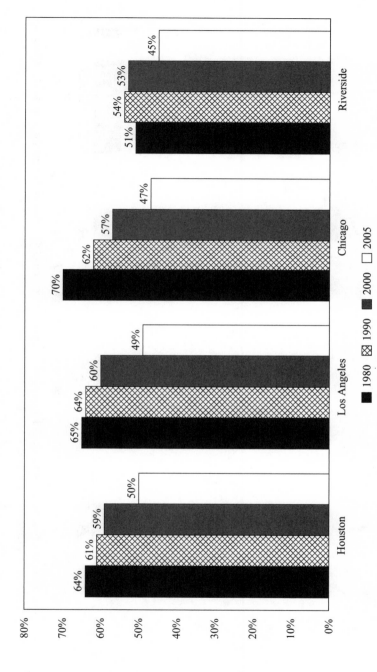

GRAPH 6.9. Percentage of Mexican Population 25 Years of Age and Older Who Have Not Graduated from High School in Houston, Los Angeles, Chicago, and Riverside, 1980–2005.

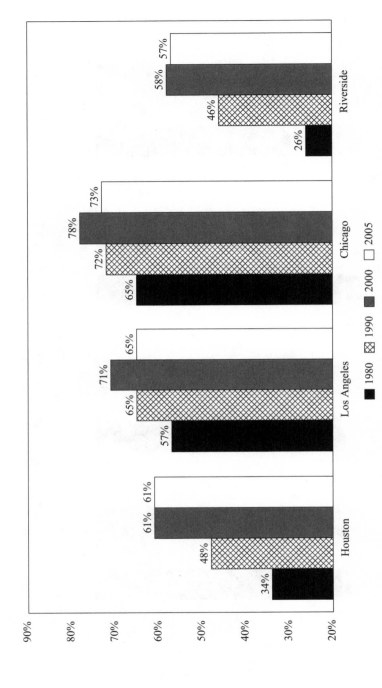

GRAPH 6.10. Percentage of Mexican Population 25 Years of Age and Older Who Were Foreign-Born in Houston, Los Angeles, Chicago, and Riverside, 1980–2005.

TABLE 6.9. *Percentage of Mexican Population 25 Years of Age or Older Who Have Achieved a B.A. Degree or Higher by Domestic- or Foreign-Born*

| | Domestic Born | | | |
	1980	1990	2000	2005
Houston	6%	8%	9%	12%
Los Angeles	6%	8%	11%	15%
Chicago	4%	9%	13%	19%
Riverside	5%	5%	8%	11%

| | Foreign Born | | | |
	1980	1990	2000	2005
Houston	3%	4%	4%	6%
Los Angeles	2%	3%	3%	4%
Chicago	3%	3%	4%	6%
Riverside	3%	3%	3%	4%

and Riverside (see Table 6.10). In contrast, the percentage those domestic-born Mexicans who had not graduated from high school fell significantly in every metropolitan area between 1980 and 2005.

One last area of analysis is diverging patterns of educational attainment by sex. Even among domestic-born non-Hispanic whites there have

TABLE 6.10. *Percentage of Mexican Population 25 Years of Age or Older Who Have Not Graduated from High School by Domestic- or Foreign-Born*

| | Domestic Born | | | |
	1980	1990	2000	2005
Houston	55%	45%	37%	31%
Los Angeles	46%	38%	30%	23%
Chicago	56%	37%	28%	21%
Riverside	43%	37%	32%	24%

| | Foreign Born | | | |
	1980	1990	2000	2005
Houston	78%	78%	73%	62%
Los Angeles	79%	77%	72%	64%
Chicago	78%	71%	66%	56%
Riverside	73%	75%	69%	61%

TABLE 6.11. *Percentage of Mexican Population 25 Years of Age or Older Who Have Achieved a B.A. Degree or Higher by Sex*

	Males			
	1980	1990	2000	2005
Houston	6%	6%	6%	8%
Los Angeles	5%	4%	5%	7%
Chicago	4%	5%	6%	9%
Riverside	6%	5%	5%	7%
	Females			
	1980	1990	2000	2005
Houston	4%	6%	6%	9%
Los Angeles	3%	4%	6%	8%
Chicago	3%	6%	7%	10%
Riverside	3%	3%	5%	7%

been significant differences emerging between rates of college graduation and/or high school dropouts by sex. But these differences are not seen among the Latino immigrants and their children. Two trends stand out between 1980 and 2005 among Mexican men and women. First, there was no substantial amelioration in the college graduation rate among either Mexican adult males or females in any of the metropolitan areas we examine here. Second, there was little difference by sex in the percentage of adult Mexicans who had achieved a B.A. degree or higher in any of the census years between 1980 and 2005. There were very slight differentials, as indicated in Table 6.11 but no major divergences in the college graduation rate between the sexes. There were also, perhaps surprisingly, no major differences in educational attainment levels among Mexican adults by sex between metropolitan areas, although college graduation rates were slightly higher in Riverside than in Houston, Los Angeles, or Chicago.

There was also a slight downward trend for both sexes in the percentages of Mexican adults who had not completed high school by 2005, with the lowest rates prevailing in Riverside. These rates were still extraordinarily high; between 44% and 51% of adult Mexican males and females had not graduated from high school in 2005 in the four metro areas under consideration here (see Table 6.12). These data reiterate the educational stratification existing among Mexican communities in the United States.

TABLE 6.12. *Percentage of Mexican Population 25 Years of Age or Older Who Have Not Graduated from High School by Sex*

	Males			
	1980	1990	2000	2005
Houston	63%	62%	61%	51%
Los Angeles	63%	64%	61%	50%
Chicago	71%	63%	59%	48%
Riverside	49%	55%	55%	47%
	Females			
	1980	1990	2000	2005
Houston	64%	60%	57%	48%
Los Angeles	66%	64%	59%	49%
Chicago	70%	60%	56%	45%
Riverside	54%	53%	52%	44%

A small percentage of Mexican adults have graduated college, and their income-earning capabilities dwarfed those of the large numbers who had not completed the most minimal educational attainment level as high school graduates, male or female (see Graph 6.11).

Among the other major Latino immigrant groups there were significant differences in educational attainment rates. In the Miami metropolitan area, Cubans were one of the best-educated Latino nationalities in the nation. The arrival of more than 125,000 Cubans during the 1980s in what is known as the Mariel boatlift slowed the pace of higher educational achievement among Miami's Cuban population since for the first time large numbers of poorer-educated working-class Cubans arrived in Miami. Some 14% of Miami Cubans 25 years of age or older had acquired B.A. degrees or higher in 1980, one of the highest rates among Latinos in the nation, but there was stagnation and a slight decline to 13% in 1990, undoubtedly because of the arrival of large numbers of Cuban adults without B.A. degrees during the 1980s. There was recovery in the 1990s as more Cubans, especially those born in the United States, acquired college educations. In 2005 some 23% of all Miami Cuban adults had graduated from college. Among adult Cuban women and men there was near parity in the rate of college graduation or higher educational attainment in 2005 (see Table 6.13).

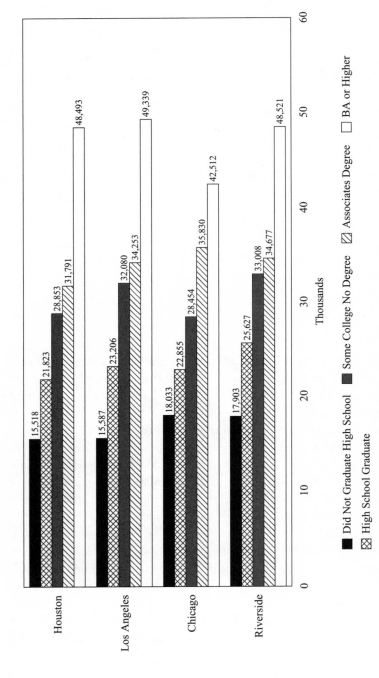

■ Did Not Graduate High School   ■ Some College No Degree   ☐ BA or Higher

▨ High School Graduate

GRAPH 6.11. Median Total Personal Income among Mexicans by Educational Attainment Levels in Houston, Los Angeles, Chicago, and Riverside, 2005.

TABLE 6.13. *Percentage of Miami Foreign and Domestic-Born Cuban Population 25 Years of Age and Older Who Have Achieved a B.A. Degree or Higher and Who Have Not Graduated from High School by Sex, 1980–2005*

	B.A. Degree or Higher		
	Males	Females	Total
1980	17%	12%	14%
1990	15%	12%	13%
2000	19%	17%	18%
2005	24%	22%	23%

	Did Not Graduate from High School		
	Males	Females	Total
1980	47%	50%	49%
1990	49%	50%	50%
2000	43%	43%	43%
2005	29%	29%	29%

More important than disparities by sex among Latinos was generational differentiations. This is clearly reflected in the percentages of domestic- and foreign-born Cubans having acquired a B.A. degree or greater. The rate of college graduation among adult Miami Cubans born in the United States more than doubled from 15% in 1980 to 39% in 2005, while among those born abroad the college graduation rate increased from 14% in 1980 to 20% in 2005. Only 12% of Cubans 25 years of age and older were born in the United States in 2005, and it may be projected that as this percentage inevitably rises in subsequent years the college graduation rate among all Miami Cubans will continue to increase significantly (see Table 6.14 and Graph 6.12).

The expected patterns of generation disparities, rather than differences by sex, also were evident at the lower end of the educational attainment hierarchy. By 2005 only 7% of domestic-born Cuban adults in Miami had not graduated from high school. Although, foreign-born Cubans saw real improvements in the high school graduation rate in Miami, in 2005 a quarter still had not finished high school.[6] These differing educational

---

[6] The discrepancies in the percentages of total Cubans not graduating from high school when males and females are quantified and when domestic- and foreign-born are analyzed was due to incomplete data on the number of domestic- and foreign-born adult Cubans.

TABLE 6.14. *Percentage of Miami Foreign and Domestic-Born Cuban Population 25 Years of Age and Older Who Have Achieved a B.A. Degree or Higher and Who Have Not Graduated from High School, 1980–2005*

	B.A. Degree or Higher		
	Domestic-Born	Foreign-Born	Total
1980	15%	14%	14%
1990	25%	13%	13%
2000	35%	16%	18%
2005	39%	20%	23%

	Did Not Graduate from High School		
	Domestic-Born	Foreign-Born	Total
1980	43%	49%	48%
1990	15%	51%	49%
2000	13%	45%	20%
2005	7%	32%	25%

attainments had a major impact on median personal income levels among Miami Cubans as may be noted in Graph 6.13.

The major Latino nationalities in New York also experienced generational differences, and variations in educational attainment levels by sex were minor for most national subgroups. Among Puerto Rican adults, only 4% had achieved a B.A. degree in 1980, and this increased to 12% in 2005. For Dominicans there was also an extraordinary increase in educational attainment from 1980 when 3% of adults had graduated college to 13% in 2005.

The third most numerous of the Latino national subgroups in New York, Mexicans, did not show any improvement in educational attainment as measured by those completing college, although there were significant differences by sex, which will be considered later. The fundamental reason for the absence of general progress was the arrival of very large numbers of poorly educated foreign-born Mexican migrants, especially men, after 1990. This is a pattern we have already observed for all the other metropolitan areas. About 11% of all Mexican adults in New York had graduated from college in 1980 and 12% had graduated in 2005.

Among Ecuadorians the increase in adults who had achieved a B.A. degree was from 6% to 14% between 1980 and 2005. One group standing in contrast to other Latino nationalities, not only in metropolitan

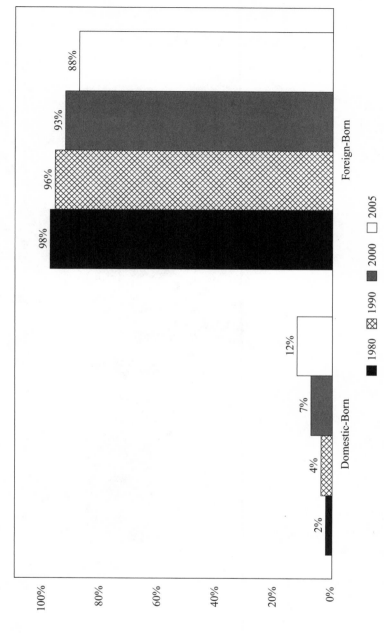

GRAPH 6.12. Percentage of Miami Cuban Population 25 Years of Age and Older Who Were Domestic- or Foreign-Born, 1980–2005.

■ 1980 ▨ 1990 ■ 2000 □ 2005

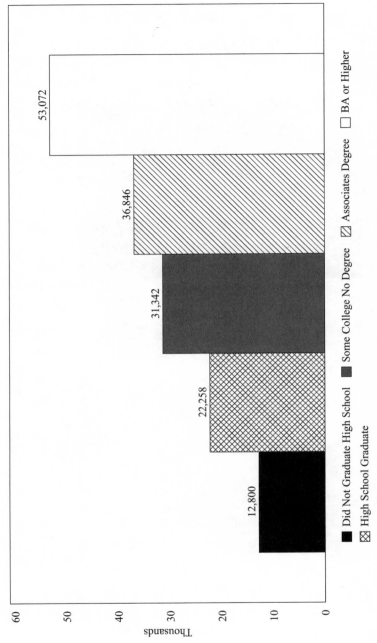

GRAPH 6.13. Median Total Personal Income among Cubans in Miami by Educational Attainment Levels, 2005.

Did Not Graduate High School ■ Some College No Degree ▨ Associates Degree □ BA or Higher ▨ High School Graduate

53,072

36,846

31,342

22,258

12,800

60

50

40

30

20

10

0

Thousands

New York but in the country as a whole, are Colombians. Some 9% of Colombian adults had graduated from college in 1980, and an astounding 27% had accomplished this by 2005, a rate that approached the 30% found among non-Hispanic white adults in the same year (see Graph 6.14).

At the lower end of the educational attainment hierarchy there were sharp declines in rates of those who had not graduated from high school for all Latino national subgroups with the exception of Mexicans who experienced a slight rise. About 52% of Mexican adults in the New York metro area had not graduated from high school in 1980, and this actually increased marginally to 54% in 2005.

There were extraordinary improvements among all other Latino national groups, even though non–high school graduates remained fairly high by 2005. Among Puerto Ricans the non–high school graduation rate fell from 64% in 1980 to 38% in 2005. For Dominicans the drop was even steeper: from 74% to 43% over the same period. Among Ecuadorian adults 52% had not graduated from high school in 1980 and 34% in 2005. For Colombians only 24% of adults did not complete high school in 2005, down from 47% in 1980. (See Graph 6.15.)

There were some marginal, but significant, differentiations in the college graduation rate and in the rates of those who had not graduated from high school by sex among Latino nationalities in New York, and these data are presented in Tables 6.15 and 6.16. With the exception of Colombians, adult women had slightly higher college graduation rates than men by 2005. The greatest differentiation was found among Mexicans where there were extraordinary improvements among Mexican women between 1980 when 8% had achieved a B.A. degree or higher to 15% in 2005. However, among Mexican adult men the college graduation rate declined from 14% in 1980 to 10% in 2005. Once again, this was the result of the migration to the region of large numbers of poorer-educated Mexican males who skewed the percentages of college graduates downward. However, among the other Latino nationalities not only had slightly greater percentages of adult females graduated from college than males, but college graduation rates rose more sharply than among males between 1980 and 2005 (see Table 6.15). This suggests that more women have been taking advantage of higher educational opportunities than men, and that it is likely that the gap in male/female educational attainment in favor of women will probably widen in subsequent years among Puerto Ricans, Dominicans, Mexicans, and Ecuadorians. However, the patterns of higher educational attainment were very different among Colombians.

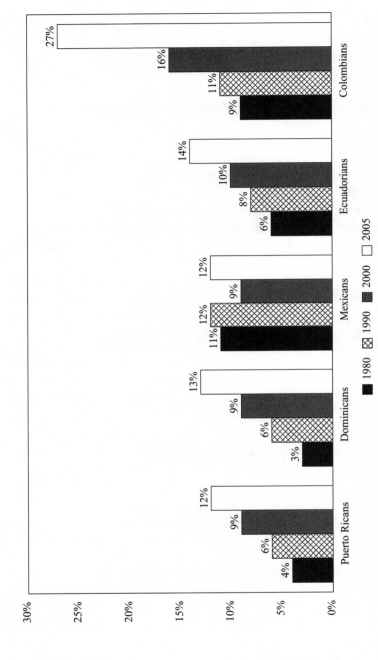

GRAPH 6.14. Percentage of New York Latino Nationalities 25 Years of Age and Older Who Have Achieved a B.A. Degree or Higher by Puerto Ricans, Dominicans, Mexicans, Ecuadorians, and Colombians, 1980–2005.

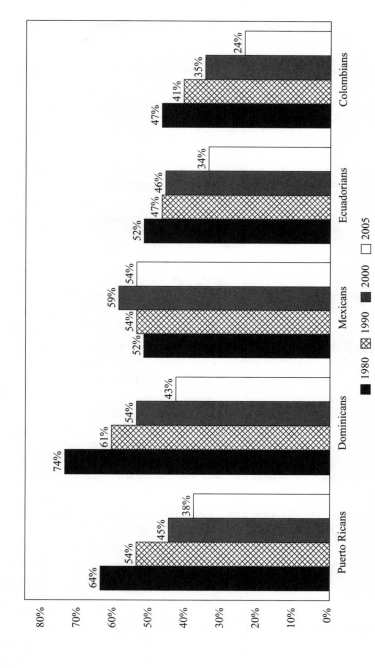

GRAPH 6.15. Percentage of New York Latino Nationalities 25 Years of Age and Older Who Have Not Graduated from High School by Puerto Ricans, Dominicans, Mexicans, Ecuadorians, and Colombians, 1980–2005.

TABLE 6.15. *Percentage of Selected New York Latino Nationalities 25 Years of Age and Older Who Have Achieved a B.A. Degree or Higher by Sex, 1980–2005*

| | Males | | | | |
	Puerto Ricans	Dominicans	Mexicans	Ecuadorians	Colombians
1980	4%	3%	14%	8%	12%
1990	6%	8%	11%	8%	12%
2000	8%	8%	8%	9%	17%
2005	11%	11%	10%	11%	30%

| | Females | | | | |
	Puerto Ricans	Dominicans	Mexicans	Ecuadorians	Colombians
1980	3%	3%	8%	4%	7%
1990	7%	6%	13%	8%	9%
2000	10%	9%	9%	11%	16%
2005	14%	14%	15%	16%	24%

Not only did they have the highest percentage of college graduates among adults, but Colombians were the only New York metro area national group in which males had higher rates than found among females in 2005, 30% to 24%, although there were marked improvements among both sexes since 1980.

TABLE 6.16. *Percentage of Selected New York Latino Nationalities 25 Years of Age and Older Who Have Not Graduated from High School by Sex, 1980–2005*

| | Males | | | | |
	Puerto Ricans	Dominicans	Mexicans	Ecuadorians	Colombians
1980	63%	71%	52%	51%	43%
1990	54%	58%	57%	47%	37%
2000	45%	55%	59%	47%	32%
2005	36%	40%	56%	36%	19%

| | Females | | | | |
	Puerto Ricans	Dominicans	Mexicans	Ecuadorians	Colombians
1980	65%	75%	52%	54%	49%
1990	54%	63%	51%	48%	45%
2000	45%	53%	59%	46%	37%
2005	39%	45%	51%	32%	28%

Among those not graduating from high school Mexican adult males and females each had the highest rates among all Latino nationalities in the New York metro area with over 50% of each sex not having completed high school in 2005, and there was absolutely no improvement since 1980. Again, these findings were linked to the arrival of large numbers of Mexicans with minimal educational achievement levels over this 25-year period. There were considerable declines among both men and women in the rates of non–high school graduation among all other Latino national subgroups as may be observed in Table 6.16.

Finally, there were extraordinary disparities in college graduation rates among those Latino nationalities, including Mexicans, who were born in the United States and those born abroad.[7] In fact, New York area Mexican adults who were domestic-born had extraordinarily high college graduation rates by 2005 at 41% compared with only 8% among the Mexican foreign-born population 25 years of age and older. Mexican adults in the New York metro area were only surpassed by domestic-born Colombians of whom 58% had achieved a B.A. degree or higher by 2005 compared with a rate of 23% among foreign-born Colombians. This college graduation rate among domestic-born Colombian adults surpassed that of Asians, the most educated race/ethnicity in the United States of whom 49% had graduated college or better in 2005.

The disparities between Puerto Ricans born in the United States, of whom 18% had finished at least a B.A. degree in 2005 and those born in Puerto Rico (8%) were pronounced. Among Dominicans 27% of domestic-born adults had achieved a B.A. degree or higher compared with 11% of the foreign-born. An even greater disparity prevailed among Ecuadorians of whom 35% of all domestic-born adults had graduated from college in 2005 compared with 12% among the foreign-born Ecuadorian population (see Table 6.17).

These higher educational attainment data among New York Latino nationalities are encouraging. The sharp upward trend in college graduation rates among all domestic-born Latino subgroups suggest that as the percentages of those born in the United States inevitably increase, overall college graduation rates will continue to rise, and in this regard the experiences of Latinos will repeat those of past immigrant groups to the United States.

[7] For Puerto Ricans we have divided the population into those born in Puerto Rico, here indicated as foreign-born even though this is not technically accurate, and those born on the U.S. mainland.

TABLE 6.17. *Percentage of Selected New York Latino Nationalities 25 Years of Age and Older Who Have Achieved a B.A. Degree or Higher by Domestic- or Foreign-Born, 1980–2005*

	Domestic-Born				
	Puerto Ricans	Dominicans	Mexicans	Ecuadorians	Colombians
1980	9%	12%	13%	23%	27%
1990	11%	14%	25%	11%	25%
2000	12%	20%	30%	26%	37%
2005	18%	27%	41%	35%	58%
	Foreign-Born				
	Puerto Ricans	Dominicans	Mexicans	Ecuadorians	Colombians
1980	3%	3%	10%	6%	9%
1990	4%	6%	8%	8%	10%
2000	6%	8%	6%	9%	15%
2005	8%	11%	8%	12%	23%

Note: For Puerto Ricans, foreign-born is born in Puerto Rico.

Compared with the foreign-born, there were also extraordinarily impressive decreases in the percentages of domestic-born Latino sub-groups in New York who had not finished high school between 1980 and 2005. A third of Puerto Rican adults born in the United States still had not graduated from high school in 2005, but among every other Latino national group these percentages had fallen meteorically from 1980 as indicated in Table 6.16. Among domestic-born Dominicans 25 years of age or older, only 12% had not graduated from high school in 2005. The rate was 17% among domestic-born Mexicans, 8% among Ecuadorians, and an astounding 2% among Colombians.

Yet, among the foreign-born, the contrast in the high school graduation rate was stark. Some 52% of Puerto Rican adults born on the island had not completed high school in 2005 compared with 47% among foreign-born Dominicans, 59% of Mexicans, 37% among Ecuadorians, and only 26% of Colombians (see Table 6.18). Once again, these data are cause for optimism. As future generations of domestic-born Latinos emerge, it is likely that there will be significant improvement in educational attainment levels.

The critical importance of educational attainment on socioeconomic status is brought into sharp focus by comparing median personal income levels and education among Latino nationalities in the New York metro area, and these are indicated in Graph 6.16. The extraordinarily higher

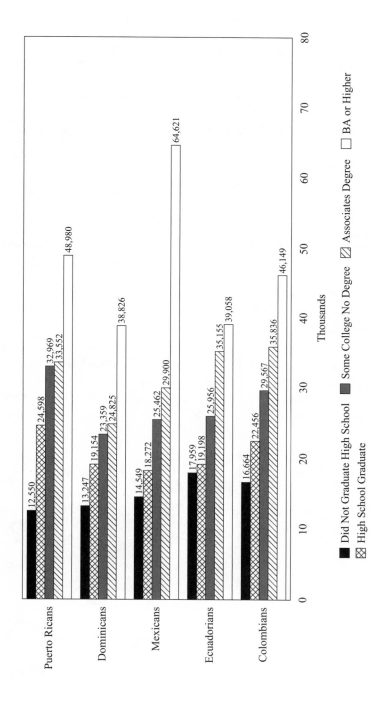

GRAPH 6.16. Median Personal Income among New York Latino Nationalities 25 Years of Age and Older by Educational Attainment Level by Puerto Ricans, Dominicans, Mexicans, Ecuadorians, and Colombians, 2005.

■ Did Not Graduate High School ■ Some College No Degree ▨ Associates Degree ☐ BA or Higher
▨ High School Graduate

TABLE 6.18. *Percentage of Selected New York Latino Nationalities 25 Years of Age and Older Who Have Not Graduated from High School by Domestic- or Foreign-Born, 1980–2005*

	Domestic-Born				
	Puerto Ricans	Dominicans	Mexicans	Ecuadorians	Colombians
1980	51%	53%	45%	31%	30%
1990	46%	40%	23%	26%	24%
2000	43%	23%	24%	17%	14%
2005	33%	12%	17%	8%	2%

	Foreign-Born				
	Puerto Ricans	Dominicans	Mexicans	Ecuadorians	Colombians
1980	69%	74%	58%	53%	47%
1990	63%	62%	64%	48%	42%
2000	58%	56%	64%	48%	37%
2005	52%	47%	59%	37%	26%

Note: For Puerto Ricans, foreign-born is born in Puerto Rico.

median incomes found among those who had graduated from college ought to serve as a major motivation for continual improvements in educational attainment, especially among subsequent generations of New York metro area Latinos.

7

Citizenship, the Latino Electorate, and Voter Participation

Between 1980 and 2005 the absolute number of citizens of Latino origin in the United States nearly tripled from about 11 million to nearly 30 million. About 81% of this increase was because of births in the United States, and 19% was because of naturalization among the foreign-born. Yet, despite this increase in the actual number of citizens, the surge in migration to the United States from Latin America and the Caribbean after 1980 resulted in a declining percentage of all Latinos who were citizens from 80% in 1980 to 71% in 2005. This immigration resulted in a more than fourfold increase in the absolute number of Latinos who were not citizens of the United States from nearly 3 million in 1980 to over 12 million in 2005. If we consider the total citizen population of the United States, in 1980, about 5% were Latinos; by 2005 this percentage had increased to 11%.

The anti-immigrant sentiment, which has swept through the United States from the mid-1990s, exemplified by the passing of Proposition 187 in California in November 1994, led to a fairly significant increase in the yearly rate of naturalization among Latinos during the 1990s.[1]

---

[1] Proposition 187 was a temporarily successful effort by anti-immigrant politicians in California to deny undocumented persons access to health care and other social services and was passed by about 59% of California voters on November 8, 1994. In March 1998 a U.S. district court judge ruled most of the law unconstitutional. Nevertheless, the successful passing of the bill prompted efforts by anti-immigrant politicians to pass similar laws in other states and "immigration reform" became a major, and polarizing, national issue. On the Latino response to these efforts see the results of the Pew Latino Opinion surveys at http://pewhispanic.org/publications/. The latest one that covers this response is Mark Hugo López and Susan Minushkin, *2008 National Survey of Latinos* (Washington, DC: Pew Hispanic Center, report dated September 18, 2008). On the

There were over 1.2 million foreign-born naturalized Latino citizens in 1980 and over 4.7 million in 2005. Latino foreign-born residents who achieved citizenship through naturalization increased at about 5% annually during the 1980s, and this rate surged to 7% yearly between 1990 and 2000. However, between 2000 and 2005 the annual rate of naturalization increase among foreign-born Latinos fell to about 4% each year.

If we consider citizens only among the Latino population of the United States, in 1980 some 11% were foreign-born and naturalized. By 2005 this had increased to 16%. If all foreign-born naturalized citizens of all nationalities in the United States are examined, Latinos made up 18% of the total in 1980. However, because of the wave of naturalization that took place among foreign-born Latinos during the 1980s and after, by 2005 Latinos had risen to almost a third (32%) of the total number of naturalized U.S. citizens. These data are summarized in Graphs 7.1 and 7.2.

Reflecting the demographic dominance of the Mexican-origin population among Latinos in the United States, the vast majority of Latino citizens were Mexicans or Mexican Americans. Mexicans made up 61% of all Latino citizens in 1980 and 63% in 2005. The second most numerous Latino national subgroup was Puerto Ricans who comprised 17% of all Latino citizens in 1980 and 13% in 2005.[2] Cubans, the third largest Latino nationality, were 4% of all Latino citizens in 1980 and the same percentage in 2005. Dominicans became the fourth largest subgroup of Latino citizens by 2005 comprising 3% of all citizens of Hispanic origin. Colombians followed at 2% of all Latinos who were citizens of the United States in 2005 (see Graph 7.3).

The absolute number of the Mexican-origin population tripled between 1980 and 2005 from about 9 million to over 27 million, while the foreign-born Mexican population who had not yet become citizens increased more than four times from a little over 1.7 million in 1980 to over 8.5 million in 2005. This large increase in foreign-born Mexicans who were not citizens resulted in a proportional decline in the overall percentage of Mexican-origin persons who were citizens, from 81% of all Mexicans in 1980 to 69% in 2005.[3]

---

origins of this important opinion survey, see F. Chris García, John A. García, Angelo Falcón, and Rodolfo O. de la Garza, "Studying Latino Politics: The Development of the Latino National Political Survey," *PS: Political Science and Politics*, 22:4 (1989), 848–52.

[2] In 1917 all people born in Puerto Rico were declared to be U.S. citizens by the Jones Act passed by the U.S. Congress in that year.

[3] There is no way to accurately estimate the number of undocumented Mexicans, or other Latino nationalities, who were foreign-born noncitizens. The Pew Hispanic Center has

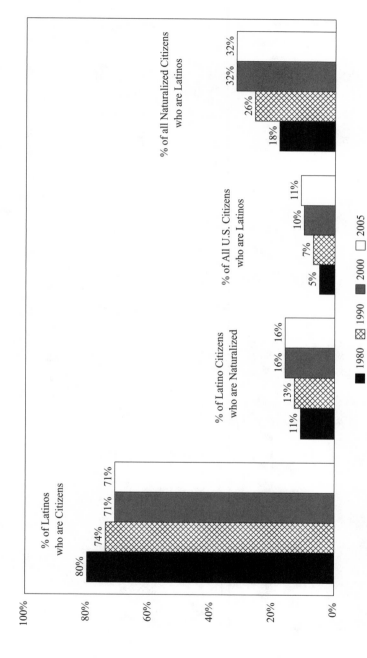

GRAPH 7.1. Citizenship Data among Latinos in the United States, 1980–2005 (in percentages).

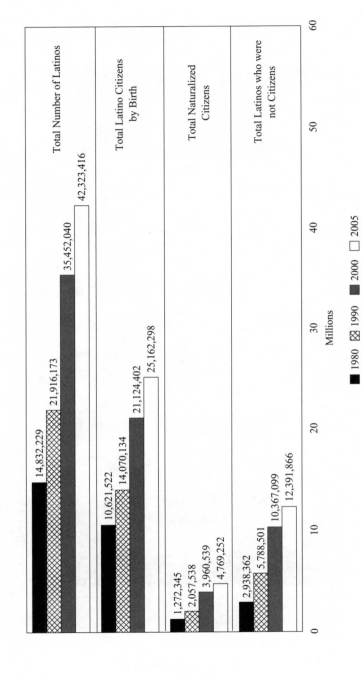

GRAPH 7.2. Citizenship Data among Latinos in the United States, 1980–2005 (in absolute numbers).

Total Number of Latinos
- 1980: 14,832,229
- 1990: 21,916,173
- 2000: 35,452,040
- 2005: 42,323,416

Total Latino Citizens by Birth
- 1980: 10,621,522
- 1990: 14,070,134
- 2000: 21,124,402
- 2005: 25,162,298

Total Naturalized Citizens
- 1980: 1,272,345
- 1990: 2,057,538
- 2000: 3,960,539
- 2005: 4,769,252

Total Latinos who were not Citizens
- 1980: 2,938,362
- 1990: 5,788,501
- 2000: 10,367,099
- 2005: 12,391,866

Millions

■ 1980 ▨ 1990 ■ 2000 □ 2005

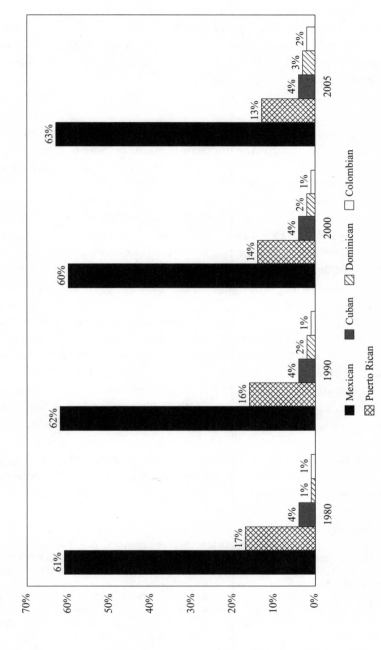

GRAPH 7.3. Percentage of Total Latino Citizens by Selected Latino Nationalities, 1980–2005.

As the rate of immigration from Cuba slowed after the Mariel boatlift of 1980, the increase in the U.S. Cuban population was not as dramatic as found among Mexicans and was largely due to natural reproduction in the United States. There were over 800,000 Cubans in the United States in 1980 and over 1.4 million in 2005. The absolute number of Cubans who were not citizens declined slightly from about 350,000 in 1980 to 344,000 in 2005. By 2005 more than three-quarters (or 76%) all Cubans were citizens, a substantial increase from the 58% who were citizens in 1980.

The pattern for all the other major Latino groups was the same: a steady increase over time in the number of citizens because of the increase in migrants who became naturalized and the rise of second and even third generations born in the United States. The Dominican population of the United States soared after 1980 from a little more than 200,000 to more than 1.2 million in 2005. Over the same period the percentage of citizens rose from 40% of all Dominicans in 1980 to 68% in 2005. Over one-quarter of all Dominicans were naturalized citizens by 2005, an increase from the 20% found in 1980. The Colombian-origin population also rose substantially in the United States from nearly 180,000 in 1980 to more than 800,000 in 2005. The citizenship rate increased from the 39% of all Colombians who were citizens in 1980 to 61% in 2005. Peruvians experienced an increase in citizenship rates from 45% to 56% between 1980 and 2005; Ecuadorians increased from 38% to 55%; and Salvadorans from 26% to 51% (see Tables 7.1, 7.2, and 7.3.)

In the six largest metropolitan areas of Latino population concentration there was a steady increase in the percentages of overall citizen populations who were of Latino origin between 1980 and 2005. The most dramatic change occurred in Miami where 25% of all citizens were Latinos in 1980 and 55% in 2005. The transformation of the Los Angeles metropolitan area was equally impressive. In 1980 21% of all citizens were Latinos; 41% in 2005. In neighboring Riverside, Latinos rose from

estimated that there were about 5.9 million undocumented Mexicans living in the United States in 2004, and 2.5 million people from the other nations of Latin America. See Jeffrey S. Passel, *Unauthorized Migrants: Numbers and Characteristics*, Pew Hispanic Center report of June 14, 2005, available at http://pewhispanic.org/files/reports/46.pdf. Also see the report issued by the Office of Immigration Statistics, U.S. Department of Homeland Security, Michael Hoefer, Nancy Rytina, and Christopher Campbell, *Estimates of the Unauthorized Immigrant Population Residing in the United States: January 2006*, available at http://www.dhs.gov/xlibrary/assets/statistics/publications/ill_pe_2006.pdf. We have decided not to include the estimates found in these studies in our calculations since there are no methods to verify accuracy.

TABLE 7.1. *Total Latino Citizenship Status by Selected Latino Nationalities, 1980–2005 (in absolute numbers)*

Mexicans

	Totals	Citizens by Birth	Naturalized Citizens	Not Citizens
1980	9,020,359	6,700,859	588,634	1,730,866
1990	13,399,858	8,959,685	996,147	3,444,026
2000	22,205,282	13,097,148	2,030,091	7,078,043
2005	27,234,036	16,308,919	2,406,568	8,518,549

Cubans

	Totals	Citizens by Birth	Naturalized Citizens	Not Citizens
1980	834,524	196,060	287,380	351,084
1990	1,058,726	300,332	381,905	376,489
2000	1,277,694	410,782	524,695	342,217
2005	1,449,647	555,115	549,977	344,555

Colombians

	Totals	Citizens by Birth	Naturalized Citizens	Not Citizens
1980	178,276	34,081	34,784	109,411
1990	386,385	99,459	80,522	206,404
2000	663,935	157,734	203,124	303,077
2005	814,978	246,472	254,555	313,951

Dominicans

	Totals	Citizens by Birth	Naturalized Citizens	Not Citizens
1980	205,281	39,937	42,042	123,302
1990	538,323	171,277	98,370	269,647
2000	1,002,412	324,911	247,314	430,187
2005	1,233,155	519,400	324,383	389,372

17% of all citizens in 1980 to 38% in 2005. In the Houston metro area, Latinos were 13% of total citizens in 1980 and 26% in 2005, while in New York the increase was from 15% to 24% between 1980 and 2005. The Chicago metro area had the smallest percentage of overall populations of whom Latinos were citizens: 6% in 1980 and 15% in 2005 (see Graph 7.4).

Among Mexicans in the four major metropolitan areas where they were demographically dominant among Latino nationalities – Houston, Los Angeles, Chicago, and Riverside – there were slightly different patterns in citizenship rates between 1980 and 2005. In Houston there was

TABLE 7.2. *Total Latino Citizenship Status by Selected Latino Nationalities, 1980–2005 (in percentages of total national populations)*

	Mexicans			
	Citizens as % of Total Populations	Citizens by Birth	Naturalized Citizens	Not Citizens
1980	81%	74%	7%	19%
1990	74%	67%	7%	26%
2000	68%	59%	9%	32%
2005	69%	60%	9%	31%

	Cubans			
	Citizens as % of Total Populations	Citizens by Birth	Naturalized Citizens	Not Citizens
1980	58%	23%	34%	42%
1990	64%	28%	36%	36%
2000	73%	32%	41%	27%
2005	76%	38%	38%	24%

	Colombians			
	Citizens as % of Total Populations	Citizens by Birth	Naturalized Citizens	Not Citizens
1980	39%	19%	20%	61%
1990	47%	26%	21%	53%
2000	54%	24%	31%	46%
2005	61%	30%	31%	39%

	Dominicans			
	Citizens as % of Total Populations	Citizens by Birth	Naturalized Citizens	Not Citizens
1980	40%	19%	20%	60%
1990	50%	32%	18%	50%
2000	57%	32%	25%	43%
2005	68%	42%	26%	32%

a steady decline in the percentage of all Mexicans who were citizens from 91% in 1980 to 79% in 2005. In part this was due to immigration of foreign-born Mexicans who had not yet acquired citizenship. Another factor was that Houston had the lowest naturalization rate among foreign-born Mexicans of the four metro areas. About 10% of Houston's total Mexican citizens were naturalized in 2005 compared with 14% in

TABLE 7.3. *Percentage of Selected Latino Nationalities Who Were Citizens, 1980–2005*

	1980	1990	2000	2005
Colombian	39%	47%	54%	61%
Cuban	58%	64%	73%	76%
Dominican	40%	50%	57%	68%
Ecuadoran	38%	47%	52%	55%
Honduran	50%	42%	42%	45%
Mexican	81%	74%	68%	69%
Peruvian	45%	44%	53%	56%
Salvadoran	26%	33%	44%	51%

Riverside, 17% in Los Angeles, and 20% in Chicago. Despite their lower rates of naturalization and thus overall citizenship compared to Mexicans in other cities, by 2005 slightly more than a quarter (26%) of Houston's total population was of Mexican origin and 21% of all Houston citizens were Mexicans or Mexican Americans. This represented a considerable increase from 1980 when 14% of Houston metro area's total population was Mexican, as was 12% of its citizen population.

Chicago's Mexican community not only had the highest naturalization rate among Mexicans but it was the one metropolitan area among the four that experienced a continually rising percentage of the total Mexican-origin population who were citizens. Chicago had the lowest percentage of all Mexicans who were citizens in 1980 at 57%, but by 2005 74% of Chicago's total Mexican population were citizens through birth or naturalization of the foreign-born. In 1980 only 5% of all Chicagoans were Mexicans as were 4% of the metro area's total citizens. By 2005 about 16% of all Chicago metro area residents were of Mexican origin, and 11% of all citizens in Chicago were Mexicans.

In Los Angeles there was a slight decline in the percentage of all Mexicans who were citizens between 1980 and 2005 from 83% to 79%, while in contiguous Riverside there was complete stability over the same period as 87% of all Mexicans were citizens in both 1980 and 2005. One slight difference between the two was that the percentage of foreign-born Mexicans who had become naturalized citizens increased sharply in Riverside from 6% of all Mexican citizens to 14% between 1980 and 2005, while in Los Angeles the rise was from 11% to 17%. Thus, although a higher percentage of Los Angeles Mexicans were naturalized by 2005,

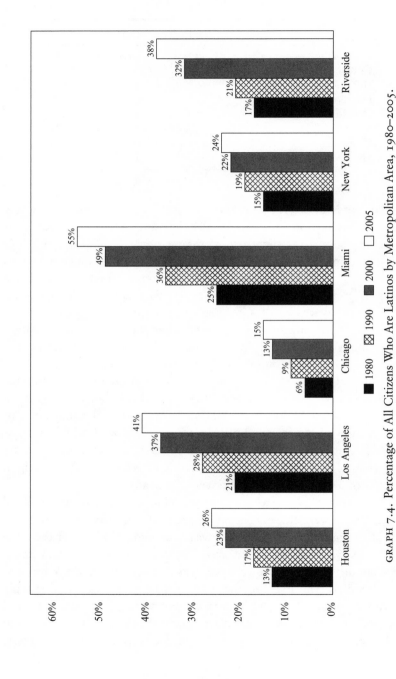

GRAPH 7.4. Percentage of All Citizens Who Are Latinos by Metropolitan Area, 1980–2005.

■ 1980 ▨ 1990 ▧ 2000 ☐ 2005

the increase was more significant in Riverside. This suggests that foreign-born Mexicans who had become citizens through naturalization moved to more suburbanized Riverside over this 25 year period.

In the Los Angeles metropolitan area 36% of the total population was of Mexican origin, and 32% of total Los Angeles citizens were Mexicans in 2005. The corresponding figures for 1980 were 22% of the total population and 17% of the Los Angeles citizen population. In Riverside only 16% of the total population was of Mexican origin in 1980, and this soared to 38% in 2005, surpassing by a small margin the percentage of Mexicans among the total Los Angeles population. Some 33% of all Riverside citizens were Mexicans in 2005, well above the 15% found in 1980. Thus, by 2005 Mexicans had established a similar presence in both urbanized Los Angeles and more suburbanized Riverside, despite the differences that had prevailed 25 years earlier. This was part of a general transformation of U.S. suburban communities that took place in the late 20th century when they began to demographically resemble contiguous urban areas. See Graphs 7.5, 7.6, and 7.7 and Table 7.4 for these data.

Miami's dominant Cuban population represents a special case when citizenship patterns are considered because of the Cuban Adjustment Act of November 1966. This law provided that permanent residence be granted to any Cuban national who had reached the United States after January 1, 1959, and had resided in the country for one year. The permanent residence status granted to nearly all Cubans was the first step in acquiring U.S. citizenship, which could be petitioned to the U.S. Immigration and Naturalization Service after residence and examination requirements had been fulfilled. The special status of Cubans is essential for explaining why Cubans had the highest naturalization rate among all Latino nationalities in the United States, and this is exemplified by examining the Miami Cuban population. Between 1980 and 2005 the percentage of Miami Cubans who were citizens increased from 50% to 71% because of the ongoing naturalization process and the birth of children to Cuban mothers. Some 68% all Miami Cuban citizens were naturalized in 1980, and as indicated previously this was the highest percentage among any Latino nationality in any of the metro areas we have considered. This rate fell to 59% by 2005, not necessarily because of a decline in the rate of naturalization but because of the birth of Cuban-origin children in the United States (see Graph 7.8). As foreign-born Cubans acquired citizenship in Miami, and more children were born to Cuban women,

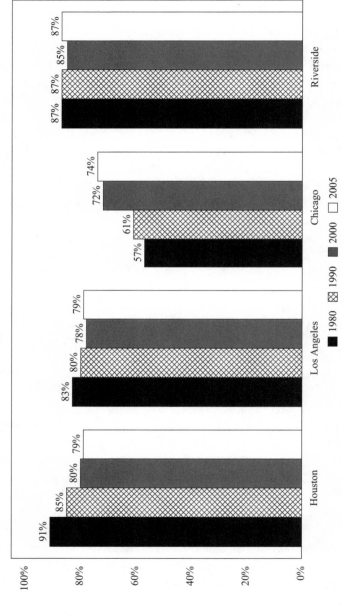

GRAPH 7.5. Percentage of Mexicans Who Were Citizens in the Houston, Los Angeles, Chicago, and Riverside Metropolitan Areas, 1980–2005.

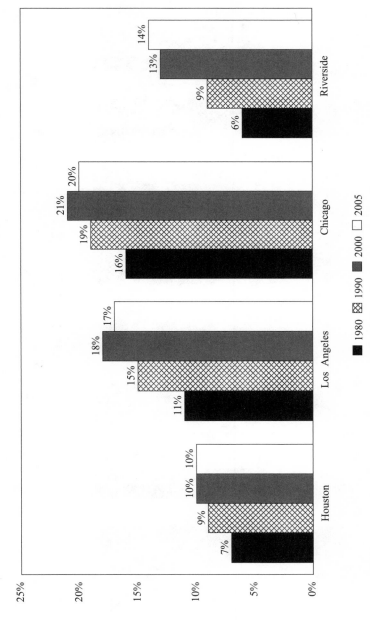

GRAPH 7.6. Percentage of Mexican Citizens Who Were Naturalized in the Houston, Los Angeles, Chicago, and Riverside Metropolitan Areas, 1980–2005.

■ 1980   ▩ 1990   ■ 2000   ☐ 2005

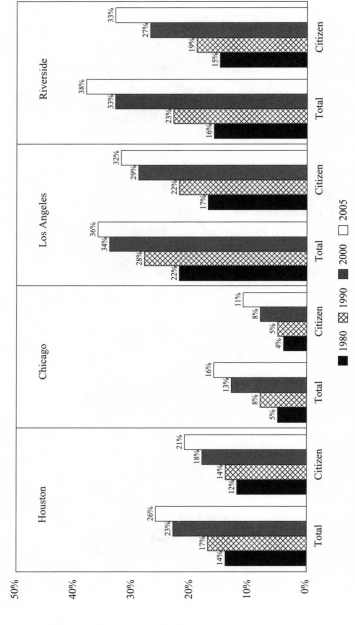

GRAPH 7.7. Mexicans as Percentage of Total Populations and as Percentage of Total Citizen Populations in the Houston, Chicago, Los Angeles, and Riverside Metropolitan Areas, 1980–2005.

■ 1980 ■ 1990 ■ 2000 □ 2005

TABLE 7.4. *Total Mexican Citizenship Status by Selected Metropolitan Areas, 1980–2005 (in absolute numbers)*

Houston			
	Total Mexicans	Citizens by Birth	Naturalized Citizens	Not Citizens
---	---	---	---	---
1980	384,718	286,677	25,935	72,106
1990	560,012	367,825	46,987	145,200
2000	977,395	554,593	89,883	332,919
2005	1,205,555	697,355	110,647	397,553

Los Angeles			
	Total Mexicans	Citizens by Birth	Naturalized Citizens	Not Citizens
---	---	---	---	---
1980	1,685,999	966,960	119,412	599,627
1990	2,501,533	1,291,429	223,195	986,909
2000	3,241,206	1,727,989	380,082	1,133,135
2005	3,550,364	2,058,823	422,096	1,069,445

Chicago			
	Total Mexicans	Citizens by Birth	Naturalized Citizens	Not Citizens
---	---	---	---	---
1980	380,200	204,123	38,195	137,882
1990	480,717	239,637	57,201	183,879
2000	1,099,863	521,750	139,159	438,954
2005	1,330,806	662,883	168,157	499,766

Riverside			
	Total Mexicans	Citizens by Birth	Naturalized Citizens	Not Citizens
---	---	---	---	---
1980	172,061	142,164	8,688	21,209
1990	587,266	395,320	37,277	154,669
2000	1,062,049	680,324	101,433	280,292
2005	1,448,798	935,268	152,704	360,826

the Miami metro area's Cuban-origin population increased from 26% of all residents in 1980 to 32% in 2005. As a percentage of total Miami citizens, there was an increase from 16% to 31% over the same period. (See Graphs 7.9 and 7.10.)

In the New York metropolitan region everyone in the largest Latino subgroup – Puerto Ricans – was a citizen, and this pushed the percentage of total Latinos who were citizens upward in comparative perspective with the other metropolitan areas. Among the four other largest Latino nationalities Dominicans and Colombians experienced extraordinary increases in citizenship rates between 1980 and 2005. Some 39% of

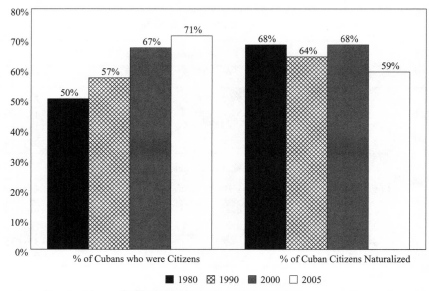

GRAPH 7.8. Percentage of Cubans in Miami Who Were Citizens and Percentage of Cuban Citizens Who Were Naturalized, 1980–2005.

New York Dominicans were citizens in 1980; and over two-thirds were citizens in 2005. Among Colombians 33% were citizens in 1980, and they were almost double that percentage in 2005. The increase in citizenship rates among Ecuadorians was lower: 36% were citizens in 1980 and 49% were citizens in 2005. Mexicans, the fastest growing Latino nationality in the New York metro area after 1980, experienced a decline in citizenship rates from 76% in 1980 to 44% in 2005, largely because of the growth of a foreign-born Mexican-origin population who had not become naturalized citizens. Accordingly, Mexicans had the lowest citizenship rate in the New York region by 2005 (see Graph 7.11).

As the most recently arrived Latino immigrant group, Mexican-origin New Yorkers had the lowest rate of naturalization among all Latino subgroups. About 14% of all New York's Mexican citizens were naturalized in 1980, and 15% were naturalized in 2005. Thus, citizenship among Mexicans was dominated by the domestic-born, more so than any other Latino subgroup.

Colombians had the highest rates of naturalization among the foreign-born in the New York metro area with 57% of all Colombian citizens having been naturalized in 2005, a slight increase from the 53% in 1980. Among Ecuadorians 53% of all citizens were foreign-born who

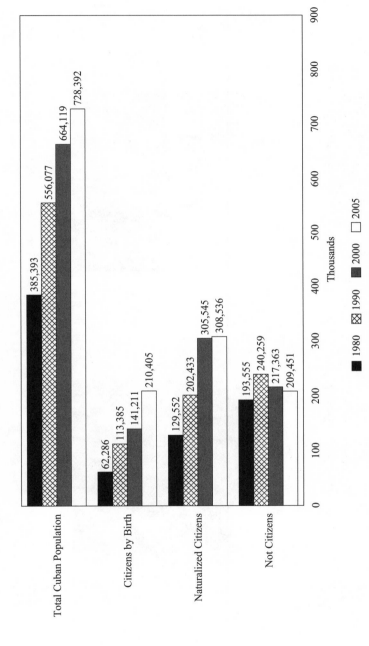

GRAPH 7.9. Cubans in the Miami Metropolitan Area by Citizenship Status, 1980–2005.

Legend: ■ 1980 ▨ 1990 ■ 2000 □ 2005

Thousands

Total Cuban Population
- 385,393
- 556,077
- 664,119
- 728,392

Citizens by Birth
- 62,286
- 113,385
- 141,211
- 210,405

Naturalized Citizens
- 129,552
- 202,433
- 305,545
- 308,536

Not Citizens
- 193,555
- 240,259
- 217,363
- 209,451

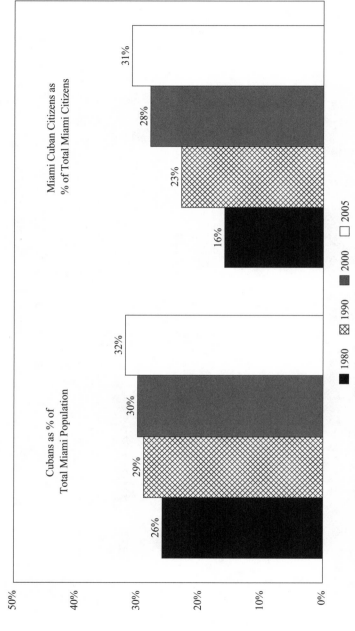

GRAPH 7.10. Percentage of Miami Population Who Were Cubans and Percentage of Miami Citizens Who Were Cuban Citizens, 1980–2005.

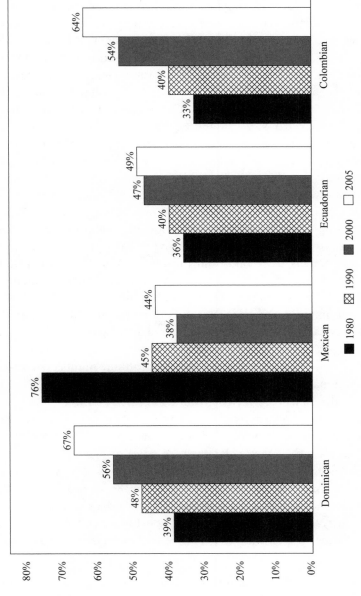

GRAPH 7.11. Percentage of Selected New York Metro Area Latino Nationalities Who Were Citizens, 1980–2005.

had been naturalized by 1980, although this fell to 44% in 2005. Among the Dominican population 50% of citizens were foreign-born who had acquired citizenship through naturalization in 1980, and 40% of all citizens were foreign-born in 2005. (See Graph 7.12.) The fall in the percentage of total foreign-born citizens who were naturalized does not mean that fewer peoples of each of these national groups sought citizenship. Rather these data reflected the increase in the domestic-born as percentages of total populations as second and third generations emerged, and these generations were all citizens through birth. The exception to this pattern was among Mexicans and Ecuadorians. The number of noncitizens among the New York metro Mexican and Ecuadorian population increased in absolute terms between 1980 and 2005 because of immigration to the region by foreign-born persons who had not yet been naturalized.

Changing citizenship rates among Dominicans in the New York metro area exemplify the connection between levels immigration and the ratio of citizens to noncitizens. Among New York Dominicans there was an increase in the percentage of the total population who were not citizens between 1980 and 2000, but the slowing of migration combined with increased numbers of second- and third-generation U.S.-born Dominicans resulted in a decline in the percentage of noncitizen Dominicans after 2000. The pattern was chronologically different for Colombians. Colombian immigration to the New York metro area was earlier than among Mexicans. The number and percentage of Colombian noncitizens rose during the 1980s but declined after 1990 as migration slowed and births to Colombian women increased. The absolute numbers of selected Latino nationalities that included citizens, naturalized citizens, and not citizens in the New York metro area are indicated in Table 7.5.

What are the implications of these patterns of citizenship among Latinos for their voting power within the United States? Specifically how many Latinos are citizens older than 18 years of age and thus eligible to vote? At the national level Latino citizens who were potential voters increased from about 6.6 million people in 1980 to nearly 17 million in 2005. Latinos comprised 4% of the total national electorate in 1980, and this increased to 9% in 2005, lagging behind their total numbers in the population.[4] They were thus still behind non-Hispanic blacks who

---

[4] The term "electorate" will be used throughout this section as being synonymous with those who were citizens and 18 years of age or older and who had the potential to vote, rather than those who actually voted.

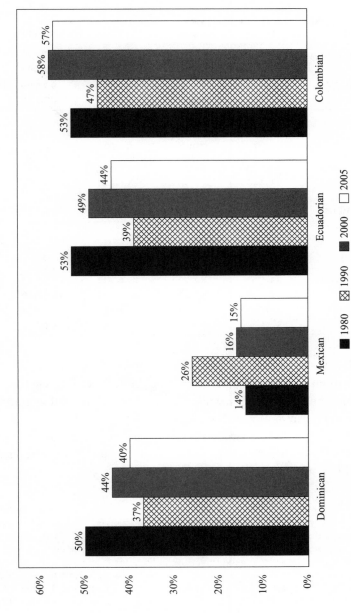

GRAPH 7.12. Percentage of New York Metro Area Total Citizens Who Were Naturalized by Selected Latino Nationalities, 1980–2005.

Legend: ■ 1980   ▨ 1990   ■ 2000   □ 2005

Dominican: 50%, 37%, 44%, 40%
Mexican: 14%, 26%, 16%, 15%
Ecuadorian: 53%, 39%, 49%, 44%
Colombian: 53%, 47%, 58%, 57%

Hispanics in the United States

TABLE 7.5. *Citizenship Status by Selected Latino Nationalities in the New York Metro Area, 1980–2005 (in absolute numbers)*

	Total Citizens			
	1980	1990	2000	2005
Dominicans	60,610	169,198	312,675	398,756
Mexicans	22,538	28,467	81,783	117,473
Ecuadorians	18,424	34,136	75,306	92,969
Colombians	19,251	38,580	62,638	77,136

	Naturalized Citizens			
	1980	1990	2000	2005
Dominicans	30,176	61,784	137,554	158,857
Mexicans	3,200	7,266	13,447	17,074
Ecuadorians	9,783	13,340	36,600	41,326
Colombians	10,184	18,167	36,093	43,994

	Not Citizens			
	1980	1990	2000	2005
Dominicans	93,177	180,368	242,741	194,917
Mexicans	29,659	63,581	212,494	268,046
Ecuadorians	32,768	51,791	84,401	95,034
Colombians	38,281	57,296	53,743	44,104

comprised 11% of the national electorate in 2005 (see Table 7.6).[5] In 1980 only about 21% of all Latinos in the electorate were foreign-born who had become naturalized citizens. The wave of naturalization among Latinos, in part inspired by anti-immigrant legislation noted previously, led to a surge in the Latino electorate after 1990. By 1990 foreign-born naturalized Latino citizens comprised 26% of the total Hispanic electorate, and this stood at 37% in 2005.[6]

---

[5] After this book was written the 2006 data were released by the U.S. Census Bureau and revealed that even though the Latino electorate had increased to over 18.6 million potential voters, they still comprised 9% of all potential voters.

[6] There is a growing literature on Latin voting patterns in recent elections from both a national and local perspective. A good survey of this literature is found in Rodney Hero, F. Chris Garcia, John García, and Harry Pachon, "Latino Participation, Partisanship, and Office Holding," *PS: Political Science and Politics*, 33:3 (2000), 529–34. For the more recent elections see Mark Hugo López, *The Hispanic Vote in the 2008 Election*, Pew Hispanic Center report of November 7, 2008; Roberto Suro, Richard Fry, and Jeffrey Passel, *Hispanics and the 2004 Election: Population, Electorate and Voters*, Pew Hispanic Center report of July 2005; David L. Leal, Matt A. Barreto, Jongho Lee, and Rodolfo O.

TABLE 7.6. *Citizens 18 Years of Age and Older by Race/Ethnicity, 1980–2005 (in absolute numbers and percentages of total citizens)*

	Absolute Numbers			
	1980	1990	2000	2005
Non-Hispanic White	131,401,304	142,025,744	147,763,693	147,253,593
Non-Hispanic Black	16,463,770	19,207,928	22,325,698	22,648,522
Latino	6,616,913	9,383,967	14,348,619	16,936,973
Asian	1,416,486	2,760,083	4,731,776	6,427,240
Other	971,257	1,337,912	4,207,380	3,681,712
TOTALS	156,869,730	174,715,634	193,377,166	196,948,040

	Percentages of Total			
	1980	1990	2000	2005
Non-Hispanic White	84%	81%	76%	75%
Non-Hispanic Black	10%	11%	12%	11%
Latino	4%	5%	7%	9%
Asian	1%	2%	2%	3%
Other	1%	1%	2%	2%
TOTALS	100%	100%	100%	100%

Reflecting the general demographic structure of Latino nationalities, the Mexican-origin population comprised 59% of the Latino electorate in both 1980 and 2005. Puerto Ricans declined from 18% to 15% of all eligible Latino potential voters, largely because of the growth of other

de la Garza, "The Latino Vote in the 2004 Election," *PS: Political Science and Politics*, 38:1 (2005), 41–49; Rodolfo O. de la Garza and Louis DeSipio, editors, *Muted Voices: Latinos and the 2000 Elections* (Lanham, MD: Rowman & Littlefield, 2005): R. Michael Alvarez and Lisa García Bedolla, "The Foundations of Latino Voter Partisanship: Evidence from the 2000 Election," *The Journal of Politics*, 65:1 (2003), 31–49. For local patterns see Daron Shaw, Rodolfo O. de la Garza, and Jongho Lee, "Examining Latino Turnout in 1996: A Three-State, Validated Survey Approach," *American Journal of Political Science*, 44:2 (2000), 338–346; David L. Leal, Valerie Martinez-Ebers, and Kenneth J. Meier, "The Politics of Latino Education: The Biases of At-Large Elections," *The Journal of Politics*, 66:4 (2004), 1224–44; R. Michael Alvarez and Tara L. Butterfield, "Latino Citizenship and Participation in California Politics: A Los Angeles County Case Study," *The Pacific Historical Review*, 68:2 (1999), 293–308. Interesting studies have also been done comparing Latino and non-Latino voting and representation; see Jonathan Nagler and R. Michael Alvarez, "Latinos, Anglos, Voters, Candidates, and Voting Rights," *University of Pennsylvania Law Review*, 153:1 (2004), 393–432; and John D. Griffin and Brian Newman, "The Unequal Representation of Latinos and Whites," *The Journal of Politics*, 69:4 (2007), 1032–46. On the representation of Latinos in specific institutions see Tim R. Sass, "The Determinants of Hispanic Representation in Municipal Government," *Southern Economic Journal*, 66: 3 (2000), 609–30.

TABLE 7.7. *Citizens 18 Years of Age and Older by Latino Nationality, 1980–2005 (in percentages of total Latino citizens 18 years of age and older)*

	1980	1990	2000	2005
Mexicans	59%	62%	57%	59%
Puerto Ricans	18%	19%	16%	15%
Cubans	5%	6%	5%	5%
Dominicans	1%	2%	2%	3%
Salvadorans	0%	1%	2%	2%
Colombians	1%	1%	2%	2%
Others	16%	9%	16%	14%
TOTALS	100%	100%	100%	100%

national groups. Cubans who were eligible to vote remained stable at 5% of voting-age citizen Latinos in both 1980 and 2005. Dominicans increased from 1% in 1980 to 3% of Latino eligible voters over the same period, and Salvadorans and Colombians comprised 2% of the Latino electorate in 2005 (see Table 7.7). In 1980 Mexicans, Puerto Ricans, and Cubans comprised 82% of all potential Latino voters, and this percentage fell only marginally to 79% in 2005.

In the metropolitan areas we have considered, Miami had the highest percentage of the total electorate that was of Latino origin by 2005 at 57%. This was an extraordinary increase from 22% in 1980. In the Los Angeles metro area 15% of all potential voters were Latinos in 1980, and this rose to 32% of all possible voters in 2005. In neighboring Riverside only 13% of the total electorate was Hispanic in 1980, but their percentage increased to 30% in 2005. Houston's Latinos comprised 10% of the total electorate in 1980 and 20% of all eligible voters in 2005. In Chicago only 11% of the electorate was Latino in 2005 compared with a miniscule 4% in 1980. Finally, in New York Latinos increased from 12% to 21% of all eligible voters between 1980 and 2005. (See Table 7.8 for these data.)

In each metropolitan area with the exception of Miami, the percentage of the Latino electorate that was comprised of foreign-born naturalized citizens increased significantly between 1980 and 2005: in Houston from 15% to 30%; from 22% to 38% in Los Angeles; from 24% to 34% in Chicago; from 19% to 31% in New York; and from 10% to 27% in Riverside. Reflecting the high percentages of naturalized Cubans in the Miami metropolitan area, 74% of eligible Latino voters were naturalized

TABLE 7.8. *Percentage of Total Electorate by Metropolitan Area by Race/Ethnicity, 1980–2005 (in percentages of total electorate)*

	Non-Hispanic Whites			
	1980	1990	2000	2005
Houston	70%	66%	58%	54%
Los Angeles	67%	58%	45%	42%
Chicago	76%	70%	67%	64%
Miami	61%	45%	27%	24%
New York	68%	58%	49%	47%
Riverside	79%	74%	61%	54%

	Non-Hispanic Blacks			
	1980	1990	2000	2005
Houston	18%	19%	20%	19%
Los Angeles	14%	14%	12%	11%
Chicago	19%	22%	20%	19%
Miami	16%	19%	19%	18%
New York	18%	22%	23%	22%
Riverside	5%	7%	8%	8%

	Latinos			
	1980	1990	2000	2005
Houston	10%	13%	17%	20%
Los Angeles	15%	20%	28%	32%
Chicago	4%	6%	9%	11%
Miami	22%	35%	51%	57%
New York	12%	16%	19%	21%
Riverside	13%	16%	25%	30%

	Asians			
	1980	1990	2000	2005
Houston	1%	2%	4%	5%
Los Angeles	4%	7%	11%	13%
Chicago	1%	2%	3%	4%
Miami	0%	1%	1%	1%
New York	1%	3%	6%	8%
Riverside	1%	2%	3%	5%

in 1980 falling to 67% in 2005 largely because of an increase in the number of Miami Latinos over 18 years of age who were born in the United States. (See Graph 7.13 for these data.)

Reflecting their overall demographic dominance, Mexicans accounted for the overwhelming share of the Latino electorate in Los Angeles, Riverside, Houston, and Chicago metropolitan areas between 1980 and 2005. There was a slight decline in their total percentages of all eligible voters in Los Angeles, Riverside, and Houston over this period because of the increase in citizenship rates among other nationalities. By 2005, however, Mexicans represented well over three-quarters of Latino eligible voters in these metro areas. In Chicago, where the Mexican community increased after 1980 and the Puerto Rican population declined, Mexicans rose as a percentage of the Latino electorate, while Puerto Ricans, the second most numerous subgroup of eligible Latino voters, declined between 1980 and 2005 (see Table 7.9 for these data).

In the Miami metropolitan area, Cubans accounted for the vast majority of the Latino electorate in 1980, 70% of all eligible Latino voters, but this declined thereafter and stood at 61% in 2005. Puerto Ricans also experienced a drop in their relative share of the Miami Latino citizen voting-age population from 14% in 1980 to 9% in 2005. These declines were due to the relative increase in Colombians, Dominicans, and Peruvian eligible voters after 1980 (see Table 7.10).

There were major transformations in the composition of the Latino electorate in the New York metro area between 1980 and 2005 and this trend will all likelihood continue into the future as the Puerto Rican population of the region continues to slowly contract in absolute numbers and as a percentage of all Latinos. The percentage of Puerto Rican eligible voters declined from 75% of all Latinos who could vote in 1980 to 52% in 2005. This was paralleled by the extraordinary growth of Dominicans who were citizens 18 years of age and older from 4% of the total New York Latino electorate in 1980 to 20% in 2005. There were also significant increases in Ecuadorian and Colombian eligible voters over the same period, although at about 5% each in 2005 they still accounted for a small share of the New York metropolitan area's Latino electorate. (See Table 7.11 for these data.)

We now turn to a consideration of the Latino electorate by nationality and by state. The order of analysis has been changed to consider the states here, after the metropolitan areas, because it is only at the state level that data are available on actual registration and voting patterns. The over 16.8 million eligible Latino voters were heavily concentrated in nine

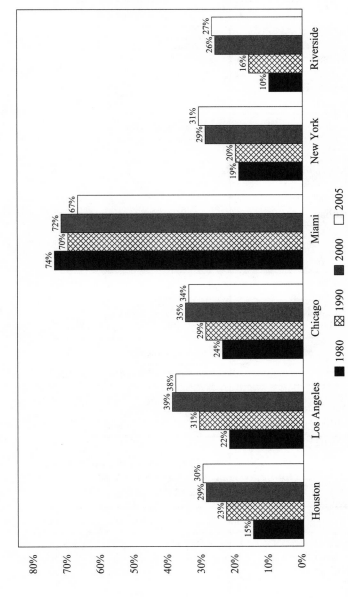

GRAPH 7.13. Percentage of Total Latino Electorate Who Were Naturalized Citizens by Metropolitan Area, 1980–2005.

■ 1980　⊠ 1990　■ 2000　☐ 2005

TABLE 7.9. *Percentage of Total Latino Electorate by Selected Latino Nationalities, 1980–2005, in Los Angeles, Riverside, Houston, and Chicago*

	Los Angeles			
	1980	1990	2000	2005
Mexican	81%	78%	76%	77%
Salvadoran	1%	3%	6%	7%
Puerto Rican	4%	3%	2%	2%
Cuban	2%	2%	2%	1%

	Riverside			
	1980	1990	2000	2005
Mexican	86%	86%	84%	85%
Puerto Rican	3%	3%	2%	2%
Salvadoran	0%	1%	2%	2%
Cuban	1%	1%	1%	1%

	Houston			
	1980	1990	2000	2005
Mexican	90%	84%	80%	78%
Salvadoran	0%	2%	4%	5%
Puerto Rican	1%	2%	2%	3%
Cuban	2%	2%	1%	2%

	Chicago			
	1980	1990	2000	2005
Mexican	54%	54%	66%	69%
Puerto Rican	33%	31%	21%	18%
Cuban	4%	3%	2%	2%

TABLE 7.10. *Percentage of Total Miami Latino Electorate by Selected Latino Nationalities, 1980–2005*

	1980	1990	2000	2005
Cuban	70%	69%	63%	61%
Puerto Rican	14%	13%	10%	9%
Colombian	3%	4%	6%	6%
Dominican	1%	2%	3%	4%
Peruvian	0%	1%	2%	3%
Mexican	3%	2%	2%	2%

TABLE 7.11. *Percentage of Total New York Latino Electorate by Selected Latino Nationalities, 1980–2005*

	1980	1990	2000	2005
Puerto Rican	75%	68%	55%	52%
Dominican	4%	9%	17%	20%
Colombian	1%	3%	4%	5%
Ecuadorian	1%	2%	4%	5%
Cuban	5%	4%	3%	3%
Mexican	2%	2%	3%	3%
Peruvian	0%	1%	1%	2%

states in 2005: California, Texas, Florida, New York, Illinois, Arizona, New Jersey, New Mexico, and Colorado. These nine states accounted for 82% of the total national-level Latino electorate in that year, and 66% were concentrated in California, Texas, Florida, and New York. (See Graph 7.14.) Potential Latino voters, citizens 18 years of age and older made up nearly 38% of the total electorate in New Mexico, 24% in Texas, 22% in California, and 17% in Arizona in 2005. In Florida, Nevada, Colorado, New York, and New Jersey, the Latino electorate ranged between 10% and 15% of all eligible voters (see Graph 7.15).

There were great differentials in the national composition of Latino electorates in each of these states. In California about 82% of all Latino eligible voters were of Mexican origin in 2005, and this was a slight increase from the 79% found in 1980. In Texas 94% of the Latino electorate was composed of Mexicans in 1980, and this fell marginally to 87% in 2005. These two states dwarfed all other states in the sheer size of eligible Latino voters in 2005: over 4.6 million Latinos could vote in California, and more than 3.3 million could vote in Texas.

The next closest state in the absolute size of eligible Latino voters was Florida with close to 1.6 million Latino citizens 18 years of age and older in 2005. But in Florida the national composition of the Latino electorate was more eclectic. Although much has been written about the "Cuban vote" in the state of Florida, in fact Cubans only comprised about one-half of the Florida Latino electorate in 1980, and this fell sharply to 36% in 2005.[7] Puerto Ricans were the second most

[7] Data released by the U.S. Census Bureau in the American Community Survey of 2006 after this manuscript was written indicate that the Cuban share of the Latino electorate continued to decline and stood at 34% in that year.

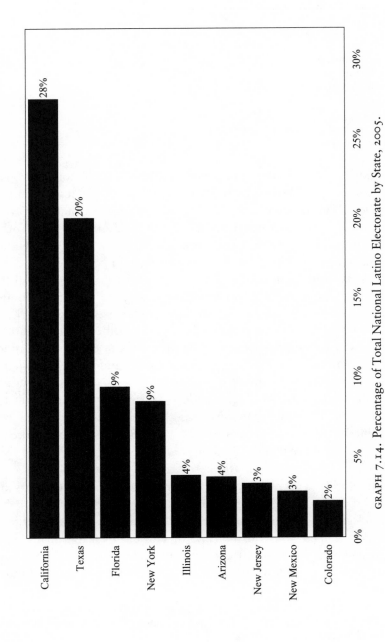

GRAPH 7.14. Percentage of Total National Latino Electorate by State, 2005.

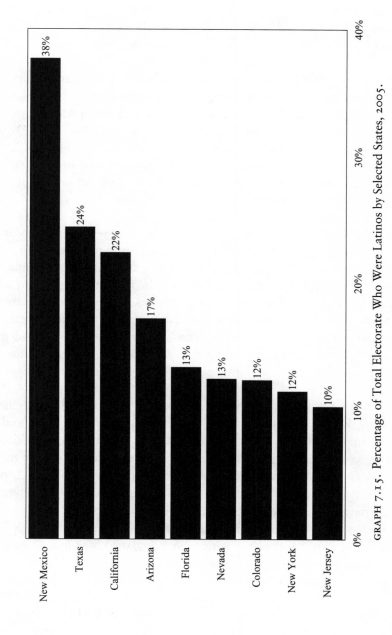

GRAPH 7.15. Percentage of Total Electorate Who Were Latinos by Selected States, 2005.

numerous Latino subgroup, increasing from 18% of Florida's potential Latino voters to 28% between 1980 and 2005 largely because of
a large Puerto Rican presence in central Florida. As percentages of all
eligible Latino voters, Mexicans (9%), Colombians (6%), and Dominicans (4%) were the next largest nationalities in the Hispanic electorate in
2005.

Finally, New York State, with over 1.4 million eligible Latino voters in
2005 manifested the same kind of diversification in terms of national origins found in Florida. Puerto Ricans had accounted for 74% of the total
Latino electorate in 1980, but this declined sharply to 52% in 2005. Over
the same period Dominican citizens 18 years of age and older increased
from 4% of all eligible New York State Latino voters in 1980 to 18%
in 2005. Colombians (5%), Ecuadorians (5%), and Mexicans (4%) were
the next largest components of the New York Latino electorate in 2005
(see Table 7.12 for these data).

An important question concerning the growth of the Latino electorate
after 1980 was the impact of California's 1994 anti-immigrant Proposition 187. In that state it appears to have had a fairly substantial impact
among the dominant Mexican community. In 1980 about 19% of all
eligible Mexican voters were naturalized citizens. This number increased
gradually to 26% in 1990. After Proposition 187 was enacted, naturalization among foreign-born Mexicans of voting age soared, and in
2000 41% of all eligible Mexican voters were foreign-born naturalized
citizens. This remained stable to 2005 when the corresponding figure
was 40%.

It is apparent, however, that the impact of Proposition 187 was confined largely to California. In Texas there was no such wave of naturalization among voting-age Mexicans. In 1980 12% of the Mexican electorate was comprised of foreign-born naturalized citizens. By 2005 this
had increased to 18%, well below the levels found in California. There
was also no measurable impact on Florida voting-age Cubans, who were
largely naturalized citizens, or in New York State where Puerto Ricans,
all citizens, were dominant among the Latino electorate. Among New
York Dominicans most of the voting-age population was composed of
naturalized citizens in 1980 (89%), and this trend continued through
2005 (65%). The relative decrease was because of the rise of a second
generation of Dominicans who were born in the United States and who
were thus citizens and eligible to vote when they reached the age of 18
between 1980 and 2005. These domestic-born Dominicans increased as

TABLE 7.12. *National Composition of Latino Electorate in California, Florida, New York, and Texas, 1980–2005 (selected nationalities)*

	California			
	1980	1990	2000	2005
Mexicans	79%	84%	84%	82%
Puerto Ricans	3%	4%	4%	2%
Cubans	1%	2%	2%	1%
Salvadorans	1%	2%	2%	4%

	Florida			
	1980	1990	2000	2005
Cubans	50%	48%	48%	36%
Puerto Ricans	18%	26%	26%	28%
Mexicans	11%	9%	9%	9%
Colombians	2%	4%	4%	6%
Dominicans	1%	2%	2%	4%

	New York			
	1980	1990	2000	2005
Puerto Ricans	74%	69%	69%	52%
Dominicans	4%	9%	9%	18%
Colombians	1%	3%	3%	5%
Ecuadorians	1%	2%	2%	5%
Mexicans	2%	3%	3%	4%
Cubans	5%	5%	5%	3%

	Texas			
	1980	1990	2000	2005
Mexicans	94%	94%	94%	87%
Puerto Ricans	1%	2%	2%	2%
Salvadorans	0%	0%	0%	1%
Cubans	0%	1%	1%	1%
Colombians	0%	0%	0%	1%

an overall percentage of eligible New York Dominican voters, and it may be projected that they will increase in the future.

Yet despite accounting for about 7% of the nation's total potential electorate in the presidential elections of 2000, Latinos made up about 5.4% of those who actually voted. In the 2004 presidential elections

Latinos comprised 8.2% of the electorate but only 6% of those who went to the polls in November 2004.[8]

Latinos had a very low rate of voter registration among citizens 18 years of age and older compared with non-Hispanic whites and non-Hispanic blacks, although it was slightly higher than Asians. About 57% of the potential Latino electorate was registered in 2000, and this rose negligibly to 58% in 2004. Among non-Hispanic whites, 75% of eligible voters were registered in 2004 and 69% of the non-Hispanic black electorate were registered in the same year. Asians had a smaller percentage of registered voters among citizens of voting age than Hispanics at 52% in 2004 (see Graph 7.16).

Once registered, however, voter turnout rates among Latinos were only marginally lower than among the other major racial/ethnic groups, although they were the lowest of all the racial/ethnic subgroups. Some 79% of registered Latino voters went to the polls in 2000, and this rose to 82% in 2004. This compares with a voter turnout rate in the 2004 presidential elections of 89% of registered voters among non-Hispanic whites, 87% among non-Hispanic blacks, and 85% among Asians (see Graph 7.17).

Because of low registration rates among those Latinos who were potentially eligible to vote, a substantially smaller share of all voting-age Latino citizens actually went to the polls when compared with non-Hispanic whites and non-Hispanic blacks, although their total voting participation rates when registered were slightly above those for Asians. In the 2004 presidential elections 47% of all potentially eligible Latino voters actually voted compared with 67% of non-Hispanic whites, 60% of non-Hispanic blacks, and 44% of Asians (see Graph 7.18).

Over 60% of the total Latino electorate was concentrated in the states of California, Texas, Florida, and New York in 2004, and these

---

[8] See the data released by the U.S. Census Bureau on its Web site "Voting and Registration in the Election of November 2000" at http://www.census.gov/population/www/socdemo/voting/p20–542.html and "Voting and Registration in the Election of November 2004" at http://www.census.gov/population/www/socdemo/voting/cps2004.html.

Also see the nuanced and most complete analysis of factors affecting registration and Latino voting patterns by Debora Upegui "Hispanic Citizenship, Registration, and Voting Patterns: A Comparative Analysis of the 2000 and 2004 Presidential Elections" on the City University of New York's Center for Latin American, Caribbean, and Latinos Studies Web site at http://web.gc.cuny.edu/lastudies. Also see Suro, Fry, and Passell *Hispanics and the 2004 Election*. All graphs on voter registration and participation in the 2000 and 2004 presidential elections in this section are based on these census data.

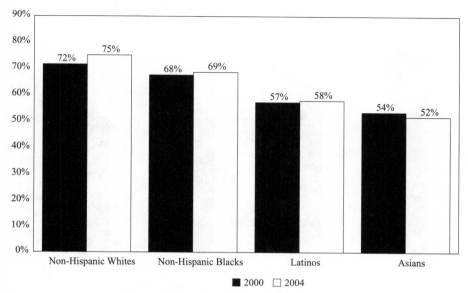

GRAPH 7.16. Percentage of Citizens 18 Years of Age and Older Registered to Vote, in the Presidential Elections of 2000 and 2004 by Race/Ethnicity.

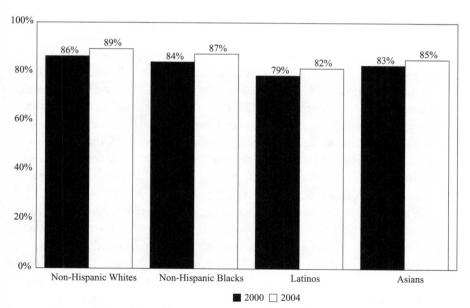

GRAPH 7.17. Percentage of Registered Voters Who Voted in the Presidential Elections of 2000 and 2004 by Race/Ethnicity.

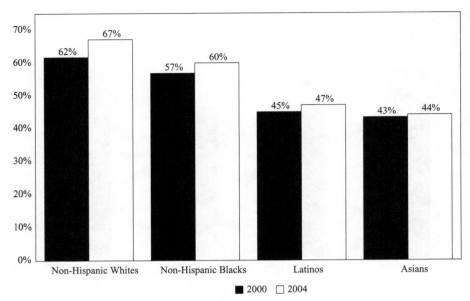

GRAPH 7.18. Percentage of Total Eligible Voting Population Who Voted in the Presidential Elections of 2000 and 2004 by Race/Ethnicity.

states serve as important indicators of Latino voter registration and participation rates at state levels. Out of all 50 states Florida had the highest rate of Latino voters registered, with 64% of all voting-age citizen Latinos registered to vote in 2004. These registrations may have been related to the strong presence of a politically mobilized Cuban citizen voting-age population, as well as the central role that the state played in both the 2000 and 2004 presidential elections. Texas followed with close to 60% of all eligible Latino voters registered to vote in 2004. In California and New York 55% and 56% of the potential Latino electorate was registered to vote in 2004 (see Graph 7.19).

When we examine the percentage of registered Latino voters who actually voted in these states, there were sharp disparities between Florida, California, and New York, where over 80% of all registered Latino voters went to the polls in 2004, and Texas where 71% voted. There is no systematic explanation for this difference. It ought to be noted that the centrality of Florida to the presidential election of 2000 apparently led to a higher voter turnout rate among Latinos in 2004. In 2000 85% of eligible Florida Latino voters actually voted, and this rose to 89% in 2004,

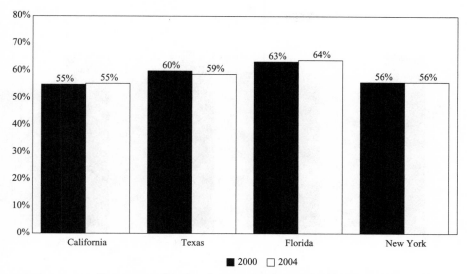

GRAPH 7.19. Percentage of Latino Citizens Aged 18 and Older Registered to Vote in the Presidential Elections of 2000 and 2004 in California, Texas, Florida, and New York.

the highest voter turnout rate among registered Latinos of any state. California was next at 85%, and in New York 81% of registered Latino voters turned out to vote in 2004, down slightly from 83% in 2000 (see Graph 7.20).

Finally, it ought to be noted that because of both lower voter registration rates and relatively low voter turnout rates among those who were registered in California, New York, and Texas, less than 50% of all potential Latino voters, citizens 18 years of age and older, actually participated in the presidential elections of both 2000 and 2004. In Texas only 42% of all Latino citizens of voting age voted. Florida stands out because of its much higher registration and turnout rates. Some 57% of all potential Latino voters voted in 2004. (See Graph 7.21.) Thus, care must be taken to distinguish between voter participation rates among registered voters, and the overall participation rates among those actually eligible to vote because they were citizens 18 years of age and older.

As the voting-age citizen Latino population of the United States inevitably increases, there are key states in which they may determine the outcome of national elections. However, this potential political weight

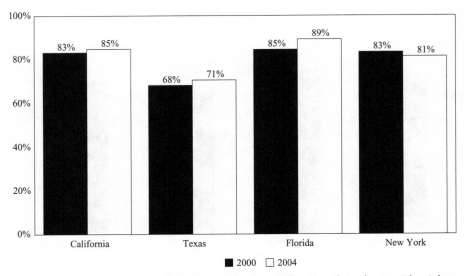

GRAPH 7.20. Percentage of Registered Latinos Who Voted in the Presidential Elections of 2000 and 2004 in California, Texas, Florida, and New York.

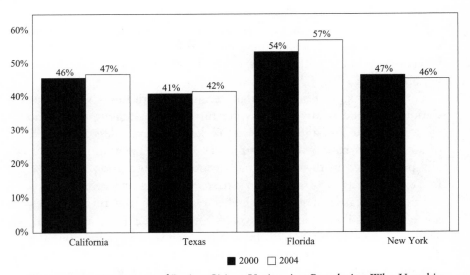

GRAPH 7.21. Percentage of Latino Citizen Voting-Age Population Who Voted in the Presidential Elections of 2000 and 2004 in California, Texas, Florida, and New York.

will be directly determined by voter registration rates and the actual turnout in local, state, and national elections. The current low registration rates that prevail across the United States within the Latino electorate inhibit the potential political impact that Hispanic voters currently exercise.

8

Occupational Structures, Employment, and Unemployment

Occupational Structures

The occupational structure of the Latino workforce was fundamentally different from the other racial and ethnic groups in the United States in that Latinos were far less likely to occupy higher-status and salaried management and professional positions than non-Hispanic whites and blacks and Asians.[1] This was closely connected to the surge in the migration

---

[1] There is a lively debate both about the first generation of Latino workers and their subsequent economic mobility. Borjas in a series of studies has argued that Mexicans and other Latinos had a different and lower level of skills and education than previous immigrant groups and that this is reflected in lower wages. See George J. Borjas, "Assimilation, Changes in Cohort Quality, and the Earnings of Immigrants," *Journal of Labor Economics*, 3 (1985), 463–89; "Self-Selection and the Earnings of Immigrants," 531–53; *Friends or Strangers: The Impact of Immigrants on the U.S. Economy* (New York: Basic Books, 1990); "Immigrants in the U.S. Labor Market: 1940–80," *The American Economic Review*, 81:2 (1991), 287–91; and "Ethnic Capital and Intergenerational Mobility," *Quarterly Journal of Economics*, 107:1 (1992): 123–50. This analysis has been challenged as being too simplistic by David Card, "Is the New Immigration Really So Bad?" 300–23, and by Kristin F. Butcher and John DiNardo, "The Immigrant and Native-Born Wage Distributions: Evidence from United States Censuses," *Industrial and Labor Relations Review*, 56:1 (2002), 97–121, both of whom are arguing that mean skills hide complex patterns and that they do not take into account national wage market changes between the Old and New Immigration and the post-1960 migration groups. If there is some rough agreement on the median educational and wage characteristics of the first generation of Hispanic males, there is much debate about Borjas's position on declining Latino mobility in the second and third generations. For a statement of his position, see George J. Borjas "Long-Run Convergence of Ethnic Skill Differentials: The Children and Grandchildren of the Great Migration," *Industrial and Labor Relations Review*, 47:4 (July 1994), 553–73; "The Intergenerational Mobility of Immigrants," *Journal of Labor Economics* 11:1 (1993): 113–35 and most recently his essay "Making It in America."

of lesser-educated persons after 1980 and the resulting lower educational attainment levels found among Latinos. In 2005 only 16.7% of all Hispanics worked in these higher-income earning professions compared with 35.4% of employed non-Hispanic whites, 23.6% of non-Hispanic blacks, and 44% of Asians. Yet, nearly 46% of the Hispanic labor force was employed in service, sales, and office occupations, and this was not too different from the other racial/ethnic groups, each of which had over 40% of their respective employed populations working in these same professions.[2]

For the opposing position see Joel Perlmann and Roger Waldinger, "Second Generation Decline? Children of Immigrants, Past and Present – A Reconsideration," *International Migration Review* 31:4 (1997), 893–922; David Card, John DiNardo, and Eugena Estes, "The More Things Change: Immigrants and the Children of Immigrants in the 1940s, the 1970s, and the 1990s," in George J. Borjas, editor, *Issues in the Economics of Immigration* (Chicago: University of Chicago Press, 2000), pp. 227–70.

[2] Some 55% of non-Hispanic blacks were employed in these occupations. A major debate has developed in the literature about the relative impact of low-skilled immigrants on the wages of low-skilled domestic-born Americans, particularly African Americans. Arguing against immigrants influencing wages of low-skilled workers is Kristin F. Butcher and David Card, "Immigration and Wages: Evidence from the 1980's," *The American Economic Review*, 81:2 (1991), 292–96; though analysis of the 1990 data by Card does suggest some influence, see David Card "Immigrant Inflows, Native Outflows, and the Local Market Impacts of Higher Immigration," *Journal of Labor Economics*, 19:1 (2001), 22–64. As Card most recently concluded, "Overall, evidence that immigrants have harmed the opportunities of less educated natives is scant." See David Card, "Is the New Immigration Really So Bad?" In contrast George J. Borjas has steadily argued for a negative impact on native workers from immigrant competition. See, for example, George J. Borjas, "The Labor Demand Curve Is Downward Sloping: Reexamining the Impact of Immigration on the Labor Market," *The Quarterly Journal of Economics*, 118:4 (2003), 1335–74. In an oft-cited major summary of all the relevant literature and applicable models used to analyze this debate, the conclusion reached was that:

Despite the popular belief that immigrants have a large adverse impact on the wages and employment opportunities of the native-born population, the literature on this question does not provide much support for this conclusion. Economic theory is equivocal, and empirical estimates in a variety of settings and using a variety of approaches have shown that the effect of immigration on the labor market outcomes of the domestic-born is small. There is no evidence of economically significant reductions in domestic-born employment. Most empirical analysis of the United States and other countries finds that a 10 percent increase in the fraction of immigrants in the population reduces domestic-born wages by at most 1 percent. Even those who should be the closest substitutes with immigrant labor have not been found to suffer significantly as a result of increased immigration. The upper bound on the wage impact is large enough to explain one-quarter of the rise in inequality in the United States in the 1980s, but the true effect is probably considerably smaller.

Rachel M. Friedberg and Jennifer Hunt, "The Impact of Immigrants on Host Country Wages, Employment and Growth," *The Journal of Economic Perspectives*, 9:2 (1995), 44.

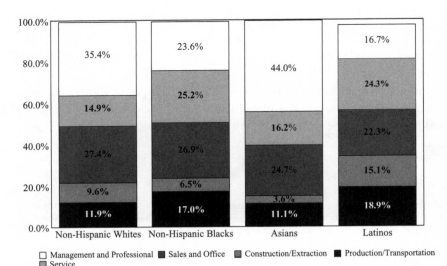

GRAPH 8.1. Percentage of the Workforce Employed by Occupational Category by Race/Ethnicity, 2005. *Note:* Small percentages of each race/ethnicity were employed in the military and in farming/fishing industries.

A major divergence was found in construction trades where there was a higher concentration of Latinos. Slightly over 15% of employed Hispanics labored in construction-related occupations compared with 9.6% of non-Hispanic whites, 6.5% of non-Hispanic blacks, and 3.6% of Asians. When construction and production occupations are examined together, the contrasts with the other racial/ethnic groups are more extreme. Just over a third of all employed Latinos worked in these two categories compared with 21.5% of non-Hispanic whites, 23.5% of non-Hispanic blacks, and only 14.7% of Asians who were employed (see Graph 8.1).

Examining these broad occupational categories by sex, just over a quarter of the male Hispanic workforce was concentrated in construction/extraction occupations, and this was nearly double the percentage found among non-Hispanic black males and significantly higher than among non-Hispanic white and Asian males. When production/transportation occupations are aggregated with the construction trades for men, nearly 49% of all employed Latino males were found in these two occupational categories compared with about 35% of non-Hispanic white males, 40% of non-Hispanic black men, and just a fifth of employed Asian males.

Some 63% of employed Latina women were concentrated in service and/or sales and office occupations, and this was about the same concentration found among non-Hispanic black women (62%), but it was

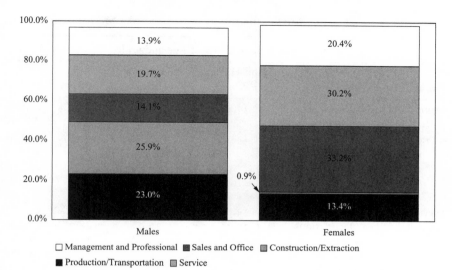

GRAPH 8.2. Percentage of the Latino Workforce Employed by Occupational Category by Sex, 2005. *Note:* Small percentages of Latino males and females were employed in the military and in farming/fishing industries.

much higher than among non-Hispanic white females (45%) or Asian women (48%). About one-fifth of Latina females worked in management and professional occupations in 2005, the lowest rate among employed females in the major racial/ethnic groups, although this rate was significantly higher than among Hispanic males (14%). (See Table 8.1 and Graph 8.2).[3]

In every single occupational category, Hispanics earned median personal incomes that were considerably lower than those found among the other racial/ethnic groups. Additionally, Hispanic women earned significantly lower median personal incomes in every occupational category compared with Hispanic men in the same occupational groups, although this pattern of comparatively lower income levels for women was found among all racial/ethnic groups. The income-earning situation among Hispanic women was particularly bleak. Some 39% of all Latinas were employed in sales or office occupations, and they earned median personal incomes of only $16,095 in 2005. Another 25% of the female

---

[3] After this book was written the Bureau of Labor Statistics published occupational structure data for 2006 and 2007, and these do not fundamentally differ from the 2005 data cited here. See the report at http://www.bls.gov/cps/cpsaat10.pdf.

TABLE 8.1. *Occupational Structure by Race/Ethnicity and Sex, 2005*

Total Population 16 Years of Age and Older

Occupational Category	Non-Hispanic White	Non-Hispanic Black	Asian	Latino
Management, Professional, and Related Occupations	35.4%	23.6%	44.0%	16.7%
Management, business, and financial operations occupations	14.3%	8.2%	14.0%	6.8%
Professional and related occupations	21.1%	15.5%	30.1%	9.9%
Service Occupations	14.9%	25.2%	16.2%	24.3%
Sales and Office Occupations	27.4%	26.9%	24.7%	22.3%
Sales and related occupations	12.5%	10.3%	12.1%	9.7%
Office and administrative support occupations	14.9%	16.6%	12.6%	12.7%
Farming, Fishing, and Forestry Occupations	0.6%	0.4%	0.2%	2.5%
Construction, Extraction, and Maintenance	9.6%	6.5%	3.6%	15.1%
Construction and extraction occupations	6.0%	3.9%	1.6%	11.7%
Installation, maintenance, and repair occupations	3.6%	2.6%	2.0%	3.4%
Production, Transportation, and Material Moving Occupations	11.9%	17.0%	11.1%	18.9%
Production occupations	6.3%	7.8%	7.9%	10.6%
Transportation and material moving occupations	5.7%	9.2%	3.2%	8.3%
Military Occupations	0.3%	0.4%	0.2%	0.2%

Total Male Population 16 Years of Age and Older

Occupational Category	Non-Hispanic White	Non-Hispanic Black	Asian	Latino
Management, Professional, and Related Occupations	33.2%	18.9%	45.8%	13.9%
Management, business, and financial operations occupations	16.2%	7.7%	14.6%	6.7%
Professional and related occupations	17.1%	11.2%	31.2%	7.2%
Service Occupations	11.6%	21.5%	13.7%	19.7%
Sales and Office Occupations	18.5%	18.6%	20.1%	14.1%
Sales and related occupations	11.8%	8.0%	11.7%	7.3%
Office and administrative support occupations	6.6%	10.5%	8.4%	6.8%

Occupational Category	Non-Hispanic White	Non-Hispanic Black	Asian	Latino
Farming, Fishing, and Forestry Occupations	0.9%	0.6%	0.3%	3.1%
Construction, Extraction, and Maintenance	17.7%	13.3%	6.6%	25.9%
Construction and extraction occupations	11.0%	8.1%	3.0%	20.2%
Installation, maintenance, and repair occupations	6.7%	5.1%	3.6%	5.8%
Production, Transportation, and Material Moving Occupations	17.7%	26.5%	13.2%	23.0%
Production occupations	8.5%	9.9%	8.1%	11.3%
Transportation and material moving occupations	9.2%	16.6%	5.1%	11.8%
Military Occupations	0.4%	0.6%	0.3%	0.3%

Total Female Population 16 Years of Age and Older

Occupational Category	Non-Hispanic White	Non-Hispanic Black	Asian	Latino
Management, Professional, and Related Occupations	37.7%	27.6%	42.2%	20.4%
Management, business, and financial operations occupations	12.2%	8.5%	13.4%	7.0%
Professional and related occupations	25.4%	19.1%	28.8%	13.5%
Service Occupations	18.4%	28.4%	18.8%	30.2%
Sales and Office Occupations	37.0%	33.9%	29.6%	33.2%
Sales and related occupations	13.1%	12.3%	12.4%	12.8%
Office and administrative support occupations	23.9%	21.7%	17.1%	20.4%
Farming, Fishing, and Forestry Occupations	0.2%	0.1%	0.2%	1.7%
Construction, Extraction, and Maintenance	0.9%	0.8%	0.5%	0.9%
Construction and extraction occupations	0.5%	0.3%	0.2%	0.6%
Installation, maintenance, and repair occupations	0.3%	0.5%	0.3%	0.3%
Production, Transportation, and Material Moving Occupations	5.8%	9.0%	8.8%	13.4%
Production occupations	3.8%	6.0%	7.6%	9.7%
Transportation and material moving occupations	1.9%	3.0%	1.2%	3.8%
Military Occupations	0.1%	0.2%	0.1%	0.1%

Hispanic workforce were employed in the service sector and earned median incomes of a paltry $10,817 in 2005 (see Table 8.2).

When we examine the Latino population by the largest nationalities, sex, and nativity, the extraordinary diversity in employment markets of this extremely heterogeneous population comes to light. Not surprisingly, the national groups with the highest educational attainment levels were those with greater percentages of their employed populations in higher-status jobs in management and professional occupations. Cubans, Colombians, Peruvians, and Puerto Ricans had relatively higher percentages of men and women in these occupations compared with the other national groups. Nearly 30% of all Cubans in the workforce were employed in management and professional occupations, whereas for Colombians, Peruvians, and Puerto Ricans roughly one-quarter of those employed were found in these categories. Hondurans and Salvadorans had the lowest portions of their workforces in higher status occupations, about 10% of those employed. Ecuadorians (17.6%), Dominicans (16.1%), and Mexicans (13.7%) were in the middle of these extremes.

Despite large numbers of men and women employed in higher status occupations, each Latino nationality had the greatest concentration of their employed populations in service, sales, and office occupations. The range was between 43% for Ecuadorians to 57% for Dominicans, with the other nationalities falling between these extremes. The differences by sex were significant. Women of all nationalities were heavily concentrated in the service, sales, and office categories and the range was between 58.5% of Cuban women to about 69% of Salvadoran women. Each of the other nationalities had over 60% of their female workforce employed in service, sales, and office professions. Yet, relatively large percentages of Puerto Rican, Cuban, Colombian, and Peruvian women were found in management and professional occupations – over one-quarter of these nationalities.

For men, there was concentration in construction, production, and transportation occupations, although there were clear discrepancies between national groups. An extraordinary 44% of Honduran males were found in the construction trades alone, and 63% of employed Honduran men were concentrated in construction, production, and transportation sectors of the workforce. Over a quarter of Mexican, Salvadoran, and Ecuadorian men were employed in construction trades, and for each of these nationalities over 50% were working in construction, production, and transportation occupations. Over one-quarter of Cuban and Colombian males in the workforce were found in management and

TABLE 8.2. *Median Personal Income by Occupational Category, Sex, and Race/Ethnicity, 2005*

	Total Population			
Occupational Category	Non-Hispanic White	Non-Hispanic Black	Asian	Hispanic
Management, Professional, and Related Occupations	45,840	38,404	50,933	35,653
Service Occupations	13,243	13,752	15,280	12,835
Sales and Office Occupations	24,448	20,373	20,373	18,336
Construction and Maintenance Occupations	32,597	25,263	32,597	22,411
Production, Transportation, and Material Moving Occupations	27,810	20,373	21,494	18,540

	Males			
Occupational Category	Non-Hispanic White	Non-Hispanic Black	Asian	Hispanic
Management, Professional, and Related Occupations	61,120	45,331	61,120	43,813
Service Occupations	20,475	16,299	18,540	17,012
Sales and Office Occupations	35,653	23,429	25,467	23,429
Construction and Maintenance Occupations	33,209	25,059	32,699	22,411
Production, Transportation, and Material Moving Occupations	31,171	23,837	25,467	22,411

	Females			
Occupational Category	Non-Hispanic White	Non-Hispanic Black	Asian	Hispanic
Management, Professional, and Related Occupations	36,061	35,653	41,424	30,560
Service Occupations	10,390	12,631	13,345	10,187
Sales and Office Occupations	20,373	19,355	18,336	16,095
Construction and Maintenance Occupations	23,429	25,467	30,560	17,623
Production, Transportation, and Material Moving Occupations	18,336	16,299	18,132	12,937

professional occupations. Hondurans (7.8%), Salvadorans (9.5%), and Mexicans (11%) had the lowest percentage of men in these higher status occupations (see Table 8.3).

Nativity was also a factor in occupational distribution by sex, although no generalizations may be applied when the Latino population is disaggregated by nationality. Some general observations may be made, however. Domestic-born men and women of every nationality had greater percentages of their employed populations in higher-status management and professional occupations than their foreign-born counterparts. This was clearly related to higher educational attainment levels for the domestic-born. For foreign-born males there were greater concentrations in construction, production, and transportation occupations than for domestic-born males. It is also interesting to note that while there were subtle differences in the percentages of foreign- and domestic-born women by nationality who were working in service, sales, and office occupations in 2005, these were not substantial. Roughly the same percentage of Latinas worked in these employment categories regardless of nativity. Complete data on labor force sector by nativity and sex are found in Table 8.4.

If there is one variable that highlights the impossibility of making sweeping generalizations about "Latinos," it is the complex mosaic of median incomes found when these variables of sex, origin, and nativity are examined.[4] In general terms, all nationalities and both sexes, whether domestic- or foreign-born, earned the greatest median incomes in higher-status professional and management occupations with the construction-related occupations falling into second place in the income hierarchy. Service, sales, and office occupations, with their high concentrations of both domestic- and foreign-born women of all national groups, generally were paid the lowest salaries as reflected in median personal income. For Mexicans, the most numerous of the Latino nationalities in the nation, there was very clear income stratification by nativity and sex. In nearly every occupational category, domestic-born males earned the highest median incomes followed by foreign-born males, domestic-born females, with foreign-born females earning the lowest incomes.[5]

---

[4] Many researchers on immigrants and their occupations and wages have stressed the need to disaggregate their findings by sex and origin, which changes the broad picture based on means that have emerged for both sexes and all Latinos. This is the position taken by Card, "Is the New Immigration Really So Bad?" and Butcher and DiNardo, "The Immigrant and Native-Born Wage Distributions."

[5] In the service, sales, and office occupations Mexican foreign-born males earned slightly more than domestic-born males.

TABLE 8.3. *Latino Occupational Structure by Nationality and Sex, 2005*

Occupational Category	Total Population 16 Years of Age and Older								
	Mexicans	Puerto Ricans	Cubans	Hondurans	Salvadorans	Colombians	Ecuadorians	Peruvians	Dominicans
Management, Professional, and Related Occupations	13.7%	23.3%	29.7%	10.7%	10.5%	26.0%	17.6%	24.0%	16.1%
Management, business, and financial operations occupations	5.7%	8.6%	12.8%	4.5%	4.4%	9.3%	6.8%	9.3%	6.5%
Professional and related occupations	8.0%	14.7%	16.8%	6.2%	6.1%	16.6%	10.8%	14.7%	9.6%
Service Occupations	24.0%	22.6%	17.3%	28.1%	33.2%	23.8%	22.8%	25.9%	31.5%
Sales and Office Occupations	20.6%	30.0%	28.5%	14.6%	16.9%	26.6%	22.9%	24.9%	25.6%
Sales and related occupations	8.9%	11.2%	13.5%	5.7%	7.3%	12.2%	9.3%	12.4%	12.2%
Office and administrative support occupations	11.7%	18.7%	15.0%	8.9%	9.6%	14.4%	13.6%	12.5%	13.5%
Farming, Fishing, and Forestry Occupations	3.7%	0.2%	0.4%	1.3%	0.9%	0.1%	0.1%	0.4%	0.2%
Construction, Extraction, and Maintenance	17.1%	8.1%	10.8%	25.1%	16.7%	8.4%	15.4%	10.1%	7.3%
Construction and extraction occupations	13.6%	4.5%	6.8%	22.3%	13.1%	5.4%	12.6%	7.3%	4.3%
Installation, maintenance, and repair occupations	3.5%	3.5%	4.0%	2.8%	3.6%	3.0%	2.8%	2.7%	3.1%
Production, Transportation, and Material Moving Occupations	20.7%	15.3%	13.3%	19.9%	21.8%	14.9%	21.1%	14.6%	19.0%
Production occupations	12.0%	7.6%	5.9%	11.5%	12.0%	8.7%	12.5%	8.0%	10.6%
Transportation and material moving occupations	8.8%	7.7%	7.4%	8.3%	9.8%	6.2%	8.6%	6.6%	8.5%
Military Occupations	0.1%	0.5%	0.1%	0.3%	0.0%	0.2%	0.1%	0.1%	0.2%

(continued)

285

TABLE 8.3 (continued)

Total Male Population 16 Years of Age and Older

Occupational Category	Mexicans	Puerto Ricans	Cubans	Hondurans	Salvadorans	Colombians	Ecuadorians	Peruvians	Dominicans
Management, Professional, and Related Occupations	11.0%	19.3%	27.5%	7.8%	9.5%	26.7%	15.8%	21.7%	14.9%
Management, business, and financial operations occupations	5.5%	8.2%	13.8%	3.5%	4.6%	11.5%	7.1%	9.9%	7.3%
Professional and related occupations	5.5%	11.1%	13.6%	4.3%	4.9%	15.2%	8.7%	11.8%	7.6%
Service Occupations	19.6%	21.5%	15.6%	18.8%	23.9%	16.3%	18.5%	21.3%	25.5%
Sales and Office Occupations	12.3%	19.7%	19.6%	8.2%	11.8%	21.1%	15.4%	20.3%	19.9%
Sales and related occupations	6.3%	8.9%	11.9%	3.3%	5.8%	10.6%	7.8%	12.0%	11.1%
Office and administrative support occupations	6.0%	10.8%	7.7%	4.9%	6.0%	10.5%	7.7%	8.3%	8.8%
Farming, Fishing, and Forestry Occupations	4.3%	0.2%	0.6%	1.8%	1.1%	0.1%	0.1%	0.6%	0.3%
Construction, Extraction, and Maintenance	28.2%	15.4%	18.9%	43.7%	28.7%	16.0%	26.3%	17.3%	14.8%
Construction and extraction occupations	22.5%	8.7%	12.1%	38.8%	22.6%	10.2%	21.7%	12.5%	8.7%
Installation, maintenance, and repair occupations	5.8%	6.7%	6.8%	4.8%	6.1%	5.8%	4.6%	4.9%	6.1%
Production, Transportation, and Material Moving Occupations	24.3%	23.0%	17.6%	19.3%	24.9%	19.5%	23.8%	18.5%	24.2%
Production occupations	12.5%	9.9%	6.1%	9.3%	11.4%	9.5%	11.3%	8.7%	10.9%
Transportation and material moving occupations	11.8%	13.1%	11.5%	10.0%	13.6%	10.0%	12.5%	9.8%	13.4%
Military Occupations	0.2%	0.9%	0.2%	0.5%	0.0%	0.3%	0.1%	0.3%	0.4%

Total Female Population 16 Years of Age and Older

Occupational Category	Mexicans	Puerto Ricans	Cubans	Hondurans	Salvadorans	Colombians	Ecuadorians	Peruvians	Dominicans
Management, Professional, and Related Occupations	17.7%	27.4%	32.3%	14.4%	11.7%	25.2%	20.1%	26.7%	17.2%
Management, business, and financial operations occupations	6.1%	9.1%	11.6%	5.7%	4.2%	7.2%	6.4%	8.6%	5.8%
Professional and related occupations	11.6%	18.4%	20.8%	8.7%	7.5%	18.1%	13.7%	18.1%	11.4%
Service Occupations	30.4%	23.7%	19.3%	40.1%	45.5%	31.1%	28.8%	31.2%	37.0%
Sales and Office Occupations	32.6%	40.2%	39.2%	22.8%	23.7%	31.9%	33.2%	30.9%	30.9%
Sales and related occupations	12.6%	13.5%	15.3%	8.6%	9.3%	13.7%	11.5%	12.9%	13.2%
Office and administrative support occupations	20.0%	26.7%	24.0%	14.1%	14.4%	18.2%	21.7%	17.3%	17.7%
Farming, Fishing, and Forestry Occupations	2.7%	0.2%	0.2%	0.6%	0.6%	0.2%	0.0%	0.2%	0.1%
Construction, Extraction, and Maintenance	1.0%	0.7%	0.9%	1.5%	0.8%	1.0%	0.5%	1.6%	0.5%
Construction and extraction occupations	0.7%	0.3%	0.3%	1.3%	0.5%	0.6%	0.1%	1.3%	0.1%
Installation, maintenance, and repair occupations	0.3%	0.4%	0.5%	0.2%	0.3%	0.4%	0.4%	0.3%	0.3%
Production, Transportation, and Material Moving Occupations	15.5%	7.6%	8.0%	20.6%	17.7%	10.5%	17.3%	10.1%	14.2%
Production occupations	11.2%	5.3%	5.7%	14.4%	12.8%	8.0%	14.1%	7.3%	10.3%
Transportation and material moving occupations	4.3%	2.4%	2.4%	6.2%	4.9%	2.5%	3.2%	2.9%	3.9%
Military Occupations	0.0%	0.1%	0.0%	0.0%	0.0%	0.0%	0.1%	0.0%	0.0%

TABLE 8.4. *Latino Occupational Structure by Nationality, Nativity, and Sex, 2005*

Occupational Category	Domestic-Born Males Population 16 Years of Age and Older								
	Mexicans	Puerto Ricans	Cubans	Hondurans	Salvadorans	Colombians	Ecuadorians	Peruvians	Dominicans
Management, Professional, and Related Occupations	18.9%	20.6%	33.6%	16.9%	18.4%	28.5%	27.2%	30.6%	22.3%
Management, business, and financial operations occupations	8.7%	8.8%	15.1%	5.1%	7.7%	11.9%	12.1%	11.3%	9.6%
Professional and related occupations	10.2%	11.8%	18.5%	11.8%	10.8%	16.6%	15.1%	19.3%	12.7%
Service Occupations	16.5%	22.2%	17.7%	16.4%	24.8%	15.2%	20.3%	17.8%	20.8%
Sales and Office Occupations	20.3%	22.0%	24.9%	21.1%	23.9%	29.0%	16.1%	19.7%	31.5%
Sales and related occupations	10.1%	10.5%	14.6%	9.8%	11.3%	15.3%	16.1%	19.7%	16.8%
Office and administrative support occupations	10.2%	11.5%	10.4%	11.3%	12.6%	13.7%	0.0%	0.0%	14.7%
Farming, Fishing, and Forestry Occupations	1.4%	0.1%	0.4%	1.1%	0.8%	0.1%	16.0%	8.7%	0.6%
Construction, Extraction, and Maintenance	20.1%	14.2%	12.6%	22.1%	13.2%	12.8%	8.9%	12.1%	9.6%
Construction and extraction occupations	13.3%	8.0%	7.7%	18.1%	10.1%	6.7%	2.4%	10.0%	5.4%
Installation, maintenance, and repair occupations	6.8%	6.2%	5.0%	4.0%	3.1%	6.0%	6.5%	2.2%	4.3%
Production, Transportation, and Material Moving Occupations	22.3%	19.9%	10.5%	17.5%	18.6%	13.7%	11.4%	10.8%	14.4%
Production occupations	9.6%	8.0%	4.0%	10.0%	5.2%	4.0%	4.8%	2.9%	3.8%
Transportation and material moving occupations	12.7%	12.0%	6.5%	7.5%	13.4%	9.7%	6.6%	7.9%	10.7%
Military Occupations	0.4%	0.9%	0.3%	4.9%	0.3%	0.6%	0.1%	0.4%	0.7%

Foreign-Born Male Population 16 Years of Age and Older

Occupational Category	Mexicans	Puerto Ricans	Cubans	Hondurans	Salvadorans	Colombians	Ecuadorians	Peruvians	Dominicans
Management, Professional, and Related Occupations	5.9%	17.2%	24.9%	7.0%	8.6%	26.3%	14.0%	20.6%	13.0%
Management, business, and financial operations occupations	3.5%	7.3%	13.3%	3.4%	4.3%	11.5%	6.3%	9.8%	6.7%
Professional and related occupations	2.4%	9.9%	11.6%	3.6%	4.3%	14.9%	7.7%	10.8%	6.3%
Service Occupations	21.6%	20.3%	14.8%	19.0%	23.8%	16.6%	18.2%	21.8%	26.7%
Sales and Office Occupations	7.3%	16.2%	17.4%	7.1%	10.5%	19.5%	12.9%	19.2%	16.8%
Sales and related occupations	4.0%	6.6%	10.8%	2.8%	5.2%	9.7%	6.5%	11.0%	9.6%
Office and administrative support occupations	3.4%	9.6%	6.5%	4.3%	5.3%	9.8%	6.4%	8.2%	7.3%
Farming, Fishing, and Forestry Occupations	6.2%	0.4%	0.7%	1.9%	1.2%	0.0%	0.2%	0.7%	0.3%
Construction, Extraction, and Maintenance	33.3%	17.3%	21.5%	45.5%	30.3%	16.7%	29.0%	18.0%	16.1%
Construction and extraction occupations	28.2%	9.9%	14.0%	40.6%	23.9%	11.0%	24.6%	12.8%	9.6%
Installation, maintenance, and repair occupations	5.1%	7.4%	7.5%	4.9%	6.4%	5.7%	4.4%	5.2%	6.6%
Production, Transportation, and Material Moving Occupations	25.6%	27.8%	20.6%	19.5%	25.6%	20.7%	25.7%	19.4%	26.8%
Production occupations	14.3%	13.0%	6.9%	9.3%	12.0%	10.7%	12.3%	9.4%	12.7%
Transportation and material moving occupations	11.3%	14.8%	13.7%	10.2%	13.6%	10.0%	13.3%	10.0%	14.1%
Military Occupations	0.0%	0.8%	0.1%	0.1%	0.0%	0.3%	0.1%	0.3%	0.3%

(continued)

TABLE 8.4 (continued)

Occupational Category	Domestic-Born Female Population 16 Years of Age and Older								
	Mexicans	Puerto Ricans	Cubans	Hondurans	Salvadorans	Colombians	Ecuadorians	Peruvians	Dominicans
Management, Professional, and Related Occupations	25.0%	28.1%	38.7%	32.3%	23.3%	35.8%	35.7%	37.4%	27.6%
Management, business, and financial operations occupations	8.6%	9.8%	13.6%	11.3%	8.7%	10.1%	8.3%	14.4%	9.4%
Professional and related occupations	16.4%	18.3%	25.1%	21.0%	14.6%	25.7%	27.4%	23.0%	18.2%
Service Occupations	23.0%	21.3%	16.4%	16.7%	23.6%	16.4%	12.9%	21.6%	20.9%
Sales and Office Occupations	43.2%	45.0%	41.6%	44.7%	47.7%	43.8%	48.2%	32.6%	48.3%
Sales and related occupations	15.6%	15.5%	14.4%	18.0%	21.3%	17.1%	16.7%	10.9%	20.0%
Office and administrative support occupations	27.7%	29.6%	27.2%	26.7%	26.3%	26.7%	31.5%	21.7%	28.3%
Farming, Fishing, and Forestry Occupations	0.6%	0.1%	0.2%	0.0%	0.0%	0.0%	0.0%	0.1%	0.3%
Construction, Extraction, and Maintenance	0.7%	0.7%	0.8%	2.7%	0.0%	0.9%	0.0%	1.0%	0.2%
Construction and extraction occupations	0.4%	0.2%	0.4%	2.7%	0.0%	0.2%	0.0%	1.0%	0.0%
Installation, maintenance, and repair occupations	0.3%	0.4%	0.4%	0.0%	0.0%	0.7%	0.0%	0.0%	0.2%
Production, Transportation, and Material Moving Occupations	7.3%	4.7%	2.3%	3.5%	5.4%	3.2%	2.4%	7.4%	2.7%
Production occupations	4.8%	2.9%	1.4%	2.4%	3.2%	1.9%	0.4%	6.3%	1.8%
Transportation and material moving occupations	2.5%	1.9%	0.8%	1.1%	2.1%	1.3%	2.0%	1.0%	1.0%
Military Occupations	0.1%	0.1%	0.0%	0.0%	0.1%	0.0%	0.9%	0.0%	0.0%

Foreign-Born Female Population 16 Years of Age and Older

Occupational Category	Mexicans	Puerto Ricans	Cubans	Hondurans	Salvadorans	Colombians	Ecuadorians	Peruvians	Dominicans
Management, Professional, and Related Occupations	9.7%	26.4%	29.3%	11.9%	10.2%	23.3%	16.8%	25.3%	14.6%
Management, business, and financial operations occupations	3.4%	7.9%	10.6%	4.9%	3.6%	6.6%	6.0%	7.9%	4.9%
Professional and related occupations	6.3%	18.5%	18.7%	7.0%	6.6%	16.6%	10.9%	17.4%	9.7%
Service Occupations	38.5%	27.7%	20.6%	43.4%	48.4%	34.0%	32.1%	32.4%	41.2%
Sales and Office Occupations	21.0%	32.2%	38.1%	19.7%	20.5%	29.6%	30.0%	29.9%	26.4%
Sales and related occupations	9.4%	10.3%	15.7%	7.3%	7.7%	13.1%	10.4%	13.1%	11.4%
Office and administrative support occupations	11.6%	21.9%	22.4%	12.4%	12.8%	16.5%	19.6%	16.8%	15.0%
Farming, Fishing, and Forestry Occupations	4.9%	0.4%	0.3%	0.7%	0.7%	0.2%	0.0%	0.2%	0.1%
Construction, Extraction, and Maintenance	1.3%	0.8%	0.9%	1.3%	0.9%	1.1%	0.6%	1.7%	0.5%
Construction and extraction occupations	1.0%	0.3%	0.3%	1.1%	0.6%	0.7%	0.1%	1.4%	0.2%
Installation, maintenance, and repair occupations	0.3%	0.4%	0.6%	0.3%	0.3%	0.3%	0.5%	0.3%	0.3%
Production, Transportation, and Material Moving Occupations	24.5%	12.5%	10.8%	23.0%	19.3%	11.9%	20.4%	10.5%	17.2%
Production occupations	18.2%	9.2%	7.7%	16.0%	14.1%	9.1%	17.0%	7.4%	12.5%
Transportation and material moving occupations	6.3%	3.2%	3.1%	7.0%	5.2%	2.8%	3.5%	3.1%	4.7%
Military Occupations	0.0%	0.1%	0.0%	0.0%	0.0%	0.0%	0.0%	0.0%	0.0%

Yet no such consistent pattern in median personal incomes was found among the other national groups. For example, island-born Puerto Rican, and foreign-born Cuban, Honduran, Salvadoran, and Peruvian males in professional and management occupations earned higher median personal incomes than their domestic-born counterparts. This implies that educational attainment was in all likelihood much more important in determining income outcomes than nativity, and that foreign-born males either arrived with greater educational attainment levels or acquired them in the United States Yet, domestic-born female Puerto Ricans and Salvadorans in the professional and management sectors earned less than foreign-born women, although for the other nationalities domestic-born women in the higher-status occupations had higher median personal incomes.

When each of the other occupational categories is considered there were no consistent patterns in income hierarchy when nativity is factored in by sex. In some occupations the foreign-born of each sex earned greater incomes than the domestic-born, while in others the opposite was true. The data are too dense to discuss in narrative form, but they nevertheless are valuable in highlighting the extraordinary economic and occupational diversity of the Latino labor force when nationality, sex, and nativity are considered and we present them in Table 8.5.

We now turn to some of the characteristics of occupational structures in the metropolitan areas with the greatest numbers of Latinos in the nation, which we have considered throughout this book.[6] There were some substantial differences in comparative occupational structures, and there were also many similarities. Miami (25%) and New York (19.5%) had the greatest percentages of the Latino workforce in professional and management positions compared with the other four metro areas among both men and women. Miami (49.3%) and New York (55.5%) also had the highest portions of the employed populations found in service, sales, and office occupations. Approximately two-thirds or more of all Latinas were employed in these occupations in each metro area with the exception of Chicago where about 53% of Latina women worked in the service, sales, and office sector. Chicago also had the highest percentage of Latino males (32.2%) and females (27.1%) who worked in production

---

[6] In this consideration of metropolitan areas and occupational structures we will not highlight the differences by sex, nativity, Latino nationality, and income differentials because the data are far too dense and the resulting narrative would, in our judgment, be much too convoluted.

TABLE 8.5. *Median Personal Income by Occupational Category by Latino Nationality, Nativity, and Sex, 2005*

Domestic-Born Males Population 16 Years of Age and Older

Occupational Category	Mexicans	Puerto Ricans	Cubans	Hondurans	Salvadorans	Colombians	Ecuadorians	Peruvians	Dominicans
Management, Professional, and Related Occupations	42,784	43,803	52,971	30,560	32,597	55,008	47,470	43,803	45,840
Service Occupations	15,280	16,910	18,540	14,669	8,302	17,827	14,465	6,112	11,715
Sales and Office Occupations	22,207	23,328	25,467	20,373	11,053	17,980	24,448	9,627	15,280
Construction, Extraction, and Maintenance	25,467	22,411	23,124	9,983	17,827	24,652	23,226	30,560	20,373
Production, Transportation, and Material Moving Occupations	23,429	22,411	20,781	12,224	14,058	15,280	8,149	26,485	14,262

Foreign-Born Male Population 16 Years of Age and Older

Occupational Category	Mexicans	Puerto Ricans	Cubans	Hondurans	Salvadorans	Colombians	Ecuadorians	Peruvians	Dominicans
Management, Professional, and Related Occupations	36,672	48,896	55,008	39,728	39,219	44,210	44,873	50,933	42,784
Service Occupations	16,299	23,429	20,373	18,336	19,355	20,373	20,373	20,934	19,966
Sales and Office Occupations	22,411	30,560	30,560	24,448	25,467	28,523	25,467	26,995	20,119
Construction, Extraction, and Maintenance	21,188	26,485	25,467	19,355	23,429	25,467	22,411	28,523	24,958
Production, Transportation, and Material Moving Occupations	21,392	26,842	22,309	20,373	22,411	27,530	22,411	24,397	21,392

(continued)

TABLE 8.5 (*continued*)

Occupational Category	Domestic-Born Females Population 16 Years of Age and Older								
	Mexicans	Puerto Ricans	Cubans	Hondurans	Salvadorans	Colombians	Ecuadorians	Peruvians	Dominicans
Management, Professional, and Related Occupations	30,560	30,560	40,747	30,560	20,883	34,024	45,840	34,635	36,672
Service Occupations	9,677	10,187	9,983	10,187	6,112	8,200	13,956	11,002	7,334
Sales and Office Occupations	15,789	15,891	19,360	11,664	10,289	12,835	12,428	17,827	8,862
Construction, Extraction, and Maintenance	20,781	17,419	21,800	3,540	—	38,709	—	29,032	6,673
Production, Transportation, and Material Moving Occupations	14,261	12,733	9,779	5,297	9,881	15,290	18,336	16,299	6,519

Occupational Category	Foreign-Born Female Population 16 Years of Age and Older								
	Mexicans	Puerto Ricans	Cubans	Hondurans	Salvadorans	Colombians	Ecuadorians	Peruvians	Dominicans
Management, Professional, and Related Occupations	22,207	32,597	36,672	28,523	27,912	30,560	30,560	28,523	28,523
Service Occupations	9,270	12,224	12,240	11,613	12,224	12,224	11,205	12,428	12,224
Sales and Office Occupations	14,159	19,864	22,207	16,299	15,280	18,336	18,743	16,299	15,280
Construction, Extraction and Maintenance	14,669	23,939	23,429	18,336	18,336	17,623	26,995	21,392	22,411
Production, Transportation, and Material Moving Occupations	12,224	15,942	12,224	11,205	14,261	15,280	12,224	12,224	13,243

and transportation occupations. The Houston metro area stands out because of the large percentage of male Latinos who worked in the construction trades – nearly 36% – and the large number of Latina women who worked in service, sales, and office professions – nearly 72% of all employed Latinas. New York had the highest concentration of male Latinos working in service, sales, and office occupations at 45% and the lowest percentage of Latino men found in the construction and production sectors when they were combined – about 38% of all employed Latino males (see Table 8.6).

A recent study that examined changes in the occupational structures among Hispanics between 1990 and 2000 found that a declining percentage of Latino males worked in management and professional occupations, in contrast to the patterns found among non-Hispanic white males.[7] Additionally, there was the tendency toward the greater concentration of Latinos, male and female, in lower-paying and lower-status jobs in the service, sales, and office sectors of the economy. In general, the study concluded that occupational mobility was more restricted for Hispanic workers than for non-Hispanics.

However, there was an important distinction between the occupational structures of recent immigrants and domestic-born Latinos or the foreign-born who have been in the United States for greater time periods. A large number of Latin American and Hispanic Caribbean–born migrants to the United States after 1990 were heavily concentrated in lower-status and lower-paying occupations. This may have statistically distorted the real opportunities for better-educated Latinos to move into higher-status occupations. It also may have created the statistical anomaly of increasing numbers of Latinos actually working in professional and management positions, even though they represented a falling percentage of the total Latino workforce because of rapidly increasing numbers of recently arrived immigrants working in lower-status jobs.

Employment and Unemployment

Unemployment rates among the laboring Latino population of the United States remained steady from 1980 to 2005 and accounted for only 9%

---

[7] See Maude Toussaint-Comeau, Thomas Smith, and Ludovic Comeau, Jr., "Occupational Attainment and Mobility of Hispanics in a Changing Economy," Pew Hispanic Center, September 2005, at http://pewhispanic.org/files/reports/59.1.pdf.

TABLE 8.6. *Latino Occupational Structure by Sex and Metropolitan Area, 2005*

Occupational Category	Total Population 16 Years of Age and Older					
	Houston	Los Angeles	Chicago	Miami	New York	Riverside
Management, Professional, and Related Occupations	11.9%	14.8%	13.3%	25.2%	19.5%	13.6%
Management, business, and financial operations occupations	5.8%	6.0%	5.7%	11.5%	7.5%	5.3%
Professional and related occupations	6.1%	8.8%	7.6%	13.6%	12.0%	8.3%
Service Occupations	16.5%	23.2%	23.5%	18.4%	30.7%	20.2%
Sales and Office Occupations	11.6%	24.5%	21.3%	30.9%	24.8%	24.8%
Sales and related occupations	5.9%	10.3%	8.2%	14.7%	9.9%	10.7%
Office and administrative support occupations	5.7%	14.2%	13.0%	16.2%	14.9%	14.2%
Farming, Fishing, and Forestry Occupations	0.4%	0.5%	0.3%	0.4%	0.2%	1.4%
Construction, Extraction, and Maintenance	35.7%	13.5%	11.4%	12.8%	10.2%	16.0%
Construction and extraction occupations	28.1%	9.8%	7.9%	8.7%	7.7%	11.3%
Installation, maintenance, and repair occupations	7.5%	3.6%	3.5%	4.0%	2.4%	4.7%
Production, Transportation, and Material Moving Occupations	23.9%	23.5%	30.1%	12.4%	14.7%	23.9%
Production occupations	11.4%	13.7%	19.6%	5.1%	7.4%	12.4%
Transportation and material moving occupations	12.5%	9.8%	10.5%	7.2%	7.3%	11.5%

296

Total Male Population 16 Years of Age and Older

Occupational Category	Houston	Los Angeles	Chicago	Miami	New York	Riverside
Management, Professional, and Related Occupations	11.9%	12.2%	9.8%	24.2%	16.8%	11.3%
Management, business, and financial operations occupations	5.8%	5.9%	5.0%	13.1%	7.6%	5.3%
Professional and related occupations	6.1%	6.3%	4.8%	11.1%	9.2%	6.0%
Service Occupations	16.5%	18.2%	24.0%	13.9%	27.6%	16.3%
Sales and Office Occupations	11.6%	17.0%	15.1%	21.2%	17.5%	14.0%
Sales and related occupations	5.9%	8.4%	6.0%	12.9%	7.8%	7.3%
Office and administrative support occupations	5.7%	8.5%	9.1%	8.3%	9.7%	6.7%
Farming, Fishing, and Forestry Occupations	0.4%	0.6%	0.4%	0.4%	0.3%	1.6%
Construction, Extraction, and Maintenance	35.7%	23.3%	18.7%	23.4%	18.5%	27.3%
Construction and extraction occupations	28.1%	17.1%	13.1%	16.1%	14.2%	19.4%
Installation, maintenance, and repair occupations	7.5%	6.1%	5.6%	7.2%	4.3%	7.9%
Production, Transportation, and Material Moving Occupations	23.9%	28.8%	32.2%	16.8%	19.5%	29.5%
Production occupations	11.4%	14.9%	18.3%	5.4%	7.8%	13.8%
Transportation and material moving occupations	12.5%	13.9%	13.9%	11.4%	11.6%	15.7%

(continued)

TABLE 8.6 (*continued*)

Total Female Population 16 Years of Age and Older

Occupational Category	Houston	Los Angeles	Chicago	Miami	New York	Riverside
Management, Professional, and Related Occupations	17.1%	18.2%	18.5%	26.2%	22.6%	16.7%
Management, business, and financial operations occupations	6.4%	6.1%	6.7%	9.7%	7.5%	5.3%
Professional and related occupations	10.7%	12.1%	11.8%	16.5%	15.1%	11.4%
Service Occupations	36.7%	29.8%	23.0%	23.6%	34.2%	25.3%
Sales and Office Occupations	35.0%	34.3%	30.2%	41.9%	33.2%	39.1%
Sales and related occupations	13.7%	12.9%	11.5%	16.8%	12.4%	15.2%
Office and administrative support occupations	21.2%	21.5%	18.8%	25.1%	20.8%	23.9%
Farming, Fishing, and Forestry Occupations	0.2%	0.3%	0.3%	0.4%	0.1%	1.1%
Construction, Extraction, and Maintenance	0.6%	0.8%	0.9%	0.7%	0.7%	1.2%
Construction and extraction occupations	0.4%	0.4%	0.3%	0.4%	0.4%	0.6%
Installation, maintenance, and repair occupations	0.2%	0.4%	0.6%	0.3%	0.3%	0.6%
Production, Transportation, and Material Moving Occupations	10.4%	16.7%	27.1%	7.3%	9.2%	16.6%
Production occupations	7.3%	12.3%	21.4%	4.9%	6.8%	10.6%
Transportation and material moving occupations	3.0%	4.4%	5.7%	2.4%	2.4%	6.0%

Note: These data are for nonmilitary occupations only. Military occupations were a fractional percentage of the total employed.

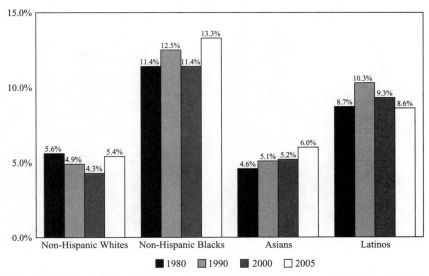

GRAPH 8.3. Unemployment Rates among Population 16 Years of Age and Older by Race/Ethnicity, 1980–2005.

of the working-age population.[8] There was a rise in unemployment during the 1980s, and rates among Hispanics peaked at 10.3% in 1990, but thereafter there was a continual decline to 9.3% in 2000 and then to 8.6% in 2005. These unemployment rates were considerably higher than found among non-Hispanic whites and Asians, but they were significantly lower than unemployment within the non-Hispanic black sector of the population. In 2005 only 5.4% of non-Hispanic whites were unemployed and among Asians the rate was 6.0%. Unemployment among non-Hispanic blacks was an extraordinarily high 13.3% in 2005 and was this was greater than the 11.4% rate of 1980, the only major racial/ethnic group in the country where unemployment increased between 1980 and 2005 (see Graph 8.3).

---

[8] The labor force is considered to be all people 16 years of age and older who were actively seeking work. These are the criteria utilized by the U.S. Department of Labor, Bureau of Labor Statistics (see their Web site at http://www.bls.gov/). Those not seeking work were not considered to be part of the labor force and thus do not enter into the calculation of unemployment rates. This category includes retired people as well as those not actively searching for a job. This is problematic in analyzing unemployment rates among Latinos since in many instances nonretired people in younger age categories may not be seeking employment. This would have the effect of keeping official unemployment statistics artificially low. We will address this issue by considering age-specific unemployment rates later in this chapter, as well as the issue of those not in the labor force by age cohort.

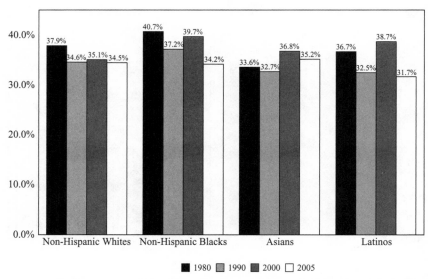

GRAPH 8.4. Percentage of Population 16 Years of Age and Older Not in the Labor Force by Race/Ethnicity, 1980–2005.

These unemployment rates among those actively seeking work must be examined within the context of the total population 16 years of age and older, and particular attention must be focused upon those who were classified as out-of-the-labor force, or not seeking work, for whatever reason. At the national level there were not major differences in the percentages of each racial/ethnic group who did not form part of the labor force and thus was not actively seeking work. By 2005 between 32% and 35% of each racial/ethnic group in the working ages was found to be out of the active labor force.[9] These data indicate that comparative unemployment rates by race/ethnicity for the 16 years of age and older population are fairly valid indicators of labor force participation (see Graph 8.4).

---

[9] A recent national-level study that surveyed the reasons for which people were out of the labor force found that about 35% of the population ages 16 years and older were out of the labor force in 2004, and this coincides with the census data we have analyzed. The study also found that of those who were out of the labor force, about 38% were retired, 19% were in school, and another 15% did not work because of chronic illness or disabilities. Among women who were not seeking work about 40% indicated that child care was the major reason.

The study further isolated Hispanics and the other race/ethnic groups between the ages of 16 and 64, or the bulk of nonretired people. It found that 40% of Latinos who were out of the workforce in 2004 indicated child care as the principal reason. This was the highest

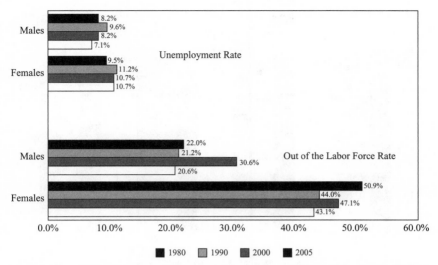

GRAPH 8.5. Unemployment Rates and Percentage of Those Not in the Labor Force among the Latino Population 16 Years of Age and Older by Sex, 1980–2005.

However, when Latino unemployment rates are examined by sex, there were disparities among men and women and an extraordinary differentiation in the proportions of those who were not part of the labor force because they were not seeking work. Among Latino males the unemployment rate dropped from 8.2% in 1980 to 7.1% in 2005, while those who were out of the labor force declined from 22% to 20.6% over the same time frame. Among Latinas older than 16 years of age the unemployment rate increased from 9.5% to 10.7% between 1980 and 2005, while the percentage of women who were out of the labor force declined from nearly 51% to 43.1%. But despite this decline, as of 2005 this out-of-the-labor force rate among Hispanic women was nearly twice that of Latino males (see Graph 8.5).

Yet these rates of non–labor force participation among Hispanic women were in line with those found among non-Hispanic white women in 2005 (41.2%) and Asian women (42.7%). However, they were much higher than the 36.7% of non-Hispanic black women who were out of

percentage of the race/ethnic groups examined. For non-Hispanic whites it was 25%; however, for non-Hispanic blacks the rate was 13.5%. See Nasrin Dalirazar, *Reasons People Do Not Work: 2004: Household Economic Studies*, Current Population Studies P70–111 (Washington, DC: U.S. Census Bureau, 2007), at http://www.census.gov/prod 207pubs/p70–111.pdf.

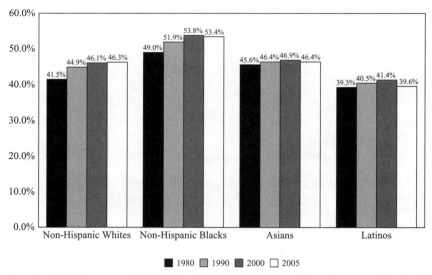

GRAPH 8.6. Women as Percentages of Total Employed Population 16 Years of Age and Older by Race/Ethnicity, 1980–2005.

the labor force in the same year. Clearly then the participation of Latina women in the labor force was roughly equal to all other groups, with African-American women being the exception.

One other important point ought to be noted about the sex division of the Latino labor force in comparison with the other major racial/ethnic groups. When we examined all of those who were employed, Latino females older than 16 years of age accounted for 39.6% of the total number of Latinos with jobs in 2005, and this was substantially lower than the 46.3% of all non-Hispanic whites employed who were women; the 53.4% of those working who were women among non-Hispanic blacks; and the 46.4% of the Asian working population that was female.

The issue of participation in the informal economy, where Hispanic women may have been working in occupations that were not enumerated by the Census Bureau, may account for these differences in the sex division of those working by race/ethnicity, although there is no empirical evidence on this aspect of the labor force (see Graphs 8.6 and 8.7).

Overall unemployment and out-of-the-workforce rates must be examined by specific age categories to have a better understanding of the nuances within the Latino labor market. Latinos had extraordinarily high rates of teenage unemployment. In 2005 nearly 24% of males and 27% of females between the ages of 16 and 19 who were in the labor force were

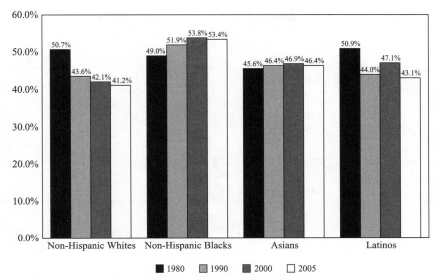

GRAPH 8.7. Percentage of All Women 16 Years of Age and Older Not in the Labor Force by Race/Ethnicity, 1980–2005.

without jobs. These were higher rates than found among non-Hispanic whites who had 19% male and 17% female teenage unemployment in 2005. The situation among non-Hispanic black teenagers, however, was far worse than that found within the Latino population. Some 43% of black males and 37% of black females between 16 and 19 years of age were unemployed in 2005. Among Asians the corresponding rates were 26% for males, about the same as for Latinos, and 16% among Asian females, which was slightly lower than found among non-Hispanic white female teenagers.

This pattern of differentiation by sex in employment rates persisted throughout the working life of Latino workers. Among Latino males fairly high rates of unemployment persisted in their 20s (8.2%), but this rate was about the same as that found among non-Hispanic white males (8%); it was slightly lower than that among Asian males (8.8%); and significantly below the 20.2% unemployment rate among non-Hispanic black males between 20 and 29 years of age. Latino males had the lowest unemployment rate (4.9%) in the 30–39 and 40–49 age cohorts, and this pattern was also found for the other racial/ethnic groups in these age categories.

Whereas Latino males seem to have had the same rates as non-Latinos (except for African Americans), among Latino females unemployment

TABLE 8.7. *Age-Specific Unemployment Rates by Race/Ethnicity and Sex, 2005*

Age Category	Non-Hispanic Whites		Non-Hispanic Blacks		Asians		Latinos	
	Males	Females	Males	Females	Males	Females	Males	Females
16–19	19.4%	16.6%	43.0%	37.4%	25.5%	16.0%	23.8%	26.7%
20–29	8.0%	7.4%	20.2%	19.3%	8.8%	8.6%	8.2%	12.5%
30–39	4.2%	4.9%	10.3%	10.7%	4.1%	4.9%	4.9%	9.5%
40–49	4.0%	4.4%	9.7%	8.9%	4.1%	4.8%	4.9%	8.1%
50–59	3.9%	3.7%	8.7%	6.9%	5.6%	5.2%	5.8%	7.3%
60–64	4.0%	3.2%	6.0%	6.4%	4.3%	4.9%	5.8%	6.7%
65+	3.4%	3.7%	7.1%	7.2%	6.4%	3.6%	6.5%	6.5%

rates in their 20s were significantly higher than for Latino males at
12.5%. These rates were also greater than the 7.4% of non-Hispanic
white women and 8.6% of Asian women 20–29 years of age who were
unemployed, but they were lower than the 19.3% of non-Hispanic black
females unemployed in 2005 (see Graph 8.8 and Table 8.7).

When the out-of-the-workforce rate was examined by sex, race, and
ethnicity for 2005, a fundamental difference was found between Latino
females and non-Hispanic white and black women: in every single age
category there were greater percentages of Hispanic women who were not
looking for work. In the core age categories of the labor force between
20 and 39 years of age, about a third of all Latinas were not seeking

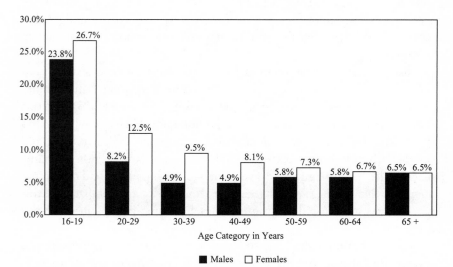

GRAPH 8.8. Age-Specific Unemployment Rates among Latinos by Sex, 2005.

TABLE 8.8. *Age-Specific Out-of-the–Labor Force Rates by Race/Ethnicity and Sex, 2005*

Age Category	Non-Hispanic Whites		Non-Hispanic Blacks		Asians		Latinos	
	Males	Females	Males	Females	Males	Females	Males	Females
16–19	49.1%	47.7%	60.9%	58.7%	68.8%	69.0%	52.8%	60.5%
20–29	13.0%	22.7%	19.0%	23.0%	26.7%	35.8%	11.4%	35.3%
30–39	7.7%	25.5%	13.4%	19.2%	11.9%	33.8%	8.4%	34.5%
40–49	9.6%	23.1%	17.9%	22.9%	11.5%	28.7%	11.7%	31.1%
50–59	17.6%	29.5%	29.0%	33.8%	17.4%	33.6%	20.2%	40.4%
60–64	42.2%	53.9%	53.1%	57.5%	36.6%	53.5%	40.5%	61.5%
65+	80.3%	89.0%	82.3%	88.3%	78.8%	90.0%	80.1%	90.6%

employment while among both non-Hispanic white and black women less than one-quarter of women were out of the labor force. Asian women, however, had out-of-the-workforce rates that were somewhat parallel to those found among Latinas in 2005 for those between the ages of 20 and 39. Among males, however, there were not such stark contrasts in age-specific out-of-the-workforce rates in 2005 compared with non-Hispanic white or Asian males, and these rates were significantly lower rates than those found among non-Hispanic blacks. (See Graph 8.9 and Table 8.8 for complete data.)

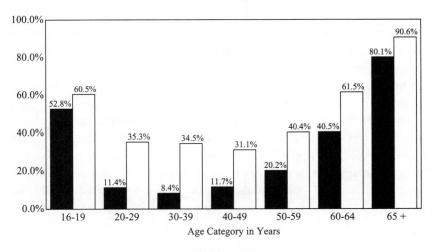

GRAPH 8.9. Age-Specific Out-of-the-Workforce Rates among Latinos by Sex, 2005.

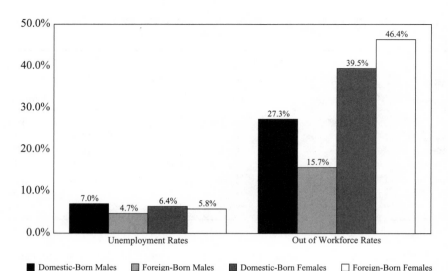

GRAPH 8.10. Unemployment Rates and Percentage of Those Not in the Labor Force among the Latino Population 16 Years of Age and Older by Nativity and Sex, 2005.

Surprisingly, foreign-born Latinos in 2005 had a lower unemployment rate (at 5.2%) than did domestic-born Latinos (6.7%). These lower rates were found among both men and women 16 years of age and older. Some 4.7% of foreign-born Latino males were unemployed in 2005 compared with 7% of domestic-born males. Among Latinas 5.8% of foreign-born women were unemployed compared with 6.4% of domestic-born Latino females. However, among Latinas there were higher out-of-the-workforce rates among the foreign-born: 46.4% of all foreign-born Latinas 16 years of age and older were out of the workforce in 2005 compared with 39.5% of the domestic-born. The exact opposite was true when male Latinos are examined. Only 15.7% of foreign-born Latino males were out of the labor force in 2005 compared with 27.3% of domestic-born Latino men older than age 16. (See Graph 8.10). It is difficult to ascertain the precise reasons for these differing patterns among foreign and domestic-born Latino males and females. One would expect the native-born to consistently do better than their foreign-born compatriots since they had better language skills, more access to contacts, and a better understanding of the U.S. economy. However, in large part these differentials have been ascribed to the integration of the foreign-born into the labor market in unskilled low-paying occupations, which the domestic-born have been reluctant

TABLE 8.9. *Unemployment Rates among Population 16 Years of Age and Older by Latino Nationality, 1980–2005*

	1980	1990	2000	2005
Dominican	12%	16%	13%	11%
Puerto Rican	11%	12%	11%	11%
Honduran	8%	13%	11%	10%
Mexican	9%	11%	9%	9%
Ecuadorian	8%	9%	9%	8%
Salvadoran	8%	11%	8%	7%
Peruvian	8%	8%	6%	7%
Colombian	7%	8%	8%	7%
Cuban	6%	7%	7%	7%

to work in.[10] Thus even for Latinos, there may be a dual labor market with domestic-born Latinos acting like other domestic-born workers in abandoning the low-status, low-skilled, less-stable, and often temporary jobs.

In considering the national level unemployment rates by the major Latino national groups, it appears that Dominicans and Puerto Ricans had the highest unemployment rates among the Hispanic nationalities. Although there were some fluctuations between 1980 and 2005, there was little change over the entire 25-year period. About 11.5% of Dominicans were unemployed in 1980; 11.4%, in 2005. There was a slight decline in the unemployment rate among Puerto Ricans from 11.2% to 10.7% over the same period. Among Mexicans, the largest Latino nationality, there was also a marginal decrease in unemployment from 9% of the labor force in 1980 to 8.5% in 2005. Salvadorans, Peruvians, Colombians, and Cubans had the lowest unemployment rates by 2005 at between 7.1% and 7.3%. (See Table 8.9.)

Although Dominicans and Puerto Ricans had the highest unemployment rates, there was a parallel decline in the percentage of each of these populations that were out of the labor force. Nearly 39% of all Dominicans 16 years of age and older were not looking for work in 1980, and

---

[10] See the report written by Rakesh Kochhar, "Latino Labor Report 2004: More Jobs for New Immigrants but at Lower Wages," Pew Hispanic Center, available at http://pewhispanic.org/files/reports/78.pdf and "1995–2005: Foreign-Born Latinos Make Progress on Wages," Pew Hispanic Center, available at http://pewhispanic.org/files/reports/45.pdf. The classic model of this dual labor market is presented in Piore, *Birds of Passage*.

TABLE 8.10. *Percentage of Population 16 Years of Age
and Older Not in the Labor Force by Latino Nationality,
1980–2005*

	1980	1990	2000	2005
Cuban	34%	35%	44%	39%
Puerto Rican	46%	39%	42%	38%
Dominican	39%	37%	43%	33%
Mexican	36%	32%	38%	31%
Colombian	32%	26%	36%	28%
Ecuadorian	28%	25%	34%	28%
Peruvian	28%	25%	34%	28%
Honduran	34%	30%	35%	26%
Salvadoran	27%	24%	36%	24%

this decreased to 33% in 2005, while among working-age Puerto Ricans
46% were out of the labor force in 1980 and 38% were not looking
for work in 2005. Mexicans also experienced a declining percentage of
people who were not looking for work over the same period as 36% of
all Mexicans were out of the labor force in 1980 and 31% in 2005 (see
Table 8.10).

When unemployment rates by sex are considered among the Latino
national subgroups, no consistent patterns were found. Among Dominicans, Puerto Ricans, Ecuadorians, and Cubans, women older than 16
years of age had slightly lower unemployment rates than men in 2005.
However, among the other nationalities the opposite was true, although
among Mexicans, the female unemployment rate (6.2%) was only
marginally higher than among Mexican men (5.6%). (See Graph 8.11.)

There were, however, extraordinary differences in the percentages of
working-age men and women who were not seeking work in 2005 among
the Latino nationalities. The most extreme example was among Mexicans
where nearly 45% of women were not in the labor force compared with
only 19.2% of men. Hondurans and Salvadorans also demonstrated great
disparities in non–labor force participation rates by sex. Only 13% of
Salvadoran men were out of the labor force compared with nearly 36%
of all Salvadoran women. For Hondurans some 14% of men were not
seeking work as opposed to 38% of women. There were extraordinarily
high percentages of Puerto Rican (44%) and Cuban (48%) women not
seeking work, and these two nationalities also had over 30% of all men
in each who were out of the labor force (see Graph 8.12).

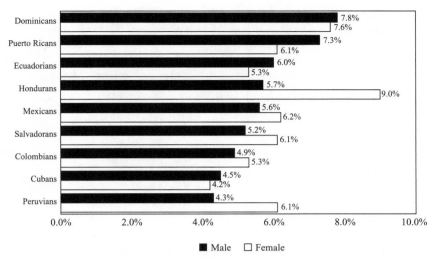

GRAPH 8.11. Unemployment Rates by Sex for Population 16 Years of Age and Older by Latino Nationality, 2005.

It is extraordinarily difficult to arrive at any analytical conclusions that could explain these disparities in the sex differentiation of labor force nonparticipation rates by national groups. One possible explanation could be a very traditional one – that higher numbers of Latina adult women remained at home taking care of younger children. However, we

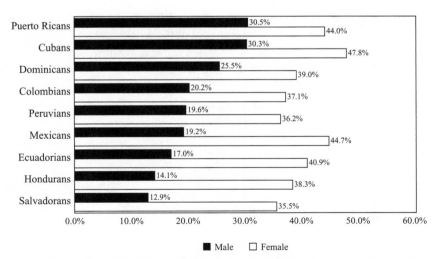

GRAPH 8.12. Out-of-the-Workforce Rates by Sex for Population 16 Years of Age and Older by Latino Nationality, 2005.

TABLE 8.11. *Unemployment Rates for Population 16 Years of Age and Older by Race/Ethnicity and Metropolitan Area, 2005*

	Non-Hispanic Whites	Non-Hispanic Blacks	Asians	Latinos
New York	5%	11%	7%	11%
Chicago	5%	19%	6%	9%
Houston	6%	14%	6%	9%
Los Angeles	6%	13%	6%	8%
Riverside	6%	10%	6%	7%
Miami	5%	15%	0%	7%

want to stress that this is not verifiable by the available quantitative data. Another possibility is underreporting of labor force participation because of work in informal economic activities such as domestic work or child care.

Examining these issues at the metropolitan level, it may be noted that, with the exception of the New York metro area, Latinos had unemployment rates that were higher than non-Hispanic whites and Asians, but lower than non-Hispanic blacks. Additionally, Latino unemployment in 2005 was highest in New York (10.8%) and lowest in Miami (6.8%) and Riverside (7.1%). In Houston, Chicago, and Los Angeles, unemployment rates among Latinos were between 8% and 9% in 2005. (See Table 8.11.)

When we examined labor markets by race and ethnicity in the major Latino metro areas, there were no significant differences in the percentages of working-age populations who were out of the workforce. In each metro area about the same percentages of non-Hispanic whites, non-Hispanic blacks, Asians, and Latinos were not seeking work (see Table 8.12).

TABLE 8.12. *Out-of-the-Workforce Rates for Population 16 Years of Age and Older by Race/Ethnicity and Metropolitan Area, 2005*

	Non-Hispanic Whites	Non-Hispanic Blacks	Asians	Latinos
New York	38%	37%	37%	38%
Miami	40%	36%	41%	37%
Riverside	40%	34%	40%	34%
Los Angeles	36%	39%	39%	33%
Houston	31%	30%	32%	30%
Chicago	31%	37%	32%	29%

However, among Latinos in these metropolitan areas there were differences. New York had the highest percentage of the working-age Latino population that was not seeking employment (38%) followed by Miami at 37%. This may be contrasted with the Chicago metro area where only 29% of all Latinos were out of the workforce in 2005. The New York and Miami metro areas had higher out-of-the-labor-force rates largely because of their older Latino populations. In New York about 32% of those out of the labor force were 60 years of age and older, while in Miami nearly 50% of those not seeking work were in the same age category. By way of contrast, in Chicago only 16% of Latinos not in the labor force were 60 years of age and older.

Additionally, the kinds of sex differentiations in both unemployment and out-of-the-workforce rates that were manifest nationally were mirrored at the metropolitan level, and this is not surprising. Latina women 16 years of age and older had unemployment rates that were consistently higher than among men in 2005 in each metropolitan area. The greatest differential was in Houston where unemployment was 6.2% among Latino males and 12.6% among females. In Los Angeles, male working-age Latinos had an unemployment rate of 6.5%; the unemployment rate for females was 10.5%. New York had both the highest Latino male (8.9%) and female (12.8%) unemployment rates, while Miami and Riverside had the lowest Latino male and female unemployment rates in 2005. In turn, Chicago stood in the middle range, with 7.3% of males and 11.5% of Latina females unemployed in 2005

Although there were extraordinary differences by sex in out-of-the-workforce rates, there was relatively little difference in female out-of-the-workforce rates among the metropolitan areas in 2005. The range of differentiation was between 42% and 48% of Latinas of working age were not seeking work in every metro area considered here. There was a greater disparity found among males. In Houston only 16.2% of Latino working-age males were out of the workforce in 2005 compared with 27.7% in Miami and 27.2% in New York, which were the metropolitan areas with the highest Latino male out-of-the-workforce rates. (See Table 8.13 for complete data.)

As we noted when analyzing the Latino workforce at the national level, it is striking that foreign-born male Latinos had both lower rates of unemployment and out-of-the-workforce rates than domestic-born Latino males in every metropolitan area. (See Table 8.14 for these data.) The out-of-the-workforce rate differentials were particularly stark in each metro area with the exception of Miami where there was a large,

TABLE 8.13. *Latino Unemployment and Out-of-the-Workforce Rates by Sex and Metropolitan Area, 2005*

Metro Area	Unemployment Rates		Out-of-the-Workforce Rates	
	Males	Females	Males	Females
Houston	6.2%	12.6%	16.2%	45.6%
Los Angeles	6.5%	10.5%	20.8%	44.6%
Chicago	7.3%	11.5%	17.8%	42.4%
Miami	5.4%	8.5%	27.7%	45.7%
New York	8.9%	12.8%	27.2%	47.0%
Riverside	6.0%	9.0%	21.3%	48.1%

and aging, foreign-born Cuban population not looking for work. In every other metropolitan region, foreign-born Latino males had relatively low percentages of all men who were out of the labor force – under 20%. Among domestic-born Latino males significantly greater rates were found, and these were highest in New York where nearly 37% of

TABLE 8.14. *Latino Unemployment and Out-of-the-Workforce Rates by Nativity, Sex, and Metropolitan Area, 2005*

	Unemployment Rates			
	Domestic-Born Males	Foreign-Born Males	Domestic-Born Females	Foreign-Born Females
Houston	8.8%	5.0%	12.3%	12.9%
Los Angeles	10.5%	4.7%	10.5%	10.5%
Chicago	11.3%	5.5%	12.5%	10.7%
Miami	7.0%	5.0%	9.4%	8.2%
New York	12.9%	6.5%	12.6%	12.9%
Riverside	8.2%	4.3%	8.4%	9.8%

	Out-of-the-Workforce Rates			
	Domestic-Born Males	Foreign-Born Males	Domestic-Born Females	Foreign-Born Females
Houston	23.4%	12.2%	37.6%	51.1%
Los Angeles	29.2%	16.2%	41.2%	46.7%
Chicago	25.3%	13.8%	38.6%	44.8%
Miami	29.0%	27.4%	38.7%	47.3%
New York	36.9%	19.5%	49.4%	44.9%
Riverside	28.5%	14.9%	42.0%	53.9%

domestic-born males were out of the workforce compared with about 20% of the foreign-born.[11]

Comparative patterns of unemployment and out-of-the-workforce rates were very different by nativity among Latino females. Although there were variations between the metro areas, there was much less of a differential in unemployment rates between domestic- and foreign-born Latino females, and near parity in Houston, Los Angeles, and New York. However, there were significant discrepancies in out-of-the workforce rates. In each metropolitan area there were significantly higher percentages of foreign-born Latinas of working age who were out of the workforce compared with domestic-born Hispanic females. This was a pattern that was exactly the opposite to the one found among Latino males, where the foreign-born consistently had lower percentages who were not seeking work for whatever reason. It is likely that there was greater participation in the informal economy by foreign-born Latinas of working age, and this employment may have been underreported. Additionally, as we have already noted, more traditional attitudes toward child care among foreign-born Latinos may have been a factor that kept many women at home taking care of children compared with domestic-born Latinas, although there are no empirical data that may support this.

Examining these issues by major Latino groups, we find that among Mexicans unemployment rates decreased between 1980 and 2005 in Chicago and Riverside, the latter having the lowest unemployment rate among Mexicans found in the four metro areas where they were the dominant Latino national group. Unemployment among Mexicans in Houston increased from 4.8% in 1980 to 8.6% in 2005, and this was related to a sharp economic downturn in the Houston economy during the 1980s. Mexican unemployment rates increased to 8.8% by 1990 after which there was no meaningful decline, despite a recovery in Houston's economy during the 1990s and after.[12] Although there was a rise in Mexican unemployment in Los Angeles between 1980 and 1990, and little improvement during the 1990s, by 2005 some 8% of Mexicans were unemployed, and this was slightly lower than the 8.2% unemployment rate found in 1980 (see Graph 8.13).

---

[11] As we have indicated previously, this was in all likelihood related to the fact that foreign-born Latinos found work in lower-paying and unskilled occupations that the domestic-born were not willing to participate in.

[12] Federal Reserve Bank of Dallas, "Houston Business – A Perspective on the Houston Economy" December 2006, at http://www.dallasfed.org/research/houston/2006/hb0604.html.

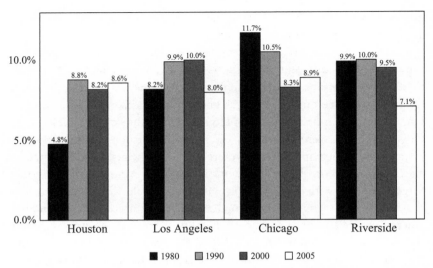

GRAPH 8.13. Unemployment Rates among Mexicans Aged 16 and Older in Houston, Los Angeles, Chicago, and Riverside, 1980–2005.

When we disaggregate Mexican unemployment rates in these metropolitan areas by sex and nativity, it is evident that foreign-born Mexican males had significantly lower unemployment rates than their domestic-born counterparts. However, for Mexican females there was no consistent pattern. In Houston and Riverside, foreign-born Mexican females had marginally higher rates of unemployment than domestic-born Mexican females; in Los Angeles and Chicago domestic-born Mexican females had slightly higher unemployment rates. When out-of-the-workforce rates are considered, there were striking similarities with national trends among Mexicans and indeed all Latinos. Nearly twice as many domestic-born Mexican males (in percentage terms) were out of the workforce compared with foreign-born Mexican males in every metro area. This may have been linked to a much younger foreign-born Mexican male population. Foreign-born Mexican females had higher out-of-the-workforce rates than domestic-born Mexican women, and these ranged between 46% and 55%. (See Table 8.15 for these data.)

Cubans in the Miami metropolitan area had the lowest unemployment rates of any Latino nationality in any of the metro areas examined here. Although there was an increase in Cuban unemployment during the 1980s and 1990s, perhaps related to the influx of political refugees linked to the Mariel boatlift of the early 1980s, by 2005 Cuban unemployment in Miami stood at 6.3%, slightly greater than the 5.7% found in 1980. Miami Cubans also demonstrated different labor-market patterns by sex

TABLE 8.15. *Mexican Unemployment and Out-of-the-Workforce Rates by Nativity, Sex, and Metropolitan Area, 2005*

	Unemployment Rates			
	Domestic-Born Males	Foreign-Born Males	Domestic-Born Females	Foreign-Born Females
Houston	9.0%	4.8%	12.3%	13.1%
Los Angeles	10.4%	4.6%	10.6%	10.2%
Chicago	10.3%	5.6%	14.2%	11.5%
Riverside	8.3%	4.3%	7.5%	10.4%
	Out-of-the-Workforce Rates			
	Domestic-Born Males	Foreign-Born Males	Domestic-Born Females	Foreign-Born Females
Houston	22.4%	12.4%	38.8%	54.1%
Los Angeles	28.5%	16.5%	41.1%	46.5%
Chicago	24.5%	13.5%	37.3%	46.4%
Riverside	28.9%	15.4%	41.3%	55.4%

and nativity than those found among Mexicans. Even though domestic- and foreign-born males and females had fairly low unemployment rates in 2005 (under 8% in each category), there were extraordinary differences in out-of-the-workforce rates among males. Miami Cubans were the only nationality in any metropolitan area for whom foreign-born males had higher out-of-the-workforce rates (34.7%) than domestic-born Cuban males (24.1%). This was not related to an older foreign-born Cuban male population that was retired or not looking for work. It is proba- ble that domestic-born Cuban males had higher skill levels, which were related to greater educational attainment levels, compared with foreign- born Cuban males, and that this made them more employable. Yet, among Cuban females the patterns found in the other metropolitan area were reproduced in Miami. Foreign-born Cuban females had much higher out-of-the-workforce rates (54.2%) than domestic-born Cuban females (35.1%). (See Graphs 8.14 and 8.15.)

In the New York metropolitan area, Puerto Ricans and Dominicans had the highest unemployment rates in 2005, each over 12%, and these were higher than in 1980 when unemployment was slightly lower than 12%. Thus, for the two largest Latino nationalities in the region, there was no improvement whatsoever in job-market possibilities. Among Mexicans, Ecuadorians, and Colombians, unemployment was somewhat lower, at between 8.8% and 9.4% in 2005 (see Graph 8.16).

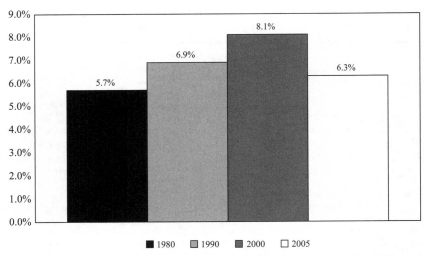

GRAPH 8.14. Unemployment Rates among Cubans 16 Years of Age and Older in Miami, 1980–2005.

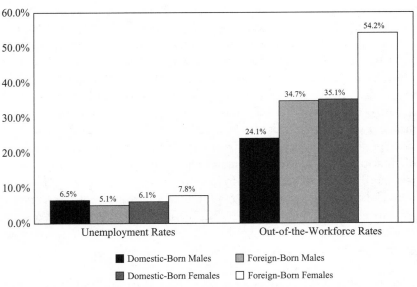

GRAPH 8.15. Unemployment and Out-of-the-Workforce Rates among Cubans 16 Years of Age and Older in the Miami Metropolitan Area by Nativity and Sex, 2005.

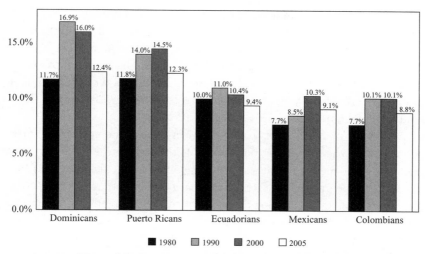

GRAPH 8.16. Unemployment Rates among Puerto Ricans, Dominicans, Mexicans, Ecuadorians, and Colombians in New York, 1980–2005.

The New York metropolitan area was the most eclectic and rapidly changing of all the regions we have considered in terms of the national composition of the Latino community. It is thus worth exploring the variations among the major Latino groups by sex and nativity in these two categories of unemployment and out-of-work ratios to the total adult labor force. There were significant disparities found among New York's Latino nationalities. First and foremost, Dominicans born in the United States had extraordinarily high unemployment rates in 2005: 19.6% for males and 15.9% for females. Among foreign-born Dominicans unemployment was considerably lower for males, but this was still the highest unemployment rate among all foreign-born adult Latino males. The unemployment rate among domestic-born Dominican women was 15.9%, while for foreign-born Dominican adult females it was 12.5%. What is also striking about the Dominican labor force is that domestic-born Dominican males also had the highest out-of-the-workforce rate among Latino men at 35.6%. Overall, only 51.7% of Dominican domestic-born adult males were employed, the lowest rate of all the Latino national groups born in the United States. In contrast, nearly 66% of all foreign-born Dominican males were employed.

Among Puerto Ricans, who had the second-highest unemployment rates, the data show that males and females born in U.S. mainland states had higher unemployment rates than those born in Puerto Rico. However, what is so striking among Puerto Ricans is the astronomically high out-of-the-workforce rates prevailing in 2005 for those born in Puerto Rico: 51.3% for males and an astounding 68.5% for adult females. Puerto Rican U.S. mainland-born females also had very high out-of-the-work force rates at 42.8%. Only 28.6% of all Puerto Rican women who were born in Puerto Rico were employed and 45% of Puerto Rican men born on the island had jobs.

Mexicans in New York had the lowest male unemployment rates among all of the Latino nationalities at 8.5% among the domestic-born and 4.7% for the foreign-born. Yet, foreign-born Mexican females had the highest unemployment rates of any Latino adult women at 26% compared with only 7.2% among domestic-born Mexican females. Mexicans also stand out as having the lowest out-of-the-workforce rates at 8.4% among foreign-born adult males and a very high rate among foreign-born females at 59.4%, which was second only to island-born Puerto Rican females. This suggests that the wave of Mexican migration to the New York metro area was paralleled by integration into the workforce by men and high unemployment among women. Additionally, nearly 60% of adult foreign-born Mexican women were out of the labor force. The unknown factor in explaining both of these high unemployment and out-of-the-workforce rates among foreign-born Mexican women is the dimension of work in the informal economy as well as the cultural differentiations, which may have resulted in the more traditional approach toward working outside of the home.

Among both Ecuadorians and Colombians in New York, foreign-born males had lower unemployment rates than the domestic-born in the New York metro area, a pattern that was found elsewhere among most Latino nationalities. Foreign-born Ecuadorian women had higher unemployment rates than their domestic-born counterparts, and among Colombian women the foreign- and domestic-born had the exact same unemployment rates. It is striking that Colombian domestic- and foreign-born males had exactly the same out-of-the-workforce rates, while among Colombian women the foreign-born had much higher rates compared with the domestic-born. The situation was very different among Ecuadorians. Only 12.9% of foreign-born males were out of the labor force compared with 29.1% of domestic-born Ecuadorian males, while 44.1% of foreign-born females and 35.1% of domestic born Ecuadorian females were not seeking work (see Table 8.16).

Among the most recent migrant groups, Mexicans and Ecuadorians, some fundamental patterns may be observed. Foreign-born males had

TABLE 8.16. *Unemployment and Out-of-the-Workforce Rates by Latino Nativity and Sex in the New York Metropolitan Area, 2005*

	Unemployment Rates			
	Domestic-Born Males	Foreign-Born Males	Domestic-Born Females	Foreign-Born Females
Puerto Ricans	9.1%	6.9%	13.2%	9.0%
Dominicans	19.6%	9.5%	15.9%	12.5%
Mexicans	8.5%	4.7%	7.2%	26.0%
Ecuadorians	10.0%	7.4%	9.0%	13.0%
Colombians	17.5%	4.5%	10.7%	10.7%

	Out-of-the-Workforce Rates			
	Domestic-Born Males	Foreign-Born Males	Domestic-Born Females	Foreign-Born Females
Puerto Ricans	23.7%	51.3%	42.8%	68.5%
Dominicans	35.6%	27.5%	42.0%	41.9%
Mexicans	28.5%	8.4%	36.5%	59.4%
Ecuadorians	29.1%	12.9%	35.1%	44.1%
Colombians	24.3%	24.3%	26.8%	40.0%

Note: For Puerto Ricans "foreign-born" is born in Puerto Rico.

significantly lower unemployment rates than domestic-born males in 2005, while the exact inverse was the case among adult women who had significantly higher unemployment rates among the foreign-born. Additionally, domestic-born Mexican and Ecuadorian males had much higher out-of-the-workforce rates than the foreign-born. This suggests that recent Mexican and Ecuadorian immigrants quickly integrated themselves into the workforce, although it is likely that they labored in lower-paying unskilled occupations. However, the patterns were completely the opposite among women. Foreign-born Mexican and Ecuadorian females had higher out-of-the-workforce rates than their domestic-born counterparts in 2005. As we have suggested previously, this may have been linked to work in the unreported informal economy as domestic workers and nannies, or to more traditional attitudes among recently arrived migrants about the household and child-rearing obligations of women. In all likelihood, a combination of the two led to these higher non–labor force participation rates among Mexican and Ecuadorian foreign-born women.

9

English Language Abilities and Domestic Usage

The importance of language skills is highlighted by a clear correlation between English language abilities, social mobility, and income levels.[1] Among Latinos, levels of English language proficiencies are, of course, linked to nativity. Nearly all adult Latinos born in the United States speak English well or very well, and in 2005 about 36% of all domestic-born Latinos 5 years of age and older spoke only English.[2] Yet, nearly 48% of all foreign-born Latinos spoke no English or did not speak English well in 2005. Since foreign-born Latinos increased from 29% of the total Hispanic population in 1980 to nearly 42% in 2005, there was a parallel rise in the percentage of the entire Latino population that did

---

[1] This theme has been constantly stressed in the literature on immigrants. See, for example, Walter McManus, William Gould, and Finish Welch, 1983, "Earnings of Hispanic Men: The Role of English Language Proficiency." *Journal of Labor Economics* 1:2 (1983), 101–03; and Evelina Tainer, "English Language Proficiency and the Determination of Earnings among Foreign-Born Men," *The Journal of Human Resources*, 23:1 (1988), 108–22. Later studies have added to these earlier findings with new datasets and more refined variables; see Barry R. Chiswick, "Speaking, Reading, and Earnings among Low-Skilled Immigrants," *Journal of Labor Economics*, 9:2 (1991), 149–70; Barry R. Chiswick and Paul W. Miller "Immigrant Earnings," 31–57. On how the isolation of Hispanic male workers into groups with low English language proficiency affects their wages, see Judith Hellerstein and David Neumark, "Ethnicity, Language, and Workplace Segregation: Evidence from a New Matched Employer-Employee Data Set, *Annales d'Économie et de Statistique*, No. 71/72 (July–December 2003), 19–78; and Thomas Bauer, Gil S. Epstein, and Ira N. Gang, "Enclaves, Language, and the Location Choice of Migrants," *Journal of Population Economics*, 18:4 (2005), 649–66.

[2] The information on mother tongue available in the U.S. census is evaluated in Gillian Stevens, "A Century of U.S. Censuses and the Language Characteristics of Immigrants," *Demography*, 36:3 (1999), 387–97.

not speak English at all or spoke English poorly. In 1980 nearly 20% of all Latinos had little domination over the English language; by 2005 this had increased to 25%, largely because of the increase in the foreign-born. There were only small differentiations in English language skills by sex among both the foreign- and domestic-born. A slightly greater percentage of foreign-born Latinas (49.4%) had poor or no English language skills compared with 45.8% of males (see Table 9.1). There were, however, distinctions based on educational backgrounds among the foreign-born. Additionally, while lower levels of English language proficiency were found among the foreign-born of all Latino subgroups, the level varied considerably by nationality.[3]

Within each Latino national subgroup the percentage of the overall population with either poor or excellent English language skills was directly linked to the volume of immigration between 1980 and 2005 and the relative importance of the foreign-born within each population. Latino nationalities with greater percentages of the foreign-born had higher portions of their populations with poor English-language skills. Among the dominant Mexican-origin population the domestic-born had great proficiency in English and by 2005 less than 5% reported that they spoke no English or did not speak English very well. More than 36% spoke English exclusively. However, with the large-scale immigration of Mexicans after 1980 the portion of foreign-born Mexicans in the United States increased from about 25% of all Mexicans and Mexican Americans in 1980 to nearly 41% in 2005. This meant that a greater share of the overall Mexican population had rudimentary English language skills

---

[3] Some studies have found a slightly higher retention of the mother tongue among third-generation Mexicans than among Asians; see Richard Alba, John Logan, Amy Lutz, and Brian Stults, "Only English by the Third Generation? Loss and Preservation of the Mother Tongue among the Grandchildren of Contemporary Immigrants," *Demography*, 39:3 (2002), 467–48. But most find a very rapid movement over time for English proficiency among Mexicans and other Hispanics. See, for example, Kristin E. Espinosa and Douglas S. Massey, "Determinants of English Proficiency among Mexican Migrants to the United States," *International Migration Review*, 31:1 (1997), 28–50; and Calvin Veltman, "Modeling the Language Shift Process of Hispanic Immigrants," *International Migration Review*, 22:4 (1988), 545–62. On the various factors that influence English adoption both in terms of experience in the home country and in the United States, see T. Espenshade and H. Fu, "An Analysis of English-Language Proficiency Among U.S. Immigrants," *American Sociological Review*, 62 (1997), 288–305; and Gillian Stevens, "The Social and Demographic Context of Language Use in the United States," *American Sociological Review*, 57:2 (1992), 171–85. On the whole separate question of bilingualism and its utility in mobility, see Tanya Golash-Boza, "Assessing the Advantages of Bilingualism for the Children of Immigrants," *International Migration Review*, 39:3 (2005):721–53.

TABLE 9.1. *English Language Ability by Sex and Nativity for Population 5 Years of Age and Older, 1980–2005* (*in percentages of total*)

1980

English Language Ability	Domestic-Born Males	Domestic-Born Females	Total Domestic-Born	Foreign-Born Males	Foreign-Born Females	Total Foreign-Born	Total Latinos
Does Not Speak English	1.4%	2.7%	2.1%	15.0%	21.2%	18.1%	7.0%
Speaks Only English	33.1%	30.8%	31.9%	4.6%	4.2%	4.4%	23.5%
Speaks English Very Well	39.4%	40.5%	40.0%	27.6%	26.3%	26.9%	36.0%
Speaks English Well	19.4%	18.7%	19.0%	27.1%	23.1%	25.1%	20.9%
Does Not Speak English Well	6.7%	7.3%	7.0%	25.8%	25.2%	25.5%	12.7%
TOTAL	100.0%	100.0%	100.0%	100.0%	100.0%	100.0%	100.0%

1990

English Language Ability	Domestic-Born Males	Domestic-Born Females	Total Domestic-Born	Foreign-Born Males	Foreign-Born Females	Total Foreign-Born	Total Latinos
Does Not Speak English	1.1%	1.6%	1.3%	13.6%	18.9%	16.1%	7.2%
Speaks Only English	35.1%	32.8%	33.9%	5.3%	5.5%	5.4%	22.7%
Speaks English Very Well	43.5%	45.4%	44.5%	29.5%	29.1%	29.3%	38.5%
Speaks English Well	14.5%	14.0%	14.2%	24.9%	21.1%	23.1%	17.7%
Does Not Speak English Well	5.8%	6.2%	6.0%	26.7%	25.4%	26.1%	13.9%
TOTAL	100.0%	100.0%	100.0%	100.0%	100.0%	100.0%	100.0%

2000

English Language Ability	Domestic-Born Males	Domestic-Born Females	Total Domestic-Born	Foreign-Born Males	Foreign-Born Females	Total Foreign-Born	Total Latinos
Does Not Speak English	1.0%	1.3%	1.1%	16.1%	20.2%	18.1%	8.8%
Speaks Only English	35.0%	32.9%	33.9%	6.0%	6.7%	6.3%	21.4%
Speaks English Very Well	46.2%	48.3%	47.2%	26.3%	26.9%	26.6%	37.9%
Speaks English Well	12.8%	12.3%	12.5%	24.1%	20.5%	22.4%	17.0%
Does Not Speak English Well	5.1%	5.2%	5.2%	27.5%	25.8%	26.7%	14.9%
TOTAL	100.0%	100.0%	100.0%	100.0%	100.0%	100.0%	100.0%

2005

English Language Ability	Domestic-Born Males	Domestic-Born Females	Total Domestic-Born	Foreign-Born Males	Foreign-Born Females	Total Foreign-Born	Total Latinos
Does Not Speak English	0.9%	1.2%	1.1%	16.6%	22.1%	19.1%	9.3%
Speaks Only English	37.2%	35.0%	36.1%	4.4%	4.5%	4.4%	21.6%
Speaks English Very Well	48.7%	50.6%	49.7%	26.0%	26.4%	26.2%	38.9%
Speaks English Well	9.2%	9.1%	9.2%	23.8%	19.6%	21.8%	15.0%
Does Not Speak English Well	4.0%	4.1%	4.0%	29.2%	27.3%	28.3%	15.2%
TOTAL	100.0%	100.0%	100.0%	100.0%	100.0%	100.0%	100.0%

by 2005 since over half of foreign-born Mexicans indicated little or no English language abilities. In 1980 about 20% of all Mexicans and Mexican Americans had poor or no English language skills; in 2005 this had risen to nearly 27% (see Table 9.2).

This general rule of increasing foreign-born resulting in the decline of overall language skills in English, did not apply to Puerto Ricans, the second largest group of Latinos. This was because U.S.-born Puerto Ricans, like Mexicans, were moving progressively toward bilingualism or exclusive use of English, and because island-born Puerto Ricans were also increasing their skill levels in English. This, of course, was related to their U.S. citizenship and the close connection of the island with the United States. Finally the decline of Puerto Rican migration to the United States after 1980 reduced the flow of non-English speakers among the Puerto Rican population. From 1980 to 2005, the number of Puerto Ricans who spoke English exclusively almost doubled from 23.4% to 40.8%, while the percentage of Puerto Ricans who did not speak English or who spoke English poorly declined from 19% to 9.7% in the same period. This was linked to the timing of migration and the emergence of multiple generations of Puerto Ricans who were born in the United States. Puerto Rican migration to the United States was concentrated in the period between roughly 1945 and 1970, and thereafter migration slowed to a trickle or ceased completely. In 1980 53% of Puerto Ricans were born in the United States. By 2005 two-thirds of Puerto Ricans were born on the continent. Each generation of Puerto Ricans born in the United States moved from speaking Spanish, to becoming bilingual, and then to an ever-greater portion who spoke English exclusively. Among Puerto Ricans residing in the United States, but born in Puerto Rico, there was a declining percentage who reported poor or no English language skills from 29.4% in 1980 to 21.7% in 2005. This suggests that English language usage and skill levels increased during this period in Puerto Rico itself or that more educated and English-proficient people of both sexes moved from the island to the U.S. mainland. In all likelihood, it was a combination of both (see Table 9.3).

Cuban language skill levels also were influenced by migration patterns and to a lesser extent by the high level of concentration of Cubans in tightly knit residential communities in the United States. The surge of Cuban migrants arriving in South Florida during the 1960s in the aftermath of Castro's seizure of power in 1959 slowed considerably after 1970. However, there was a renewal of large-scale migration to the United States during the early 1980s related to what has become known as the

TABLE 9.2. *English Language Ability by Sex and Nativity for Mexican-Origin Population 5 Years of Age and Older, 1980–2005 (in percentages of total)*

1980

English Language Ability	Domestic-Born Males	Domestic-Born Females	Total Domestic-Born	Foreign-Born Males	Foreign-Born Females	Total Foreign-Born	Total Mexicans
Does Not Speak English	1.2%	1.9%	1.5%	18.5%	25.7%	21.9%	7.3%
Speaks Only English	32.4%	30.7%	31.5%	2.9%	2.6%	2.7%	23.4%
Speaks English Very Well	40.5%	41.9%	41.2%	21.8%	21.8%	21.8%	35.7%
Speaks English Well	20.1%	19.5%	19.8%	26.6%	22.0%	24.4%	21.1%
Does Not Speak English Well	5.9%	6.1%	6.0%	30.2%	28.0%	29.1%	12.5%
TOTAL	100.0%	100.0%	100.0%	100.0%	100.0%	100.0%	100.0%

1990

English Language Ability	Domestic-Born Males	Domestic-Born Females	Total Domestic-Born	Foreign-Born Males	Foreign-Born Females	Total Foreign-Born	Total Mexicans
Does Not Speak English	0.7%	1.1%	0.9%	15.9%	22.3%	18.8%	7.5%
Speaks Only English	36.3%	34.2%	35.3%	4.2%	4.6%	4.4%	23.9%
Speaks English Very Well	43.7%	45.7%	44.7%	25.7%	26.1%	25.9%	37.8%
Speaks English Well	14.2%	13.8%	14.0%	24.4%	19.8%	22.4%	17.1%
Does Not Speak English Well	5.0%	5.2%	5.1%	29.7%	27.2%	28.6%	13.7%
TOTAL	100.0%	100.0%	100.0%	100.0%	100.0%	100.0%	100.0%

(continued)

TABLE 9.2 (continued)

2000

English Language Ability	Domestic-Born Males	Domestic-Born Females	Total Domestic-Born	Foreign-Born Males	Foreign-Born Females	Total Foreign-Born	Total Mexicans
Does Not Speak English	0.9%	1.0%	0.9%	18.6%	23.9%	21.0%	10.2%
Speaks Only English	35.4%	33.8%	34.6%	5.6%	6.5%	6.0%	21.4%
Speaks English Very Well	46.0%	48.0%	47.0%	22.7%	23.4%	23.0%	35.9%
Speaks English Well	13.0%	12.5%	12.7%	23.6%	19.0%	21.5%	16.8%
Does Not Speak English Well	4.8%	4.7%	4.8%	29.5%	27.3%	28.5%	15.7%
TOTAL	100.0%	100.0%	100.0%	100.0%	100.0%	100.0%	100.0%

2005

English Language Ability	Domestic-Born Males	Domestic-Born Females	Total Domestic-Born	Foreign-Born Males	Foreign-Born Females	Total Foreign-Born	Total Mexicans
Does Not Speak English	0.8%	1.1%	1.0%	18.8%	26.2%	22.1%	10.6%
Speaks Only English	37.0%	35.8%	36.4%	3.5%	3.6%	3.6%	21.4%
Speaks English Very Well	48.8%	50.5%	49.7%	22.3%	22.4%	22.4%	37.2%
Speaks English Well	9.5%	9.1%	9.3%	23.6%	18.2%	21.2%	14.7%
Does Not Speak English Well	3.7%	3.5%	3.6%	31.8%	29.5%	30.8%	16.0%
TOTAL	100.0%	100.0%	100.0%	100.0%	100.0%	100.0%	100.0%

TABLE 9.3. *English Language Ability by Sex and Nativity for Puerto Rican–Origin Population 5 Years of Age and Older,* 1980–2005 *(in percentages of total)*

1980

English Language Ability	U.S.-Born Males	U.S.-Born Females	Total U.S.-Born	Island-Born Males	Island-Born Females	Total Island-Born	Total Puerto Ricans
Does Not Speak English	1.3%	1.7%	1.5%	5.3%	11.7%	8.7%	5.3%
Speaks Only English	27.0%	23.4%	25.2%	4.6%	3.7%	4.2%	14.3%
Speaks English Very Well	46.2%	49.7%	48.0%	38.4%	34.8%	36.4%	42.0%
Speaks English Well	18.9%	19.2%	19.0%	32.7%	27.6%	30.0%	24.7%
Does Not Speak English Well	6.5%	6.0%	6.3%	18.9%	22.2%	20.7%	13.7%
TOTAL	100.0%	100.0%	100.0%	100.0%	100.0%	100.0%	100.0%

1990

English Language Ability	U.S.-Born Males	U.S.-Born Females	Total U.S.-Born	Island-Born Males	Island-Born Females	Total Island-Born	Total Puerto Ricans
Does Not Speak English	0.9%	0.7%	0.8%	4.4%	7.8%	6.2%	3.3%
Speaks Only English	32.9%	28.1%	30.5%	6.7%	5.3%	6.0%	18.9%
Speaks English Very Well	48.0%	53.8%	50.9%	45.2%	42.6%	43.9%	47.6%
Speaks English Well	12.7%	12.4%	12.5%	27.9%	24.8%	26.3%	19.0%
Does Not Speak English Well	5.5%	5.0%	5.2%	15.9%	19.4%	17.7%	11.1%
TOTAL	100.0%	100.0%	100.0%	100.0%	100.0%	100.0%	100.0%

(continued)

TABLE 9.3 (*continued*)

2000

English Language Ability	U.S.-Born Males	U.S.-Born Females	Total U.S.-Born	Island-Born Males	Island-Born Females	Total Island-Born	Total Puerto Ricans
Does Not Speak English	0.2%	0.2%	0.2%	4.3%	7.0%	5.7%	2.5%
Speaks Only English	40.0%	34.4%	37.2%	8.6%	6.9%	7.7%	24.8%
Speaks English Very Well	47.3%	53.4%	50.4%	47.5%	45.0%	46.2%	48.6%
Speaks English Well	8.9%	9.0%	8.9%	25.2%	23.5%	24.3%	15.4%
Does Not Speak English Well	3.6%	3.1%	3.4%	14.4%	17.5%	16.1%	8.7%
TOTAL	100.0%	100.0%	100.0%	100.0%	100.0%	100.0%	100.0%

2005

English Language Ability	U.S.-Born Males	U.S.-Born Females	Total U.S.-Born	Island-Born Males	Island-Born Females	Total Island-Born	Total Puerto Ricans
Does Not Speak English	0.2%	0.3%	0.3%	3.8%	6.2%	5.1%	2.0%
Speaks Only English	46.7%	40.8%	43.7%	9.6%	6.7%	8.0%	30.5%
Speaks English Very Well	45.3%	51.4%	48.4%	50.4%	45.4%	47.7%	48.2%
Speaks English Well	5.3%	5.2%	5.3%	21.6%	23.3%	22.5%	11.6%
Does Not Speak English Well	2.5%	2.3%	2.4%	14.5%	18.4%	16.6%	7.6%
TOTAL	100.0%	100.0%	100.0%	100.0%	100.0%	100.0%	100.0%

Mariel boatlift. Thereafter, migration slowed again. Accordingly, the percentage of Cubans born outside of the United States fell gradually, and this affected overall language proficiency levels. In 1980 about 76% of all Cubans in the United States were born in Cuba, and this declined to 63% by 2005. Among these foreign-born Cubans poor English language skills remained significant and in fact increased slightly. In 1980 some 40% of foreign-born Cubans could not speak English or spoke poorly, and this increased to nearly 43% in 2005. Since foreign-born Cubans remained such a large percentage of the overall Cuban population, this affected overall Cuban English language proficiency levels. As to be expected, nearly all domestic-born Cubans spoke English fluently, but about 29% of all Cubans spoke no English or could not speak very well in 2005. This was slightly higher than the rate found among Mexicans (27%) and extraordinarily higher than the some 10% of Puerto Ricans who had poor English language skills in the same year (see Table 9.4).

Salvadorans were the fourth largest Latino nationality in the nation. In many ways they were similar to Mexicans in that immigration continued to be a major factor after 1980 since large numbers of Salvadorans fled the civil wars raging in that country during the 1980s. Still, the foreign-born Salvadoran population declined from nearly 87% of all Salvadorans in 1980 to 67% in 2005 because of high fertility and birth rates among Salvadorans in the United States. Like Mexicans and others, nearly all domestic-born Salvadorans spoke English fluently. However, Salvadorans had an extraordinarily high percentage of their total population with poor or no English language skills in 2005 (37.5%), which was significantly greater than the 27% rate found among all Mexicans. This was because of the extraordinary high rate of foreign-born Salvadorans who had not acquired English language abilities. In 2005 nearly 49% had no or poor English language skills (see Table 9.5). In all likelihood, this was connected to the socioeconomic origins of Salvadorans who tended to be poorer and less educated compared with Cubans, for example.

To some extent Dominicans demonstrated patterns of English language abilities and acquisition found among Salvadorans. The constant arrival of foreign-born Dominicans after 1980, mostly to the New York metropolitan area, reinforced the sector of the Dominican population with poor English language skills. In 1980, when over 80% of all Dominicans in the United States were foreign-born, 47% of the total Dominican population spoke little or no English. The growth of the domestic-born sector, nearly all of whom spoke English fluently by 2005 and who made up 40% of all Dominicans in the United States by 2005, reduced

TABLE 9.4. *English Language Ability by Sex and Nativity for Cuban-Origin Population 5 years of Age and Older, 1980–2005 (in percentages of total)*

1980

English Language Ability	Domestic-Born Males	Domestic-Born Females	Total Domestic-Born	Foreign-Born Males	Foreign-Born Females	Total Foreign-Born	Total Cubans
Does Not Speak English	1.0%	1.4%	1.2%	14.0%	22.6%	18.6%	15.1%
Speaks Only English	29.2%	28.6%	28.9%	3.3%	2.1%	2.7%	7.9%
Speaks English Very Well	54.2%	54.8%	54.5%	37.5%	31.7%	34.4%	38.5%
Speaks English Well	11.9%	11.7%	11.8%	24.7%	21.2%	22.9%	20.6%
Does Not Speak English Well	3.7%	3.5%	3.6%	20.5%	22.3%	21.4%	17.8%
TOTAL	100.0%	100.0%	100.0%	100.0%	100.0%	100.0%	100.0%

1990

English Language Ability	Domestic-Born Males	Domestic-Born Females	Total Domestic-Born	Foreign-Born Males	Foreign-Born Females	Total Foreign-Born	Total Cubans
Does Not Speak English	0.5%	0.4%	0.5%	13.2%	20.6%	17.0%	13.0%
Speaks Only English	29.9%	28.8%	29.4%	5.1%	4.4%	4.7%	10.7%
Speaks English Very Well	58.6%	60.8%	59.7%	37.3%	33.0%	35.1%	41.1%
Speaks English Well	7.7%	7.5%	7.6%	22.3%	19.8%	21.0%	17.7%
Does Not Speak English Well	3.3%	2.5%	2.9%	22.2%	22.2%	22.2%	17.5%
TOTAL	100.0%	100.0%	100.0%	100.0%	100.0%	100.0%	100.0%

2000

English Language Ability	Domestic-Born Males	Domestic-Born Females	Total Domestic-Born	Foreign-Born Males	Foreign-Born Females	Total Foreign-Born	Total Cubans
Does Not Speak English	0.4%	0.3%	0.4%	15.5%	20.3%	18.0%	13.0%
Speaks Only English	33.6%	33.6%	33.6%	6.2%	6.0%	6.1%	13.9%
Speaks English Very Well	57.3%	58.7%	58.0%	34.5%	33.2%	33.9%	40.7%
Speaks English Well	6.2%	5.6%	5.9%	20.7%	18.0%	19.3%	15.5%
Does Not Speak English Well	2.4%	1.9%	2.2%	23.1%	22.5%	22.8%	16.9%
TOTAL	100.0%	100.0%	100.0%	100.0%	100.0%	100.0%	100.0%

2005

English Language Ability	Domestic-Born Males	Domestic-Born Females	Total Domestic-Born	Foreign-Born Males	Foreign-Born Females	Total Foreign-Born	Total Cubans
Does Not Speak English	0.4%	0.2%	0.3%	15.4%	21.4%	18.5%	12.5%
Speaks Only English	36.3%	34.2%	35.3%	5.7%	4.6%	5.1%	15.1%
Speaks English Very Well	58.6%	60.2%	59.4%	33.5%	33.5%	33.5%	42.0%
Speaks English Well	3.1%	3.8%	3.4%	19.7%	17.3%	18.5%	13.5%
Does Not Speak English Well	1.6%	1.7%	1.6%	25.7%	23.2%	24.4%	16.9%
TOTAL	100.0%	100.0%	100.0%	100.0%	100.0%	100.0%	100.0%

TABLE 9.5. *English Language Ability by Sex and Nativity for Salvadoran-Origin Population 5 Years of Age and Older, 1980–2005 (in percentages of total)*

1980

English Language Ability	Domestic-Born Males	Domestic-Born Females	Total Domestic-Born	Foreign-Born Males	Foreign-Born Females	Total Foreign-Born	Total Salvadorans
Does Not Speak English	1.5%	3.8%	2.6%	14.5%	18.0%	16.5%	15.4%
Speaks Only English	13.5%	10.9%	12.3%	2.5%	2.3%	2.4%	3.2%
Speaks English Very Well	52.5%	55.2%	53.8%	22.6%	20.1%	21.2%	23.7%
Speaks English Well	20.5%	23.5%	21.9%	29.1%	26.5%	27.6%	27.2%
Does Not Speak English Well	12.0%	6.6%	9.4%	31.3%	33.1%	32.3%	30.6%
TOTAL	100.0%	100.0%	100.0%	100.0%	100.0%	100.0%	100.0%

1990

English Language Ability	Domestic-Born Males	Domestic-Born Females	Total Domestic-Born	Foreign-Born Males	Foreign-Born Females	Total Foreign-Born	Total Salvadorans
Does Not Speak English	2.6%	2.9%	2.8%	14.2%	20.1%	17.0%	15.4%
Speaks Only English	16.2%	12.2%	14.2%	3.0%	3.6%	3.3%	4.6%
Speaks English Very Well	51.9%	53.5%	52.7%	26.0%	22.8%	24.4%	27.8%
Speaks English Well	18.6%	20.1%	19.3%	26.5%	22.9%	24.8%	24.1%
Does Not Speak English Well	10.7%	11.3%	11.0%	30.3%	30.7%	30.5%	28.2%
TOTAL	100.0%	100.0%	100.0%	100.0%	100.0%	100.0%	100.0%

2000

English Language Ability	Domestic-Born Males	Domestic-Born Females	Total Domestic-Born	Foreign-Born Males	Foreign-Born Females	Total Foreign-Born	Total Salvadorans
Does Not Speak English	1.1%	1.4%	1.3%	13.4%	18.4%	15.8%	13.2%
Speaks Only English	13.6%	12.0%	12.8%	4.6%	5.4%	5.0%	6.4%
Speaks English Very Well	63.2%	64.9%	64.1%	26.5%	24.0%	25.3%	32.3%
Speaks English Well	16.1%	15.8%	16.0%	26.6%	22.9%	24.8%	23.2%
Does Not Speak English Well	6.0%	5.9%	5.9%	28.9%	29.3%	29.1%	24.9%
TOTAL	100.0%	100.0%	100.0%	100.0%	100.0%	100.0%	100.0%

2005

English Language Ability	Domestic-Born Males	Domestic-Born Females	Total Domestic-Born	Foreign-Born Males	Foreign-Born Females	Total Foreign-Born	Total Salvadorans
Does Not Speak English	0.9%	1.3%	1.1%	15.8%	21.9%	18.7%	14.1%
Speaks Only English	12.7%	11.8%	12.2%	3.2%	3.2%	3.2%	5.5%
Speaks English Very Well	69.5%	71.6%	70.6%	25.9%	23.6%	24.8%	36.7%
Speaks English Well	11.8%	11.1%	11.4%	25.6%	20.7%	23.2%	20.2%
Does Not Speak English Well	5.1%	4.2%	4.6%	29.5%	30.6%	30.0%	23.4%
TOTAL	100.0%	100.0%	100.0%	100.0%	100.0%	100.0%	100.0%

the overall percentage of Dominicans with poor English language skills to 41% of all Dominicans – lower than for Ecuadorians but much higher then was the case among Mexicans, Puerto Ricans, or Cubans (see Table 9.6).

Among the Colombian-origin population, migration to the United States slowed during the late 1990s, and accordingly both the percentage of the overall Colombian population born in the United States and English language proficiency increased. About 18% of all Colombians were domestic-born in 1980, and 29%, in 2005. However, even though a very large percentage of Colombians were foreign-born in 2005 (71%), they had a comparatively lower percentage of people with poor English language skills than the other Latino nationalities. In 2005 about 30% of foreign-born Colombians reported speaking no English or did not speak English very well. Among Mexicans, Hondurans, and Salvadorans about 50% of the foreign-born had little command of English, while for Dominicans and Cubans more than 40% of the foreign-born had poor English language skills.[4] The English language skills of foreign-born Colombians were clearly linked to the higher educational attainment levels, which we considered in Chapter 6.

These higher educational attainment levels were also found among foreign-born Peruvians, and it is conspicuous that they too had a relatively low percentage with poor English language skills (29%) when compared to other Latino nationalities, which was roughly the same as for the Colombian foreign-born. It is also not coincidental that among total Peruvian and Colombian populations in the United States about the same percentage (about 24%) possessed poor English language skills, the lowest among all of the Latino nationalities with the exception of Puerto Ricans at 9.7% (see Tables 9.7 and 9.8).

Finally, Hondurans had the poorest overall English language abilities of any major Latino national subgroup in the United States. Nearly 41% of all Hondurans spoke little or no English in 2005, and this was a substantial increase from the 25% who had few English language skills in 1980. In part, this was linked to the immigration after 1990. About 50% of foreign-born male and female Hondurans spoke little English in 2005. Very low educational attainment levels among the adult Honduran population was another factor accounting for these very high rates of poor or no English-language skills (see Table 9.9).

[4] Puerto Ricans are a special case because of extensive English-language instruction on the island. Some 22% of island-born Puerto Ricans had poor English language skills.

TABLE 9.6. *English Language Ability by Sex and Nativity for Dominican-Origin Population 5 Years of Age and Older, 1980–2005 (in percentages of total)*

1980

English Language Ability	Domestic-Born Males	Domestic-Born Females	Total Domestic-Born	Foreign-Born Males	Foreign-Born Females	Total Foreign-Born	Total Dominicans
Does Not Speak English	2.4%	2.0%	2.2%	18.1%	27.8%	23.5%	20.8%
Speaks Only English	8.7%	7.6%	8.1%	2.3%	1.9%	2.1%	2.8%
Speaks English Very Well	47.4%	54.8%	51.1%	22.6%	19.8%	21.0%	24.8%
Speaks English Well	29.9%	25.6%	27.7%	28.8%	21.6%	24.7%	25.1%
Does Not Speak English Well	11.6%	10.1%	10.8%	28.2%	28.9%	28.6%	26.4%
TOTAL	100.0%	100.0%	100.0%	100.0%	100.0%	100.0%	100.0%

1990

English Language Ability	Domestic-Born Males	Domestic-Born Females	Total Domestic-Born	Foreign-Born Males	Foreign-Born Females	Total Foreign-Born	Total Dominicans
Does Not Speak English	1.8%	1.8%	1.8%	14.0%	21.0%	17.8%	13.9%
Speaks Only English	12.4%	11.6%	12.0%	4.1%	3.7%	3.9%	5.8%
Speaks English Very Well	58.6%	60.8%	59.7%	30.9%	26.3%	28.4%	36.0%
Speaks English Well	19.6%	18.8%	19.2%	24.9%	20.3%	22.4%	21.6%
Does Not Speak English Well	7.6%	7.0%	7.3%	26.0%	28.7%	27.5%	22.6%
TOTAL	100.0%	100.0%	100.0%	100.0%	100.0%	100.0%	100.0%

(continued)

TABLE 9.6 (*continued*)

2000

English Language Ability	Domestic-Born Males	Domestic-Born Females	Total Domestic-Born	Foreign-Born Males	Foreign-Born Females	Total Foreign-Born	Total Dominicans
Does Not Speak English	0.6%	0.6%	0.6%	13.1%	18.5%	16.0%	12.0%
Speaks Only English	13.6%	10.3%	12.0%	5.7%	5.7%	5.7%	7.4%
Speaks English Very Well	64.6%	71.0%	67.8%	29.9%	27.0%	28.3%	38.7%
Speaks English Well	16.3%	14.2%	15.3%	26.2%	21.9%	23.9%	21.6%
Does Not Speak English Well	4.8%	3.9%	4.3%	25.1%	26.9%	26.1%	20.4%
TOTAL	100.0%	100.0%	100.0%	100.0%	100.0%	100.0%	100.0%

2005

English Language Ability	Domestic-Born Males	Domestic-Born Females	Total Domestic-Born	Foreign-Born Males	Foreign-Born Females	Total Foreign-Born	Total Dominicans
Does Not Speak English	0.4%	0.3%	0.4%	10.2%	18.3%	14.8%	9.8%
Speaks Only English	16.0%	16.2%	16.1%	4.6%	4.3%	4.4%	8.5%
Speaks English Very Well	69.2%	70.4%	69.8%	34.8%	27.9%	30.9%	44.4%
Speaks English Well	11.5%	10.6%	11.1%	25.4%	21.7%	23.3%	19.1%
Does Not Speak English Well	2.8%	2.5%	2.7%	25.0%	27.7%	26.5%	18.3%
TOTAL	100.0%	100.0%	100.0%	100.0%	100.0%	100.0%	100.0%

TABLE 9.7. *English Language Ability by Sex and Nativity for Colombian-Origin Population 5 Years of Age and Older, 1980–2005 (in percentages of total)*

1980

English Language Ability	Domestic-Born Males	Domestic-Born Females	Total Domestic-Born	Foreign-Born Males	Foreign-Born Females	Total Foreign-Born	Total Colombians
Does Not Speak English	1.4%	3.9%	2.7%	7.3%	13.4%	10.6%	9.5%
Speaks Only English	17.7%	14.0%	15.8%	4.7%	4.3%	4.5%	6.1%
Speaks English Very Well	56.8%	57.7%	57.3%	35.1%	28.1%	31.4%	35.0%
Speaks English Well	15.9%	17.9%	17.0%	33.4%	28.7%	30.9%	28.9%
Does Not Speak English Well	8.1%	6.5%	7.3%	19.5%	25.5%	22.7%	20.5%
TOTAL	100.0%	100.0%	100.0%	100.0%	100.0%	100.0%	100.0%

1990

English Language Ability	Domestic-Born Males	Domestic-Born Females	Total Domestic-Born	Foreign-Born Males	Foreign-Born Females	Total Foreign-Born	Total Colombians
Does Not Speak English	0.4%	0.6%	0.5%	6.2%	11.5%	9.0%	7.5%
Speaks Only English	22.7%	23.4%	23.1%	7.3%	5.5%	6.4%	9.3%
Speaks English Very Well	59.9%	60.3%	60.1%	35.3%	30.7%	32.8%	37.7%
Speaks English Well	12.0%	11.3%	11.7%	30.2%	27.6%	28.8%	25.7%
Does Not Speak English Well	4.9%	4.5%	4.7%	21.1%	24.8%	23.0%	19.8%
TOTAL	100.0%	100.0%	100.0%	100.0%	100.0%	100.0%	100.0%

(continued)

TABLE 9.7 (*continued*)

2000

English Language Ability	Domestic-Born Males	Domestic-Born Females	Total Domestic-Born	Foreign-Born Males	Foreign-Born Females	Total Foreign-Born	Total Colombians
Does Not Speak English	0.4%	0.6%	0.5%	8.0%	12.6%	10.5%	8.6%
Speaks Only English	22.6%	21.5%	22.1%	6.4%	6.1%	6.2%	9.3%
Speaks English Very Well	63.9%	68.0%	65.9%	35.8%	30.4%	32.8%	39.2%
Speaks English Well	10.0%	7.3%	8.6%	28.6%	26.2%	27.3%	23.7%
Does Not Speak English Well	3.2%	2.7%	2.9%	21.3%	24.6%	23.1%	19.2%
TOTAL	100.0%	100.0%	100.0%	100.0%	100.0%	100.0%	100.0%

2005

English Language Ability	Domestic-Born Males	Domestic-Born Females	Total Domestic-Born	Foreign-Born Males	Foreign-Born Females	Total Foreign-Born	Total Colombians
Does Not Speak English	0.0%	0.3%	0.2%	5.7%	10.8%	8.5%	6.5%
Speaks Only English	33.2%	25.8%	29.5%	5.7%	5.5%	5.6%	11.4%
Speaks English Very Well	59.5%	65.4%	62.5%	42.7%	34.4%	38.1%	44.0%
Speaks English Well	5.1%	7.4%	6.3%	26.9%	26.2%	26.5%	21.6%
Does Not Speak English Well	2.1%	1.1%	1.6%	19.0%	23.1%	21.3%	16.5%
TOTAL	100.0%	100.0%	100.0%	100.0%	100.0%	100.0%	100.0%

TABLE 9.8. *English Language Ability by Sex and Nativity for Peruvian-Origin Population 5 Years of Age and Older, 1980–2005 (in percentages of total)*

1980

English Language Ability	Domestic-Born Males	Domestic-Born Females	Total Domestic-Born	Foreign-Born Males	Foreign-Born Females	Total Foreign-Born	Total Peruvians
Does Not Speak English	–	–	–	3.5%	7.3%	5.4%	4.5%
Speaks Only English	29.4%	29.1%	29.2%	7.2%	5.7%	6.5%	10.3%
Speaks English Very Well	46.6%	50.8%	48.6%	40.5%	35.4%	37.9%	39.7%
Speaks English Well	21.1%	15.1%	18.2%	33.7%	30.3%	31.9%	29.6%
Does Not Speak English Well	2.9%	5.0%	3.9%	15.2%	21.3%	18.3%	15.9%
TOTAL	100.0%	100.0%	100.0%	100.0%	100.0%	100.0%	100.0%

1990

English Language Ability	Domestic-Born Males	Domestic-Born Females	Total Domestic-Born	Foreign-Born Males	Foreign-Born Females	Total Foreign-Born	Total Peruvians
Does Not Speak English	0.5%	0.1%	0.3%	4.7%	8.1%	6.4%	5.4%
Speaks Only English	35.0%	28.3%	31.5%	5.4%	4.7%	5.0%	9.5%
Speaks English Very Well	50.5%	58.7%	54.8%	38.1%	37.3%	37.7%	40.6%
Speaks English Well	9.6%	9.4%	9.5%	30.5%	27.9%	29.2%	25.9%
Does Not Speak English Well	4.3%	3.5%	3.9%	21.3%	21.9%	21.6%	18.7%
TOTAL	100.0%	100.0%	100.0%	100.0%	100.0%	100.0%	100.0%

(continued)

TABLE 9.8 (continued)

2000

English Language Ability	Domestic-Born Males	Domestic-Born Females	Total Domestic-Born	Foreign-Born Males	Foreign-Born Females	Total Foreign-Born	Total Peruvians
Does Not Speak English	0.4%	0.2%	0.3%	5.6%	8.5%	7.1%	5.8%
Speaks Only English	28.0%	28.8%	28.4%	5.9%	5.7%	5.8%	10.2%
Speaks English Very Well	59.3%	60.8%	60.1%	39.4%	36.5%	37.9%	42.1%
Speaks English Well	8.5%	8.2%	8.3%	28.1%	26.9%	27.5%	23.8%
Does Not Speak English Well	3.8%	2.0%	2.9%	21.1%	22.4%	21.7%	18.1%
TOTAL	100.0%	100.0%	100.0%	100.0%	100.0%	100.0%	100.0%

2005

English Language Ability	Domestic-Born Males	Domestic-Born Females	Total Domestic-Born	Foreign-Born Males	Foreign-Born Females	Total Foreign-Born	Total Peruvians
Does Not Speak English	0.1%	0.5%	0.3%	5.2%	9.5%	7.3%	6.0%
Speaks Only English	29.4%	27.1%	28.3%	5.8%	5.3%	5.5%	10.0%
Speaks English Very Well	61.9%	62.8%	62.4%	38.0%	34.7%	36.4%	41.5%
Speaks English Well	6.9%	7.7%	7.3%	31.4%	26.2%	28.8%	24.6%
Does Not Speak English Well	1.6%	1.9%	1.8%	19.6%	24.3%	22.0%	18.0%
TOTAL	100.0%	100.0%	100.0%	100.0%	100.0%	100.0%	100.0%

TABLE 9.9. *English Language Ability by Sex and Nativity for Honduran-Origin Population 5 Years of Age and Older, 1980–2005 (in percentages of total)*

1980

English Language Ability	Domestic-Born Males	Domestic-Born Females	Total Domestic-Born	Foreign-Born Males	Foreign-Born Females	Total Foreign-Born	Total Hondurans
Does Not Speak English	–	0.9%	0.5%	5.9%	10.5%	8.6%	7.0%
Speaks Only English	39.1%	34.1%	36.4%	10.7%	9.3%	9.9%	15.0%
Speaks English Very Well	38.1%	43.1%	40.7%	36.8%	31.4%	33.6%	35.0%
Speaks English Well	16.2%	16.6%	16.4%	27.3%	26.3%	26.7%	24.7%
Does Not Speak English Well	6.6%	5.4%	6.0%	19.3%	22.4%	21.1%	18.2%
TOTAL	100.0%	100.0%	100.0%	100.0%	100.0%	100.0%	100.0%

1990

English Language Ability	Domestic-Born Males	Domestic-Born Females	Total Domestic-Born	Foreign-Born Males	Foreign-Born Females	Total Foreign-Born	Total Hondurans
Does Not Speak English	1.1%	1.3%	1.2%	11.7%	15.0%	13.6%	11.6%
Speaks Only English	38.3%	33.3%	35.8%	7.4%	7.6%	7.5%	12.0%
Speaks English Very Well	44.5%	49.8%	47.2%	32.0%	30.7%	31.2%	33.7%
Speaks English Well	10.6%	12.0%	11.3%	25.6%	21.1%	23.1%	21.2%
Does Not Speak English Well	5.5%	3.6%	4.5%	23.3%	25.7%	24.6%	21.5%
TOTAL	100.0%	100.0%	100.0%	100.0%	100.0%	100.0%	100.0%

(continued)

TABLE 9.9 (continued)

2000

English Language Ability	Domestic-Born Males	Domestic-Born Females	Total Domestic-Born	Foreign-Born Males	Foreign-Born Females	Total Foreign-Born	Total Hondurans
Does Not Speak English	1.7%	2.0%	1.8%	16.7%	17.6%	17.2%	14.7%
Speaks Only English	25.1%	20.8%	22.9%	6.1%	6.3%	6.2%	8.9%
Speaks English Very Well	54.3%	59.2%	56.8%	25.8%	27.7%	26.8%	31.6%
Speaks English Well	13.9%	14.0%	13.9%	22.7%	21.4%	22.1%	20.8%
Does Not Speak English Well	5.1%	4.0%	4.5%	28.6%	27.0%	27.8%	24.1%
TOTAL	100.0%	100.0%	100.0%	100.0%	100.0%	100.0%	100.0%

2005

English Language Ability	Domestic-Born Males	Domestic-Born Females	Total Domestic-Born	Foreign-Born Males	Foreign-Born Females	Total Foreign-Born	Total Hondurans
Does Not Speak English	2.3%	1.1%	1.7%	21.0%	21.3%	21.1%	17.2%
Speaks Only English	17.7%	18.8%	18.3%	5.6%	5.6%	5.6%	8.2%
Speaks English Very Well	61.0%	67.4%	64.3%	23.1%	26.6%	24.8%	32.8%
Speaks English Well	11.0%	7.4%	9.1%	20.4%	20.8%	20.6%	18.3%
Does Not Speak English Well	8.0%	5.4%	6.6%	29.9%	25.8%	27.9%	23.6%
TOTAL	100.0%	100.0%	100.0%	100.0%	100.0%	100.0%	100.0%

In the metropolitan areas we have considered throughout this book there were very different patterns in English language skills, and these were closely linked to the timing of immigration and the percentages of populations who were foreign-born. The most extreme examples were Houston and Riverside where foreign-born Latinos 5 years of age and older increased substantially between 1980 and 2005 and where the percentage of overall Latino populations with poor English language skills also rose. In 1980 about 30% of Houston's Latino population 5 years of age and older was foreign born, and this increased to nearly 52% by 2005. Those Latinos who spoke little or no English in Houston increased over the same time frame from 22% to nearly 32%. In Riverside, foreign-born Latinos in the same age category increased from about 20% of the overall Latino population to 40%. Those who spoke little or no English rose from 11% in 1980 to nearly 20% in 2005.

In Los Angeles and Miami there were marginal changes in the percentage of foreign-born Latinos 5 years of age and older between 1980 and 2005, and in fact there was a slight decrease in the portion of the population with poor English-language skills. About half of Los Angeles Latinos were foreign-born in both 1980 and 2005, while in Miami there was a slight decrease from 78% to 73%. Those who spoke little or no English experienced almost no change in Los Angeles (about 27%) and declined from 38% to 33% in Miami. A similar modest change occurred in Chicago, even though there was a major increase in the foreign born. Here the foreign-born Latino population 5 years of age and older rose from 42% to 52% between 1980 and 2005 but those with poor English language abilities increased marginally from 27% to 29%.

New York was very different from the patterns found in the other five metropolitan areas, largely because of the presence of a large Puerto Rican population with good English language abilities. In 1980 30% of the Latino population of New York 5 years of age and older were foreign-born, and this increased to 46% in 2005. However, there was little change in the overall percentage of this population with poor English language abilities – about one-quarter of all Latinos in both years (see Table 9.10).

The level of total median personal income earned by Latino men and women was directly connected to English language skills among other factors. Latino men and women who spoke no English, and were 25 years of age and older, earned incomes that were less than half those of either sex who spoke only English. Those who did not speak English well earned significantly lower median incomes than those with better English

TABLE 9.10. *Percentage of Population 5 Years of Age and Older Who Have Poor English Language Skills and Percentage of the Population Who Were Foreign-Born by Metro Area, 1980 and 2005*

	1980		2005	
	Does Not Speak or Speaks English Poorly	% Population Foreign-Born	Does Not Speak or Speaks English Poorly	% Population Foreign-Born
Houston	21.6%	29.7%	31.6%	51.6%
Los Angeles	28.4%	49.7%	26.8%	50.8%
Chicago	26.9%	42.4%	28.6%	51.7%
Miami	37.5%	77.7%	32.7%	72.9%
New York	25.1%	29.8%	24.4%	46.3%
Riverside	11.2%	19.7%	19.7%	40.4%

language skills. The situation was particularly dire for Latinas with poor spoken English language abilities. Those women who spoke no English whatsoever earned median incomes of about $3,700 in 2005 and those who hardly spoke English earned only $7,000 in median incomes. At all levels of spoken English ability, male Latinos earned significantly more than female Latinos (see Graph 9.1).

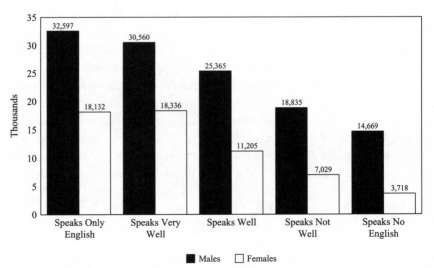

GRAPH 9.1. Median Total Personal Income by Sex and Ability to Speak English among All Latinos, 2005 Population 25 Years of Age and Older.

Regardless of ability to speak English, there was widespread use of Spanish as the dominant language within Latino households.[5] The language spoken at home reflected the linguistic preference of the household head who often was foreign-born and who may have even acquired adequate English language skills. Although, nearly all domestic-born Latinos spoke fluent English, bilingualism was widespread, and many spoke the language of their parents or grandparents in the home environment. When we examine the trends in language spoken at home, it is remarkable that there was little change between 1980 and 2005 despite the fact that immigration patterns shifted and the relative percentages of domestic and foreign-born Latinos also were transformed. In 1980 nearly 76% of all Latinos were classified as living in households where Spanish was the dominant spoken language. By 2005 this percentage had increased slightly to about 78%. Even among domestic-born Latinos there was little change. In 1980 two-thirds of all Latinos born in the United States lived in households that spoke Spanish, and this fell marginally to about 63% in 2005. Among the foreign-born, as to be expected, nearly 94% spoke Spanish at home in 2005, and this was the exact same percentage found in 1980. There was little variation by sex as Latino men and women had about the same rates of language usage at home (see Table 9.11).

While this does not reflect on the ability of individual Latino householders to speak English, it does indicate that continual migration to the United States by Latinos reinforced the usage of Spanish in the home environment when the entire Latino population is considered. This is brought into focus by examining the radically changed nativity of household heads between 1980 and 2005 and their use of language at home. In 1980 63% of all Latino household heads were domestic-born. By 2005 the majority of Latino household heads – 55% – were born outside of

---

[5] Language spoken at home is defined as follows by the Census Bureau: "In households where one or more people (5 years old and over) speak a language other than English, the household language assigned to all household members is the non-English language spoken by the first person with a non-English language in the following order: householder, spouse, parent, sibling, child, grandchild, in-laws, other relatives, stepchild, unmarried partner, housemate or roommate, and other non-relatives. Thus, a person who speaks only English may have a non-English household language assigned to him/her in tabulations of individuals by household language." Additionally, the Census Bureau noted that "Most people who reported speaking a language other than English at home also speak English." See *2000 Census of Population and Housing, Public Use Microdata Sample 2000* Issued December 2005. p. B-30–1, available at http://www.census.gov/prod/cen2000/doc/pums.pdf.

TABLE 9.11. _Percentage of Latino Population That Spoke Spanish at Home by Nativity and Sex, 1980–2005_

Nativity and Sex	1980	1990	2000	2005
Domestic-Born Males	66.6%	64.6%	64.8%	62.6%
Domestic-Born Females	68.8%	67.0%	66.8%	64.8%
Total Domestic-Born	67.7%	65.8%	65.8%	63.7%
Foreign-Born Males	94.1%	93.5%	92.9%	94.0%
Foreign-Born Females	94.4%	93.2%	91.8%	93.7%
Total Foreign-Born	94.2%	93.3%	92.4%	93.9%
Total Males	75.0%	76.3%	77.9%	77.6%
Total Females	76.5%	76.9%	77.7%	77.4%
Total Latinos	75.8%	76.6%	77.8%	77.5%

the United States. However, quite remarkably, and despite the constant increase in the foreign-born portion of Latino household heads between 1980 and 2005, there was absolutely no change in the percentage of Latino household heads who spoke Spanish at home – 80% in both 1980 and 2005. (See Graph 9.2.)

These patterns of Spanish language usage at home were reproduced within each Latino nationality. Only among Puerto Ricans, who experienced a steady increase in the percentage of domestic-born Puerto Ricans

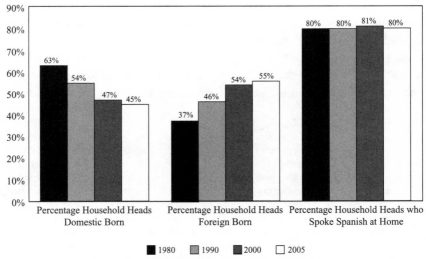

GRAPH 9.2. Percentage of Latino Household Heads by Nativity and Who Spoke Spanish at Home, 1980–2005.

TABLE 9.12. *Percentage of Persons 5 Years of Age and Older Who Spoke Spanish at Home by Latino Nationality, 1980–2005*

	1980	1990	2000	2005
Mexican	76.7%	76.3%	78.5%	78.6%
Cuban	92.0%	89.3%	86.0%	84.8%
Honduran	84.9%	88.1%	91.0%	91.8%
Salvadoran	96.8%	95.3%	93.6%	94.4%
Colombian	93.8%	90.7%	90.6%	88.6%
Ecuadoran	95.4%	92.1%	92.2%	91.5%
Peruvian	89.6%	90.5%	89.6%	89.8%
Dominican	97.1%	94.1%	92.6%	91.5%
Puerto Rican	85.6%	81.0%	75.1%	69.4%

between 1980 and 2005, was there a significant decrease in the use of Spanish as the primary language at home. In 1980 about 86% of Puerto Rican households spoke Spanish. This percentage fell to 69% in 2005, still a very large portion of all Puerto Rican homes in which Spanish was the dominant language. Among Hondurans, Salvadorans, Ecuadorians, Peruvians, Colombians, and Dominicans, around 90% or more of all households reported the use of Spanish as the dominant language in 2005, and the changes from 1980 were not significant. Within Mexican-headed households Spanish was the dominant language in nearly 79% in 2005, up marginally from 77% in 1980. Finally, within Cuban homes 85% spoke Spanish, a decrease from the 92% found in 1980 (see Table 9.12).

When we examined Spanish language use by household in the major metropolitan areas, we have found little differentiation. In Miami, however, with its large foreign-born Cuban population, about 87% of all Latino households reported Spanish as the dominant language in 2005. In Houston, Los Angeles, Chicago, and New York about three-quarters of all Latino households spoke Spanish as the principal language, and in Riverside it was about two-thirds. Riverside is the only metropolitan area that stands out because the percentage of people living in households where Spanish was the major language spoken increased from 55% in 1980 to 66% in 2005, largely because of an influx of foreign-born Mexicans (see Table 9.13).

We now turn to the changing percentage of the Latino population living in linguistically isolated households between 1990 and 2005. These households were defined as having no person 14 years of age and older

TABLE 9.13. *Percentage of Latinos Who Spoke Spanish at Home by Metro Area, 1980–2005*

	1980	1990	2000	2005
Houston	74.8%	73.4%	73.5%	76.1%
Los Angeles	72.6%	73.8%	74.9%	75.8%
Chicago	75.0%	74.8%	75.5%	75.2%
Miami	91.6%	88.8%	88.2%	87.4%
New York	81.9%	79.4%	78.2%	76.3%
Riverside	54.6%	59.2%	63.4%	65.8%

who spoke English exclusively or spoke English "very well."[6] About one-quarter of all Latinos lived in households that were classified by the U.S. Census Bureau as linguistically isolated in both 1990 and 2005. Among domestic-born Latinos there was a slight decline from the 12.8% living in such homes in 1990 to 11.2% in 2005; for foreign-born Latinos there was a slight increase from about 40% to 43% over the same period (see Graph 9.3). Comparing these data with the language-spoken-at-home levels we have considered indicates a fairly widespread implicit bilingualism within Latino households. A significantly lower percentage of Latinos were found to be living in linguistic isolation in 2005 (26%) than the population that lived in households where Spanish was the dominant language (80%).

Nevertheless, as the percentage of households headed by foreign-born Latinos continues to rise, the problem of increasing levels of linguistic isolation may lead to increasing poverty. This is brought into very sharp focus by examining income levels for households that were linguistically isolated, compared with those that were not. In 2005 the median household income for Latino household heads classified as linguistically isolated was $25,467, while for non–linguistically isolated household heads it was $44,618, some 75% higher. Clearly language isolation and socioeconomic status have been closely connected, and such isolation

[6] Linguistic isolation was first measured systematically in 1990 and is defined as follows: "Linguistic isolation. A household in which no person 14 years old and over speaks only English and no person 14 years old and over who speaks a language other than English speaks English 'Very well' is classified as 'linguistically isolated.' In other words, a household in which all members 14 years old and over speak a non-English language and also speak English less than 'Very well' (have difficulty with English) is 'linguistically isolated.' All the members of a linguistically isolated household are tabulated as linguistically isolated, including members under 14 years old who may speak only English." See *2000 Census of Population and Housing, Public Use Microdata Sample 2000.*

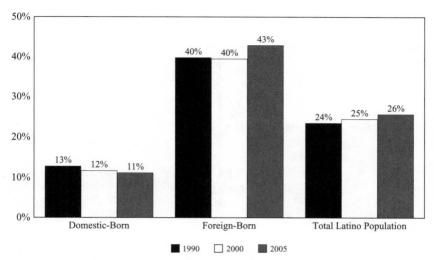

GRAPH 9.3. Percentage of Latinos Living in Linguistically Isolated Households, 1990–2005.

had a negative impact on the relative economic success of foreign-born Hispanics.

When we examine the changes in linguistic-isolation patterns among Latino nationalities, there were three major groupings. First were those Latino subgroups that experienced a declining overall percentage of their total populations that were linguistically isolated. These were Salvadorans, Colombians, Dominicans, and Puerto Ricans. Each of these groups experienced contraction in the overall portion of their populations that were foreign-born. Puerto Ricans had the lowest percentage of total populations living in linguistically isolated homes at nearly 12% in 2005, a decline from 18% in 1990. Dominicans also experienced a decline in people living in linguistically isolated homes from 38% in 1990 to 29% in 2005. Colombians experienced a decline of their linguistically isolated population from 33% to 25% between 1990 and 2005. Salvadorans, also dropped from 48% of their total population living in linguistic isolation in 1990 to 38% in 2005, but they still had the second-highest percentage of all Latino nationalities living in linguistically isolated households, behind Hondurans, at 42% in 2005.

The second group was those nationalities that experienced marginal change in the percentages of linguistically isolated persons. These included Cubans, Ecuadorians, and Peruvians. Some 28% of Cubans were living in linguistically isolated homes in 1990; 30%, in 2005. For Ecuadorians

TABLE 9.14. *Linguistic Isolation by Latino Nationality and Nativity,*
1990–2005

Nationality	Nativity	1990	2000	2005
Mexican	Domestic-Born	12.0%	11.8%	11.7%
	Foreign-Born	42.6%	42.3%	46.3%
	TOTAL	23.3%	26.0%	27.5%
Cuban	Domestic-Born	7.3%	4.2%	4.4%
	Foreign-Born	34.8%	37.9%	42.4%
	TOTAL	28.3%	28.5%	29.9%
Honduran	Domestic-Born	14.2%	20.0%	23.7%
	Foreign-Born	39.9%	41.5%	47.2%
	TOTAL	35.9%	38.1%	42.4%
Salvadoran	Domestic-Born	33.2%	25.5%	21.3%
	Foreign-Born	49.6%	40.6%	44.1%
	TOTAL	47.7%	37.9%	38.2%
Colombian	Domestic-Born	17.2%	12.6%	8.2%
	Foreign-Born	35.9%	33.5%	30.2%
	TOTAL	32.6%	29.5%	24.9%
Ecuadorian	Domestic-Born	17.5%	11.9%	12.2%
	Foreign-Born	34.4%	36.1%	35.4%
	TOTAL	30.7%	31.0%	29.8%
Peruvian	Domestic-Born	10.3%	10.7%	9.8%
	Foreign-Born	32.5%	28.3%	32.8%
	TOTAL	28.9%	24.9%	28.3%
Dominican	Domestic-Born	26.4%	19.5%	15.5%
	Foreign-Born	42.2%	36.6%	35.9%
	TOTAL	38.4%	32.2%	28.8%
Puerto Rican	Domestic-Born	10.1%	5.9%	4.3%
	Foreign-Born	26.9%	23.8%	24.4%
	TOTAL	18.1%	13.5%	11.7%

Note: In the case of Puerto Ricans "Foreign-Born" means born in Puerto Rico.

the corresponding figures were 31% and 30%, while for Peruvians some
29% of total populations lived in linguistic isolation in 1990, and 28%,
in 2005.

Finally, the third group experienced an increase in linguistically isolated individuals. Large-scale Mexican migration to the United States
after 1990 was paralleled by a slight rise in the linguistically isolated population from 23% to 27% in 2005, while among Hondurans the increase
was substantial, from 36% to 42% over the same period (see Table 9.14).

Differentiation in household income by linguistic isolation status
for heads of households was extraordinary among the Latino national

TABLE 9.15. *Median Household Income by Household Head, Linguistic Isolation Status, and Latino Nationality, 2005*

	Not Linguistically Isolated	Linguistically Isolated	% Differential
Mexicans	42,784	25,976	64.7%
Puerto Ricans	42,784	15,280	180.0%
Cubans	61,120	20,373	200.0%
Hondurans	39,789	30,560	30.2%
Salvadorans	45,942	31,579	45.5%
Colombians	55,212	30,560	80.7%
Ecuadorians	53,989	32,597	65.6%
Peruvians	55,008	31,889	72.5%
Dominicans	39,728	19,558	103.1%

groups. The most extreme differential was found among Cubans. Household heads who did not live in linguistically isolated households earned three times as much as those who were found living in linguistic isolation in 2005. Puerto Rican household heads living in linguistic isolation earned about 36% the median income level of those who were not linguistically isolated, while Dominicans earned half (see Table 9.15).

It is clear that language skills were an important determinant of socioeconomic status and income levels. While an increasing percentage of Latinos developed better English language skills between 1980 and 2005, there was continuity in the domestic use of Spanish, and in the percentage of linguistically isolated Latinos of every nationality. Although detailed data on bilingualism is not provided in the U.S. census or in other inclusive databases, it is clear that it is widespread. The continuity in the use of Spanish at home, while English language skills improve, is evidence of this. Naturally, the use of English or Spanish, and linguistic isolation, is determined largely by the percentage of the foreign-born within the total Latino population and within each national group and metropolitan area we have considered. It may be expected that as the relative portion of domestic-born Latinos increase, overall English language abilities will improve, and linguistic isolation will diminish.

10

Hispanic Business Ownership

Hispanic business ownership soared between 1987 and 2002 when the last economic census was undertaken measuring business ownership in the United States.[1] The number of Hispanic-owned business more than tripled over this period from 489,973 to 1,573,600 firms, while gross revenues more than quadrupled from $61.3 billion to $242 billion.[2] Additionally, the gross receipts per Hispanic-owned business increased from about $125,000 in 1987 to about $154,000 in 2002. There was some stagnation in receipts per business between 1987 and 1992; a sharp rise between 1992 and 1997; and then a decline between 1997 and 2002. (See Table 10.1.) Yet, while these Latino-owned businesses increased from 3.6% of all business enterprises in the United States in 1987 to 6.8% in 2002, their collective share of total gross business receipts fell from 1.6% in 1987 to 1.0% in 2002.

This was related to the small-scale nature of most Hispanic-owned firms, which is revealed by several indicators. First and foremost, more

---

[1] Data on Hispanic business ownership were collected by the U.S. Bureau of the Census as part of the economic census, which is undertaken every five years for years that end in "2" and "7". The 2002 data used here were part of the Survey of Business Owners (SBO), which replaced the previous data-gathering surveys used in 1992 and 1997, the Surveys of Minority- and Women-Owned Business Enterprises (SMOBE/SWOBE). For a discussion of the different business classification systems and comparability of data from various census years see the SBO Web page at http://www.census.gov/csd/sbo/. Hispanic businesses were defined as firms in which those of Latino origin owned 51% or more of the overall business and for which yearly receipts were over $1,000 in nominal prices. For a description of the methods used in the survey see the following Web page: http://www.census.gov/econ/overview/muo200.html.

[2] These, and all subsequent values, are in 2005 dollars adjusted for inflation using the inflation calculator available at the Bureau of Labor Statistics Web site at http://www.bls.gov.

TABLE 10.1. *Hispanic Business Ownership in the United States, 1987–2002*

Year	Number of Businesses	Nominal Gross Receipts in Billions of Dollars	Gross Receipts in Billions of 2005 Dollars	Gross Receipts per Business in 2005 Dollars	% of All Businesses in the United States	% of Gross Receipts of All Businesses in the United States	Number of Employees	% of All U.S. Employees
1987	489,973	32.8	61.3	125,182	3.6%	1.6%	NA	NA
1992	862,605	76.8	106.8	123,824	5.0%	2.3%	772,453	2.8%
1997	1,199,896	186.3	227.3	189,396	5.8%	1.0%	1,388,746	1.3%
2002	1,573,600	222.0	242.0	153,759	6.8%	1.0%	1,537,801	1.4%

Notes: Values in 2005 dollars were converted from nominal prices using the consumer price indices and the "inflation calculator" found on the Bureau of Labor Statistics Web site at http://www.bls.gov. NA is not available.

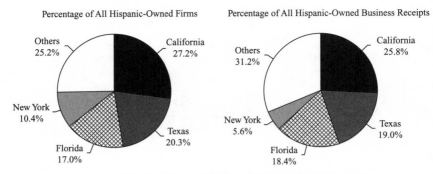

Percentage of All Hispanic-Owned Firms   Percentage of All Hispanic-Owned Business Receipts

Others 25.2%   California 27.2%   New York 10.4%   Florida 17.0%   Texas 20.3%

Others 31.2%   California 25.8%   New York 5.6%   Florida 18.4%   Texas 19.0%

GRAPH 10.1. Hispanic-Owned Businesses in the United States, 2002.

than 87% of all Hispanic business enterprises had no paid employees in 2002, while the corresponding portion for all businesses was about 75%. Thus, most Hispanic-owned businesses were relatively small-scale, family-owned and -operated firms. Second, among all firms in the United States with paid employees the average number of workers was about 20 per enterprise, while among Hispanic-owned enterprises there were 7.7 workers per firm, which is again indicative of the small-scale nature of these businesses.

It is not surprising that these Hispanic-owned businesses were concentrated in the states with the largest Latino populations. In 1987, 1992, 1997, and 2002 about three-quarters of all Latino businesses were located in the states of California, Texas, Florida, and New York, and California and Texas alone accounted for about one-half of all firms. In 2002 these four states accounted for 69% of total revenues generated by Hispanic-owned businesses. While the number of Hispanic businesses across the United States nearly tripled and gross revenues increased nearly five times between 1987 and 2002, there were marked variations by state. New York experienced the largest gains in overall Hispanic-owned businesses over these 15 years (479%), while their revenues rose by 404%. In Texas, revenues increased by 551%, the largest rise among the four states, although the number of businesses increased by a much smaller 237%. (See Table 10.2 and Graph 10.1 for complete data.)

When considering the metropolitan areas we have examined in this study – Chicago, Houston, Los Angeles, Miami, New York, and Riverside – we find that 55% of the nation's total Hispanic-owned businesses in 2002 were concentrated in these six metro areas and that 44% of the total were found in Los Angeles, New York, and Miami alone. The

TABLE 10.2. *Number of and Receipts of Hispanic-Owned Firms by Selected States, 1987–2002 (in 2005 dollars adjusted for inflation)*

	1987		1992		1997		2002			
	No. of Firms	Sales and Receipts in Thousands Dollars	No. of Firms	Sales and Receipts in Thousands Dollars	No. of Firms	Sales and Receipts in Thousands Dollars	No. of Firms	Sales and Receipts in Thousands Dollars	% Increase in No. of Firms 1987–2002	% Increase in Receipts 1987–2002
California	132,212	13,966,147	249,717	27,178,165	336,405	63,052,040	427,727	62,315,228	224%	346%
Texas	94,754	7,065,891	155,909	16,396,858	240,396	48,168,040	319,339	45,988,974	237%	551%
Florida	64,413	8,512,540	118,208	22,416,811	193,902	43,128,220	266,727	44,575,364	314%	424%
New York	28,254	2,675,978	50,601	6,577,868	104,189	12,579,420	163,639	13,495,984	479%	404%
Others	102,740	10,317,797	197,274	28,656,034	246,541	60,327,270	396,168	75,579,187	286%	633%
Total U.S.	422,373	42,538,352	771,709	101,225,737	1,121,433	227,254,990	1,573,600	241,954,737	273%	469%

Notes: All values have been converted to 2005 dollars using the consumer price index from the Bureau of Labor Statistics.

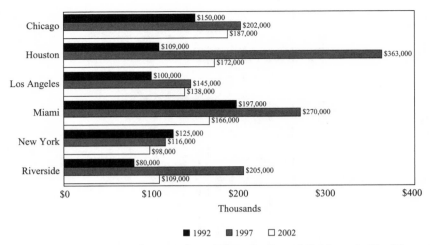

GRAPH 10.2. Revenues Generated per Hispanic-Owned Business in Six Metro Areas, 1992–2002.

growth in the absolute number of businesses owned by Latinos rose by an extraordinary 439% between 1992 and 2002 in New York, although these were mostly comparatively small-scale. New York's Hispanic businesses recorded very low revenues compared with the other metro areas, an average of $98,000 per establishment in 2002. In Chicago, business enterprises owned by Hispanics generated the highest revenues per business at $187,000 in 2002. Yet in all of these metro areas, after a general rise in revenues per business between 1992 and 1997, there was contraction thereafter to 2002, and this was indicative of the opening of smaller-scale establishments. (See Table 10.3 and Graph 10.2 for complete data.)

At the national level it was to be expected that Mexicans were the most numerous Hispanic business owners. However, even though their share of the national Latino population was about 60% in 2002, Mexicans owned 44% of all Hispanic businesses.[3] Cubans owned roughly 10% of

---

[3] Data on the nationality of Hispanic business owners was only collected for Mexicans, Puerto Ricans, and Cubans. All other Latino nationalities were grouped together as "other Hispanics." It also should be noted that it is nearly impossible to compare these kinds of data with 1997 and 1992 because of the changes in the way data was collected. From 1987 the Standard Industrial Classification (SIC) system was used to collect data on Hispanic and other minority-owned businesses. In 2002 this was changed to North American Industry Classification System (NAICS). For a discussion of changes and data incompatibility see http://www.census.gov/econ/census02/text/sbo/sbomethodology.htm. Accordingly, the discussion in the rest of this chapter will be confined to the 2002 data.

TABLE 10.3. *Number of and Receipts of Hispanic-Owned Firms by Selected Metro Areas, 1992–2002 (in 2005 dollars adjusted for inflation)*

	1992		1997		2002		% Increase in No. of Firms 1992–2002	% Increase in Receipts 1992–2002
	No. of Firms	Sales and Receipts in Thousands Dollars	No. of Firms	Sales and Receipts in Thousands Dollars	No. of Firms	Sales and Receipts in Thousands Dollars		
Chicago	16,663	2,496,309	27,482	5,556,266	38,766	7,260,455	133%	191%
Houston	33,765	3,684,686	41,769	15,146,765	75,562	12,983,963	124%	252%
Los Angeles	109,104	10,903,298	136,678	19,820,036	277,858	38,242,901	155%	251%
Miami	77,300	15,219,463	120,605	32,610,641	206,047	34,204,906	167%	125%
New York	39,175	4,882,636	84,880	9,825,474	211,024	20,780,233	439%	326%
Riverside	21,380	1,718,280	32,198	6,593,901	48,756	5,292,354	128%	208%

Notes: All values have been converted to 2005 dollars using the consumer price index from the Bureau of Labor Statistics.

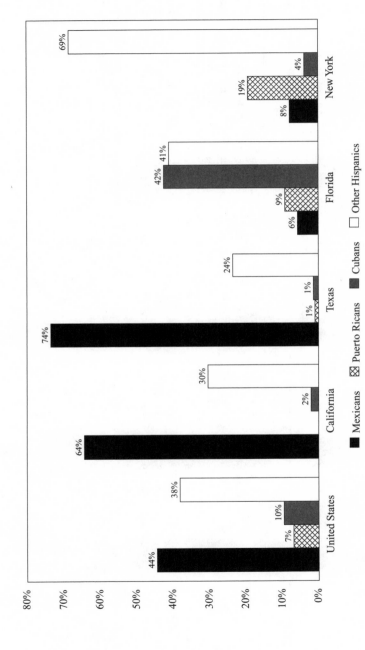

GRAPH 10.3. Percentage of Total Hispanic-Owned Businesses by Latino Nationality Nationwide and Selected States, 2002.

all Latino businesses in 2002 followed by Puerto Ricans at 7%. Other Latino nationalities owned a large share of businesses, 38% of the total, but it is unfortunate that there are no data on these business owners.

At the state level, Hispanic business ownerships patterns reflected the dominant national Latino subgroups. In California nearly two-thirds were owned by Mexicans, while in Texas they owned nearly three-quarters of the total. It is hardly surprising that Cubans owned 42% of all of Florida's Hispanic-owned businesses, while in New York State Puerto Ricans owned 19% of the total. It is unfortunate that data were not collected on New York State's other Hispanic national subgroups since they owned about 69% of all Latino businesses in the state. In Florida there was also a large portion of businesses owned by "other Hispanic" nationalities – 41% of the total. (See Graph 10.3 for these data.)

The same expected patterns of business ownership by Latino nationality were found in the metropolitan areas we have considered here and reflect the demographic predominance of national groups found in the states where these metro areas are located. These data are summarized in Graph 10.4.

Hispanic-owned businesses in 2002 were heavily concentrated in four overarching sectors: services, trade, construction, and health care and social assistance. About 80% of both the total number of businesses and the total gross revenues produced by all business enterprises owned by Hispanics were found in these broadly defined industries. (See Table 10.4.) However, when disaggregated into subsectors, there was a heavy concentration of the revenues generated by these businesses in trade, services, and construction. Retail and wholesale trading establishments owned by Latinos accounted for about 12% of all businesses, but 36% of all revenues. Service industries of various types were the largest single national-level sector – 42% of all Hispanic-owned businesses – but they generated 22% of all revenues. Construction industries accounted for 14% of all businesses and the same percentage of total revenues.

There were variations in these patterns when we examine the states with the largest concentrations of Latinos, although these were not major. In California, Florida, and New York the service sector accounted for between 42% and 45% of all Hispanic-owned businesses. In Texas some 37% were in the service sector. The major differentiation was in the construction business. In Texas nearly a quarter of all Hispanic businesses were in the construction sector compared with between 7% and

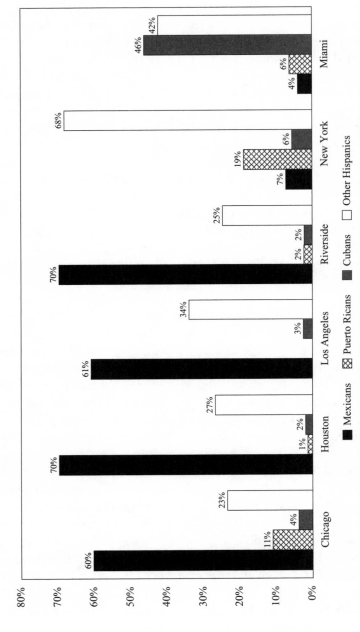

GRAPH 10.4. Percentage of Total Hispanic-Owned Businesses by Latino Nationality and Selected Metro Areas, 2002.

TABLE 10.4. *Hispanic Businesses by Sector in the United States, 2002*

Business Sector	% of Total Businesses	% of Total Receipts
Services	42.2%	22.4%
Other services (except public administration)	15.8%	4.5%
Administrative, support, waste management, remediation service	13.2%	5.5%
Professional, scientific, technical services	8.8%	6.8%
Accommodation, food services	3.1%	5.1%
Educational services	1.2%	0.5%
Trade	11.8%	36.0%
Retail trade	9.6%	18.2%
Wholesale trade	2.2%	17.7%
Construction	13.5%	14.2%
Health Care and Social Assistance	11.5%	6.2%
Transportation and Warehousing	8.0%	4.8%
Real Estate, Rental, Leasing	4.4%	2.8%
Arts, Entertainment, Recreation	2.8%	0.8%
Finance, Insurance	2.1%	2.3%
Manufacturing	2.0%	8.1%
Information	0.9%	1.0%
Others	0.8%	1.5%
TOTALS	100.0%	100.0%

11% in California, Florida, and New York. It is impossible to determine the reasons for this significant difference in the state of Texas. (See Graph 10.5.)

There were also some differences in the percentage of revenues derived from the various economic sectors by state. In Florida 44% of total business receipts generated by Hispanic-owned businesses were from the retail and wholesale trades compared with 39% in New York, 36% in Texas, and 32% in California. In Texas, despite the numeric importance of the construction industries, about 18% of all revenues produced by Latino-owned businesses in 2002 were derived from construction industries. These revenues were not extraordinarily higher than the 10% found in New York, 11% in Florida, and 12% in California. (See Graph 10.6.)[4]

---

[4] The data on Hispanic business sectors for the metropolitan areas we have considered here have too many missing values to consider statistically, and so we have decided not to include an analysis of the incomplete data in this chapter.

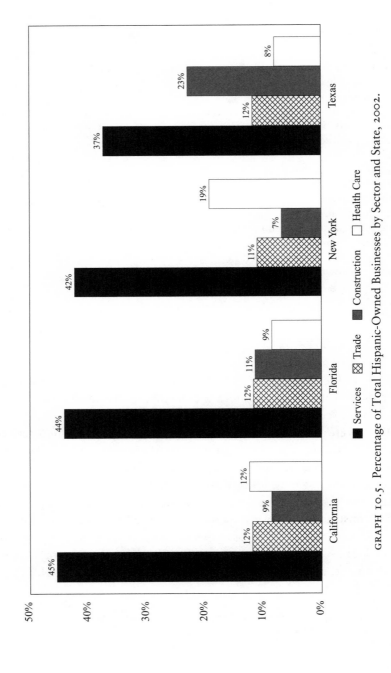

GRAPH 10.5. Percentage of Total Hispanic-Owned Businesses by Sector and State, 2002.

■ Services   ⊠ Trade   ■ Construction   ☐ Health Care

362

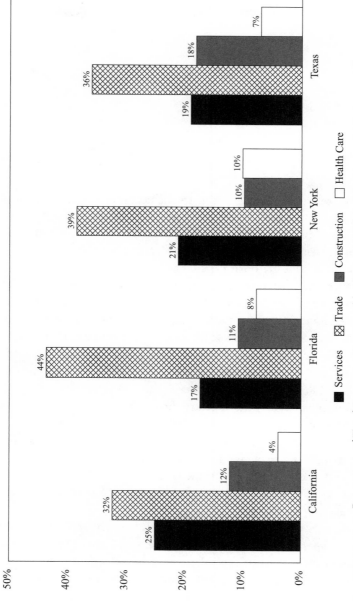

GRAPH 10.6. Percentage of Total Revenues Generated by Hispanic-Owned Businesses by Sector and State, 2002.

11

Race

The issue of race and its relation to socioeconomic status and mobility among Latinos in the United States has become an issue of importance among academics from different disciplines. Yet, the concept of race within Latin American and Caribbean cultures, in the region and among their foreign- and domestic-born populations in the United States, is entirely different. Racial conceptualizations in the United States have historically been bifurcated into the extremes of black and white; however, race perceptions within Latin America and the Caribbean have been extraordinarily more complex because of the extensiveness of race mixture.

First and foremost, there never has been a finite, absolute, or static definition of race within Latin America and the Caribbean from the onset of Spanish and Portuguese colonization in the late 15th and early 16th centuries. Europeans, of white ancestry, brought free and enslaved Africans to the Americas from the first voyages of discovery initiated by Columbus in the 1490s. Whether white or of African origin, free or slave, they all interacted extensively with indigenous women voluntarily or through the use of force, and this began the construction of complex multiracial societies whose characteristics evolved in distinctive rhythms over time and by geographical region.

The density of indigenous populations in Central Mexico and the Andes before Spanish colonization meant that those of native-American origin would remain majority populations even as their cultures experienced demographic disasters of various magnitudes during the 16th century.[1] In

---

[1] Alfred W. Crosby, *The Columbian Exchange; Biological and Cultural Consequences of 1492* (Westport, CT: Greenwood, 1972).

these regions large numbers of African slaves were introduced by European colonizers as indigenous populations declined and the resulting population mix, referred to as *mestizaje* or race mixture, produced multiracial societies in which it was nearly impossible to quantify the myriad racial categories that evolved over the ensuing five centuries. This was despite a near obsession by political power elites during the colonial period and even after independent nationhood was achieved in the early 19th century, to classify people according to race. At the extremes, those of pure European, African, or indigenous ancestry could be visually identified by their skin tones and physical characteristics. However, color and physiognomy became extraordinarily varied over five centuries of continuous race mixture, and peoples who were the products of miscegenation often could not be categorized or identified by using a tripartite system of racial classification. Finally, notions of "race" would become bound together with social constructs, cultural affinities, and class and wealth criteria rather than skin color. For example, a *mestizo*, or a person with indigenous and European ancestry who spoke Spanish only, dressed in European-style clothing and worshipped in Catholic churches, often conceived of themselves as "white" despite the fact that outsiders may have labeled them as *indios* or *mestizos*. By the same token a person with the exact same skin color and physical attributes, who spoke an indigenous language at home, dressed in indigenous clothing, and continued in private to maintain indigenous religious beliefs may have identified themselves as an *indio* despite having the exact same appearance as a person who conceived of themselves as "white."

As noted previously, in these same Meso-American and Andean societies African slaves were introduced in considerable numbers during the 16th and early 17th centuries, and this furthered the process of race and cultural mixture. It also exacerbated the problem of precise racial identification for people who were not of pure African descent. The emergence of the mulatto, or person of mixed African/European heritage, or the *zambo*, of mixed indigenous/African heritage further complicated the issue of racial identification by elites and self-identification by these new racial groups.

In the Hispanic Caribbean, indigenous peoples succumbed to the ravaging impact of European diseases during the 16th century. When labor demands escalated because of the demand and profitability of producing tropical export products such as sugar, coffee, and tobacco, massive numbers of African slaves were imported by the European colonial powers. This same process first occurred in Brazil, which would become the

largest destination of the transatlantic slave trade. Although the indigenous population did not disappear, as was the case in the Caribbean, the
racial configurations of both regions initially became tripartite. Whites,
or Europeans, stood apart from those of pure African descent and could
be easily identified by their physical characteristics. However, the large-
scale emergence of mixed-race individuals, mulattos, turned these societies into multiracial cultures in which people did not identify themselves
using the U.S.-based dualistic concepts of black and white. The problem
of racial identification was further exacerbated because of the large-scale
emergence of a population of free blacks and mulattos, who eventually
became the majority population sector in Brazil, as well as important
components of each Hispanic Caribbean culture. From the point of view
of comparative race relations between the United States and the region,
this is an important point to take note of. In the United States some
90% of peoples of African descent were slaves, and the entire concept of
"black" was often synonymous with "slave." But in Latin American and
the Caribbean the association of "black" and "slave" was not necessarily
part of the vocabulary on race and social or legal status.

This was because free mulattos and even those who would be clearly
classified as "black" in the United States who acquired education, skills,
or even wealth may have self-identified as "white" despite skin color or
the way in which they were labeled by elites and other "outsiders."[2] Thus,
the concept of race, in this example, had nothing to do with "color" or
other physical attributes of a person but with how they "constructed"
their identities socially and culturally as well as their self-perceptions of
social and economic status.

Social constructions of identity, race, and skin color evolved differ-
ently in each region, culture, and eventual nation state, and this makes
overarching classifications such as "black" and "white" nearly impossible. The concept of who could be labeled as black, mulatto, or *mestizo*
became blurred. Racial notions evolved as social and cultural constructs
and were woven together with class and status, rather than having to
do with skin color or physical appearance. For Dominicans, to cite but
one example, blacks are Haitians, and a Dominican with the exact same
skin color as a Haitian would take great offense at being referred to as

[2] See Magnus Morner, *Race Mixture in the History of Latin America* (Boston: Little, Brown,
1967); Peter Wade, *Race and Ethnicity in Latin America* (London: Pluto Press, 1997);
Nancy P. Appelbaum, Anne S. Macpherson, and Karin Alejandra Rosemblatt, editors,
Race and Nation in Modern Latin America (Chapel Hill: University of North Carolina
Press, 2003).

black.[3] For Cubans and Puerto Ricans, people who may be labeled by outsiders as mulattos or even blacks, especially those of lighter skin tones, most often self-identify as whites irrespective of skin color. These Latin American and Caribbean constructions of race would carry over to the United States within Latino communities, and they would be somewhat transformed by the racial notions that were and are extant throughout the United States.

This discussion of racial conceptualizations within Latin American and Caribbean societies could go on interminably. The key question is how did Mexicans and later immigrants to the United States fit into the racial classification system in the United States? This must be considered from three perspectives. First, how did outsiders – or extant populations who could be black or white – classify Latinos as their populations evolved in the United States because of changing migration patterns? Second, how did different Latino subgroups in the United States conceive of themselves in terms of race within the context of a society that had very different definitions from those that prevailed in their countries of origin? Third, how did the U.S. Census Bureau enumerate the racial characteristics of this extraordinarily diverse population, which has been constantly transformed by changing migration patterns, especially after the Second World War?

First and foremost, it is generally accepted that Latinos do not constitute a race. Although outsiders may generalize about Hispanics as a separate race, social scientists and the U.S. Census Bureau recognize that Latinos may be of any race. Some scholars have attempted to classify "Hispanics" as a separate ethnic group based on an assumed communality of language, religion, traditions, and other characteristics of a common heritage that define an ethnicity. However, while this may be convenient to outside observers who cannot appreciate the nuances of an extraordinarily diverse population, the reality is that most Latinos first define themselves by their national origins, and these emphasize uniqueness and separateness from other Hispanics, rather than any shared traits.[4] Latinos also

---

[3] See Ernesto Sagás, *Race and Politics in the Dominican Republic* (Gainesville: University Press of Florida, 2000).

[4] The 2002 National Survey of Latinos conducted by the Pew Hispanic Center found that 54% of Latinos identify themselves primarily by their parents' country of origin while only 24% first identify themselves as "Latino" or "Hispanic." See Pew Hispanic Center/Kaiser Family Foundation, "2002 National Survey of Latinos," available at http://pewhispanic .org/reports/report.php?ReportID=15. Another 2006 survey revealed that 48% of Latinos who were adults referred to themselves by their country of origin first: 26% used "Hispanic" or "Latino," and 24% used "American" as their first self-identification. See Jeffrey Passel and Paul Taylor, "Who's Hispanic?" report of Pew Hispanic Center,

do not first identify themselves by any race. This does not mean that the terms "Latino" or "Hispanic" are rejected, but that nationality is first and foremost in Latino self-identification. But, it is exceedingly rare that people of Hispanic heritage identify themselves by the racial nomenclatures used either in Latin American and the Caribbean or in the United States.

Second, even though Latinos clearly first identify with their national origins, they have been forced to confront the issues of "race," which have been so central to the evolution of the United States. This means that in many contexts Latinos have had to "create" a racial identity to satisfy the imperative of racial classifications that have been critical to elites and within popular culture. However, this creation of a racial identity may have little to do with actual skin color, or the conceptualizations of race that prevailed within the United States prior to the large-scale arrival of Latin American and Caribbean immigrants in the aftermath of World War II. This is brought into focus by the Latino conception of white.

White may have a very different meaning among Hispanics when compared with how white is perceived by those of pure European heritage. Although notions of white differ within each Latino national subgroup because of different racial configurations in their home societies, clearly the concept may be more closely connected to what has been called a "measure of belonging, stature, and acceptance" rather than physical appearance.[5] Latinos who have achieved social and economic success may identify as white regardless of actual racial characteristics in order to socially distance themselves from other Latinos who have not been as fortunate. Additionally, since white is in some ways perceived as "fitting in," many Latinos who have not experienced upward social and economic mobility may also adopt self-perceptions of whiteness. This is not universal, however, and does not imply that within particular Latin American and Caribbean nationalities and individuals there is not pride at indigenous or African heritage. The extraordinary diversity among Latinos ensures that there are a wide range of individual attitudes and concepts about racial identities. Yet in this context, race is hardly an absolute concept based on common assumptions about skin color or other physical characteristics but rather a social and cultural construct that can be fluid and changing through time.

May 28, 2009, issued after the nomination of Sonia Sotomayor to the U.S. Supreme Court, available at http://pewhispanic.org/reports/report.php?ReportID=111.

[5] Sonya Tafoya, "Shades of Belonging," Pew Hispanic Center, December 2004 available at http://pewhispanic.org/reports/report.php?ReportID=35.

The third point revolves around how data on the racial components
and classifications on Hispanics have been collected by official government agencies such as the U.S. Census Bureau. In 1976 the U.S. Congress
mandated the collection of data on "Americans of Spanish Origin or
Descent" and in 1977 the U.S. Office of Management and Budget issued
a directive on gathering data on race and ethnicity.[6] These directives,
however, did not mean that the racial characteristics of Hispanics were
enumerated. It was only in the 1980 decennial census that Hispanics
were asked to self-identify both their race and whether or not they were
Hispanic. The way these questions on race and Hispanic origin were
asked and the order in which they appear were changed for the 1990 and
2000 decennial censuses, and in the American Community Survey data
collected from 2001 onward.[7] What is critical to take note of is that all

---

[6] See *Spotlight on Heterogeneity: The Federal Standards for Racial and Ethnic Classification*, (Washington, DC: National Academy Press, 1996), Appendix B Office of Management and Budget Statistical Directive No. 15, Race And Ethnic Standards For Federal Statistics And Administrative Reporting, available at http://books.nap.edu/openbook
.php?record_id=9060&page=65. A central objective of the 1976 law was that federal
agencies keep records of the characteristics of the people they served. On the implications
of this change in race identification and the subsequent decision to allow more than one
race to be declared; see C. Matthew Snipp, "Racial Measurement in the American Census:
Past Practices and Implications for the Future," *Annual Review of Sociology*, 29 (2003),
563–88.

[7] See Clara E. Rodríguez, *Changing Race: Latinos, the Census, and the History of Ethnicity
in the United States* (New York: New York University Press, 2000).
  For a discussion of the various categories and questions on race and Hispanic origin
used by the U.S. Bureau of the Census, and the revisions which took place in 1996, see
U.S. Bureau of the Census, Staff of the Special Population Statistics Population Division,
"Findings on Questions on Race and Hispanic Origin Tested in the 1996 National Content Survey" Population Division Working Paper No. 16, December 1996, available at
http://www.census.gov/population/www/documentation/twps0016/twps0016.html.
  A major difference with respect to data collection on race for the 2000 census and
subsequent American Community Surveys was the inclusion of multiracial categories as
options. A person could report more than one race for the first time, as opposed to simply
black, white, Indian, and so on. Additionally, the order of the questions on race and
Hispanic origin was changed. Prior to the 2000 census the question on race preceded
the question on whether an individual was of Spanish or Hispanic or Latino origin.
This created confusion for Latinos filling out census forms as many were unsure as to
whether "Hispanic" was considered a race. For 2000 and later, the question on whether
one was Spanish/Hispanic/Latino preceded the question on race. For a discussion on
these changes in the way data were collected for the 2000 census see U.S. Bureau of the
Census, "Questions and Answers for Census 2000 on Race," March 14, 2001, available
at http://www.census.gov/Press-Release/www/2001/raceqandas.html.
  For the precise wording of the question on race in each U.S. decennial census and
American Community Surveys see the IPUMS Web page at http://usa.ipums.org/usa-
action/variableDescription.do?mnemonic=RACE. Go to the section that lists "Questions

of these data were gathered on the basis of self-declarations. People had
the option to declare whether they were Hispanic or not Hispanic and
to self-identify their race. Thus, the data collected by the Census Bureau
on the racial characteristics of Hispanics had little to do with pre-1980
U.S.-based concepts of race, which largely revolved around a black/white
polarity. Rather these data were entirely the result of the racial self-images
of individual Latinos from different national subgroups. These images
and subsequent declarations to census workers could be social and cultural constructions rather than having anything to do with skin color, as
was the historical "marker" for racial classifications in the United States.
Thus, the data on race among Hispanics presented in the remainder of
this chapter are the results of self-perceptions and cannot be utilized as
absolute indicators of racial categories. Yet, despite their imperfections,
they may be used as broad, if imprecise, indicators of important social and
economic differences between those Hispanics who perceived themselves
as white and those who did not.[8]

There are several general observations to be made about the data on
racial self-declarations among Hispanics between 1980 and 2005. First,
the percentage of Latinos who declared that they were white decreased
marginally from 58% to 54% between 1980 and 2005, although there
had been a decline to 48% in 2000, probably because of the differing
methodologies in collecting data on race. Second, the percentage who
reported that they were of some other race, or of mixed racial ancestry
(other designation), increased from 40% to 44%. Third, Latinos who
reported that they were black were under 3% in each decennial census year, and only 1.5% of all Hispanics in 2005. (See Table 11.1.)[9]

---

to Respondents" and click on the census year for the exact census questionnaire. On the
difficulty of using the multiple-race question and various attempts to analyze this new
identifier, see Carolyn A. Liebler and Andrew Halpern-Manners, "A Practical Approach
to Using Multiple-Race Response Data: A Bridging Method for Public Use Microdata,"
Demography, 45:1 (February 2008), 143–55.

[8] Although there has been much written about Afro-Latinos, Latinos who self-identify as
being "black" have been very marginal quantitatively and are most prevalent among
Hispanic Caribbean nationalities and Panamanians. See the essays in Anani Dzidzienyo
and Suzanne Obler, editors, *Neither Enemies nor Friends: Latinos, Blacks, Afro-Latinos*
(New York: Palgrave Macmillan, 2005).

[9] Our estimates differ slightly from those put forth by John Logan "How Race Counts for
Hispanic Americans," Lewis Mumford Center, University of Albany, July 14, 2003, p. 3,
available at http://mumford.albany.edu/census/BlackLatinoReport/BlackLatino1.htm.
Although he used the same data sets, we have recoded Latinos to exclude Europeans
and we have included Brazilians in our definitions. The differences for 2000 are statistically insignificant.

TABLE 11.1. *Racial Composition of the Latino Population of the United States Based on Self-Declarations, 1980–2005*

	1980		1990		2000		2005	
White	8,573,751	57.8%	10,776,646	51.4%	16,920,644	47.9%	22,784,788	54.3%
Some Other Race	5,856,456	39.5%	9,562,284	45.6%	17,760,660	50.3%	18,557,037	44.2%
Black	402,022	2.7%	619,750	3.0%	655,665	1.9%	619,411	1.5%
TOTAL	14,832,229	100.0%	20,958,680	100.0%	35,336,969	100.0%	41,961,236	100.0%

Note: For 1980 and 1990 people had the option of "writing in" Spanish under the race question. Since there was not racial specificity, we have labeled these individuals as belonging to "some other race." For 2000 and 2005 this option was removed and "other race" became the preferred alternative to white, black, or mixed race. For the 1980 and 1990 data we have also added those designated as "other race" to those writing in "Spanish" to arrive at our data for "some other race." For all years we have added those who did not declare black or white to "some other race."

371

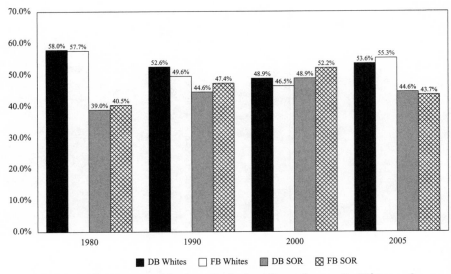

GRAPH 11.1. Percentage of Latinos Declaring Themselves to Be White or Some Other Race by Foreign- or Domestic-Born, 1980–2005. *Note:* DB is domestic-born; FB is foreign-born; SOR is "some other race."

Additionally, there were no significant differences in the percentages of foreign-born or domestic-born Latinos who self-declared as white, some other race, or black. (See Graph 11.1.)

There were, however, significant differences in racial self-conceptions among the different Latino national subgroups and in the major metropolitan areas we have examined. Cubans were at the extreme in identifying themselves as white. Some 84% of all Cubans declared themselves to be white in 2005, and this was significantly greater than among any other Latino nationality. There was almost no statistical difference between foreign and domestic-born Cubans who self-identified as white.[10] There is no way to verify the accuracy of these self-declaration data, although it is well-known that in the migratory flows that followed the 1959 triumph of the Castro-led revolution upper- and middle-class Cubans who were predominantly white dominated those who fled the island. However, there was a marked change in migration during the 1980 Mariel boatlift and after when poorer Cubans emigrated, and they have been

---

[10] 84% of foreign-born Cubans identified themselves as white, while 83% of domestic-born Cubans also indicated they were white in 2005.

TABLE 11.2. *Percentage of People Declaring Themselves to Be White, Some Other Race, or Black by Latino Nationality, 2005*

	% White	% SOR	% Black
Cuban	84.0%	13.3%	2.7%
Colombian	62.3%	36.4%	1.4%
Mexican	54.8%	44.7%	0.6%
Honduran	53.8%	43.5%	2.7%
Peruvian	52.5%	46.9%	0.6%
Ecuadoran	49.8%	49.6%	0.6%
Salvadoran	48.4%	51.1%	0.4%
Puerto Rican	48.2%	46.9%	4.9%
Dominican	28.0%	64.2%	7.8%

Note: SOR is "some other race."

observed to have been of darker skin colors. How this impacted the over-all racial composition of the Cuban population in the United States is unknown. It is conspicuous, however, that the exact same percentage of Cubans classified themselves as white in 1980 (84%).

Colombians also stand out for the relatively higher percentage of persons who identified themselves as white at 62% in 2005. Dominicans were exceptional because only 28% considered themselves to be white in 2005, 64% considered themselves as belonging to some other race, and nearly 8% identified themselves as black, which was the highest among all of the Latino nationalities. Among all other Latino national subgroups between 48% and 55% self-identified as white, while most others considered themselves to be of some other race. Nearly 5% of Puerto Ricans declared themselves to be black in 2005, the second-highest national subgroup behind Dominicans. (See Table 11.2 for data.)

The racial self-conceptions of Latinos in the major metropolitan areas we have considered were closely related to the national origins of the most numerous national subgroups. In Miami, with its high concentration of Cubans, an extraordinary 87% of all Latinos self-identified as white in 2005, while in New York with its eclectic mix of Latino nationalities, and where Puerto Ricans and Dominicans were the most numerous nationalities, only 36% of all Latinos considered themselves to be white in the same year. New York also had the highest percentage of Latinos who considered themselves to be black at 5.4%, and this reflected the concentration of Dominicans in the New York metropolitan area.

There were interesting disparities in race conceptions within the Mexican-dominant metro areas. In Houston some 65% of all Latinos considered themselves to be white, while in Chicago only 45% of all Latinos identified as white in 2005, about the same percentage as in the Los Angeles metro area (46%). It is relevant to compare the Los Angles race data among Latinos with neighboring, and more suburban, Riverside where 51% of all Latinos self-identified as white. There is absolutely no empirical evidence that the racial origins of Mexicans in each of these four metropolitan areas were any different, and there are no scientific data that may be used to explain the different racial configurations the Census Bureau enumerated based on self-declarations. Despite the similar percentages of Mexican-origin persons in each of these four metro areas, how may we explain the different racial self-conceptions? It has been suggested that Hispanics tend to identify themselves racially according to the overall racial structure of the region, or metro area, in which they live. In other words, in regions where there is a higher percentage of whites among the overall population, Latinos may be more prone to label themselves as white.[11] This is consistent with the notion advanced above that racial self-conceptions among Hispanics are influenced to some extent by a desire to fit in.

However, this conclusion does not coincide with the data on the overall racial structures within the Mexican-dominant metro areas. In Houston about 42% of the total population was white in 2005, while in Chicago 55% of all residents were white. Despite the fact that a higher percentage of the general population self-identified as white in Chicago, a lower percentage of Latinos identified themselves as white (45%) than in Houston (65%). Yet, in Riverside, where the overall population was 41% white, a higher percentage of Latinos self-identified as white (51%) than in neighboring Los Angeles where 46% of Latinos considered themselves to be white and where only 29% of the total population was white in 2005. It is difficult to speculate on precisely why racial self-conceptions differ in these Mexican-dominant metropolitan areas. This underscores the difficulty of measuring racial structures among Latinos when data are derived exclusively from self-declarations. (See Table 11.3.)

Yet, based on the available data there were socioeconomic differentiations based upon racial self-declarations among the Latino population. We will examine three indicators: household income, poverty, and educational attainment and how these changed over time. First and foremost, those Latinos who declared themselves to be white earned higher median

---

[11] Logan, "How Race Counts for Hispanic Americans."

TABLE 11.3. *Percentage of Latinos Declaring Themselves
to Be White, Some Other Race, or Black by
Metro Area, 2005*

	% White	% SOR	% Black
Miami	87.4%	10.5%	2.1%
Houston	64.9%	34.5%	0.6%
Riverside	51.2%	48.2%	0.6%
Los Angeles	45.8%	53.7%	0.5%
Chicago	44.9%	54.3%	0.8%
New York	36.0%	58.5%	5.4%

Note: SOR is "some other race."

household incomes than those who identified as some other race and black between 1980 and 2005. Yet what is important to take note of is that the gap in median household income between these racial classifications narrowed considerably over this 25-year period. In 1980 Latinos who considered themselves to be some other race earned 87% of the median household incomes of those who declared as whites, and Latino blacks earned 71% of that earned by Latino whites. Yet by 2005 there were negligible differences in the median household incomes of those who were of some other race – 98% the income level of Latino whites – while Latino blacks had closed the gap to 86% of the median household incomes of Latino whites. Additionally, while median household income among Latino whites increased by 11% between 1980 and 2005, it increased by 25% among those of some other race, and 36% among Latino blacks.[12] What is unknown, and impossible to determine, is how the changes in the way the Census Bureau collected race data among Latinos between 1980 and 2005 affected these household-income data.[13] (See Table 11.4 and Graph 11.2.)

Among the demographically dominant Mexican-origin population, similar patterns may be observed. In 1980 Mexicans who identified themselves as belonging to some other race earned 96% of the median household income level of those who declared themselves to be white. Thus, there was no significant difference in household incomes for 99%

[12] These percentages have been calculated in 2005 inflation-adjusted dollars.
[13] We examined the 2007 data after this manuscript was written to check whether there was any differential with the 2005 data and found that Latinos of some other race earned 99% the level of median household incomes of Latino whites and that Latino blacks had closed the gap considerably and earned 95% the median household incomes of Latino whites. Thus, by 2007 there was practically no differentiation in median household incomes by race among Latinos.

TABLE 11.4. *Median Household Income among Latinos by Racial Self-Declarations, 1980–2005*

	1980	1990	2000	2005	% Increase 1980–2005
White	40,232	43,334	45,366	44,821	11%
Some Other Race	34,968	39,299	43,098	43,803	25%
Black	28,470	38,029	40,546	38,709	36%
SOR Income as % of White Income	86.9%	90.7%	95.0%	97.7%	
Black Income as % of White Income	70.8%	87.8%	89.4%	86.4%	

Note: Values are in 2005 dollars adjusted for inflation.
SOR is "some other race."

of all Mexicans since less than 1% self-identified as black. In fact, by 2005 some-other-race Mexicans earned marginally higher median household incomes than those who were white, which calls into question the generalized assumption that Latino whites were generally better off than the two other major racial subgroups. (See Table 11.5 for these data.)

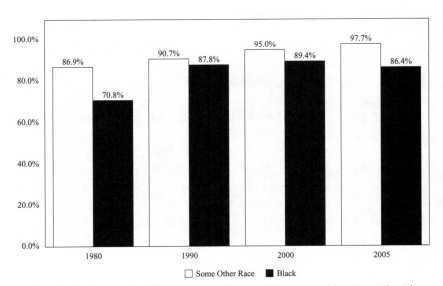

GRAPH 11.2. Percentage of the Median Household Income of Latinos Who Identify as White Earned by Latinos Who Identify as Some Other Race and as Black, 1980–2005.

TABLE 11.5. *Median Household Income among Mexicans by Racial Self-Declarations, 1980–2005*

	1980	1990	2000	2005	% Increase 1980–2005
White	38,501	40,494	43,098	41,256	7%
Some Other Race	36,865	39,209	42,984	42,784	16%
Black	24,711	35,862	39,582	38,302	55%
SOR Income as % of White Income	95.7%	96.8%	99.7%	103.7%	
Black Income as % of White Income	64.2%	88.6%	91.8%	92.8%	

Note: Values are in 2005 dollars adjusted for inflation.
SOR is "some other race."

Among the Puerto Rican population this was not the case. Puerto Ricans who declared themselves to be white (about 48% of all Puerto Ricans in 2005) earned significantly more than some other race or black Puerto Ricans in 2005, although as was the case with the Mexican population, the income differential narrowed between 1980 and 2005. In 1980 Puerto Ricans who identified themselves as belonging to some other race earned 72% of the median household incomes reported by whites. By 1980 they earned 84% of white Puerto Rican income levels. On the other hand, those Puerto Ricans who identified themselves as black (5% of the total Puerto Rican population in 2005) experienced an increasing gap in income compared with both white and some-other-race Puerto Ricans between 1980 and 2005. (See Table 11.6.)

TABLE 11.6. *Median Household Income among Puerto Ricans by Racial Self-Declarations, 1980–2005*

	1980	1990	2000	2005	% Increase 1980–2005
White	32,762	44,888	47,634	49,915	52%
Some Other Race	23,727	32,874	38,561	41,765	76%
Black	28,405	34,647	37,427	35,653	26%
SOR Income as % of White Income	72.4%	73.2%	81.0%	83.7%	
Black Income as % of White Income	86.7%	77.2%	78.6%	71.4%	

Note: Values are in 2005 dollars adjusted for inflation.
SOR is "some other race."

TABLE 11.7. *Median Household Income among Cubans by Racial Self-Declarations, 1980–2005*

	1980	1990	2000	2005	% Increase 1980–2005
White	47,454	52,308	52,965	55,976	18%
Some Other Race	39,450	46,023	47,861	49,762	26%
Black	34,932	44,828	42,077	39,790	14%
SOR Income as % of White Income	83.1%	88.0%	90.4%	88.9%	
Black Income as % of White Income	73.6%	85.7%	79.4%	71.1%	

Note: Values are in 2005 dollars adjusted for inflation.
SOR is "some other race."

Cubans were the Latino national subgroup with the greatest percentage who self-identified as white – 84% in 2005 – and indeed they generally earned higher median household incomes compared with some-other-race Cubans and blacks. However, as was the case with Puerto Ricans, the median household income gap separating some-other-race Cubans narrowed slightly between 1980 and 2005, although it widened marginally among Cuban blacks. Among Dominicans, who had the lowest percentage of the overall population identifying as white and the highest percentage of all Latinos who declared themselves to be black, the patterns of median household income differentiation were similar to that of Cubans. By 2005 both of the nonwhite categories earned 83% the median household incomes of Dominican whites. (See Tables 11.7 and 11.8.)

TABLE 11.8. *Median Household Income among Dominicans by Racial Self-Declarations, 1980–2005*

	1980	1990	2000	2005	% Increase 1980–2005
White	32,685	39,114	42,746	43,090	32%
Some Other Race	26,104	37,357	38,788	35,653	37%
Black	28,191	33,448	39,468	35,653	26%
SOR Income as % of White Income	79.9%	95.5%	90.7%	82.7%	
Black Income as % of White Income	86.3%	85.5%	92.3%	82.7%	

Note: Values are in 2005 dollars adjusted for inflation.
SOR is "some other race."

TABLE 11.9. *Median Household Income among Colombians by Racial Self-Declarations, 1980–2005*

	1980	1990	2000	2005	% Increase 1980–2005
White	45,082	53,793	52,171	55,008	22%
SOR	40,339	50,366	52,454	54,397	35%
Black	47,169	49,759	55,800	44,007	−7%
SOR Income as % of White Income	89.5%	93.6%	100.5%	98.9%	
Black Income as % of White Income	104.6%	92.5%	107.0%	80.0%	

Note: Values are in 2005 dollars adjusted for inflation.
SOR is "some other race."

Among Colombians, the Latino national subgroup with the second-largest percentage of self-declared whites – 62% in 2005 – the patterns in the development median household incomes by race were similar to those found among Mexicans. By 2005 both Colombian whites and those of some other race earned about the same, although Colombian blacks lagged behind. However, they were only 1.4% of all Colombians according to the self-identification data. (See Table 11.9.)

When poverty rates are examined by race among Latinos between 1980 and 2005, similar findings are forthcoming. Fewer self-declared Latino whites lived in poverty than those of some other race or blacks, although the differential closed significantly by 2005. In 1980 21% of Latino whites lived in poverty compared with 27% of Latinos who considered themselves to be of some other race and 36% of Latino blacks. By 2005 21% of Latino whites, 22% of some other race, and 27% of blacks lived in poverty according to Census Bureau data. Once again there was almost no difference in poverty rates between whites and those of some other race, although Latino self-declared blacks had greater poverty rates. Although Latino blacks had significantly higher poverty rates in all years between 1980 and 2005, it must be kept in mind that they represented only 1.5% of the total Latino population in 2005. Thus, overall poverty rates in 2005 were about the same for nearly 99% of all Latinos, irrespective of their racial self-perceptions. What is unknown is whether these statistical results were affected by the different methodologies used by the Census Bureau to gather data on the race of Latinos in the different census years. (See Table 11.10.)

TABLE 11.10. *Percentage of Latinos Living in Poverty by Racial Self-Declarations, 1980–2005*

	1980	1990	2000	2005	% Increase 1980–2005
White	20.6%	23.5%	21.1%	20.8%	1%
SOR	26.8%	28.1%	24.4%	21.9%	−18%
Black	35.6%	30.6%	27.9%	26.9%	−24%

Among Mexicans there were almost no differences whatsoever in poverty rates by race from 1980 through 2005, although Mexicans who declared themselves to be black – only 0.6% of all Mexicans in 2005 – had higher rates. Thus, among Mexicans race was absolutely not a factor in determining who lived in poverty. (See Table 11.11.)

This was not the case among Puerto Ricans. Puerto Ricans who self-identified as white had consistently lower poverty rates than the other two racial groupings, although the differential declined significantly between 1980 and 2005. This was not the case among Cubans, the only Latino national group whose poverty rates by race remained relatively stable between 1980 and 2005. Dominicans also demonstrate different patterns in the evolution of poverty rates by race than the demographically dominant Mexicans, although there were some similarities in trends with Puerto Ricans. As was the case with all other Latino subgroups, Dominican whites did have lower poverty rates than those who declared themselves to be of some other race or black, but the differences were not by wide margins. In 2005 23% of Dominican whites, 29% of Dominicans who declared as being of some other race, and 27% of blacks lived in poverty. This same pattern was found among Colombians. There were not major statistical differences in poverty levels by race among Colombians in 2005 when 12% of whites, 13% of those who declared as some other race, and 14% of Colombian blacks lived in poverty. (See Tables 11.12 through 11.15 for these data).

TABLE 11.11. *Percentage of Mexicans Living in Poverty by Racial Self-Declarations, 1980–2005*

	1980	1990	2000	2005	% Increase 1980–2005
White	22.1%	26.0%	23.2%	23.6%	7%
SOR	23.9%	27.6%	24.6%	22.3%	−7%
Black	42.7%	32.2%	29.7%	30.7%	−28%

TABLE 11.12. *Percentage of Puerto Ricans Living in Poverty by Racial Self-Declarations, 1980–2005*

	1980	1990	2000	2005	% Increase 1980–2005
White	29.8%	23.2%	20.7%	19.5%	−34%
SOR	42.5%	36.3%	29.2%	25.6%	−40%
Black	37.3%	34.8%	31.2%	31.8%	−15%

TABLE 11.13. *Percentage of Cubans Living in Poverty by Racial Self-Declarations, 1980–2005*

	1980	1990	2000	2005	% Increase 1980–2005
White	12.0%	13.2%	13.5%	12.8%	7%
SOR	17.6%	18.0%	19.4%	19.1%	8%
Black	21.2%	22.4%	26.2%	23.6%	11%

TABLE 11.14. *Percentage of Dominicans Living in Poverty by Racial Self-Declarations, 1980–2005*

	1980	1990	2000	2005	% Increase 1980–2005
White	27.5%	29.0%	24.6%	23.3%	−15%
SOR	36.2%	31.9%	28.5%	29.2%	−19%
Black	29.3%	36.0%	26.6%	27.2%	−7%

TABLE 11.15. *Percentage of Colombians Living in Poverty by Racial Self-Declarations, 1980–2005*

	1980	1990	2000	2005	% Increase 1980–2005
White	13.3%	14.3%	16.6%	11.5%	−13%
SOR	17.5%	14.7%	16.6%	12.6%	−28%
Black	17.6%	21.1%	19.9%	13.7%	−22%

Hispanics in the United States

Of the three socioeconomic indicators on racial disparities among Latinos, it was only in educational attainment that there were significant differentials between the three major racial groups. A greater percentage of some-other-race Latinos 25 years of age and older did not graduate from high school in all years, although by 2005 the gap had narrowed considerably, and in this regard – the reduced differential between race groups over time – educational attainment indicators were similar to median household income and poverty trends. Additionally, a significantly higher percentage of self-declared white Latinos graduated from college or acquired higher degrees than some-other-race Latinos, and the differential remained significant even in 2005.[14] Some 16% of white Latinos older than 25 years of age had achieved a B.A. degree or higher in 2005 compared with 11% of some-other-race Latinos. (See Graph 11.3.)

It should be recalled that there was a surge in migration from Latin America and the Caribbean after 1980 and that by 2005 this resulted in a larger foreign-born Latino population than those who were born in the United States. If we isolate the population 25 years old and older, the standard criteria for examining educational attainment, about 60% of all Latinos were foreign-born in 2005. This is important to take note of because foreign-born Latinos had extraordinarily lower high school graduation rates, and somewhat lower college graduation rates, than domestic-born Latinos. Among domestic-born Latinos the differential in rates among those who did not graduate from high school by race was small: 24% for whites, 27% for some-other-race Latinos, and 22% for black Latinos. Among foreign-born Latinos 50% of whites, 52% of those who declared themselves to be of some other race, and 35% of blacks did not graduate from high school in 2005. Thus, the high rates of non–high school graduates among the foreign-born resulted in overall higher rates among the entire Latino adult population. It ought to be underlined, however, that the variation in rates of those who did not graduate from high school by race was small in both foreign- and domestic-born Latinos.

When college graduation rates are examined by race, the differences between domestic- and foreign-born Latinos were not as stark, although the foreign-born had lower graduation rates. White Latinos, whether domestic- or foreign-born, had marginally higher rates than Latinos who

---

[14] We have elected to include data on Latino blacks here, but the sample size on the Latino black population 25 years of age and older is fairly small and the statistical reliability of the results is highly questionable. The sample size for blacks was further reduced when national groups were considered.

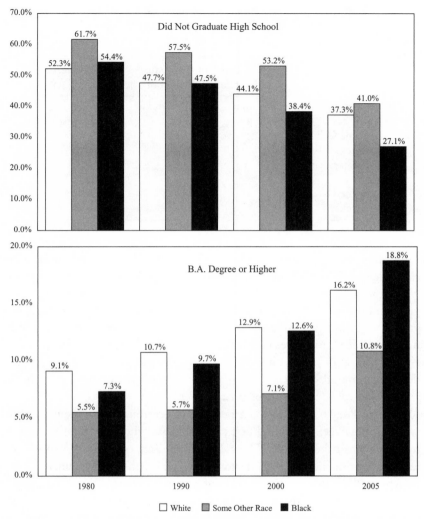

GRAPH 11.3. Percentage of Latinos 25 Years of Age or Older Who Did Not Graduate from High School or Who Achieved a B.A. Degree or Higher by Racial Self-Identification, 1980–2005.

were of some other race, although because of small sample sizes Latino blacks had higher college graduation rates than the other groups for both the domestic- and foreign-born. (See Table 11.16.)

Among Mexicans there was a slight difference in rates of non–high school graduates by race between 1980 and 2000 with those who had declared themselves to be of some other race having marginally higher

TABLE 11.16. *Percentage of Foreign- and Domestic-Born
Latinos Who Did Not Graduate from High School
or Graduated from College by Race, 2005*

	Did Not Graduate from High School	B.A. Degree or Higher
Domestic-Born		
Whites	23.5%	17.3%
Some Other Race	26.5%	13.3%
Blacks	21.7%	20.6%
Foreign-Born		
Whites	50.1%	12.0%
Some Other Race	52.4%	8.0%
Blacks	35.4%	17.0%

rates than whites. However, by 2005 the gap had closed to statistical insignificance, and both Mexicans who considered themselves to be white and some-other-race Mexicans had about identical non–high school graduation rates for the population 25 years of age and older. College-graduation rates increased for all racial groups between 1980 and 2005; however, Mexican whites experienced somewhat higher rates in all years. By 2005 some 11% of white Mexican adults had achieved a B.A. or higher degree compared with 8.3% of those who considered themselves to be of some other race.[15] (See Graph 11.4.)

Among Puerto Ricans two aspects of educational attainment by race stand out between 1980 and 2005. First, those who declared themselves to be of some other race had both lower high school graduation and college graduation rates, than Puerto Ricans who considered themselves to be white. Black Puerto Ricans – about 5% of all Puerto Ricans in 2005 – performed better than those of some other race but generally lagged behind Puerto Rican whites. Second, the trends in educational attainment by race group were about identical between 1980 and 2005. Over time there were decreasing non–high school graduation rates among all races at about the same pace, and college graduation rates also increased significantly for the three major self-declared races. (See Graph 11.5.)[16]

[15] Although Mexican blacks had significantly lower non–high school graduation rates and higher college graduation rates, the sample size was very small, and more importantly they accounted for less than 1% of the overall Mexican population in the United States.
[16] Non–high school graduation rates declined at 3.6% yearly and college graduation rates increased 3.9% yearly between 1980 and 2005 for all Puerto Rican racial groups.

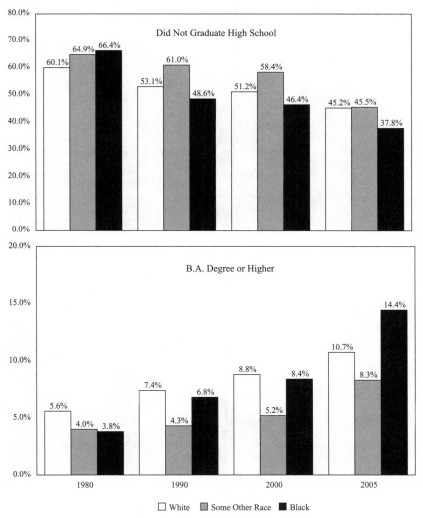

GRAPH 11.4. Percentage of Mexicans 25 Years of Age or Older Who Did Not Graduate from High School or Who Achieved a B.A. Degree or Higher by Racial Self-Identification, 1980–2005.

Among Cubans, of whom 84% declared themselves to be white in 2005, there were marginal differences in high school graduation rates by race, and by 2005 some-other-race and black Cubans had slightly lower non-high school graduation rates than Cuban whites. White Cubans, however, had higher college graduation rates than the other two racial groups, although not by extraordinary margins, and in fact black Cuban

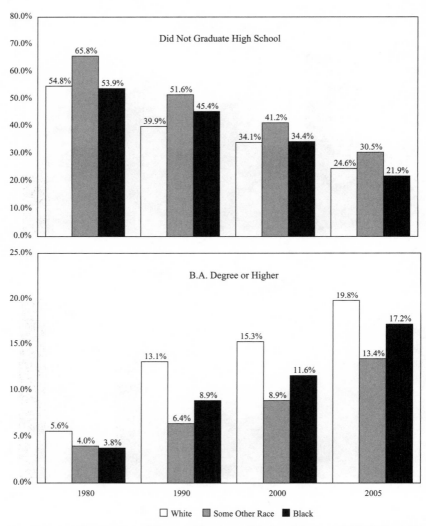

GRAPH 11.5. Percentage of Puerto Ricans 25 Years of Age or Older Who Did Not Graduate from High School or Who Achieved a B.A. Degree or Higher by Racial Self-Identification, 1980–2005.

adults achieved a B.A. degree or higher at higher rates than some-other-race Cubans in all years between 1980 and 2005. (See Graph 11.6.)

Among Dominicans it is striking that there were similar patterns in educational attainment rates by race despite the fact that the racial components of the Dominican population were so different from Cubans. It will be recalled that only 28% of Dominicans considered themselves

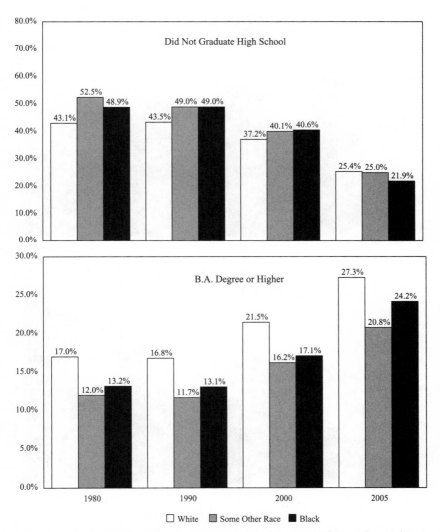

GRAPH 11.6. Percentage of Cubans 25 Years of Age or Older Who Did Not Graduate from High School or Who Achieved a B.A. Degree or Higher by Racial Self-Identification, 1980–2005.

to be white. Yet, non–high school graduation rates were fairly close by self-declared racial groups, and the college graduation rates of Domini-can whites were, as was the case with Cubans, only slightly higher than among the other racial groups. (See Graph 11.7.)

Finally, among the nation's Colombian population, 62% of whom declared themselves to be white in 2005, there was a racial hierarchy.

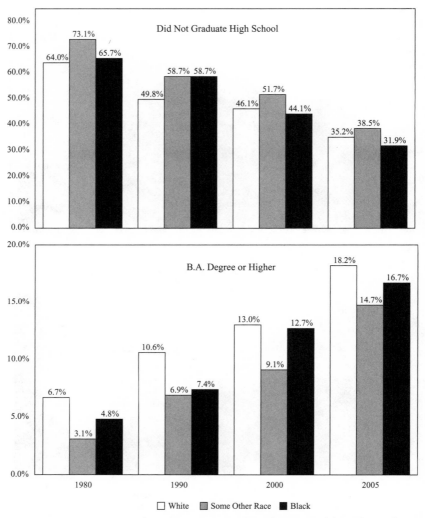

GRAPH 11.7. Percentage of Dominicans 25 Years of Age or Older Who Did Not Graduate from High School or Who Achieved a B.A. Degree or Higher by Racial Self-Identification, 1980–2005.

Whites had both lower non–high school completion rates and higher college graduation rates than the other two race groups. (See Graph 11.8.)

These data on race must be used with caution because of the extraordinary difficulty of ascertaining accuracy since race was self-declared rather than the result of any objective criteria that was universally applied to

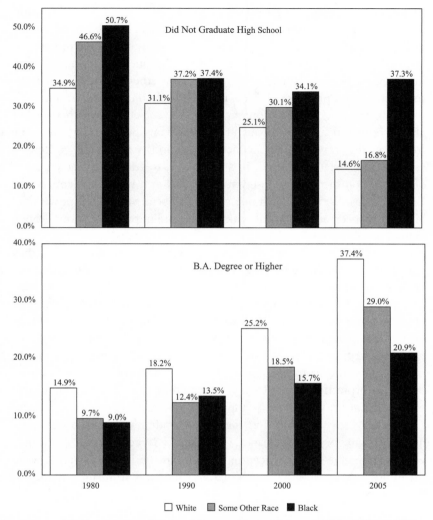

GRAPH 11.8. Percentage of Colombians 25 Years of Age or Older Who Did Not Graduate from High School or Who Achieved a B.A. Degree or Higher by Racial Self-Identification, 1980–2005.

determine the race of the person responding to Census Bureau questions. Measuring changes in race among Latinos over time is also difficult because between 1980 and 2005 the U.S. Census Bureau changed the way it asked the questions on race and the order in which the questions were placed. Yet, the evidence on social and economic inequality by race for all Latinos and for the different national subgroups we have considered here suggests a complex mosaic with some overtones of the U.S. traditional racial classification system. Whites do seem to have been marginally more successful in educational and economic terms than mixed-race Latinos and blacks, though these differences are disappearing in most groups over time. However, the nagging question is whether or not success in the socioeconomic sphere reinforced people's self-conceptions about their particular race within the context of a U.S. society in which race has always been conceived of through the black/white polarity. Latinos came from societies in which racial conceptualizations were entirely different, yet they have been obligated, in some ways, to transform their visions of race to conform more closely to the black and white concepts of the United States. Within their home countries social status and power had historically been concentrated within the white population. Even though many Latinos would not have been considered to be white in their countries of origin, given the opportunity to declare their racial identities, they may have chosen white not only because this offered the opportunity to fit in with the dominant white majority in the United States, but also because it conferred upon them a measure of social status in contrast with the other racial groups. It is also clear that the increasing percentage of self-declared mixed-race Latinos, which seems to closely resemble the *mestizo* and mulatto traditional categories in their countries of origin, is becoming an ever more important element within U.S. society. Given the recent projection by the Census Bureau that non-Hispanic whites will become a minority of the U.S. population by the middle of the 21st century, it may very well be that mixed-race individuals will become the new third category in the formerly dualistic U.S. racial system. This may very well change racial conceptualizations in the United States toward the multiracial models that have long prevailed in Latin America and the Caribbean.

12

Endogamous and Exogamous Marriage Patterns among Latino Household Heads

One measure of acculturation into the host society among immigrant populations is the changing frequency they choose to marry outside of their particular national, racial, or ethnic groups. The databases we have used throughout this book provide a number of ways to examine changing marriage patterns among Latinos. We have chosen to use data on household heads and their spouses as indicators of shifting marriage choices between 1980 and 2005.[1] These household data are not ideal in that they do not represent marriage patterns among the entire Hispanic population, as there may have been more than one family living within a household. There could have been cross-generational related families or multiple families living in the same household. However, the Census Bureau designated only one person as the head of the household. Despite their imperfections, these data on household heads and their spouses are suggestive of general

---

[1] The variable "relate" was used to determine "head of household" and the "spouse" of the head of household. Spouse is defined as follows: "Spouse – Includes a person married to and living with a householder who is of the opposite sex of the householder. The category 'husband or wife' includes people in formal marriages, as well as people in common-law marriages." The sample sizes for each nationality other than Mexicans, who comprise over two-thirds of all U.S. Latinos, were fairly small as indicated in the graphs presented in this chapter. However, these are the only existent data that suggest marriage patterns.

When examining marriage patterns to non-Latinos, it would be desirable to measure the race of these non-Latinos in order to determine whether white Latinos had a greater propensity to marry non-Hispanic whites or if nonwhite Latinos married non-Hispanic blacks or Asians. However, the sample sizes were so small that they were deemed to be statistically unreliable to include in this discussion. For a consideration of this issue for 1990 see Zhenchao Qian and José A. Cobas, "Latinos' Mate Selection: National Origin, Racial, and Nativity Differences," *Social Science Research*, 33:2 (June 2004), 225–47.

TABLE 12.1. *Percentage of Latino Household Heads Married to Latinos,*
Non-Hispanic Whites, Non-Hispanic Blacks, and Asians by Sex, 2005

Spouses	Foreign-Born Latino Household Heads		Domestic-Born Latino Household Heads		Total Latino Household Heads	
	Males	Females	Males	Females	Males	Females
Latinos	91.5%	87.8%	68.8%	66.3%	82.5%	76.9%
Non-Hispanic Whites	7.5%	10.6%	28.6%	28.6%	15.9%	19.8%
Non-Hispanic Blacks	0.5%	1.0%	1.1%	3.1%	0.7%	2.1%
Asians	0.5%	0.5%	1.5%	1.9%	0.9%	1.2%
TOTAL	100.0%	100.0%	100.0%	100.0%	100.0%	100.0%

endogamous and exogamous marriage patterns among the Latino population.

As expected, there were significant differences in marriage patterns
when domestic-born Latinos are compared with their foreign-born counterparts. By 2005 roughly 90% of Latino foreign-born household heads,
both male and female, married other Latinos, while a significantly lower
portion – about two-thirds – of domestic-born Latino household heads
of both sexes married other Latinos. (See Table 12.1.) Between 1980
and 2005, the percentage of domestic-born male Latino household heads
who married other Latinos fell from 75% to 69%, while there was almost
no change in the percentage of female domestic-born Latino household
heads who married other Latinos – 65% in 1980 and 66% in 2005.
Over the same period there was marginal change in the percentage of
male and female foreign-born Latinos who married other Latinos. (See
Graph 12.1.) When marrying non-Latinos, most household heads married
non-Hispanic whites, and only a very small percentage chose to marry
non-Hispanic blacks or Asians.[2] (See Graph 12.2.)

Among Mexican, Puerto Rican, and Cuban household heads the changing trends in marriage preferences between 1980 and 2005 were similar, although the absolute numbers differed for each nationality.[3] (All

---

[2] Less than 2% of Latino household heads married non-Hispanic blacks in 2005, and about
1% were married to Asians.

[3] We are confining our analysis of changing marriage patterns to these three Latino nationalities because we have deemed that the sample sizes for the other national groups are too
small to be statistically reliable.

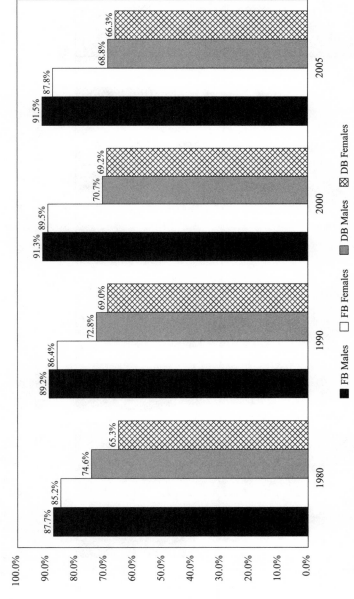

GRAPH 12.1. Percentage of Foreign- and Domestic-Born Latino Household Heads Married to Other Latinos, by Sex, 1980–2005.

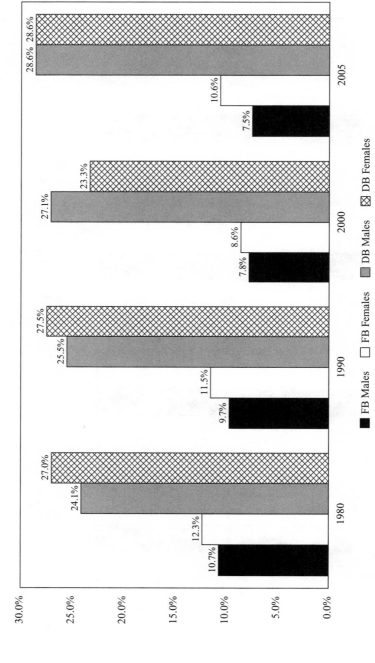

GRAPH 12.2. Percentage of Foreign- and Domestic-Born Latino Household Heads Married to Non-Hispanic Whites, by Sex, 1980–2005.

data for the subsequent discussion are presented in Table 12.2.) As expected, there was an extraordinary difference in the marriage patterns of those who were domestic-born and those foreign-born. Foreign-born household heads of each nationality, both male and female, preferred to marry spouses of their own nationality or other Latinos, rather than non-Hispanic whites, blacks, or Asians, and this did not change significantly over time. Yet, among domestic-born household heads there were significant changes in marriage choices, especially among Puerto Ricans and Cubans. Over time, both male and female household heads married their national counterparts or other Latinos less frequently and increasingly married non-Hispanic whites.

Puerto Ricans were the most likely of all the Latino nationalities to marry outside of their national-origin group and to marry non-Latinos. This holds true for Puerto Ricans born on the island and in the United States, although those who were born on the U.S. mainland had significantly lower rates of marriage to other Puerto Ricans. Some 77% of Puerto Rican males and 83% of females who were born in Puerto Rico married other Puerto Ricans in 1980. After 1980 there was a gradual decline, and by 2005 about two-thirds of Puerto Rican–born male and female household heads living in the United States married other Puerto Ricans. Among domestic-born Puerto Rican household heads a little over half of all males married other Puerto Ricans in 1980 and this fell to 37% by 2005. In 2005 about 40% of female Puerto Rican household heads married other Puerto Ricans, a sharp decline from the 64% rate prevailing in 1980.

By 2005 over 80% of male and female Puerto Rican–born household heads married either Puerto Ricans or other Latinos. A significantly lower 57% of United States–born Puerto Rican household heads of both sexes married Puerto Ricans or other Latinos. There was no great concentration among these Latino marriage partners in 2005. About 6% were marriages to Mexicans, nearly 3% of marriages were to Dominicans and Cubans, and about 2% were to Colombians. No other Latino nationality accounted for more than 1% of marriages to domestic-born Puerto Ricans.

There were extraordinary contrasts in the percentage of Puerto Rican household heads who married non-Hispanic whites by birthplace. In 2005 about 15% of those born in Puerto Rico were married to non-Hispanic whites compared with about one-third of both male and female Puerto Rican household heads born in the United States. About 2% of island-born Puerto Ricans and 6% of United States-born Puerto Ricans of both sexes married non-Hispanic blacks.

TABLE 12.2. *Percentage of Foreign- and Domestic-Born Household Heads and Marriage Partners by Sex and Latino Nationality, 1980–2005*

Married to Others of Same Nationality

	Puerto Ricans				Cubans				Mexicans			
	Foreign-Born Males	Foreign-Born Females	Domestic-Born Males	Domestic-Born Females	Foreign-Born Males	Foreign-Born Females	Domestic-Born Males	Domestic-Born Females	Foreign-Born Males	Foreign-Born Females	Domestic-Born Males	Domestic-Born Females
1980	77.3%	82.6%	52.6%	63.9%	82.5%	65.2%	28.5%	31.3%	90.7%	89.5%	78.0%	74.2%
1990	71.5%	76.4%	46.6%	57.7%	77.6%	67.1%	27.5%	27.4%	91.6%	89.7%	73.9%	68.1%
2000	71.4%	72.3%	60.2%	61.4%	74.7%	74.0%	31.4%	33.4%	91.9%	91.6%	68.7%	68.7%
2005	67.1%	64.4%	37.2%	39.8%	72.3%	72.3%	31.1%	28.0%	92.6%	91.0%	67.0%	66.7%

Married to Other Latinos Including Spouses of Same Nationality

	Puerto Ricans				Cubans				Mexicans			
	Foreign-Born Males	Foreign-Born Females	Domestic-Born Males	Domestic-Born Females	Foreign-Born Males	Foreign-Born Females	Domestic-Born Males	Domestic-Born Females	Foreign-Born Males	Foreign-Born Females	Domestic-Born Males	Domestic-Born Females
1980	87.3%	92.3%	64.4%	75.2%	90.9%	76.3%	42.6%	47.9%	93.5%	92.0%	80.1%	76.5%
1990	83.8%	89.2%	58.3%	70.0%	88.6%	79.3%	41.4%	45.3%	94.4%	93.3%	75.4%	71.0%
2000	86.0%	89.6%	71.1%	74.8%	88.2%	85.0%	49.4%	50.9%	95.4%	95.1%	72.7%	73.3%
2005	82.5%	81.6%	56.3%	57.1%	86.8%	84.4%	50.3%	45.3%	95.8%	94.8%	70.7%	70.4%

Married to Non-Hispanic Whites

	Puerto Ricans				Cubans				Mexicans			
	Foreign-Born Males	Foreign-Born Females	Domestic-Born Males	Domestic-Born Females	Foreign-Born Males	Foreign-Born Females	Domestic-Born Males	Domestic-Born Females	Foreign-Born Males	Foreign-Born Females	Domestic-Born Males	Domestic-Born Females
1980	11.1%	6.1%	29.2%	17.2%	8.3%	19.3%	52.3%	39.6%	6.2%	6.8%	19.1%	21.8%
1990	14.3%	9.6%	34.8%	21.5%	10.5%	18.5%	53.3%	48.7%	5.3%	5.6%	23.5%	26.7%
2000	12.2%	7.6%	24.2%	17.5%	11.0%	13.2%	47.0%	42.9%	4.2%	4.2%	25.8%	23.3%
2005	15.5%	14.9%	36.2%	32.0%	11.7%	14.6%	45.9%	49.6%	3.8%	4.5%	27.4%	26.8%

Married to Non-Hispanic Blacks

	Puerto Ricans				Cubans				Mexicans			
	Foreign-Born Males	Foreign-Born Females	Domestic-Born Males	Domestic-Born Females	Foreign-Born Males	Foreign-Born Females	Domestic-Born Males	Domestic-Born Females	Foreign-Born Males	Foreign-Born Females	Domestic-Born Males	Domestic-Born Females
1980	1.3%	1.2%	3.5%	5.6%	0.6%	2.9%	4.8%	12.5%	0.1%	0.9%	0.3%	1.3%
1990	1.4%	0.9%	4.1%	6.7%	0.6%	2.0%	4.0%	5.1%	0.1%	0.4%	0.3%	1.4%
2000	1.2%	2.4%	3.1%	6.7%	0.5%	1.4%	2.6%	5.4%	0.1%	0.4%	0.5%	2.5%
2005	1.5%	3.2%	4.7%	9.6%	1.2%	0.8%	1.9%	4.7%	0.1%	0.3%	0.4%	2.0%

The disparities between foreign- and domestic-born Cuban household heads in their marriage choices were stark. First and foremost, there was only marginal change between 1980 and 2005 in the percentage of both domestic- and foreign-born Cubans, males and females, who married other Cubans. By 2005 about 72% of foreign-born Cuban household heads of both sexes married other Cubans. However, when we examine domestic-born Cuban household heads, only 31% of males and 28% of females were married to Cuban spouses.

These same patterns were evident when examining marriages to all Latinos including Cubans. Change over the 25-year period between 1980 and 2005 was slight. However, by 2005 the differences between foreign- and domestic-born household heads were significant. About 85% of male and female Cuban household heads were married to other Latinos including Cubans, while 50% of domestic-born Cuban males and 45% of Cuban females chose to marry Latinos. Puerto Ricans and Mexicans were the spousal choices for 4% each of the domestic-born followed by Colombians at 2%. Some 3% of foreign-born Cubans married Puerto Ricans followed by Mexicans and Colombians at 2% each. Very few Cuban household heads, domestic or foreign, between 1% and 2%, married non-Hispanic blacks. The principal marriage choice was non-Hispanic whites. Some 12% of foreign-born male and 15% of females married non-Hispanic whites, compared with 46% of domestic-born males and 50% of females. By 2005 nearly 5% of domestic-born female Cubans were married to non-Hispanic blacks, compared with 2% of domestic-born males, and 1% of foreign-born Cuban males and females.

The demographically dominant Mexican population, both domestic and foreign born, were more likely to marry other Mexicans or Latinos, and less inclined to marry non-Hispanic whites than Cubans or Puerto Ricans. However, there were expected differences between those who were born in the United States and household heads born in Mexico. About 90% of all foreign-born Mexican household heads married other Mexicans in all years between 1980 and 2005, and there was little differentiation between males and females in spousal choices. Among domestic-born Mexicans about three-quarters of both male and female household heads married other Mexicans in 1980 although this declined to about two-thirds by 2005. About 95% of male and female foreign-born household heads married Mexicans or other Latinos, compared with 70% of their domestic-born counterparts in 2005. There were no significant concentrations of marriage to any particular Latino nationality among either the domestic- or foreign-born.

However, there were extreme contrasts in the frequency of marriage to non-Hispanic whites by birthplace, and in this sense Mexicans were similar to Cubans and Puerto Ricans. By 2005 between 4% (males) and 5% (females) of foreign-born Mexican household heads were married to non-Hispanic whites. These data are well below the over one-quarter domestic-born Mexicans, male and female, married to non-Hispanic whites. About 2% of domestic-born Mexican females were married to non-Hispanic blacks, although less than 1% of domestic- and foreign-born males and females had non-Hispanic black spouses.

Although the other major Latino national groups do not have sample sizes of household heads and their spouses that are large enough to parse them into domestic- and foreign-born, we may use their total numbers as indicators of endogamous or exogamous marriage patterns in comparison with the other Latino nationalities. There was a hierarchy in the structure of Latino nationalities – both male and female household heads – married to spouses of their own nationality, and Mexicans led this ranking at 81%. At the other extreme were Puerto Ricans of whom 53% married other Puerto Ricans in 2005. (See Graph 12.3.) Yet, Salvadorans were most likely to marry other Latinos – 93% of them did in 2005 – while over 80% of Dominicans, Mexicans, and Colombians chose other Latinos as their spouses. Cubans (77%) and Puerto Ricans (70%) were at the lower end of the spectrum in marriages to other Latinos. (See Graph 12.4.) The exact reverse order was evident in the frequency of Latino nationalities married to non-Hispanic whites in 2005. About one-quarter of all Puerto Ricans and 21% of all Cubans were married to non-Hispanic white spouses, while at the other extreme only 8% of Dominicans and 6% of Salvadorans were married to non-Hispanic whites in 2005. (See Graph 12.5.) Puerto Ricans and Dominicans were more likely to marry non-Hispanic blacks than the other nationalities, but the overall percentage for both was under 5%. Less than 1% of Colombians, Mexicans, and Salvadorans were married to non-Hispanic blacks in 2005. (See Graph 12.6.)

There are a number of issues raised by the data we have used to calculate exogamous and endogamous marriage patterns and how they changed between 1980 and 2005. First and foremost, those national populations that have had a longer presence in the United States, and thus a larger domestic-born component of their populations, were more likely to marry non-Latinos than more recent groups with larger percentages of foreign-born persons. Domestic-born Cubans were the most extreme example. Over 45% of all marriages were to non-Hispanic whites. They

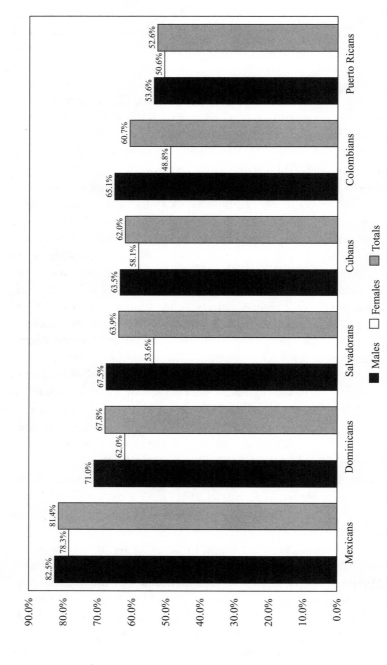

GRAPH 12.3. Percentage of Heads of Households by Nationality and Sex Married to Spouse of Same Nationality in the United States, 2005.

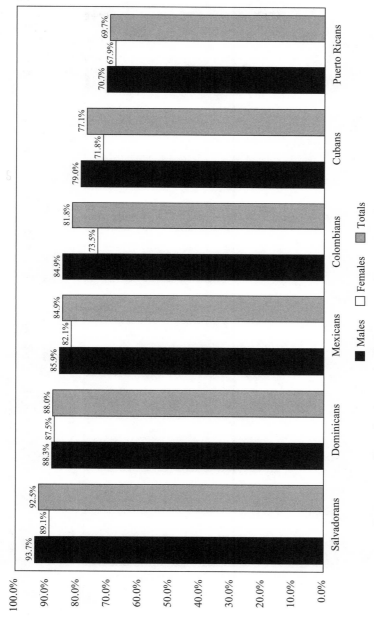

GRAPH 12.4. Percentage of Heads of Households by Nationality and Sex Married to Spouse Who Was a Latino in the United States, 2005.

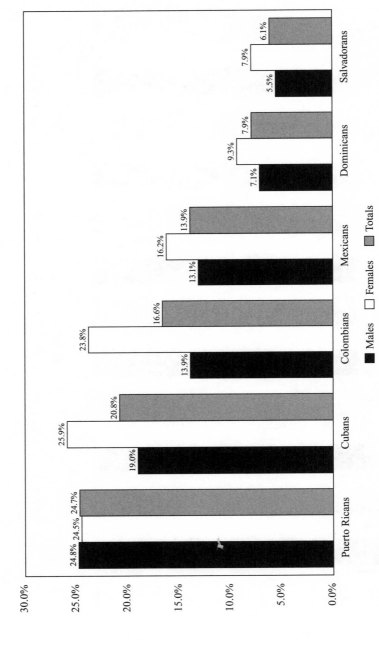

GRAPH 12.5. Percentage of Heads of Households by Nationality and Sex Married to a Spouse of Opposite Sex Who Was Non-Hispanic White, 2005.

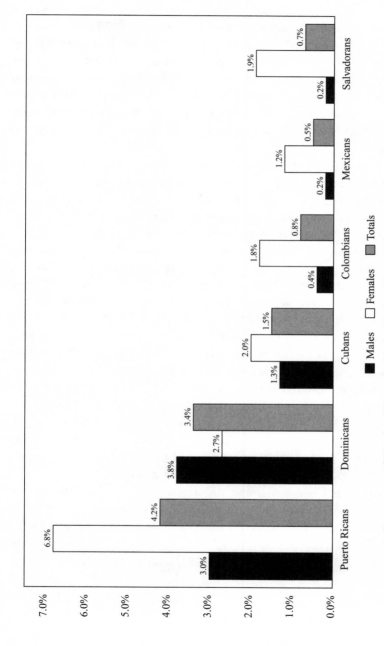

GRAPH 12.6. Percentage of Heads of Households by Nationality and Sex Married to a Spouse of Opposite Sex Who Was Non-Hispanic Black, 2005.

403

were followed by domestic-born Puerto Ricans at about one-third, and
Mexicans of whom over one-quarter married non-Hispanic whites in
2005. This suggests, of course, a process of acculturation and a likely, if
immeasurable, degree of assimilation into a changing U.S. society in the
same way as past immigrant groups. It also may be used as a predictor
for future behavior patterns of more recent Latino immigrant groups who
still have large foreign-born populations. It is likely that the longer they
are in the United States, and domestic components of populations increase
proportionally, there will be a greater degree of exogenous marriages in
the future.

A second issue revolves around socioeconomic status. In earlier chapters we have noted that the domestic-born have achieved higher educational attainment levels, developed a better command of English, and
earned more income than the foreign-born. The role and impact of exogamous marriage patterns as a determinant factor cannot be properly
measured by the data we have considered because the sample sizes are
too small to produce statistically reliable correlations, in our estimation.
However, it is likely that marriage to non-Latino spouses did have some
impact on socioeconomic status since non-Hispanic whites generally had
achieved higher educational attainment levels and had greater median
household incomes than the other ethnic and racial groups in U.S. society. A related, and indeterminate, factor is whether there was a process
of self-selection in mate choices by Latinos. For example, we don't know
if more educated or higher-income-earning Latinos chose to marry more
educated and wealthier non-Hispanic whites, although this is likely. If this
is true, then issues of social class in mate selection were probably much
more important than race, ethnicity, or national origin. In this sense
Latinos were, in all likelihood, no different from the other components
of the U.S. population or previous immigrant groups.[4]

A third issue revolves around the use of data on the national origins of Latinos in current and future databases produced by the Census
Bureau and other government agencies. Each person enumerated by the
census selects a unique "nationality," which they either write in or check
boxes provided only for Puerto Ricans, Cubans, and Mexicans. However, the data on intermarriage among Latinos, and the high proportion
of exogenous marriages by domestic-born Latinos, calls into question the

---

[4] See the discussion of endogamy data by race for 2005 in Michael J. Rosenfeld, "Racial,
Educational and Religious Endogamy in the United States: A Comparative Historical
Perspective," *Social Forces*, 87:1, (September 2008).

precise statistical validity of nationality designations used to enumerate the Latino population. This is an important issue since it is certain that the frequency of these exogenous marriages will grow in the future. We have chosen not to address "identity issues" in this book, but clearly a fundamental question arises for each Latino national group. There is however a question of "who" are Mexicans, Puerto Ricans, Cubans, and so forth in the many instances of children who are the products of "mixed" marriages with other Latinos or non-Hispanic whites or blacks. If a person is married to a non-Latino, how do their children self-classify themselves with respect to national origin?

It is, of course, easy to raise this fundamental question despite the difficulty of producing a valid answer. It is clear that individual choice and self-conceptualization are paramount in these identity issues since all individuals queried by the Census Bureau self-declare their national origin and race, as we indicated previously. However, producing accurate statistical profiles of socioeconomic indicators by Latino national subgroup will becomes an even more challenging task as exogenous marriages increase in frequency in the future. Perhaps this will reinforce an even more widespread use of the term "Latino," which of course circumvents the statistical problems of measuring each national group because of the increasing exogenous marriage patterns we have described in this chapter.

13

Conclusion

The presidential election of 2008 and the confirmation of Judge Sonia Sotomayor as the first Hispanic justice of the U.S. Supreme Court in 2009 have highlighted the extraordinary, and growing, political clout of the Latino population in the United States. It may be argued that President Barack Obama's electoral victory in at least four swing states in November 2008 – Florida, New Mexico, Colorado, and Nevada – was closely linked to the overwhelming support he received from Hispanic voters in each of these states.[1] Latinos, along with African Americans, have struggled to secure civil rights and end institutionalized and less-formal forms of discrimination for decades. Shear demographics, however, have placed Latinos front and center as a political and economic force of extraordinary importance that must be reckoned with today and certainly in the future.

In July 2008 the Census Bureau estimated that Latinos numbered approximately 47 million persons, about 15.4% of the total U.S. population. It has been projected that by 2050 this population will triple in absolute size and will comprise 30% of the population of the United States.[2] Latinos have been as mobile as the rest of the U.S. population and have

---

[1] See López, *The Hispanic Vote in the 2008 Election*, and Mark Hugo López and Paul Taylor, "Dissecting the 2008 Electorate: Most Diverse in U.S. History," April 30, 2009, available at http://pewhispanic.org/reports/report.php?ReportID=108. For the data released by the U.S. Census Bureau on voter participation in the 2008 elections go to http://www.census.gov/population/www/socdemo/voting/cps2008.html.

[2] Currently the United States has a larger Latino population than any country in Latin America and the Caribbean with the exception of Brazil (190 million) and Mexico (110 million people). For population projections see http://www.census.gov/Press-Release/www/releases/archives/facts_for_features_special_editions/013984.html.

migrated from the traditional southwestern and western states to areas of the nation where there have never been many Latinos, such as the Southern and Southeastern states. Latino demographic projections have politicians and marketing professionals in the private sector in a state of near frenzy. Not only did the Hispanic vote help elect President Obama, but the Democratic Party succeeded in reversing the trend in Hispanic voting patterns toward the Republican Party, which had been evident in the 2000 and 2004 presidential elections. This growing political importance on the national stage was accomplished despite the fact that Hispanics continued to have the lowest political participation rate of the major racial/ethnic groups in the United States. In November 2008 only half of all Latino citizens 18 years of age and older voted compared with about two-thirds of non-Hispanic whites and blacks. However, the Hispanic vote doubled in its portion of the total U.S. electorate that voted from 3.6% in the 1988 presidential elections to 7.4% in 2008.[3] It is certain that the Latino political participation rate will increase in the future, and as the Hispanic population continues to expand, the percentage of total voters who are Latinos may lead to a veritable upheaval in the U.S. political system.

The critical future role that Latinos will play in local, state, and national politics will be paralleled by a huge expansion of the Latino consuming market and overall impact on the U.S. economic system. This market has increased from approximately $212 billion in 1990; $489 billion in 2000; to $951 billion in 2008, and it is estimated that it will be about $1.4 trillion in 2013 when it will account for about 10% of total U.S. consumption.[4] To put this into another perspective, the Latino market in the United States is the third-largest market for a Latin American and Caribbean origin population in the western hemisphere behind only Brazil and Mexico. If these rates of Latino market expansion continue into the future, by 2050 it may amount to an astronomical $32 trillion. It is no wonder that dissecting the Latino market for major U.S.

[3] About the same portion of Asians voted, but their overall numbers were relatively small. It also should be noted that despite the comparatively low participation rate of 50% this was an increase from the 47% participation rate in the 2004 presidential elections.
[4] See Jeffrey M. Humphreys, "The Multicultural Economy 2008," Terry College of Business, Selig Center for Economic Growth, The University of Georgia, available at http://www.terry.uga.edu/selig/docs/buying_power_2008.pdf. In states where Hispanics are concentrated demographically, the overall percentage of Hispanic consumer market share was much higher in 2008: 30% in New Mexico, 20% in Texas, 18% in California, 16% in Arizona, 15% in Florida and Nevada, and 12% in Colorado.

corporations, advertising agencies, and direct marketers has become a veritable industry.[5]

Latinos have "arrived." In this book we have demonstrated important social, economic, and demographic aspects of their journey to the present juncture. Unlike many studies on Hispanics in the United States we have presented a dynamic vision of change over time among the Latino population between 1980 and 2005 rather than a static portrait of a particular chronological moment, geographic area, or national subgroup. We have emphasized that despite a well-documented and widely discussed pattern of historical discrimination against Latinos of every nationality, Hispanics are very much like previous waves of immigrant groups who have come to the United States in their socioeconomic and demographic dynamics. It is clear that an anti-Latino and implicitly anti-immigrant sentiment is still pervasive among some population sectors in the United States and in many geographic regions, even if it has diminished to some degree. But these retrograde anti-immigrant and sometimes racist attitudes were all too common in the remote and even recent past and are unfortunately part and parcel of the complex history of the United States. "Nativist" political movements and popular anti-immigrant sentiments were directed against Scotch, German, and Irish immigrants in the mid 19th century. The Chinese, first recruited as laborers for the construction of the transcontinental railroad, bore the brunt of anti-immigrant nativism as well, often perpetrated by prior waves of immigrants and their offspring. Italians, Jews, and other Eastern Europeans during the great waves of migration of the late 19th and early 20th centuries were often not welcomed by extant populations, almost always of immigrant origin. The degrading use of an anti-immigrant vocabulary was hardly pioneered against Latinos. Anti-immigrant sentiments, arguments, and discriminatory practices have been similar through time, and lamentably there is nothing very original in their utilization against Latinos. A series of myths and symbols, which have had nothing to do with "reality," have been always invoked by those who have sought, and seek, to fan the flames of hatred and bigotry. They will be familiar to most readers. Immigrants "steal" jobs that could have gone to "native" workers because they labor for lower wages. Immigrants are not patriotic like "real Americans." Immigrants are an "economic burden" to the public because

---

[5] Note the results generated by typing "Latino market research" into any internet search venue such as Google or Yahoo.

they absorb local, state, and national, government funds in programs such as "welfare." Since they speak different languages, immigrants isolate themselves and are not part of the "American" mainstream, and never will be. And it goes on and on in a similar vein.

Yet, every prior immigrant group in the history of the United States has overcome each and every one of these lamentable obstacles and has become mainstream "Americans," whatever it is that this means in the context of an extraordinarily diverse society that is constantly changing and reinventing itself. In fact, there may not be a "mainstream" despite the imagery that there is some kind of American cultural homogeneity projected by the use of this term. The supposed mainstream consists of many very diverse strands, and it is clear that Latinos are very much part and parcel of this. This is true in spite of the anti-Latino and anti-immigrant extremists who make headlines, host political talk shows, or even report the "news" with a clear message of prejudice, whether it is subtle or overt. It is ironic that much of this anti-Latino sentiment, and even legislation, is centered in the southwestern states, which account for the largest Latino populations in the nation. Perhaps there is a collective amnesia in these regions, which were first populated by Mexicans long before a United States of America ever existed.

The integration of immigrants over time is central to the history of the United States. It may have been second-generation domestic-born populations for some groups and even third and fourth generations for others. But inevitably there has been acceptance and integration to varying degrees, however grudgingly this has been recognized by some. Latinos are not exceptions to this pattern although it might not appear to be the case because of ongoing migration and the arrival of so many Latin American and Caribbean migrants who do not speak English, who are undocumented, and who do in fact tend to cluster together in national or ethnic enclaves precisely because of these factors. Yet, their visibility and utilization as public scapegoats for so many of our nation's ills by anti-immigrant groups obfuscates the fact that most Latinos have in fact become part and parcel of U.S. society and play a critical role as a labor force in many industries, especially agriculture. It should be kept in mind that by 2005 some 60% of the nation's Latino population was born in the United States despite ongoing migration.

Throughout this book we have emphasized that despite the popular nomenclatures and labels applied to peoples of Latin American and Caribbean origin – Latinos or Hispanics – this is an extraordinary diverse population to which overarching generalizations may not be applied. Labels are convenient to outsiders who have difficulty recognizing differentiation, and in fact we employ the popularly recognized labels ourselves precisely because they have become part and parcel of the national idiom. But differentiation is precisely the most important aspect of Latino society and culture from a wide variety of perspectives. Each Hispanic national group has its unique cultural characteristics that make it different to varying degrees from other Latinos. Mexicans and Puerto Ricans, Dominicans and Colombians, Central Americans and Peruvians, to note just some examples, share little in common beyond language and religion. The fact that they are of immigrant origin makes them, in the popular imagination, all Latinos. This observation is not meant to debunk the idea of an emerging set of communalities that make people Latinos and this is especially the case with second and subsequent generations. Yet, even domestic-born Latinos first identify themselves by their national origins and only second as Latinos or Hispanics, and this is most often done to and for outsiders. To one another Latinos are Puerto Ricans, Dominicans, Mexicans and so forth.

Differentiation because of nationality is only the beginning of the story. If it is common practice by outsiders to refer to Latinos as one homogeneous mass of people, it is equally common to encounter repeated references to Mexicans, Chicanos, Puerto Ricans, and the other national subgroups comprising the Latino population, as if within each group there is uniformity simply because of national origins. The very terms "Latino" or "Hispanic" have distinct and changing meanings in different geographical regions. In our consideration of the major metropolitan areas where Latinos are concentrated, we have indicated this quite clearly. To be a Latino in Los Angeles, for example, invokes an image of Mexicans, Chicanos, and more recently of Central Americans as well. Yet, in New York, where Latino was once exclusively synonymous with Puerto Rican, Latino now may mean Dominican, and increasingly Mexican or other Latino national subgroups. Mexicans are the fastest-growing Latino nationality in the New York metropolitan region, and it may very well be that sometime in the future the terms "Latino" and "Mexican" will become closely associated. In Miami, where Latino once meant Cuban, there has been a process of extraordinary national diversification as many Puerto Ricans, Central Americans, and Mexicans have arrived from the 1980s on. Some are internal domestic-born migrants, while others have immigrated from Latin America and the Caribbean. Cubans are now a distinct, and vocal, minority among the Miami Latino population. The predominance of Mexicans in Chicago was not always the case since Puerto Ricans established a major presence by the 1970s and 1980s, although their relative share of the Latino population has since declined. Houston and Riverside most resemble Los Angeles in the national makeup of their Latino populations. Thus, the very "concept" and meanings of the terms "Latino" or "Hispanic" are fluid and ever changing if shifting national origins are carefully considered from regional or local perspectives. This is not the case with the other two major racial/ethnic groups – non-Hispanic whites and blacks – although among Asians there is the same kind of dynamic as migration patterns change.

We have systematically shown throughout this book that there is a very hierarchical social and economic structure within each Latino national subgroup that is in fact a class structure very similar to that of the other major racial and ethnic groups. The unfortunate stereotypical image of enduring poverty is emphatically false. There are impoverished sectors, some of significant size among each Latino nationality, but there are sizeable percentages of families and households who are quite well off from a purely economic point of view measured by their median household incomes and other indicators. As in all racial/ethnic groups in the United States, the vast majority of Latinos, irrespective of nationality, fall between rich and poor.

Yet, even this observation must be recognized as static. To better understand the varied Latino experience, it is important to measure changes over time. These indicate that more and more Latinos of every nationality have experienced improvements in their lives between 1980 and 2005, measured by increasing median incomes, notwithstanding continued rates of poverty that afflict those at the bottom of the Latino socioeconomic hierarchy. In fact, a smaller percentage of the Latino population lived in poverty in 2005 than in 1980, and median household incomes in after-inflation dollars grew considerably among Latinos over this same period. Although these median incomes continued to lag behind non-Hispanic whites and Asians by 2005, Latinos in general were significantly better off than non-Hispanic blacks. There were, however, differentiations by sex, and most importantly by national origin. Latino males tended to earn more than females, but this was not fundamentally different from other U.S. racial/ethnic groups. There was a major difference between the domestic-born who earned higher incomes in general than those who were foreign born. But this also has been common among all previous immigrant populations and their subsequent generations. Again, Latinos were not any different in this regard than prior immigrant communities established in the United States.

Educational attainment patterns also suggest constant and substantive improvements for Latinos between 1980 and 2005. The percentage of adults who had not graduated from high school plummeted over these 25 years, and more importantly for its socioeconomic implications, the portion of Latino adults who had graduated from college increased steadily to some 14% by 2005, nearly doubling from 1980. This still lagged behind the other major racial and ethnic groups in the United States, but it is certain that college graduation rates will continue to improve, especially for domestic-born Latinos who are almost always fluent in English, which offers a clear advantage over immigrants whose English-language skills lag behind. For particular Latino national sub-groups – Colombians, Peruvians, and Cubans – college graduation rates paralleled or even surpassed those of non-Hispanic whites in 2005. As more Latinos complete university degrees, and they will, there will be a narrowing of the gap in median incomes when compared to non-Hispanic whites, blacks, and Asians because of the close correlation between income-earning capacity and educational attainment.

In the preceding chapters we have examined a whole range of other variables that underscore our theme of a diverse population that defies generalizations. There were differences in English language abilities by nationality, although Latinos who exclusively speak English or speak the language very well have continually increased in absolute terms. The waves of migration after 1980 and the increase of the foreign-born population meant that overall data do not indicate a major change in the percentage of Latinos who dominate the English language. However, as the domestic-born population expands and foreign-born Latinos struggle to learn the dominant language of the United States, the linguistic impediment to socioeconomic progress will, in all likelihood, diminish.

The percentage of Latinos who are citizens continues to increase because of a surge in naturalizations that resulted from the anti-immigrant Proposition 187 passed in the state of California in 1994, as well as the steady expansion in the absolute number of domestic-born Latinos because of very high fertility rates. This will impact the potential Latino electorate by increasing the number eligible voters, as we noted previously.

With respect to occupational structures it is likely that increasing educational attainment levels will lead to more Latinos working in higher-paid skilled labor jobs and in professional occupations. The meteoric increase in Hispanic business ownership during the 1990s and after

2000 will undoubtedly continue into the future, although there is no way to predict the economic sectors that will attract Latino investment capital.

Latinos in the United States live within the framework of a society that has historically defined itself in racial terms using the fairly rigid notions of a black and white dichotomy. This doesn't work for Latinos because it is nonexistent within Latin America and the Caribbean. In their various countries of origin racial concepts are much more complex because of the intricate patterns of race mixture that resulted in *mestizos*, mulattoes, and a range of racial categories that are impossible to delineate with precision in general terms because they are different in each country or region. Since they were asked from 1980 on by the U.S. Census Bureau to identify themselves by race, Latinos have responded in different ways. So much confusion has arisen because Hispanics and non-Hispanics alike have misunderstood the whole concept of "race." A common mistake is to identify Latino or Hispanic as a race, rather than an ethnicity or collection of nationalities. One result of this confusion is that more and more Latinos have declared themselves to be of some other race – or neither black nor white – when obligated to respond to changing and confusing questions on census forms and in other data-collecting venues. This is intriguing for its implications. As Latinos move toward becoming one-third of the U.S. population by the middle of the 21st century, they may shatter the black/white polarity, which historically has been used to label people. Race conceptualizations in the United States may move in the direction of a more subtle and nuanced appreciation of what a multiracial society really is – a conglomeration of many races rather than simply two. It may very well be that the notions of race in the United States become more similar to those used in Latin America and the Caribbean in the future.

The tendency of domestic-born Latinos of every nationality to marry outside of their national-origin group to other Latinos, and more frequently to non-Hispanic whites, may make the convenient hanging of labels upon those of Latino descent a bit more complex. Since the U.S. Census Bureau began collecting systematic data on Latinos, it asks people to declare whether they are Hispanic or non-Hispanic. This is the same dualistic manner in which people are labeled to be either black or white. This may no longer be a valid question since we have noted that one-third of domestic-born Puerto Ricans, more than 45% of Cubans, and more than one-quarter of Mexicans were married to non-Hispanic whites in 2005. A fundamental question is whether their children are or are not Latinos. For the descendants of Latinos and non-Hispanic whites, blacks, or Asians, the term "Hispanic" may simply become an arbitrary question of self-identification in the same way that race is for Latinos. This will certainly complicate the task of data gathering on Latinos for government agencies in the future.

The economic recession that began in 2007 resulted in a sharp decrease in the number of Mexican migrants arriving in the United States, documented and undocumented, as labor markets contracted. It should be stressed that Mexicans account for two-thirds of all Latin American and Caribbean migrants to the United States and a third of all foreign-born residents in the nation. There is, however, little evidence that the recession has produced any significant spike in return migration to Mexico or elsewhere in Latin America and the Caribbean.[6] A fundamental question is whether or not this will have any impact on the development of Mexican and overall Latino populations in various regions of the nation. It is likely that this decline in migration will be temporary. When the U.S. economy fully recovers, it may be expected that migration from Mexico and elsewhere will return to the patterns evident before the current economic downturn.

This book has shown that the Latino population of the United States is not only extraordinarily diverse but also dynamic and adaptable. Like all previous migrant populations to the United States, there has been a constant quest for upward social mobility, often in the face of prejudice, discrimination, and many other obstacles. Yet, the trends indicated on a wide range of social and economic variables suggest that numerically significant sectors of the Latino population, of every national subgroup, have already been successful at moving up the social hierarchy. It is certain that with rising levels of educational attainment there will be a decrease in the number and portion of Latinos living in poverty. This does not mean that in the near future upward social mobility will be any more pervasive than it has been already. However, Latinos, in the long term will probably consolidate the extant social and economic structures that are similar to those prevailing among other racial/ethnic groups in the United States. There is little evidence that Latinos are very different from previous immigrant groups in this regard. One difference however is critical to take note of. There are no immigrant-origin groups who have ever accounted for nearly a third of the total U.S. population, which

---

[6] See Jeffrey S. Passel and D'Vera Cohn, "Mexican Immigrants: How Many Come? How Many Leave?" Pew Hispanic Center, July 22, 2009, available at http://pewhispanic.org/files/reports/112.pdf.

may be the case by 2050. It is difficult to make population projections for the last half of the 21st century. But there is the distinct possibility that Latinos may very well comprise close to, or a majority, of the U.S. population sometime in the 22nd century.

We have emphasized, over and again, the difficulty of generalizing about Latinos because of the extraordinary differentiation existing within the Hispanic population. One of the other themes we have stressed is the similarity in historical experiences that Latinos share with previous immigrant groups in terms of "integration" into U.S. society. Yet, we want to stress that there are also some important differences with previous groups of migrants who have melded to varying degrees into the U.S. mainstream, even though these have not been a focus of this book. There seems to be a pattern of linguistic retention that has transcended the time frame of prior waves of immigrants. Bilingualism is pervasive within Latino communities, and even second- and third-generation Latinos speak some Spanish, although it is not as fluent as their parents or grandparents. The retention of Latin American and Caribbean and particular national cultural practices in all of their complex manifestations seems to have continued much longer, and at a much more intense level, than was the case with previous migrant populations. This is because these cultural manifestations are continually reinforced by the ongoing arrival of migrant populations who infuse new energy into Latino communities. This steady stream of immigration contributes to the strong maintenance and continual reinforcement of Latin American and Caribbean cultures, and this has had an important impact even on those Latinos who have lived in the United States all of their lives because they were born here.

Prior waves of migrants were separated physically from their countries of origin by vast oceans. Additionally it was difficult, if not impossible, to come to the United States without official documentation. This is in sharp contrast with the existence of a long and historically porous border with Mexico that has provided a well-known, and much discussed, overland route for entrance into the United States for those without legal documents. Unlike prior waves of migrants, this has meant that people from the region have continued to arrive, regardless of efforts to stem this "illegal" migratory flow, most recently manifested by the construction of a wall along the U.S.-Mexican border. It is certain that even this will not stop migration as long as there are jobs to be had in *El Norte* and poverty and unemployment in the nations of the region, principally Mexico, that push people to seek opportunities to better themselves and support their families.

Another major difference with previous immigrant communities is the constant movement of Latinos to and from their countries of origin, especially if they have legal documentation. Throughout each year, and especially during holidays, Latinos in the United States "go home" to visit family, as there are extensive, and somewhat affordable, air routes that connect all major U.S. urban centers with every single country in the region. An important connection with countries of origin revolves around the constant remission of money. Often, families at "home" depend upon these funds transfers for survival, and in many countries remissions from the United States account for an extraordinary percentage of foreign exchange earned.[7] Previous migrants to the United States undoubtedly sent money home to help family members, but the ease and rapidity of money transfers has made this aspect of life for immigrant communities much more central than ever before.

The continual arrival of new migrants and the constant interaction with families in countries of origin is unique in its intensity in the history of migration to the United States. As noted previously, this reinforces the dynamic regeneration of each Latino national group and all of Latino culture in its multifaceted totality. Latinos may be similar in their socioeconomic evolution to previous immigrant groups, but they are different in the size, intensity, and ongoing movement that connect them to their countries of origin, and because of the ongoing process of migration that will undoubtedly continue into the future. Here is another great difference with Eastern Europeans, Southern Europeans, Asians, and so forth. Most of these different groups arrived within a demarcated time frame. Large-scale migration began in the late 19th century and generally ended by the First World War, although small numbers of migrants continued to arrive until the Great Depression. For Latinos there have been fluctuations in migration from various countries to be sure, but the migratory process continues, and will continue, into the foreseeable future.

---

[7] Latin America and the Caribbean received nearly $68 billion in remissions in 2006. For some of the smaller nations, remissions from the United States accounted for an extraordinary percentage of Gross Domestic Product: Honduras, 25%, El Salvador, 18%, Nicaragua, 15%, Bolivia 9%, Dominican Republic 9%, and Ecuador 8%. In 2008 Mexico was the largest recipient at $25 billion, about 35% of the total, followed by Brazil at $7 billion, Colombia at $4.8 billion, Guatemala at $4.3 billion, and El Salvador at about $3.8 billion. See the International Fund for Agricultural Development Web page at http://www.ifad.org/events/remittances/maps/latin.htm and the data presented by the Inter-American Development Bank at http://www.iadb.org/mif/remesas_map.cfm? language=English&parid=5.

The creation of a Latino "identity," a theme of considerable scholarly and popular interest, is a broad and complex topic we have chosen not to consider in this book. As indicated in the introduction, we have focused on social, economic, and demographic themes, which we feel are central to an understanding of Latino society. Scholarship on any theme or overarching topic is in many ways a collective enterprise, and not only have there been exemplary studies on Latino identity and culture, but it is certain that in the future there will be the continued publication of important works on these themes. We have provided in this book an empirical database on Latinos, which we hope will be useful for current and future generations of scholars who will move in new and innovative directions in their research and writing on a sector of the U.S. population that is poised to play a critical role in the future of our nation.

Bibliography

Abraido-Lanza, Ana F., Bruce P. Dohrenwend, Daisy S. Ng.-Mak, and J. Blake Turner. "The Latino Mortality Paradox: A Test of the 'Salmon Bias' and Healthy Migrant Hypotheses," *American Journal of Public Health*, 89:10 (October 1999), 1543–48.

Alanis Enciso, Fernando Saúl. "¿Cuántos fueron?: La repatriación de mexicanos en los Estados Unidos durante la Gran Depresión: Una interpretación cuantitativa 1930–1934," *Aztlán: A Journal of Chicano Studies*, 32:2 (Fall 2007), 65–91.

Alba, Richard, John Logan, Amy Lutz, and Brian Stults. "Only English by the Third Generation? Loss and Preservation of the Mother Tongue among the Grandchildren of Contemporary Immigrants," *Demography*, 39:3 (2002), 467–48.

Alba, Richard, Amy Lutz, and Elena Vesselinov. "How Enduring Were the Inequalities among European Immigrant Groups in the United States?" *Demography*, 38:3 (August 2001), 349–56.

Alvarez, R. Michael and Lisa García Bedolla. "The Foundations of Latino Voter Partisanship: Evidence from the 2000 Election," *The Journal of Politics*, 65:1 (2003), 31–49.

Alvarez, R. Michael, and Tara L. Butterfield. "Latino Citizenship and Participation in California Politics: A Los Angeles County Case Study," *The Pacific Historical Review*, 68:2 (1999), 293–308.

Alvarez, Robert R. *Familia: Migration and Adaptation in Baja and Alta California, 1800–1975*. Berkeley: University of California Press, 1987.

American Community Survey of 2005 summary tables, available at http://www2.census.gov/acs2005/SPP/Race_Ancestry_Hispanic_Origin/Mexican/.

Appelbaum, Nancy P., Anne S. Macpherson, and Karin Alejandra Rosemblatt, eds. *Race and Nation in Modern Latin America*. Chapel Hill: University of North Carolina Press, 2003.

Ayala, César J., and Rafael Bernabe. *Puerto Rico in the American Century: A History since 1898*. Chapel Hill: University of North Carolina Press, 2007.

Baganha, María Ioannis Benis. "The Social Mobility of Portuguese Immigrants in the United States at the Turn of the Nineteenth Century," *International Migration Review*, 35:2 (1999), 277–99.

Balderrama, Francisco E., and Raymond Rodríguez. *Decade of Betrayal, Mexican Repatriation in the 1930s* (2nd rev. ed.). Albuquerque: University of New Mexico Press, 2006.

Bauer, Thomas, Gil S. Epstein, and Ira N. Gang. "Enclaves, Language, and the Location Choice of Migrants," *Journal of Population Economics*, 18:4 (2005), 649–66.

Bean, Frank D., and Marta Tienda. *The Hispanic Population of the United States*. New York: Russell Sage Foundation, 1987.

Bean, Frank D., Rodolfo Corona, Rodolfo Tuirán, and Karen A. Woodrow-Lafield. *Migration Between Mexico and the United States, Binational Study*, Vol. 1. Mexico City and Washington, DC: Mexico Ministry of Foreign Affairs; U.S. Commission on Immigration Reform, 1998.

Borjas, George J. *Friends or Strangers: The Impact of Immigrants on the U.S. Economy*. New York: Basic Books, 1990.

———. "Assimilation, Changes in Cohort Quality, and the Earnings of Immigrants," *Journal of Labor Economics*, 3 (1985), 463–89.

———. "Ethnic Capital and Intergenerational Mobility," *Quarterly Journal of Economics*, 107:1 (1992): 123–50.

———. "The Labor Demand Curve Is Downward Sloping: Reexamining the Impact of Immigration on the Labor Market," *Quarterly Journal of Economics*, 118 (November 2003), 1335–74.

———. "Long-Run Convergence of Ethnic Skill Differentials: The Children and Grandchildren of the Great Migration," *Industrial and Labor Relations Review*, 47:4 (July 1994), 553–73.

———. "Immigrants in the U.S. Labor Market: 1940–80," *The American Economic Review*, 81:2 (1991), 287–91.

———. "The Intergenerational Mobility of Immigrants," *Journal of Labor Economics*, 11:1 (1993), 113–35.

———. "Self-Selection and the Earnings of Immigrants," *American Economic Review*, 77 (1987), 531–53.

———. "Long-run Convergence of Ethnic Skill Differentials, Revisited," *Demography*, 38:3 (August 2001), 357–61.

———. "Long-Run Convergence of Ethnic Skill Differentials: The Children and Grandchildren of the Great Migration," *Industrial and Labor Relations Review*, 47 (July 1994), 553–73.

———. "Making It in America: Social Mobility in the Immigrant Population," NBER Working Paper 12088 (March 2006).

———. "The Labor Demand Curve Is Downward Sloping: Reexamining the Impact of Immigration on the Labor Market," *The Quarterly Journal of Economics*, 118:4 (2003), 1335–74.

Borjas, George J., and Lawrence F. Katz. "The Evolution of the Mexican-Born Workforce in the United States," in George J. Borjas, ed. *Mexican Immigration to the United States*. Chicago: University of Chicago Press, 2007.

Borjas, George J., Jeffrey Grogger, and Gordon H. Hanson. "Immigration and African-American Employment Opportunities: The Response of Wages, Employment, and Incarceration to Labor Supply Shocks," NBER Working Paper 12518 (September 2006).

Briggs, John W. *An Italian Passage: Immigrants to Three American Cities.* New Haven, CT: Yale University Press, 1978.

Bureau of Vital Statistics, New York City Department of Health and Mental Hygiene, "Summary of Vital Statistics, 2005," The City of New York, Table 30, p. 44.

Bush, Virgilio Partida, et al. "Situación actual y perspectivas demográficas" in *La situación demográfica de México, 2000* (2nd rev. ed.). México: CONAPO, 2001.

Butcher, Kristin F., and David Card. "Immigration and Wages: Evidence from the 1980's," *The American Economic Review*, 81:2 (1991), 292–96.

Butcher, Kristin F., and John DiNardo. "The Immigrant and Native-Born Wage Distributions: Evidence from United States Censuses," *Industrial and Labor Relations Review*, 56:1 (2002), 97–121.

Camarillo, Albert. *Chicanos in a Changing Society From Mexican Pueblos to American Barrios in Santa Barbara and Southern California, 1848–1930.* Cambridge, MA: Harvard University Press, 1979.

Camposortega Cruz, Sergio. *Análisis demográfico de la mortalidad en México, 1940–1980.* México: El Colegio de México, 1992.

Card, David. "Immigrant Inflows, Native Outflows, and the Local Market Impacts of Higher Immigration," *Journal of Labor Economics*, 19:1 (2001), 22–64.

———. "Is the New Immigration Really So Bad?" *Economic Journal*, 115:507 (November 2005), 300–23.

Card, David, John DiNardo, and Eugena Estes. "The More Things Change: Immigrants and the Children of Immigrants in the 1940s, the 1970s, and the 1990s," in George J. Borjas, ed. *Issues in the Economics of Immigration.* Chicago: University of Chicago Press, 2000, 227–70.

Cárdenas, Rosario. "Las causas de muerte en México," in Gómez de León and Rebell, eds. *La población de México, cuadro 1,* 22–23.

Carpenter, Niles. *Immigrants and Their Children, 1920.* Bureau of the Census, Census Monographs VII, Washington, DC: GPO, 1927.

Carter, Susan B., et al. *Historical Statistics of the United States: Earliest Times to the Present,* 5 vols. Millennial edition. New York: Cambridge University Press, 2006.

Castillo, Pedro G., and Antonio Ríos Bustamanete. *México en los Ángeles. Una historia social y cultural, 1781–1985.* México: Alianza Editorial Mexicana, 1989.

CDC, NCHS (Center for Disease Control and Prevention, National Center for Health Statistics). "Births: Final Data for 2003," *National Vital Statistics Reports,* 54:2 (September 8, 2005), 37, Table 6.

———. *Health, United States, 2005 with Chartbook on Trends in the Health of Americans.* Hyattsville, MD: National Center for Health Statistics, 2005.

_____. *Health, United States, 2006 With Chartbook on Trends in the Health of Americans*. Hyattsville, MD: U.S. Department of Health and Human Services, Centers for Disease Control and Prevention and National Center for Health Statistics, 2006, 177–78, Table 28.

_____. *National Vital Statistics Reports*, 51:12 (August 4, 2000), Table 2.

_____. *National Vital Statistics Reports*, 51:1 (December 11, 2002), 6–8, Tables 1 and 2.

_____. *National Vital Statistics Reports*, 54:13 (April 19, 2006), Table 5.

_____. *National Vital Statistics Reports*, 55:1 (September 29, 2006), 41, Table 5.

_____. "Topics in Minority Health: Childbearing Patterns Among Puerto Rican Hispanics in New York City and Puerto Rico," *Morbidity and Mortality Weekly Report [MMWR]*, 36:3 (January 30, 1987), 39–41.

_____. *Vital Statistics of the US, 2001*, I, "Natality," Table 3–1. "Live Births and Birth Rates: Puerto Rico, 1943–2001."

_____. *Vital Statistics of the US 2002*, Part 1 "Natality."

CEED (Centro de Estudios Económicos y Demográficos). *Dinámica de la población de México* (2nd ed.). México: El Colegio de México, 1981.

"Census 2000 ACS 2005 Comparison Issues," available at http://dola.colorado.gov/dlg/demog/census/ACS2005comparison.pdf.

Center for Puerto Rican Studies, Hunter College, City University of New York, special edition of the *Centro Journal*, (Fall 2001), XIII.

Chesnais, Jean-Claude. *The Demographic Transition: Stages, Patterns, and Economic Implications*. Oxford: Clarendon Press, 1992.

Chiquiar, Daniel, and Gordon H. Hanson. "International Migration, Self-Selection, and the Distribution of Wages: Evidence from Mexico and the United States," *Journal of Political Economy*, 113:2 (2005), 239–81.

Chiswick, Barry R. "Differences in Education and Earnings Across Racial and Ethnic Groups: Tastes, Discrimination, and Investments in Child Quality," *The Quarterly Journal of Economics*, 103:3 (1988), 571–97.

_____. "Speaking, Reading, and Earnings among Low-Skilled Immigrants," *Journal of Labor Economics*, 9:2 (1991), 149–70.

Chiswick, Barry R., and Paul Miller. "Immigrant Earnings, Language Skills, Linguistic Concentration and the Business Cycle," *Journal of Population Economics*, 15 (2002), 31–57.

CONAPO (Consejo Nacional de Población), Cuadro A. "Indicadores sobre migración a Estados Unidos, índice y grado de intensidad migratoria por entidad federativa, 2000," available at http://www.conapo.gob.mx/publicaciones/migra4.htm.

_____. *Índice de Intensidad migratoria México-Estados Unidos, 2000*. México: CONAPO, 2002.

_____. *Indicadores demográficos, 1990–2050*, available at http://www.conapo.gob.mx/index.php?option=com_content&view=article&id=149&Itemid=14.

_____. *La situación demográfica de México*, 2000; found at http://www.conapo.gob.mx/publicaciones/2000.htm

Corona, Rodolfo. "Estimación del número de emigrantes permanentes de México a Estados Unidos 1850–1990," in Rodolfo Tuirán, ed. *Migración México-EU,*

Continuidad y cambio. México: CONAPO, 1998, cuadro 3, available at www.conapo.gob.mx/publicaciones/migra3/03.pdf.

Crosby, Alfred W. *The Columbian Exchange; Biological and Cultural Consequences of 1492*. Westport, CT: Greenwood, 1972.

Dalirazar, Nasrin. *Reasons People Do Not Work: 2004: Household Economic Studies*. Current Population Studies, P70–111. Washington, DC: U.S. Census Bureau, September 2007.

Dirección General de Inmigración, *Resumen estadístico del movimiento migratorio en la República Argentina, años 1857–1924*. Buenos Aires: Ministerio de Agricultura de la Nación, 1925.

Durand, Jorge. "Origen y destino de una migración centenaria," in Marina Ariza and Alejandro Portes, eds. *El país transnacional: Migración Mexicana y Cambio Social a través de la frontera*. Mexico: UNAM, 2007, 55–82.

Durand, Jorge, Douglas S. Massey, and Fernando Charvet. "The Changing Geography of Mexican Immigration to the United States: 1910–1996, "*Social Science Quarterly*, 81:1 (March 2000): 1–15.

Durand, Jorge, Douglas Massey, and Rene Zentino. "Mexican Immigration to the United States: Continuities and Changes," *Latin American Research Review*, 36:1 (2001), 107–27.

Dzidzienyo, Anani, and Suzanne Obler, *eds. Neither Enemies nor Friends: Latinos, Blacks, Afro-Latinos*. New York: Palgrave Macmillan, 2005.

Easterlin, Richard A. "The American Baby Boom in Historical Perspective," *American Economic Review*, LI:5 (December 1961), 869–911.

Eltis, David, editor. *Coerced and Free Migration: Global Perspectives*. Stanford, CA: Stanford University Press, 2002.

———. *Economic Growth and the Ending of the Transatlantic Slave Trade*. New York: Oxford University Press, 1987.

———. *The Rise of African Slavery in the Americas*. New York: Cambridge University Press, 2000.

———. "Slavery and Freedom in the Early Modern World," in Stanley L. Engerman, ed. *Terms of Labor. Slavery, Serfdom and Free Labor*. Stanford, CA: Stanford University Press, 1999.

Elo, Irma T., Cassio M. Turra, Bert Kestenbaum, and B. Reneé Ferguson. "Mortality among Elderly Hispanics in the United States: Past Evidence and New Results," *Demography*, 41:1 (February 2004), 109–28.

Erickson, Charlotte J. "Emigration from the British Isles to the USA in 1841: Part 1. Emigration from the British Isles," *Population Studies*, 43 (1989), 347–67.

Espenshade, T., and H. Fu. "An Analysis of English-Language Proficiency Among U.S. Immigrants." *American Sociological Review*, 62 (1997), 288–305.

Espinosa, Kristin E., and Douglas S. Massey. "Determinants of English Proficiency among Mexican Migrants to the United States," *International Migration Review*, 31:1 (1997), 28–50.

Federal Reserve Bank of Dallas. "Houston Business – A Perspective on the Houston Economy" December 2006, available at http://www.dallasfed.org/research/houston/2006/hb0604.html.

Feliciano, Cynthia. "Educational Selectivity in U.S. Immigration: How Do Immigrants Compare to Those Left Behind?" *Demography*, 42:1 (February 2005), 131–52.

Feliciano, Zadia M. "The Skill and Economic Performance of Mexican Immigrants from 1910 to 1990," *Explorations in Economic History*, 38 (2001), 386–409.

Ferenczi, Imre, and Walter F. Willcox. *International Migrations*, 2 vols. New York: National Bureau of Economic Research, 1929.

Fligstein, Neil. *Going North. Migration of Blacks and Whites from the South, 1900–1950.* New York: Academic Press, 1981.

Fogelman, Aaron. "From Slaves, Convicts and Servants to Free Passengers: The Transformation of Immigration in the Era of the American Revolution," *Journal of American History*, 85:1 (June 1998), 43–76.

———. "Migrations to the Thirteen British North American Colonies, 1700–1775: New Estimates," *Journal of Interdisciplinary History*, XXII:4 (Spring 1992), 691–709.

Friedberg, Rachel M., and Jennifer Hunt. "The Impact of Immigrants on Host Country Wages, Employment and Growth," *The Journal of Economic Perspectives*, 9:2 (1995), 44.

Fussell, Elizabeth. "Sources of Mexico's Migration Stream: Rural, Urban, and Border Migrants to the United States," *Social Forces*, 82:3 (March 2004), 937–67.

Galenson, David W. "The Rise and Fall of Indentured Servitude in the Americas: An Economic Analysis," *The Journal of Economic History*, 44:1 (March 1984), 1–26.

García, F. Chris, John A. Garcia, Angelo Falcon, and Rodolfo O. de la Garza. "Studying Latino Politics: The Development of the Latino National Political Survey," *PS: Political Science and Politics*, 22:4 (1989), 848–52.

García, Juan R. "History of Chicanos in Chicago Heights," *Aztlán: A Journal of Chicano Studies*, 7:2 (Summer 1976), 291–306.

García, María Cristina. "Exiles, Immigrants and Transnationals: The Cuban Communities of the United States," in David G. Gutiérrez, ed. *The Columbia History of Latinos in the United States Since 1960*. New York: Columbia University Press, 2004, 146–86.

———. *Havana USA: Cuban Exiles and Cuban Americans in South Florida, 1959–1994.* Berkeley: University of California Press, 1996.

García, Mario T. *Desert Immigrants: The Mexicans of El Paso, 1880–1920*. New Haven, CT: Yale University Press, 1981.

García, Matt A. *World of Its Own. Race, Labor and Citrus in the Making of Greater Los Angeles, 1900–1970.* Chapel Hill: University of North Carolina Press, 2001.

García y Grego, Manuel. "The importation of Mexican Contract Laborers to the United States, 1942–1964," in David G. Gutiérrez, ed. *Between Two Worlds: Mexican Immigrants in the United States*. Wilmington, DE: Scholarly Resources, 1996, 45–85.

Garza O., Rodolfo de la, and Louis DeSipio, *eds. Muted Voices: Latinos and the 2000 Elections*. Lanham, MD: Rowman & Littlefield, 2005.

Georges, Eugenia. *The Making of a Transnational Community. Migration, Development and Cultural Change in the Dominican Republic.* New York: Columbia University Press, 1990.

Gibson, Campbell J., and Emily Lennon. *Historical Census Statistics on the Foreign-born Population of the United States: 1850–1990.* U.S. Bureau of the Census, Population Division, Working Paper Series No. 29 (February 1999).

Gibson, Campbell J., and Kay Jung. *Historical Census Statistics on Population Totals by Race, 1790 to 1990, and by Hispanic Origin, 1970 to 1990, for The United States, Regions, Divisions, and States.* U.S. Bureau of the Census, Population Division, Working Paper Series No. 56 (September 2002).

Golash-Boza, Tanya. "Assessing the Advantages of Bilingualism for the Children of Immigrants," *International Migration Review,* 39:3 (2005), 721–53.

Gómez de León Cruces, José, and Virgilio Partida Bush. "Niveles, tendencias y diferenciales de la mortalidad," in José Gómez de León Cruces and Cecilia Rabell Romero, eds. *La población de México: Tendencias y perspectivs sociodemográficas hacia el siglo XXI.* México: CONAPO and Fondo de Cultura Económica, 2001, 81–108.

Gonzáles, Manuel G. *Mexicans. A History of Mexicans in the United States.* Bloomington: Indiana University Press, 1989.

Gould, J. D. "European Inter-Continental Emigration – The Road Home: Return Migration from the U.S.A.," *Journal of European Economic History,* 9 (1980), 79–87.

Grasmuck, Sherri, and Patricia R. Pessar. *Between Two Islands: Dominican International Migration.* Berkeley: University of California Press, 1991.

Griffin, John D., and Brian Newman, "The Unequal Representation of Latinos and Whites," *The Journal of Politics,* 69:4 (2007), 1032–46.

Griswald del Castillo, Richard. *The Los Angeles Barrio, 1850–1890: A Social History.* Berkeley: University of California Press, 1979.

———. *La familia: Chicano Families in the Urban Southwest, 1848 to the Present.* Notre Dame, IN: University of Notre Dame Press, 1984.

Grubb, Farley. "The End of European Immigrant Servitude in the United States: An Economic Analysis of Market Collapse, 1772–1835," *The Journal of Economic History,* 54:4 (December 1994), 794–824.

Haines, Michael R. "The Urban Mortality Transition in the United States, 1800–1940," NBER Historical Research Paper No. 134 (July 2001).

———. "The White Population of the United States, 1790–1920," in Michael R. Haines and Richard H. Steckel, eds. *A Population History of North America.* Cambridge: Cambridge University Press, 2000.

Hamilton, Brady E. "Reproduction Rates for 1990–2002 and Intrinsic Rates for 2000–2001: United States." *National Vital Statistics Reports,* 52:17 (March 18, 2004).

Hamilton, Nora, and Norma Stoltz Chinchilla. *Seeking Community in a Global City: Guatemalans and Salvadorians in Los Angeles.* Philadelphia: Temple University Press, 2001.

Haslip-Viera, Gabriel. "The Evolution of the Latino Community in New York City: Early Nineteenth Century to the Present," in Gabriel Haslip-Viera and

Sherry L. Baver, eds. *Latinos in New York. Communities in Transition.* Notre Dame, IN: University of Notre Dame Press, 1994, 3–29.

Hatton, Timothy J., and Jeffrey G. Williamson. "What Drove the Mass Migrations from Europe in the Late Nineteenth Century?" *Population and Development Review*, 20:3 (September 1994), 533–59.

Health United States, 1983. Washington, DC: National Center for Health Statistics, Public Health Service, 1983, p. 155, Table 19.

Hellerstein, Judith, and David Neumark. "Ethnicity, Language, and Workplace Segregation: Evidence from a New Matched Employer-Employee Data Set," "*Annales d'Économie et de Statistique*, No. 71/72 (July–December 2003), 19–78.

Hernández Alvarez, José. *Return Migration to Puerto Rico.* Population Monographs No.1. Berkeley: University of California Press, 1967.

Hernández, Ramona, and Silvio Torres-Saillant. "Dominicans in New York: Men, Women and Prospects," in Gabriel Haslip-Viera and Sherry L. Baver, eds. *Latinos in New York. Communities in Transition.* Notre Dame, IN: University of Notre Dame Press, 1994, 30–56.

Hero, Rodney, F. Chris Garcia, John Garcia, and Harry Pachon. "Latino Participation, Partisanship, and Office Holding," *PS: Political Science and Politics*, 33:3 (2000), 529–34.

Higham, John. *Strangers in the Land: Patterns of American Nativism, 1860–1925.* New York: Atheneum Press, 1963.

Historical Statistics of the United States: Earliest Times to the Present. 5 vols.; Millennial edition: New York: Cambridge University Press, 2006.

Hobbs, Frank, and Nicole Stoops. *Demographic Trends in the 20th Century.* U.S. Census Bureau, Census 2000, Special Reports, Series CENSR-4. Washington, DC: Government Printing Office, 2002.

Hoefer, Michael, Nancy Rytina, and Christopher Campbell. *Estimates of the Unauthorized Immigrant Population Residing in the United States: January 2006.* Office of Immigration Statistics, U.S. Department of Homeland Security, available at http://www.dhs.gov/xlibrary/assets/statistics/publications/ill_pe_2006.pdf.

Humphreys, Jeffrey M. "The Multicultural Economy 2008," Terry College of Business, Selig Center for Economic Growth, The University of Georgia, available at http://www.terry.uga.edu/selig/docs/buying_power_2008.pdf.

INEGI (Instituto Nacional de Estadística, Geografía e Informática). *Estadísticas históricas de México* (3rd ed.). México: INEGI, 2000.

———. *Estados Unidos Mexicanos. XII Censo General de Población y Vivienda, 2000. Tabulados Básicos y por Entidad Federativa. Bases de Datos y Tabulados de la Muestra Censal* (Aguascalientes, Ags., México, 2001), available at http://www.inegi.gob.mx/estadistica/espanol/sociodem/asentamientos/ase_02.htm1.

———. *Indicadores Sociodemográficos de México (1930–2000).* Aguascalientes, Ag., 2001.

———. "Tasa de mortalidad infantil por entidad federativa, 2000 a 2006," available at http://www.inegi.gob.mx/est/contenidos/espanol/rutinas/ept.asp?t=mpob55&c=3232.

Instituto Centrale di Statistica, *Bolletino mensile de Statistica* (Gennaio, 1975), Anno 5, Appendix 2: "Espatriati e Rimpatriati, anno 1876–1973," 254–55.

Itzigsohn, José. *Encountering American Fault Lines: Race, Class, and the Dominican Experience in Providence.* New York: Russell Sage Foundation, 2009.

Johnson, Daniel M., and Rex R. Campbell. *Black Migration in America: A Socio-Demographic History.* Durham, NC: Duke University Press, 1981.

Kasinitz, Philip, John H. Mollenkopf, Mary C. Waters, and Jennifer Holdaway. *Inheriting the City: The Children of Immigrants Come of Age.* New York: Russell Sage Foundation, 2008.

Kasinitz, Philip, John H. Mollenkopf, and Mary C. Waters, eds. *Becoming New Yorkers: Ethnographies of the New Second Generation.* New York: Russell Sage Foundation, 2004.

Kerr, Louise Año Nuevo. "The Chicano Experience in Chicago, 1920–1970." Ph.D. dissertation, University of Illinois, 1976.

———. "Chicano Settlements in Chicago: A Brief History," *Journal of Ethnic Studies*, 2:4 (Winter 1975), 22–32.

Kitagawa, Evelyn M. "Differential Fertility in Chicago, 1920–40," *American Journal of Sociology*, 58:5 (March 1953), 481–92.

Klein, Herbert S. "A integração dos imigrantes italianos no Brasil, na Argentina e nos Estados Unidos," *Novos Estudos CEBRAP* (São Paulo), 25 (Outubro 1989), 95–117.

———. *The Atlantic Slave Trade.* New York: Cambridge University Press, 1999.

———. "The Integration of Italian Immigrants into Argentina and the United States: A Comparative Perspective," *American Historical Review*, 88:2 (April 1983), 306–29.

———. *Population History of the United States.* New York: Cambridge University Press, 2002.

Klein, Herbert S., and Daniel C. Schiffner. "The Current Debate About the Origins of the Paleoindians of America," *Journal of Social History*, 37:2 (Winter 2003), 483–92.

Kochhar, Rakesh. "Latino Labor Report 2004: More Jobs for New Immigrants but at Lower Wages," Pew Hispanic Center, available at http://pewhispanic.org/files/reports/45.pdf.

———. "1995–2005: Foreign-Born Latinos Make Progress on Wages," Pew Hispanic Center, available at http://pewhispanic.org/files/reports/78.pdf.

Kolata, Gina, "Data on Hispanic Immigrants Presents Puzzle on Aging," *New York Times*, January 3, 2007, p. A16.

Leal, David L., Matt A. Barreto, Jongho Lee, and Rodolfo O. de la Garza. "The Latino Vote in the 2004 Election," *PS: Political Science and Politics*, 38:1 (2005), 41–49.

Leal, David L., Valerie Martinez-Ebers, and Kenneth J. Meier. "The Politics of Latino Education: The Biases of At-Large Elections," *The Journal of Politics*, 66:4 (2004), 1224–44.

Leon, Arnaldo de. *The Tejano Community, 1836–1900.* Dallas: Southern Methodist University Press, 1997.

León Cruces, José Gómez de, and Virgilio Partida Bush. "Niveles, tendencias y diferenciales de la mortalidad," in José Gómez de León Cruces and Cecilia

Rabell Romero, eds. *La población de México: Tendencias y perspectivas sociodemográficas hacia el siglo XXI.* México: CONAPO and Fondo de Cultura Económica, 2001.

Levitt, Peggy. *The Transnational Villagers.* Berkeley: University of California Press, 2001.

Liebler, Carolyn A., and Andrew Halpern-Manners. "A Practical Approach to Using Multiple-Race Response Data: A Bridging Method for Public Use Microdata," *Demography,* 45:1 (February 2008), 143–55.

Livi Bacci, Massimo. *L'immigrazione e l'assimilazione degli italiani negli Stati Uniti secondo le statistiche demografiche americane.* Milano: Giuffrè, 1961.

Livingston, Gretchen, and Joan R Kahn. "An American Dream Unfulfilled: The Limited Mobility of Mexican Americans," *Social Science Quarterly,* 83:4 (September 2002), 1003–12.

Logan, John. "How Race Counts for Hispanic Americans," Lewis Mumford Center, University of Albany, July 14, 2003, available at http://mumford.albany.edu/census/BlackLatinoReport/BlackLatino01.htm.

———. "The New Latinos: Who They Are, Where They Are," available at http://mumford.albany.edu/census/report.html.

López Nistal, Libia Miriam A. Gran Álvarez, and Ana Maria Felipe Ramos. "Evolución de la fecundidad en Cuba en las últimas cinco décadas," *Revista Temas Estadísticos de Salud* (Habana), No 2 (Diciembre 2006).

López, Mark Hugo. "The Hispanic Vote in the 2008 Election," Pew Hispanic Center, Report of November 7, 2008, available at http://pewhispanic.org/files/reports/98.pdf.

López, Mark Hugo, and Paul Taylor. Pew Research Center, "Dissecting the 2008 Electorate: Most Diverse in U.S. History," April 30, 2009, available at http://pewhispanic.org/reports/report.php?ReportID=108.

López, Mark Hugo, and Susan Minushkin. *2008 National Survey of Latinos.* Washington, DC: PEW Hispanic Center, report dated September 18, 2008.

Maldonado Turra, Cassio. "Living and Dying at Older Ages: Essays on the Hispanic Mortality Paradox and the Annuity Puzzle in the United States." Ph.D. dissertation, Department of Sociology, University of Pennsylvania, 2004.

Martin, Joyce A, B. E. Hamilton, P. D. Sutton, et al. "Births: Final Data for 2003," *National Vital Statistics Reports,* 54:2 (2005).

Martin, Joyce A., et al. "Births: Final Data for 2004," *National Vital Statistics Reports,* 55:1 (September 29, 2006), 54, Table 13.

Massey, Douglas S., Jorge Durand, and Nolan J. Malone. *Beyond Smoke and Mirrors: Mexican Immigration in an Era of Economic Integration.* New York: Russell Sage Foundation, 1992.

Mayer, Albert, and Carol Klapprodt. "Fertility Differentials in Detroit, 1920–1950," *Population Studies,* 9:2 (November 1955), 148–58.

McCaa, Robert. "El poblamiento de México: de sus orígenes a la Revolución," in José Gómez de León Cruces and Celia Rabell Romero, eds. *La población de México, tendencias y perspectivas sociodemográficas hacia el siglo XXI.* México: CONAPO & Fondo de Cultura Económica, 2001.

Mccall, Leslie. "Explaining Levels of Within-Group Wage Inequality in U.S. Labor Markets," *Demography,* 37:4 (2000), 415–30.

McClelland, Peter D., and Richard J. Zeckhauser. *Demographic Dimensions of the New Republic: American Interregional Migration, Vital Statistics and Manumissions, 1800–1860.* Cambridge: Cambridge University Press, 1982.

McKenziea, David, and Hillel Rapoport. "Self-Selection Patterns in Mexico-U.S. Migration: The Role of Migration Networks," World Bank, Policy, Research Working Paper No. WPS 4118 (August 2006).

McManus, Walter, William Gould, and Finish Welch. "Earnings of Hispanic Men: The Role of English Language Proficiency," *Journal of Labor Economics*, 1:2 (1983), 101–03.

Menchaca, Martha. *The Mexican Outsiders: A Community History of Marginalization and Discrimination in California.* Austin: University of Texas Press, 1995.

Mier y Terán, Marta. "La fecundidad en México: 1940–1980. Estimaciones derivadas de la información del registro civil y de los census," in Beatriz Figueroa Campos, ed. *Le fecundidad en México: Cambios y perspectivas.* México: El Colegio de México, 1989, 21–23.

Missouri Census Data Center. "Ten Things to Know about the American Community Survey (2005 Edition)," available at http://mcdc2.missouri.edu/pub/data/acs2005/Ten_things_to_know.shtml.

Mitchell, B. R. *International Historical Statistics: Europe, 1750–1993* (3rd ed.). New York: Stockton Press, 1992.

Monroy, Douglas. *Rebirth: Mexican Los Angeles from the Great Migration to the Great Depression.* Berkeley: University of California Press, 1999.

Montejano, David. *Anglos and Mexicans in the Making of Texas, 1836–1986.* Austin: University of Texas Press, 1987.

Morgan, S. Philip, Susan Cotts Watkins, and Douglas Ewbank. "Generating Americans: Ethnic Differences in Fertility," in Susan Cotts Watkins, ed. *After Ellis Island: Newcomers and Natives in the 1910 Census.* New York: Russell Sage Foundation, 1994, 83–124.

Morner, Magnus. *Race Mixture in the History of Latin America.* Boston: Little, Brown, 1967.

Mortara, Gregorio "A inmigração italiano no Brasil e algumas caracteristicas do grupo italiano de São Paulo," *Revista Brasileira de Estadistica*, 11 (1950), 65–95.

Nagler, Jonathan, and R. Michael Alvarez. "Latinos, Anglos, Voters, Candidates, and Voting Rights," *University of Pennsylvania Law Review*, 153:1 (2004), 393–432.

Nguyenn, Anh, Getinet Hailenn, and Jim Taylor. "Ethnic and Gender Differences in Intergenerational Mobility: A Study of 26-Year-Olds in the USA." *Scottish Journal of Political Economy*, 52:4 (2005), 544–64.

Nugent, Walter. *Crossings: The Great Transatlantic Migrations, 1870–1914.* Bloomington: Indiana University Press, 1992.

Ottaviano, Gianmarco I. P., and Giovanni Peri. "Rethinking the Gains from Immigration: Theory and Evidence from the U.S.," NBER Working Paper 11672 (September 2005).

Padilla, Elena. *Up From Puerto Rico.* New York: Columbia University Press, 1958.

Padilla, Felix M. *Puerto Rican Chicago*. Notre Dame, IN: University of Notre Dame Press, 1987.

Palloni, Alberto, and Elizabeth Arias, "Paradox Lost: Explaining the Hispanic Adult Mortality Advantage," *Demography*, 41:3 (August 2004), 385–415.

Passel, Jeffrey S. *Unauthorized Migrants: Numbers and Characteristics*, Pew Hispanic Center report of June 14, 2005, available at http://pewhispanic.org/files/reports/46.pdf.

Passel, Jeffrey S., and D'Vera Cohn. "Mexican Immigrants: How Many Come? How Many Leave," Pew Hispanic Center, July 22, 2009, available at http://pewhispanic.org/files/reports/112.pdf.

Passel, Jeffrey S., and Paul Taylor. "Who's Hispanic?" report of Pew Hispanic Center, May 28, 2009, available at http://pewhispanic.org/reports/report.php?ReportID=111.

Patel, Kushang V., Karl Eschbach, Laura A. Ray, and Kyriakos S. Markides. "Evaluation of Mortality Data for Older Mexican Americans: Implications for the Hispanic Paradox," *American Journal of Epidemiology*, 159:7 (2004), 707–15.

Pérez, Lisandro. "Growing Up in Cuban Miami: Immigration, the Enclave and New Generations," in Rubén G. Rumnaut and Alejandro Portes. *Ethnicities. Children of Immigrants in America*. New York: Russell Sage Foundation, 2001, 91–126.

Pérez Astorga, Javier. "Mortalidad por causas en México, 1950–1980," in Mario Branfman and José Gómez de León, eds. *La mortalidad en México: niveles, tendencias y determinantes*. México: Colmex, 1988.

Pérez, Jr., Louis A. *Essays on Cuban History: Historiography and Research*. Gainesville: University of Florida Press, 1995.

Perlmann, Joel, and Roger Waldinger. "Second Generation Decline? Children of Immigrants, Past and Present – A Reconsideration," *International Migration Review*, 31:4 (1997), 893–922.

Pew Hispanic Center/Kaiser Family Foundation, "2002 National Survey of Latinos," available at http://pewhispanic.org/reports/report.php?ReportID=15.

PEW Latino Opinion surveys, available at http://pewhispanic.org/publications/.

Piore, Michael J. *Birds of Passage: Migrant Labor and Industrial Society*. Cambridge, MA: MIT Press, 1979.

Polenberg, Richard. *One Nation Divisible: Class, Race and Ethnicity in the United States Since 1938*. New York: Viking Press, 1980.

Pitti, Stephen J. *The Devil in Silicon Valley: Northern California, Race, and Mexican Americans*. Princeton, NJ: Princeton University Press, 2002.

Portes, Alejandro, and Robert Bach. *Latin Journey: Cuban and Mexican Immigrants in the United States*. Berkeley: University of California Press, 1985.

Portes, Alejandro, and Alex Stepick. "Unwelcome Immigrants: The Labor Market Experiences of 1980 (Mariel) Cuban and Haitian Refugees in South Florida," *American Sociological Review*, 50:4 (August 1985), 493–514.

PUMA (Public Use Microdata Sample). "Census 2000 Super-Public Use Microdata Area (PUMA) Maps," available at http://www.census.gov/geo/www/maps/sup_puma.htm.

"PUMS Accuracy of the Data, 2005," available at http://www.census.gov/acs/
www/Downloads/2005/AccuracyPUMS.pdf.

Qian, Zhenchao, and José A. Cobas. "Latinos' Mate Selection: National Origin,
Racial, and Nativity Differences," *Social Science Research*, 33:2 (June 2004),
225–47.

Ramos-Zayas, Ana Yolanda. *Nationalist Performances: Race, Class, and Space
in Puerto Rican Chicago.* Chicago: University of Chicago Press, 2003.

Reed, Deborah. "Immigration and Males' Earnings Inequality in the Regions of
the United States," *Demography*, 38:3 (August 2001), 363–73.

Roberts, Bryan, and Erin Hamilton. "La nueva geografía de la emigración: zonas
emergentes de atracción y expansión, continuidad y cambio," in Marina Ariza
and Alejandro Portes, eds. *El país transnacional: Migración Mexicana y Cambio Social a través de la frontera.* México: UNAM, 2007, 83–118.

Rodríguez, Clara E. *Changing Race: Latinos, the Census, and the History of
Ethnicity in the United States.* New York: New York University Press, 2000.

Rodríguez, Clara E., and Virginia Sánchez Korrol, editors. *Historical Perspectives
on Puerto Rican Survival in the U.S.* Princeton, NJ: Markus Wiener Publishers,
1996.

Romo, Ricardo. *East Los Angeles: History of a Barrio.* Austin: University of
Texas Press, 1983.

Rosenfeld, Michael J. "Racial, Educational and Religious Endogamy in the United
States: A Comparative Historical Perspective," *Social Forces*, 87:1 (September
2008), 1–31.

Ruggles, Steven, Matthew Sobek, Trent Alexander, Catherine A. Fitch, Ronald
Goeken, Patricia Kelly Hall, Miriam King, and Chad Ronnander. *Integrated
Public Use Microdata Series: Version 3.0* [machine-readable database]. Minneapolis, MN: Minnesota Population Center [producer and distributor], 2004,
available at http://usa.ipums.org/usa/.

Sagas, Ernesto. *Race and Politics in the Dominican Republic.* Gainesville: University Press of Florida, 2000.

Sánchez, George Joseph. "Becoming Mexican American: Ethnicity and Acculturation in Chicano Los Angeles, 1900–1943." Ph.D. dissertation, Stanford
University, 1989.

———. *Becoming Mexican American: Ethnicity, Culture, and Identity in Chicano
Los Angeles, 1900–1945.* New York: Oxford University Press, 1993.

Sánchez Korrol, Virginia. *From Colonia to Community: The History of Puerto
Ricans in New York City, 1917–1948.* Westport, CT: Greenwood Press, 1983.

Sass, Tim R. "The Determinants of Hispanic Representation in Municipal Government," *Southern Economic Journal*, 66:3 (2000), 609–30.

Schoen, Robert. "Timing Effects and the Interpretation of Period Fertility,"
Demography, 41:4 (November 2004), 815–16.

Shaw, Daron, Rodolfo O. de la Garza, and Jongho Lee. "Examining Latino
Turnout in 1996: A Three-State, Validated Survey Approach," *American Journal of Political Science*, 44:2 (2000), 338–46.

Snipp, C. Matthew. "Racial Measurement in the American Census: Past Practices
and Implications for the Future," *Annual Review of Sociology*, 29 (2003),
563–88.

Southern California Association of Governments. "Population Estimates and Projections by County, Ethnicity, Region, and State, 1990–1996, and 1997–2040,"
available at http://www.scag.ca.gov/economy/econdata.html.

*Spotlight on Heterogeneity: The Federal Standards for Racial and Ethnic Clas-
sification,* (Washington, DC: National Academy Press, 1996), Appendix B
Office of Management and Budget Statistical Directive No. 15 Race and Ethnic Standards for Federal Statistics and Administrative Reporting, available at
http://books.nap.edu/openbook.php?record_id=9060&page=65.

Stevens, Gillian. "A Century of U.S. Censuses and the Language Characteristics
of Immigrants," *Demography,* 36:3 (1999), 387–97.

———. "The Social and Demographic Context of Language Use in the United
States," *American Sociological Review,* 57:2 (1992), 171–85.

Suro, Robert. "Counting the "Other Hispanics": How Many Colombians, Dominicans, Ecuadorians, Guatemalans and Salvadorans Are There in the United
States?" Pew Hispanic Center, available at http://pewhispanic.org/reports/
report.php?ReportID=8.

Suro, Roberto, Richard Fry, and Jeffrey Passel. *Hispanics and the 2004 Election:
Population, Electorate and Voters.* Washington, DC: PEW Hispanic Center,
Report, July 2005, available at http://www.pewhispanic.org.

Tafoya, Sonya. "Shades of Belonging," Pew Hispanic Center, December 2004,
available at http://pewhispanic.org/reports/report.php?ReportID=35.

Tainer, Evelina. "English Language Proficiency and the Determination of Earnings
among Foreign-Born Men," *The Journal of Human Resources,* 23:1 (1988),
108–22.

Thompson, Warren S., and P. K. Whelpton. *Population Trends in the United
States.* New York: McGraw-Hill, 1933.

Toussaint-Comeau, Maude. "The Occupational Assimilation of Hispanic Immigrants in the U.S.: Evidence from Panel Data," *International Migration Review,*
40:3 (Fall 2006), 508–36.

Toussaint-Comeau, Maude, Thomas Smith, and Ludovic Comeau, Jr. "Occupational Attainment and Mobility of Hispanics in a Changing Economy."
Pew Hispanic Center, September 2005, available at http://pewhispanic.org/files/
reports/59.1.pdf.

Tuirán, Rodolfo Virgilio Partida, Octavio Mojarro, and Elena Zúñiga. "Tendencias y perspectivas de la fecundidad," in *La situación demográfica de México,
2002.* México: CONAPO, 2002.

U.S. Bureau of Citizenship and Immigration Services. Table HS-9. "Immigration
by Leading Country or Region of Last Residence: 1901 to 2001," reproduced
in U.S. Bureau of the Census. *Statistical Abstract of the United States: 2003,*
(Washington DC: Government Printing Office, 2004) Mini-Historical Statistics,
16.

———. For immigration legislation, see http://www.immigration.gov/graphics/
shared/aboutus/statistics/legishist/index.htm.

U.S. Bureau of Labor Statistics. Occupational structure data for 2006 and 2007,
available at http://www.bls.gov/cps/cpsaat10.pdf.

U.S. Bureau of the Census. "American Community Survey, 2005,"available at
http://www2.census.gov/acs2005/SPP/Race_Ancestry_Hispanic_Origin/
Mexican/.

_____. "American Community Survey, Puerto Rico Community Survey, 2005, Subject Definitions," available at http://www.census.gov/acs/www/Downloads/2005/usedata/Subject_Definitions.pdf.

_____. American Factfinder, Census 2000. "GCT-P6: Race and Hispanic or Latino: 2000," Summary File 1. United States – States and Puerto Rico, available at http://factfinder.census.gov/servlet/GCTTable?_bm=y&-state=gct&-ds_name=DEC_2000_SF1_U&-_box_head_nbr=GCT-P6&-mt_name=DEC_2000_SF1_U_GCTP6_CO1&-_caller=geoselect&-geo_id=&-format=US-9&-_lang=en.

_____. *1860 Census of the United States*, vol. 2. Washington DC: Government Printing Office, 1864.

_____. *1910 Census of the United States*. Washington, DC: Government Printing Office, 1913.

_____. *1980 Census of the United States, Characteristics of the Population, General Social and Economic Characteristics*, vol. 1. Washington, DC: Government Printing Office, 1983.

_____. *1980 Census of the United States*, Summary Volumes, vol. 1, PC80-1-B1. Washington DC: Government Printing Office, 1983.

_____. *1980 Census of the Population*, "United States Summary," vol. 1, chapter C, part 1, PC80-l-C1. Washington, DC: Government Printing Office, 1983.

_____. *2000 Census of Population and Housing, Public Use Microdata Sample 2000*, issued December 2005, B-30–1, available at http://www.census.gov/prod/cen2000/doc/pums.pdf.

_____. *2000 Census of Population and Housing*, Summary File 2, "PCT9. Household Size, Household Type, And Presence Of Own Children – Universe: Households," available at http://factfinder.census.gov/servlet/DTTable?_bm=y&-geo_id=01000US&-ds_name=DEC_2000_SF2_U&-_lang=en&-_caller=geoselect&-state=dt&-format=&-mt_name=DEC_2000_SF2_U_PCT009.

_____. "Chapter 4, Sample Design and Estimation," *1990 Census of Population and Housing: Public-use Microdata Samples Technical Documentation*, Washington, DC: U.S. Department of Commerce, Bureau of the Census, 1992, pp. 4–1 to 4–7, reprinted by IPUMS at http://usa.ipums.org/usa/voliii/1990samp.shtml.

_____. "Chapter 4, Sample Design for the Public-Use Microdata Samples," *Census of Population and Housing, 1980: Public-Use Microdata Samples Technical Documentation*, Washington, DC: U.S. Department of Commerce, Bureau of the Census, 1983, pp. 35–42, reprinted by IPUMS at http://usa.ipums.org/usa/voliii/1980samp.shtml.

_____. Cost of living indexes for metropolitan areas for the fourth quarter 2005, available at http://www.census.gov/compendia/statab/2007/prices/consumer_price_indexes_cost_of_living_index.html.

_____. Consolidated Metropolitan Statistical Area (CMSA) and Metropolitan Statistical Area (MSA) definitions, available at http://www.census.gov/acs/www/UseData/index.htm.

_____. *Estimates of the Population by Race Alone or in Combination and Hispanic or Latino Origin for Counties with 1,000,000 or more population as of July 1, 2005 sorted by total population size: July 1, 2005*, internet release of

August 4, 2006, available at http://www.census.gov/Press-Release/www/2006/cb06–123table2.xls.

———. "Fertility of American Women, Current Population Survey – June 2004, Table 7, available at http://www.census.gov/population/www/socdemo/fertility/cps2004.html.

———. *Historical Statistics of the United States, Colonial Times to 1970.* 2nd. ed. Washington, DC: U.S. Department of Commerce, Bureau of the Census, 1976.

———. Poverty thresholds estimates, available at http://www.census.gov/hhes/www/poverty/threshld.html.

———. Projections of the Population by Sex, Race, and Hispanic Origin for the United States: 2010 to 2050 (NP2008-T4); Release date: August 14, 2008.

———. "PUMS Accuracy of the Data, 2000," available at http://www.census.gov/acs/www/Downloads/C2SS/AccuracyPUMS.pdf.

———. "PUMS Accuracy of the Data, 2005," available at http://www.census.gov/acs/www/Downloads/2005/AccuracyPUMS.pdf.

———. "Questions and Answers for Census 2000 on Race," March 14, 2001, available at http://www.census.gov/Press-Release/www/2001/raceqandas.html.

———. Simulated Totals For Hispanic National Origin Groups [in Census 2000] By State, Place, County, And Census Tract: [United States] [computer file]. ICPSR release. Washington, DC: U.S. Dept. of Commerce, Bureau of the Census [producer], 2003. Ann Arbor, MI: Inter-university Consortium for Political and Social Research [distributor], 2004, available at http://webapp.icpsr.umich.edu/cocoon/CENSUS-STUDY/03907.xml#methodology.

———. *The Social and Economic Status of the Black Population in the United States, 1790–1978: An Historical View.* Current Population Reports, P-23, No. 80. Washington, DC: Government Printing Office, 1978.

———. *Statistical Abstract: 2007 Edition*, Table 709, available at http://www.census.gov/compendia/statab/2007/2007edition.html.

———. *Thirteenth Census of the United States, 1910.* Washington, DC: n.p., 1918, Vol. 1, Chapter 2, p. 130, Table 8.

———. Vital Statistics of the US 2002, Part 1, Table 41.

———. "Voting and Registration in the Election of November 2000," available at http://www.census.gov/population/www/socdemo/voting/p20–542.html.

———. "Voting and Registration in the Election of November 2004," available at http://www.census.gov/population/www/socdemo/voting/cps2004.html.

U.S. Bureau of the Census, Staff of the Special Population Statistics Population Division, "Findings on Questions on Race and Hispanic Origin Tested in the 1996 National Content Survey" Population Division Working Paper No. 16, December 1996, available at http://www.census.gov/population/www/documentation/twps0016/twps0016.html.

U.S. Commission on Immigration Reform. *Migration Between Mexico and the United States, Binational Study*, Vol. 1. Mexico City and Washington, DC: Mexico Ministry of Foreign Affairs, 1998.

U.S. Department of Justice, Immigration and Naturalization Service. *Statistical Yearbook of the Immigration and Naturalization Service, 1998.* Washington, DC: Government Printing Office, 2000.

————. *Statistical Yearbook of the Immigration and Naturalization Service, 2000.* Washington, DC: Government Printing Office, 2002.

University of Minnesota, Minnesota Population Center's Integrated Public Use Microdata Series (IPUMS), available at http://www.ipums.org.

Upegui, Debora. "Hispanic Citizenship, Registration, and Voting Patterns: A Comparative Analysis of the 2000 and 2004 Presidential Elections," City University of New York, Center for Latin American, Caribbean, and Latinos Studies, available at http://web.gc.cuny.edu/lastudies.

Valdés, Dionicio Nodín. *Barrios norteños: St. Paul and Midwestern Mexican Communities in the Twentieth Century.* Austin: University of Texas Press, 2000.

Vargas, Zaragosa. *Proletarians of the North: A History of Mexican Industrial Workers in Detroit and the Midwest, 1917–1933.* Berkeley: University of California Press, 1993.

Vázquez Calzada, José L. *La población de Puerto Rico y su trayectoria histórica.* Rio Piedras: Raga Printing, 1988.

Veltman, Calvin. "Modeling the Language Shift Process of Hispanic Immigrants," *International Migration Review,* 22:4 (1988), 545–62.

Verduzco, Gustavo. "La migración mexicana a Estados Unidos: Estructuración de una selectividad histórica," in Rodolfo Tuirán, ed. *Migración México-Estados Unidos Opciones de política.* México: CONAPO, 2000, 23–25.

Wade, Peter. *Race and Ethnicity in Latin America.* London: Pluto Press, 1997.

Waldinger, Roger. "From Ellis Island to LAX: Immigrant Prospects in the American City," *International Migration Review,* 30:4 (Winter 1996), 1078–86.

Wildsmith, Elizabeth. "Race/Ethnic Differences in Female Headship: Exploring the Assumptions of Assimilation Theory," *Social Science Quarterly,* 85:1 (March 2004), 89–106.

Yans-McLaughlin, Virginia. *Family and Community: Italian Immigrants in Buffalo, 1880–1930.* Ithaca, NY: Cornell University Press, 1977.

Index

African-Americans, 11, 63
  educational attainment, 194
Africans, forced migration of, 3, 364,
    365
Alabama, 75
Albuquerque, New Mexico, 85
American Community Surveys (ACS),
    4–6
American FactFinder, 4, 126
Amerindian peoples, 9
anti-immigration sentiment, 237, 268,
    408
Argentina, 13
Arizona, 67, 72
  voter participation, 265
Arkansas, 71, 75
Asia, post-war, 36
Asians
  childhood poverty, 160
  concentration of wealth, 166, 181
  educational attainment, 194, 206,
    211
  female head-of-household, 128
  fertility levels, 109
  head-of-household birthplace, 55
  immigration ban, 27
  median income, 126, 163
  occupational structures, 276
  poverty rates, 159, 169
  settlement patterns, 32

unemployment, 299, 303
vote registration, 270

baby boom, 57
Bean, Frank, 7
Bexar County, Texas, 79
Brazil, 13, 365
Brazilians, 7

California, 67, 72
  business ownership, 354, 359
  voter
    participation, 265
    registration, 272
Caribbean, 1, 2, 36
census
  1870, 16
  1950, 54
  1970, 54
  1980, 54
Center for Disease Control, 8, 54, 99
Central Americans, 66
Chicago metropolitan area, 85
  business ownership, 356
  demographics, 243
  domestic language, 347
  educational attainment, 214–15
  electorate, 260
  English language proficiency, 343
  income, 177

Chicago metropolitan area (*cont.*)
   production and transportation
      occupations, 292
   racial self-declaration, 374
   service, sales, and office
      occupations, 292
   unemployment, 310
   upward mobility, 177
Chinese, 36
Colombians
   concentration of wealth, 169
   demographics, 238, 242
   domestic language, 347
   educational attainment, 153, 199,
      206, 229, 233–4, 387, 412
   English language proficiency, 334
   head-of-household birthplace, 153
   in Florida, 143
   in management and the professions,
      282
   in Miami metropolitan area, 262
   in New York metropolitan area, 94,
      142, 152, 188, 252, 262
   linguistically isolated households,
      349
   marriage patterns, 399
   median income, 130
   percentage of electorate, 260
   poverty rates, 160, 168, 380
   racial self-declaration, 373, 379
   unemployment, 307, 315
Colorado
   voter participation, 265, 406
cost-of-living indices, 147, 156
criollo, 7
Cuba, 1, 36
Cuban Adjustment Act (1966),
      247
Cuban Revolution (1959), 39
Cuban War for Independence
      (1895–1898), 37, 89
Cubans
   average age of mothers at first birth,
      106
   business ownership, 356
   childhood poverty, 163
   concentration of wealth, 169

demographics, 238
domestic language, 347
educational attainment, 148, 199,
   206, 213, 223, 385, 412
English language proficiency, 324
fertility rates, 100
head-of-household birthplace, 150,
   156
in Florida, 37, 40, 68, 89, 142
in Louisiana, 37
in management and the professions,
   282
in Miami metropolitan area, 186,
   247, 262
in New Jersey, 41
in New York metropolitan area, 37,
   40
in service, sales, and office
   occupations, 282
in Tampa, Florida, 37
in U.S., after 1950, 39
linguistically isolated households,
   349
marriage patterns, 398–9
median income, 133
percentage of electorate, 260
poverty rates, 160, 168, 380
racial notions, 367
racial self-declaration, 372, 378
tobacco workers, 1
unemployment, 307–8, 314
Current Population Survey (1969), 54

Dallas County, Texas, 82
Dallas-Fort Worth metropolitan area,
   82
data sets, 4–8
demographic structure, pre-modern,
   47
demographic transition, 13
Denver, Colorado, 85
Diaz, Porfirio (1876–1911), 48
discrimination, 3
Dominican Republic, 94
Dominicans
   childhood poverty, 162, 176
   concentration of wealth, 169

demographics, 238, 242
domestic language, 347
educational attainment, 153, 199,
    206, 226, 229, 233–4, 386
English language proficiency, 329
head-of-household birthplace,
    153
in Florida, 143
in management and the professions,
    282
in Miami metropolitan area, 262
in New York metropolitan area, 42,
    94, 142, 152, 186, 188, 251,
    256, 262
in service, sales, and office
    occupations, 282
in the northeast, 68
in U.S.
    after 1970, 41
linguistically isolated households,
    349
marriage patterns, 399
percentage of electorate, 260
poverty rates, 160, 168, 380
racial notions, 366
racial self-declaration, 373, 378
settlement patterns, 94–5
single-mother households, 109
unemployment, 307, 315
upward social mobility, 188

Ecuadorians
childhood poverty, 176
concentration of wealth, 169
demographics, 242
domestic language, 347
educational attainment, 199, 206,
    226, 229, 233–4
English language proficiency, 334
head-of-household birthplace, 153
in construction, 282
in management and the professions,
    282
in New York metropolitan area, 94,
    142, 152, 188, 252, 262
in service, sales, and office
    occupations, 282

linguistically isolated households,
    349
median income, 130
poverty rates, 160, 168
unemployment, 315
El Barrio, 37
El Salvador, 66

fertility rate differential, 58
Florida, 68, 72, 406
business ownership, 354, 359
Cuban vote, 265
voter
    participation, 265
    registration, 272

Georgia, 68, 75
Germany, 16
Greece, 17

Harris County, Texas, 79
Hispanic Paradox, 115
Hispanics
as other category persons, 6
birth rates, 103–11
business ownership, 361
Caribbean, 41–2, 142, 365
    in Florida, 1
    in New York metropolitan area,
        1
citizenship, 237–75
consumer market, 407
dependency ratio, 113
economic performance, 123–91
educational attainment, 193–236,
    412
employment, 276–319
factors influencing migration, 97
family size, 113–14
fertility rate, 99–103, 412
Iberian, 7
in California, 55
in construction, 278
in management or professions, 279
in New York metropolitan area, 55
in service, sales or office
    occupations, 278

Hispanics (*cont.*)
  in Texas, 55
  in the U.S.
    1980, 57
  language skills and domestic usage,
    3, 320–51, 415
  management and professional
    occupations, 295
  marriage patterns, 114–16, 413
  median age, 113
  median income, 191, 279, 411
  mortality rates, 115–21
  national subgroups, 6
  occupational structures, 276–95,
    412
  percentage of electorate, 256
  population growth, 53, 63–98
    projected, 1, 406, 415
  poverty rates, 159
  racial and ethnic diversity, 2, 367,
    390, 410
  self-identification, 6, 7, 54, 413
  settlement patterns, 2, 55
  sex ratio, 114
  unemployment, 276–319
  voter
    participation, 237–75, 407
    turnout, 270
history, measuring change over
  time, 3
Hondurans
  concentration of wealth, 169
  domestic language, 347
  educational attainment, 199, 204,
    206
  English language proficiency, 334
  in construction, 282
  in management and the professions,
    282
  linguistically isolated households,
    349
  unemployment, 308
Houston metropolitan area, 81
  construction, 295
  demographics, 243
  domestic language, 347

  educational attainment, 216
  electorate, 260
  English language proficiency, 343
  income, 177
  racial self-declaration, 374
  service, sales and office occupations,
    295
  unemployment, 310

Illinois, 67
  voter participation, 265
Imperial County, California, 83
income
  family, 124
  household, 125
  measurement indicators, 124
  personal, 125
    educational attainment, 292
indio, 365
infant mortality, 60
infectious diseases, in Mexico, 48
Integrated Public Use Microdata Series
    (IPUMS, University of
    Minnesota, Minnesota
    Population Center), 4
Ireland, 16
Italy, 17

Jones Act (1917), 91

Kansas, 78
Key Biscayne, Florida, 89

labor globalization, 12
Las Vegas, Nevada, 85
Latin America, 2
  post-war, 36
Latinos
  identity, 2, 417
  in California, 55, 66
  in Florida, 55, 66
  in Illinois, 55
  in New Jersey, 55
  in New York metropolitan area, 55,
    66
  in Texas, 55, 66

in western and southwestern states, 66
population growth, 53, 64
Los Angeles County, California, 81, 83
Los Angeles metropolitan area, 83
 business ownership, 354
 demographics, 242
 domestic language, 347
 educational attainment, 214, 215
 electorate, 260
 English language proficiency, 343
 income, 177
 racial self-declaration, 374
 unemployment, 310
 upward mobility, 177

Mariel Boatlift, 40, 168, 175, 223, 242, 329, 372
Mayan Indians, 2
median income
 adjusted, 144, 147
 cost-of-living, 150
 English language proficiency, 343
 linguistically isolated households, 348, 350
 racial self-declaration, 374
mestizaje (race mixture), 365
mestizo (Spanish speaker with Indigenous and European ancestry), 7, 365
Mexican-American War (1848), 1, 43
Mexicans, 36, 66, 142
 1900 census, 43
 1990 census designations, 7
 average age of mothers at first birth, 105
 birth rates, 103–5
 business ownership, 356
 childhood poverty, 163, 175, 177
 concentration of wealth, 169
 domestic language, 347

dominance of, 66–90, 238, 243
educational attainment, 143, 146–7, 199, 204, 206, 213, 217, 226, 229, 233–4, 383
employment, 50
English language proficiency, 321
factors influencing migration to U.S., 47–53
fertility rates, 99, 103
growth rates, 49
head-of-household birthplace, 144, 153
household gender distribution, 144
in Arizona territory, 43
in California, 43, 45, 71
in Chicago metropolitan area, 45, 184, 245, 262
in construction, 282
in Florida, 45, 71
in Georgia, 45
in Houston metropolitan area, 184, 262
in Kansas, 45
in Los Angeles metropolitan area, 184, 245, 262
in management and the professions, 282
in New Mexico, 43
in New York metropolitan area, 72, 142, 152, 184, 252
in Riverside metropolitan area, 184, 247, 262
in Southwest and California, 1
in Texas, 43, 71, 244
in the U.S., 45
infant mortality rates, 60
linguistically isolated households, 350
marriage patterns, 398, 404
percentage of electorate, 259
poverty rates, 160, 380
racial self-declaration, 375
single mother households, 109
twentieth century, 48
unemployment, 307, 313, 315

Mexico, 364
Miami metropolitan area, 85
   business ownership, 354
   demographics, 242
   domestic language, 347
   educational attainment, 214, 216
   electorate, 260
   English language proficiency, 343
   income, 177
   management and professionals, 292
   racial self-declaration, 373
   service, sales, and office
      occupations, 292
   unemployment, 310
   upward mobility, 181
Miami-Dade County, Florida, 79
migration
   bracero, 52
   demarcated time frames, 415
   to Canada (1826–1835), 13
   to U.S.
      1821–1924, 13
      1821–61, 13
      colonial, 9–11
      from Northwestern Europe, 13
      Hispanic-Caribbean
         1940s, 37
         1960s, 39
      New Immigrant (from Eastern
         and Southern Europe), 13
      New New Immigrant (from Asia,
         Latin America, Hispanic
         Caribbean), 13
      nineteenth century, 12
      uniqueness of, 3
   to U.S. to 1850, 35
   universality of experience, 39
mulatto (person of mixed
   African/European heritage),
   365

nationalism, 2
Nevada, 72, 406
New Immigrant, 17, 24, 26
New Jersey
   voter
      participation, 265

New Mexico, 72, 406
   voter participation,
New York metropolitan area, 85, 89,
   93, 152–6
   business ownership, 354, 359
   construction and production,
      295
   demographics, 243
   domestic language, 347
   educational attainment, 214–15
   electorate, 260
   English language proficiency, 343
   income, 177
   management and professionals, 292
   racial self-declaration, 373
   service, sales, and office
      occupations, 292, 295
   unemployment, 310
   upward mobility, 181
   voter
      participation, 265
      registration, 272
Nicaragua, 66
Nicaraguans, in Florida, 143
non-Hispanic blacks
   educational attainment, 194, 211
   occupational structures, 276
   percentage of electorate, 256
   poverty rates, 159, 163
   unemployment, 299
   voter
      registration, 270
      turnout, 270
non-Hispanic whites
   educational attainment, 194, 211
   median income, 128
   occupational structures, 276
   unemployment, 299
   voter
      registration, 270
      turnout, 270
North Carolina, 68, 75

Obama, Barack, 406
Orange County, California, 83
Oregon, 68
Ottoman Empire, 17

Peruvians
  concentration of wealth, 169
  demographics, 242
  domestic language, 347
  educational attainment, 199, 206,
    412
  English language proficiency,
    334
  in management and the professions,
    282
  in Miami metropolitan area, 262
  linguistically isolated households,
    349
  median income, 130
  poverty rates, 160, 168
  unemployment, 307
Phoenix, Arizona, 85
Pima County, Arizona, 83
Poland, 17
population
  nineteenth century, 11
  post-1830, 11
Portugal, 17
poverty
  childhood, 162, 171–7
  indices, 156–91
Proposition 187 (California), 237,
    268, 412
Public Use Microdata Sample (PUMS,
    U.S. Census Bureau), 4, 6
Puerto Ricans
  business ownership, 359
  childhood poverty, 163, 176
  concentration of wealth, 169
  demographics, 238
  domestic language, 346
  educational attainment, 153, 199,
    206, 213, 215, 226, 229, 233,
    234, 384
  English language proficiency, 324
  fertility rates, 100–2
  head-of-household birthplace,
    153
  in Chicago metropolitan area, 38,
    262
  in Florida, 37, 89, 143
  in Hartford, Connecticut, 38

  in Hawaii, 37, 91
  in management and the professions,
    282
  in Miami metropolitan area, 262
  in New York metropolitan area, 37,
    91, 142, 186, 251, 262
  in Philadelphia, Pennsylvania, 38
  in the northeast, 68
  in U.S.
    after 1950, 37
  infant mortality rates, 60
  linguistically isolated households,
    349
  marriage patterns, 395, 404
  median income, 133
  percentage of electorate, 259
  poverty rates, 160, 168, 380
  racial notions, 367
  racial self-declaration, 373, 377
  settlement patterns, 88, 91–4
  single-mother households, 109
  unemployment, 307, 308, 315
  upward social mobility, 188
Puerto Rico, 1, 36
  U.S. occupation of (1898), 37
  unincorporated territory of U.S.
    (1898), 37

quota
  laws (1920s), 43
  system reform (1965), 36

race
  conceptualizations, 367
racial/ethnic categories
  educational attainment, 382
  poverty rates, 379
  self-declaration, 370
  U.S. government, 54, 369
racism, 3
refugees
  economic, 2
  political, 2
reproduction
  colonial, 11
  population expansion through, 39
Riverside County, California, 83

Riverside metropolitan area
  demographics, 242
  domestic language, 347
  educational attainment, 214–15
  electorate, 260
  English language proficiency, 343
  income, 177
  racial self-declaration, 374
  unemployment, 310
Russian Empire, 17

Salvadorans, 82, 83, 85
  concentration of wealth, 169
  demographics, 242
  domestic language, 347
  educational attainment, 199, 204,
    206
  English language proficiency, 329
  in construction, 282
  in management and the professions,
    282
  in service, sales, and office
    occupations, 282
  linguistically isolated households,
    349
  marriage patterns, 399
  percentage of electorate, 260
  poverty rates, 160, 168
  unemployment, 307, 308
San Antonio metropolitan area, 79
San Bernardino County, California,
    83
San Diego
  County, 83
  metropolitan area, 85
San Francisco-Oakland metropolitan
    area, 85
Sandinista revolution (1979), 66
Scotland, 16
self-identification, 2
Sotomayor, Sonia, 406
South Carolina, 68, 75

Spain, 17
Sweden, 16

Takima County, Washington, 78
Tejano, 7
Tennessee, 75
Texas, 67, 72
  business ownership, 354, 359
  voter
    participation, 265
    registration, 272
Tienda, Marta, 7
Treaty of Guadalupe Hidalgo (1848),
    43

U.S. Census Bureau, 4
United Kingdom, 16
United States
  demographic change
    1860–1900, 16
    after 1880, 17
urbanization, in Mexico, 51

wages, 12
War of U.S. Intervention (1848),
    1, 43
War on Poverty, 171
workers
  agricultural, 1
  contract, 10
  free, 9, 11
  indentured servant, 11, 12
  Mexican, 1
  railroad, 1
  seasonal, 1
  slave, 9
  tobacco, 1

Yuma County, Arizona, 83

zambo (person of mixed Indigenous/
    African heritage), 365